LATIN AMERICAN STUDIES

LATIN AMERICAN STUDIES

CRITIQUES OF CINEMA, LITERATURES, POLITICS AND REVOLUTION

DAVID GALLAGHER, EDITOR

ACADEMICA PRESS
BETHESDA - DUBLIN - PALO ALTO

Library of Congress Cataloguing-in-Publication Data

Latin American studies : critiques of contemporary cinema, literatures, politics and revolution / [edited by] David Gallagher.
   p. cm.
Includes bibliographical references and index.
ISBN 978-1-936320-20-2
1. Latin America—Civilization. I. Gallagher, David, 1944-
F1408.3.L39 2012
980—dc23

2011034556

Copyright 2012 by David Gallagher

All rights reserved. Printed in the United States of America. No part of this book may be used or reproduced in any manner whatsoever without written permission except in the case of brief quotations embodied in critical articles and reviews.

Academica Press, LLC
Box 60728
Cambridge Station
Palo Alto, CA. 94306

Website: www.academicapress.com

to order: 650-329-0685

CONTRIBUTORS

Stacey Van Dahm earned her Ph.D. in Comparative Literature at the University of California, Santa Barbara. Her research is in nationalism and transnational models for community and belonging. Her work focuses on Latino and Latina experience in the United States, especially during the Cold War period.

Dorian Lugo-Bertrán was born in Santurce, Puerto Rico. He received his doctorate in Philosophy with a specialization in Hispanic Studies from the Universidad de Puerto Rico, Recinto de Rio Piedras. He works as an Assistant Professor for the School of Communications of the same institution. Lugo-Bertrán teaches theory courses that deal with signification, information, and cultural studies. His line of research explores the implications of gender and queer theories in different objects of study, including cinema, Renaissance literature, and plastic arts. Lugo-Bertrán has published in various journals, as well as an anthology of cultural production and artist's book that stages the performativity of the same book, *Saqueos* (2002). He has been twice elected Co-Chair of the Film Studies Section of the Latin American Studies Association (2009-2010 and 2010-2011).

Ana Ros is Assistant Professor of Latin American Literature and Culture at Binghamton University (State University of New York). She is interested in young filmmakers and narratives in Argentine, Chile and Uruguay. Her research reflects on how the Southern Cone post dictatorship generations reshape the collective memory of the dictatorial past through political activism and forms of artistic expression (cinema, literature, comics and photography). Ros has presented her research at national and international conferences and is currently working on a book manuscript entitled *Rediscovering Revolutionaries, Rethinking Bystanders Postdictatorship Generation and Collective Memory in Argentina, Chile and Uruguay*. Her recent publications include: 'Leaving and Letting Go as Possible Ways of Living Together, in Jorge Gaggero's *Live-in Maid*' in *New Trends in Argentine and Brazilian Cinema* (Bristol: Intellect, 2010) edited by Cacilda Rêgo and Carolina Rocha; '*La asesina de Lady Di*: Deseo y mercado en la Argentina de fin de milenio' in AA. VV. *Trauma, Historia y Subjetividad*, edited by AASM (Buenos Aires: Serie Conexiones, 2010), pp. 467-70; '¿Cómo heredar la militancia política del 60 y 70? Reflexiones en torno a tres narrativas recientes de/sobre la generación de posdictadura en el Río de la Plata' in *Letral. Revista Electrónica de Estudios Transatlánticos de Literatura/Letral Electronic Journal of Transatlantic Studies in Literature*, 3 (2009), 12-27, and 'Tropicália en Brasil y movimiento estudiantil en México: entrando y saliendo de las estructuras consensuales de 1968' in *Tiresias: University of Michigan Graduate Students Online Journal*, 1 (2007), 55-71. She would like to acknowledge Jakob Feinig, for making this essay possible in many ways.

David Gregory was born in San Juan, Puerto Rico in 1978. He has carried out research on the role of aesthetics and the artist figure since his graduate studies at the University of Puerto Rico. His latest research focuses on the role of art within different political conditions in a transnational frame in Hispano-America, including an ongoing project on Cuban film. He has also written short stories and his poetry has been read during a series of artistic events in San Juan. Presently, he is a Doctoral Candidate at the University of Notre Dame and his dissertation is entitled: 'Dissertation Title: *Aesthetics as an Alter Voice: Contemporary Literature and Filmic Representations of Alterity within the Polis.*'

He has published an online article in *Tiresias: Culture, Politics and Critical Theory* entitled 'The Righteous Empire: An Imposition to the Other in *Why We Fight?* and *Syriana*'. Other articles include 'Babel sigue siendo Babel', *Diálogo* (2007) and 'Apuntes de memoria', again online with the journal *Tiresias*.

Rubén Pelayo is Professor of twentieth-century Latin American Literature at Southern Connecticut State University and his research interests include 'The Life and Works of Gabriel García Márquez', literary criticism, textual experimentation in Contemporary Latin American Literature, the merging of genres, pedagogy, translation, and Spanish Language Acquisition. His publications include *Gabriel García Márquez: A Biography* (Westport, CT: Greenwood Press, 2009), and he is co-author of *La voz: Fonética y fonología españolas* (New York: Prentice Hall, 2007), *Pupazzo's Colorful World* (New Haven, CT: Keylock Kreations, 2006), 'Love in the Time of Cholera' in *Gabriel García Márquez's Love in the Time of Cholera*, edited by Harold Bloom (Philadelphia: Chelsea House Publishers, 2005), *Gabriel García Márquez: A Critical Companion* (Westport, CT: Greenwood Press, 2001) as well as numerous essay publications. His essay publications include poststructuralist and linguistic studies, literary criticism, and the merging of genres. Professor Pelayo has presented his research both nationally and internationally.

Itzá A. Zavala-Garrett is from Mexico City. She holds a Ph.D. in Latin American Literature from the University of Colorado at Boulder. Currently, she is an Assistant Professor at Morehead State University. Before her present academic position, Dr. Zavala-Garrett worked for five years as a Visiting Professor at Wake Forest University. In addition, she has worked in numerous universities in Mexico as a Spanish and Literature Professor including: Tecnológico y de Estudios Superiores de Monterrey (ITESM), Universidad del Valle de México and Universidad Autónoma de Querétaro. Her area of concentration is Contemporary Latin American Literature and Culture with an emphasis on twentieth century Mexican Literature, anthropological and sociological approaches to literature, cultural studies, and film and gender studies. She has published various articles about Mexican writers such as Carlos Monsiváis, María Luisa Puga and Elena Poniatowska.

Briah Luther is a World Comparative Literature Postgraduate student at San Francisco State University. She has taken an active role in the university's Comparative Literature Student Association as Vice President and Treasurer, and works hard to create academic networks and social activities for students in her program. She has been an editor for San Francisco State University's online journal, *Portals*. She recently spoke at San Francisco State University's Comparative Literature Graduate Student Annual Symposium and ACLA's annual conferences in Long Beach, Boston, and New Orleans. She received her Bachelor of Arts in Comparative World Literature from Long Beach State University. Her personal academic interests include the Feminine Gothic, Spanish Feminine Neo-Gothic, Feminism, Gender and Sexuality, and other various concepts involving identity. She is currently working on her thesis, 'Knowledge: The Currency for Power and Monstrosity among Shelley's *Frankenstein* and García Morales' *La lógica del vampiro*.'

Hilarie Ashton is a second-year student in the John W. Draper Interdisciplinary Master's Program in Humanities and Social Thought at New York University; her focus is on critical and cultural theory in a postmodern context. Her master's thesis is entitled Life of the Author: Embodied Authorship in Paul Auster's *City of Glass* and Edgardo Vega Yunqué's *The Lamentable Journey of Omaha Bigelow into the Impenetrable Loisaida Jungle*. She is also a research associate with NYU's Office for University Development and Alumni Relations. She is an inaugural member of the program board of NYU's Masters College and communications chair and board member of the Greater New York Chapter of the International Association of Professional Researchers for Advancement. From 2006 to 2008, she was a member of the editorial board of *Eyes on the ICC*, a publication of the Council for American Students in International Negotiations. She also worked as a writing tutor for the Williams College Writing Workshop from 2004 to 2005. She received her Bachelor of Arts in English and philosophy from Williams College. She has published the article: "My Name is Johnny Cash' The Artistic Persona through Jameson and Foucault', *Anamesa*, 7.1 (2010).

Ghazala Hashmi is Professor of English as J. Sargeant Reynolds Community College in Richmond, Virginia. Her areas of specialization include modern and contemporary American literature, and postcolonial literature. Dr. Hashmi's recent research focuses upon Edwidge Danticat, Arundhathi Roy, and other postcolonial women writers.

Marika Preziuso is a Fellow of the Virginia Foundation for the Humanities and following a Masters in Gender and Cultural Studies, graduated with a Doctorate in English from Birkbeck College, University of London. She holds a Masters in Translation Studies from the Università La Sapienza, Rome, and a United Kingdom Diploma in English and American Literature from the University of Kent at Canterbury. She first graduated with a First Class Honours Degree in Modern European Languages and Literature from the Università di Salerno, Italy. Her areas of specialization include Postcolonial Literature, World Literature, Caribbean Literature (Francophone/Anglophone), Comparative Literature, Transnational Literature, Latino/a, Women's Fiction, Literary Theory, Writing and Composition.

Mariana Past (Dickinson College) concentrates on Twentieth- and twenty-first century Spanish and Francophone Caribbean literature, and her current projects focus on Haitian-Dominican relations and representations of the Haitian Revolution in literary and historical texts written in Spanish, French, and Haitian Creole. Her interests also include questions of migration/exile in Caribbean and Latin American literature. She has published articles in the *Revista de la Casa de las Américas*, *The Journal of Haitian Studies*, Del Caribe, and *The Global South*.

Patrick Sylvain is a poet, writer, photographer and social critic. He works as a Haitian language and culture instructor at Brown University, a language coach at Harvard University, and has taught in the anthropology department of the University of Massachusetts at Boston. In 1998, as a Conant Fellow, Sylvain graduated from the Harvard Graduate School of Education. His work has been published in numerous anthologies and journals, including: *African American Review*, *Agni*, *American Poetry Review*, *Callaloo*, *Caribbean Writers*, *Crab Orchard Review*, *Haiti Noir*, *Haitian Times*, *Massachusetts Review* and *Ploughshares*. His latest bilingual poetry collection is 'Love, Lust & Loss,' which was published in 2005 by Memoire D'Encrier. Sylvain is also a frequent contributor to the *Boston Haitian Reporter* and is currently working on two collections of poetry, 'Spirit Chaser' and 'Windows of Exile' and a multidisciplinary book on Haiti entitled 'Framing Structural Violence.'

Alexandra Fitts is Professor of Spanish and Women's & Gender Studies at the University of Alaska Fairbanks. Her interests include women writers of Latin America and Spain, Chicana literature, translation, and film. She has published on Alejandra Pizarnik, Luisa Valenzuela, Armonía Somers, Sandra Cisneros, and Rosario Ferré.

Priscilla Archibald is an Associate Professor in the Department of Literature and Languages at Roosevelt University. She has written about urbanization and modern Peruvian culture, José María Arguedas, transnationalism and transculturation, and indigeneity and indigenous video. Her publications include *Imagining Modernity in the Andes* (Bucknell University Press, 2010), as well as articles in *Social Text*, *Literatura Iberoamericana* (a special volume on the Andes), and *Revista canadiense de estudios hispánicos* among other journals. She is currently working on the politics of trans-American literary discourse in the nineteen-twenties, thirties and forties.

Natalie M. Léger is a PhD candidate in English at Cornell University whose research interests include Haitian Revolutionary Studies, Caribbean women writers, Caribbean philosophy as well as postcolonial literature and theory. She is currently completing a dissertation entitled, *"'A Tragedy of Success': Haiti and the Promise of Revolution,"* which reads Caribbean literature to access the significance of Haiti and the Haitian Revolution to Caribbean theorizations of modernity.

CONTENTS

Contributors   v
Abbreviations   xv
Introduction   1

1. Desire, Arenas, and Cold War Discourse: Reinaldo Arenas as Protagonist in Julian Schnabel's *Before Night Falls*.   15

Stacey Van Dahm (Philadelphia University)

2. No Strength: Flaccidity and Resonance in the Films of Lucrecia Martel

Dorian Lugo-Bertrán (University of Puerto Rico, Río Piedras)   33

3. Young Argentine Filmmakers: Remembering the Past from a Present of Crisis

Ana Ros (Binghamton University)   45

4. Beneath the surface: Violent representations of a collective trauma in

Dos veces junio and *Garage Olimpo*
David Gregory (University of Notre Dame)   65

5. The Mythical South: From Mississippi to the Magdalena and into the Mainstream

Rubén Pelayo (Southern Connecticut State University)   83

6. Fraternal Dialogue between José Manuel Prieto and Fernando Del Paso's Fiction Works

Itzá A. Zavala-Garrett (Morehead State University)   107

7. The Bordering of Identities within Gloria Anzaldúa's *Borderlands/La Frontera: The New Mestiza* and Audre Lorde's 'Age, Race, Class, and Sex'

Briah Luther (San Francisco State University)   119

8. 'Urban (as) Flâneur: Narrator and City in *The Lamentable Journey of Omaha Bigelow Into The Impenetrable Loisaida Jungle*'

Hilarie Ashton (New York University)   133

9. 'What will we do with our beast?': Reversing the Spectacle in Edwidge Danticat's *The Dew Breaker*

Ghazala F. Hashmi (J. Sargeant Reynolds Community College)   147

10. Liberating Borders: Edwidge Danticat's Poetics of Haiti's 'Vulnerability' in *The Farming of Bones*

Contents   xiii

Marika Preziuso (Virginia Foundation for the Humanities)   161

11. What's in a name? Reading transformative farce in Césaire's *La Tragédie du roi Christophe* and Najman's 'Royal bonbon'

Mariana Past (Dickinson College)   183

12. Gastronomical Metaphors: Their Presence within the Sexual and Socio-Political Context of Haitian Culture

Patrick Sylvain (Brown University)   201

13. Recipes for Disaster? The Kitchen as Creative Space in Latin American Women's Fiction

Alexandra Fitts (University of Alaska, Fairbanks)   227

14. American Friendships and Hemispheric Discourse

Priscilla Archibald (Roosevelt University)   241

15. From Anacaona we are born, through Défilée we remember: an Istwa (History/Story) of mourning and revolution

Natalie M. Léger (Cornell University)   261

Bibliography   281
Notes   321
Index   353

ABBREVIATIONS

AC   Aimé Césaire, *La tragédie du roi Christophe* (Paris: Présence africaine, 1963)

AL   Audre Lorde, 'Age, Race, Class, and Sex,' in *Sister Outsider*, ed. by Cheryl Clarke (Berkeley: The Crossing Press, 2007)

DB   Edwidge Danticat, *The Dew Breaker* (New York: Vintage Books, 2004)

FB   Edwidge Danticat, *The Farming of Bones* (London: Abacus, 1998)

GA   Gloria Anzaldúa, *Borderlands/La Frontera: The New Mestiza* (New York: Aunt Lute Books, 1987)

KK   Edwidge Danticat, *Krik? Krak!* (New York: Vintage Contemporaries, 1996)

NTS   'Nineteen Thirty Seven' from *Krik? Krak!* (New York: Vintage Contemporaries, 1996)

INTRODUCTION

As the title to this volume suggests, the essays on Latin American studies in this volume are critiques of contemporary cinema, literature, politics and revolution. Many of these contributions were originally conceived as conference papers for the ACLA Conference in New Orleans, Louisiana which took place from April 1-4, 2010. Following the conference the contributors agreed to revise, amend, expand, rewrite or carry out further research on their papers to produce the finished articles in this collective volume.

The history of the colonization of Latin America has already been subject to detailed expert research over many decades and all students who wish to acquaint themselves with this history have a number of publications available to them, including *Early Latin America* by Lockhart and Schwartz, *Colonial Latin America* by Burkholder and Johnson, and *The Americas* by Felipe Fernández-Armesto.[1] It is perhaps pertinent here to outline some brief points about the early colonization.

Genoese adventurer Christopher Columbus famously 'sailed the ocean blue', and was the first to land in these territories now regarded as Latin America, but it is not always appreciated that his mission was in fact to discover Asia and his avowed aim and purpose of this voyage was always to find the island of Japan. The substantial financial assistance of Ferdinand of Aragon and Isabella of Castile had enabled him to send three ships out in search of Japan and China, the *Santa Maria*, the *Pinta* and the *Niña*, to acquire sovereignty, bring back wealth and gold deposits, and provide Castile with a direct sea link with Asia. It was only mistakenly that his ship arrived at Hispaniola (Haiti), which was then taken over by the arriving Spanish and colonized after bitter struggles with the natives.

The subsequent history of the colonization of South America was one involving battles between Spanish conquistadors in search of gold, who with their comparatively meagre Spanish forces managed many times to overcome the natives. There were casualties on both sides, of course: the conquering Spanish forces were depleted by catching tropical diseases and the natives, who had never been exposed to and thus built up an immunity to European diseases such as smallpox, contracted them and died in their thousands. Legends such as the Man of Gold, El Dorado and the promise of riches spurred on conquistadors and Spanish adventurers who went out in search of riches in Mexico, Peru, Brazil, Ecuador, Colombia, and Venezuela, and encountered previously unchartered and hostile regions of the Americas. In addition, the physical battles reduced the number of settlers and there were also battles akin to civil wars involving Spanish against Spanish.[2] Latin America has always been since 1492 a place involving battles for wealth, territory, and political supremacy, and if we add to this mix its ecological and natural disasters such as recent mudslides, tropical storms and earthquakes, its variety of music, dance and literature, political uprisings, the struggle to maintain the rainforests, rebellions and the passionate nature of its people, one cannot deny that the diverse area of Latin America is one that requires constant revisitation and whose cinema, literatures, politics and revolution flourish against the background of its special geographical position, the battles for sovereignty that created its own political history and its continued fight against the challenges faced by its own very special natural environment.

Geographically Latin America covers a wide region and the languages spoken in its various parts vary from Spanish and Portuguese to French and some Creole languages. The region traditionally includes the territories where the

Spanish and Portuguese languages prevail as well as Mexico, most of Central and South America and in the Caribbean, Cuba, the Dominican Republic and Puerto Rico. For the purposes of this book Latin America encompasses all of the Americas south of the United States, including French-speaking Haiti. Argentina, Chile, Colombia, Cuba, Haiti, Mexico, Peru, and Puerto Rico are the principal countries, whose cinema, literature, politics and revolution is here the subject of investigation.

Cinematic analysis focuses on Argentine filmmakers Lupe Pérez García, Lucía Cedrón, Lucrecia Martel and the Chilean-Italian film screenwriter and director, Marco Bechis. The writers that come under the spotlight here include the Puerto Rican poet William Carlos Williams and novelist Edgardo Vega Yunqué, the Peruvian Marxist and essayist, José Carlos Mariátegui; Argentina's novelists Jorge Luis Borges and Martín Kohan, Julio Cortázar and Manuel Puig, the Colombian Gabriel García Márquez, the Haitian writer Edwidge Danticat, the Mexicans Fernando Del Paso and Gloria Evangelina Anzaldúa, the Cuban writers Reinaldo Arenas and José Manuel Prieto and Audre Lorde, whose family were Caribbean immigrants to America. As regards the political issues within the Latin Americas, the revolutions of Cuba and Haiti are given close attention.

Starting off with papers examining cinema, Stacey Van Dahm indicates that *Antes que anochezca*, the 1992 memoir by Reinaldo Arenas, is one of the first Latin American autobiographies to openly represent homosexuality, and it does so with bold disregard for the potential homophobia of its reading audience. Arenas' style, a fantastic blend of fact and fiction that portrays Cuba, Castro and revolutionary persecution with passion, anger and biting mockery, is transformed significantly by Julian Schnabel in his film adaptation of the memoir, *Before Night Falls* (2000). Schnabel's adaptation, artistically beautiful, alters Arenas' portrayal of self and Cuban gender and sexuality, taming Arenas' desire to be more palatable to a mainstream American movie viewership. Van Dahm explores what is lost and gained in this translation of the Cuban author, particularly in its social and political settings: the extreme persecution of homosexuals in Cuba in the 60s and U.S. anticommunism and homophobia of the 80s when Arenas lived in exile in the United States. Van Dahm argues that the film silences the queer identities and desires that Arenas' text implies, framing Arenas within U.S. paradigms of gender and sexuality and offering the author's story as a counter to communist persecution. The film purchases tolerance of homosexuality at the cost of embedding the terms of freedom in the binary discourses of the Cold War period. In fact, the memoir's complicated portrayal of desire suggests pathways outside of binary limitations and towards more productive discussions about human experience and how it is shaped by nationalist discourses.

In 'No Strength: Flaccidity and Resonance in the Films of Lucrecia Martel' Dorian Lugo-Bertrán reveals that the constitutive 'strangeness' of Latin American production is no secret. Many thinkers, from the early European *cronistas* to later Latin American theorists, have elaborated that what was perceived in this context as out of the ordinary by the 'outside' gaze is taken as day-to-day experience by the local ones. It is not that Latin American production is in essence disquieting. More likely, instances of Latin American production unsettle fixed identity constructions, including the ethnic one. Outside of some cultural hegemonies, production from these poetic zones converges in motivation and traces with Creole, diasporic, populous elaborations, whether from a dependent or dominant geography. One could state that the more political instances of Latin American production stem from a Creole subjectivity, that is to say, that which stages or propounds liminal points of contact in things. From this very context, of strangeness and 'creolité', he discusses the films of contemporary Argentinean director Lucrecia Martel. As a matter of fact, 'strange' is one of the signifiers that surface most often by critics to describe Martel's films. With three feature films to her credit, this director's production does little to present a 'strong story-line', to explain or justify fully her characters' motivations and liminalities, or even to expound any 'great truth' upon narrative closure. Queer theory assists in reading the historical and artistic specificities of this strangeness and 'creolité', there where fallogocentric tropes collapse one by one on the deliberately precarious grounds of these films.

In 'Young Argentine Filmmakers' Perspectives on the Past of Activism and Repression' Ana Ros reflects on how young filmmakers intervene in the formation of collective memory concerning the last Argentine dictatorship (1976-1983), contributing to the renewed societal interest in the subject. The two films which she analyzes share a concern with creating a more instructive and inclusive collective memory by encouraging different societal groups to learn from the past to inform decisions in the present. This includes not only the repressors and the victims, but also the so-called bystanders. In an experimental documentary, *Diario argentino/Argentine Journal* (2007), Lupe Pérez García focuses on the so-called 'bystanders' – those who were neither activists nor repressors. She challenges their typical image as passive spectators in a war between 'two demons' and highlights their role as political actors in the past and the present. Secondly, in the feature film *Cordero de Dios/Lamb of God* (2008), Lucía Cedrón, herself daughter of a 'disappeared' activist, proposes a way of taking the past as a guide for acting in present situations of hate and violence.

David Gregory in 'Beneath the surface: Violent representations of a collective trauma in *Dos veces junio* and *Garage Olimpo*' explains how the moment of shock has the potential to shape a collective psyche and its future neurosis. Through aesthetics, literature has the potential to make a representation of that collective trauma and its fragmented consequences on that collective identity. Literature insists on underlining the collective wound recreating subjective narratives, providing an alternate space to represent a psyche that cannot exist beyond that catalytic moment. Renouncing any claim to justice, truth or revenge, both *Dos veces junio*, written by Martín Kohan, and Marco Bechis' *Garage Olimpo*, insist on new ways of representing the past as part of a traumatic experience of a violent political regime. Both novel and film recreate the literary-visual echoes of a world that insists on its violence from two fronts: the imposition of the collective identity and its national 'glory' along with the exclusion of the other as an enemy. In that negotiation, the novel sets in motion a reflection of a fragmented voice-nation, a reflection of an Argentina that is both the horror of its violence and the prosperity of those who failed to recognize its trauma. His intention is to explore how the novel and film respond from and to the *polis*, providing a connection to the past that insists on its scars and the obscure consequences that lie beneath the surface.

For Rubén Pelayo's contribution 'The Mythical South: From Mississippi to the Magdalena and into the Mainstream', the *mythical south* that frames his writing refers to the American Deep South and South America, where Argentina's Borges, Cortázar, Puig, and Peronism all immediately are evoked. The phrase *From Mississippi to the Magdalena*, on the other hand, makes an allusion to two large southern rivers, the former in the United States, the latter in Colombia. This connects his analysis with Nobel-prize winners William Faulkner and Gabriel García Márquez. The idea of *Into the Mainstream* that closes the title makes reference to the 1940s and beyond, when Latin American writers, personalities, and political events came to world-wide awareness and became truly cosmopolitan. His paper's core, however, brings forward two parallel lines: firstly, a brief biographical account of Latin American figures, and secondly, confronting the traditional literary criticism that views Latin American writing of the second half of the twentieth century as an echo of either American or European authors as viewed by critics like Harold Bloom. His essay points out that while Faulkner can be traced in García Márquez's writing, among others, Cervantes is actually the one who can be credited as 'the influence.' Thus what we have is a Spanish tradition, all along, as opposed to an English school of writing. He concludes his article with the observation that *One Hundred Years of Solitude* (*Cien años de soledad*) has much more of *Don Quixote* (*Don Quijote de la Mancha*) as an influence than Faulkner's writings.

In 'Fraternal Dialogue between José Manuel Prieto and Fernando Del Paso's Fiction Works', Itzá A. Zavala-Garrett elucidates that the short stories book *El tartamudo y la rusa* (2002) by José Manuel Prieto may be considered as a microcosm of the whole work of this Cuban writer. This book, with a post modernist accent like his novel *Rex* (2008) and other fiction works written by this successful author remind us of Del Paso's fiction works, especially his novel *Palinuro de México* (1977). Both Del Paso and Prieto use intertextual displays and the fine arts to expose the reader to a total renovation of language. In addition, they make us aware of contemporary topics such as social movements, the political ideological breakdowns of governments, cosmopolitanisms and interdisciplinary fields. The objective of Zavala-Garrett's paper is to connect the aesthetic perspectives of these writers; Del Paso's playful and encyclopaedic style and Prieto's intercultural and new baroque style. Both literary styles develop a similar dialogue that is essential to discover in order to understand the new Latin American literature and culture.

Briah Luther discusses Gloria Anzaldúa's unapologetic hybridization of Spanish and English to create a utopian Creole-like concept outside the hegemonic binary system alongside Audre Lorde's stark representation of the hegemony as a call to unite for a new movement beyond the old way of thinking. In a society where the good is defined in terms of profit rather than in terms of human need, she examines Lorde's article 'Age, Race, Class, and Sex: Women Redefining Difference' with Anzaldúa's *Borderlands/La Frontera: The New Mestiza* as a platform where binary guidelines are challenged through an effort to unify one's identity with a positive awareness of our differences. She considers these guidelines within the hegemonic patriarchal system, which confine Anzaldúa and Lorde, as well as the authors' individual efforts to create a new consciousness, stemming from continual creative motions that break down the unitary aspects of each paradigm by not accepting the superficial aspects of social change. Within the paper, Luther compares Anzaldúa's language project, *The New Mestiza* (a creative response inspired by the natural evolution of Chicano Spanish), with Lorde's desire to use each person's respective experiences that arise due to one's differences in order to create positive change that does not place the pressure of teaching this harmfulness solely upon the oppressed individuals.

Anzaldúa's *The New Mestiza* also urges everyone to piece together the segregated parts of one's self to make a whole person. This, connected with Lorde's idea that people are more than their binary parts from which they are often labelled, argues how essential it is for everyone (including those who fit comfortably within the binary system but want to deviate) to build an inclusive and integrative system. Furthermore, *The New Mestiza*'s unwavering commitment to use both languages without translation coupled with Lorde's strategic methods of uniting the separate shows the importance for a shift in focus, along with the need for the dominant culture to claim responsibility for their part in producing the gap in equality.

In 'Urban (as) Flâneur: Narrator and City in *The Lamentable Journey of Omaha Bigelow Into The Impenetrable Loisaida Jungle*', Hilarie Ashton adverts to the fact that despite the quixotic appeal of Edgardo Vega Yunqué's fiction, much of which chronicles the lives of Puerto Rican New Yorkers, his oeuvre has received sparse critical attention. An interest in what his work would look like under different critical and theoretical lenses is one of the motivating forces behind her study. More specifically, her project examines how Vega Yunqué's magical realist novel *The Lamentable Journey of Omaha Bigelow into the Impenetrable Loisaida Jungle* explodes its Lower East Side locale out of the realm of pure setting and pushes it into the realm of character/motive force. In probing different aspects of the tension between city-as-environment/city-as-character, she argues that in their combination, they present a twist on Benjamin's theory of the *flâneur*, updating it to the specifics of a new century, a new city, and a new type of protagonist while leaving room for the aspects of this novel's narratology that cannot be viewed through Baudelairean eyes. Although the city as portrayed in *Lamentable Journey* derives a great deal of additional force from its author's structure and plot (or lack of plot) choices, it turns out that the author himself is just as intriguing a figure as the version of the *flâneur* that his protagonist or his location enacts. The degree to which the combination of his incarnations shapes the text aligns him even more closely with his text's version of the *flâneur*, distinct from Benjamin's original form.

Ghazala F. Hashmi's essay examines Edwidge Danticat's *The Dew Breaker* in the context of the author's transfer of power away from the torturers and towards those who survive state-sponsored trauma. *The Dew Breaker* enacts an ironic reversal of Foucault's examination of the panopticon: the individual stories and testimonies of victims, when brought together and connected into meaningful narrative by the reader, become a broader and encompassing gaze from which scrutiny the torturer cannot evade. Hashmi suggests that Danticat's purpose in creating this ironic reversal is to pass control and meaning back to those who suffer; to place the abuser under a gaze that strips away his amalgamation of deceptions; and to disrupt the traditional narrative impulse towards hope for a just resolution. Memory and testimony exist with valid purpose in Danticat's text, and the stories' re-telling of terrible violence moves the reader not toward closure but toward reclamation of the various truths that exist within both victim and victimizer.

Marika Preziuso's paper uses *The Farming of Bones* (1998), the acclaimed novel by Haitian author Edwidge Danticat, for the challenge it poses – both in its language and as a cultural product intended for a transnational readership – of what have been the most conventional representations of Haiti. 'Authenticity' has historically been used as the discursive violence that has coated the Haitians' revolutionary enterprise (the successful slaves' Revolution in 1803) with images of unruliness, which attached the island to the most negative stereotypes of 'blackness'. Danticat, on the other hand, conceptualizes 'vulnerability' as a transgressive poetics that reflects Haiti's anti-colonial 'modernity'. She does so in the novel through the many physical demonstrations of liberation enacted by the bodies of her Haitian and Haitian-Dominican characters. Furthermore, Danticat equates the experience of crossing the Haitian-Dominican border as that of wearing a 'veil', evanescent yet physically present. The 'veil' of the border between Haiti and the Dominican Republic, which recurs throughout her novel, becomes the platform for her poetics of vulnerability. The vulnerability and sensuality of the 'veil/border' also leads to questions around the ways in which certain border-spaces such as patrols and checkpoints, when they are imagined in their vulnerability, can realize a transcultural potential. This argument is confirmed by one of Danticat's latest novels, *The Dew Breaker* (2004). Here she plays out the Haitians' liberation from the violence of colonialism and historical marginalization through the narrative of the 'Ka' spirit and soul purification, as described in the Egyptian *The Book of the Dead*. By literally 'remapping' the Caribbean by expanding its geographical and ideological borders, Preziuso demonstrates that Danticat's poetics of vulnerability responds successfully to the violence of certain discourses and representations of Haiti.

Mariana Past in 'What's in a name? Reading transformative farce in Césaire's *La Tragédie du roi Christophe* and Najman's *Royal bonbon*' refers to Aimé Césaire's *La tragédie du roi Christophe* (1963), which is arguably the most canonical work of literature to address the Haitian Revolution and its history. The apparent excesses of Césaire's protagonist have shaped readers' assumptions that the dramatic text is a cautionary tale for revolutionary leaders in the era of African Independences. Charles Najman's film *Royal bonbon* (2002) poignantly interrogates the famous *devise* of Christophe – '*Je renais de mes cendres*' – as the bicentenary of Haitian Independence looms large on the horizon. Through a farcical re-enactment of Christophe's reign in present-day Haiti, which repeatedly echoes Césaire's *Tragédie*, *Royal bonbon* uncovers the phenomenon of 'wa kaka', a literal example of postcolonial *folie*, and critiques the impulse to glorify and revive Haitian history and its heroes. Past's study contends that the ostensible parody of geographical names in the *Tragédie*'s court scene (Act I, Scene 3), closely replicated in Najman's film, reflects the significance of name changes in Afro-Caribbean cultures; also, the apparently farcical royal titles subtly evoke the Amerindian past which gave the new black republic its name in 1804. This scene simultaneously highlights and obscures aspects of Haitian history and ultimately alters understandings of the world's first black republic in an awkward, if perhaps inadvertent way. Placing the literary and visual texts in dialogue with one another, Past unravels the multiple layers of meaning involved in the court scene and shows how, through further humanizing king Christophe, they simultaneously challenge historical legends and participate in their re-articulation and deformation.

In 'Gastronomical Metaphors: Their Presence within the Sexual and Socio-Political Context of Haitian Culture', Patrick Sylvain argues that the indisputable existence of metaphorical patterns in Haitian speech provides an interdisciplinary blueprint for a culture that is heavily influenced by agricultural activities and a language pregnant with food attributive metaphors. The metaphors used in Haitian reflect the overall disposition of the people and an acceptance of certain views that are represented through speech and text. The 'woman as food' metaphor is a consequence of the patriarchal nature of the Haitian society; the overall permeation of gastronomical metaphors in the language is a product of a culture that has a strong preoccupation with food. The predominance of these gastronomical metaphors that are couched in cultural analogies proves that language is not only reflective, but it is also constitutive of social realities. His objective is to demonstrate that Haitian consumptive language is the manifestation of the conscious in a state of non-escape that consumes time, being and material condition. Here, in the act of consumption, to devour another becomes a potent metaphor because of the exploitative totality in which the speaker exists. In Haitian, not only does hunger carry its own symbolisms, but also the act of eating (*manje*, to eat) often serves as the metaphorical 'container' to embed the suggested meaning. In Haitian Creole, the verb, *manje* (eating/consuming), may have various connotations (sexual, political, competitive, sacred, symbolic), but is at the same time a gastronomical act. What is operating at the core of the culture is an obsession with eating, while giving special consideration to the constructive and destructive properties of food. Sylvain refers to this obsession as a psychology of consumption, but this in reality represents a fear of being consumed.

Alexandra Fitts in 'Recipes for Disaster?: The Kitchen as Creative Space in Latin American Women's Fiction' draws our attention to the fact that while

Virginia Woolf may not have been thinking of the kitchen as 'the room of one's own' that women need to engage in literary activity, the kitchen has long served as the site of women's production. But the kitchen is also a powerful symbol of women's oppression and of the demands of domestic labour. Latin American (and Latina) women writers have taken up both sides of the debate on cooking and food – condemning the kitchen for its representation of confinement by stereotypical gender roles, or celebrating it as the locus of feminine power and creativity. Alexandra's paper looks at works by Rosario Castellanos, Laura Esquivel, Isabel Allende, and Coco Fusco and Nao Bustamante to examine their treatments of the heavily fraught relationships between women, cooking, eating, sexuality, and stereotype.

Priscilla Archibald indicates that American avant-garde movements from the 1920s and 30s are often contextualized in an international arena, because of the nature of the work itself and the international character of the movement. Paris has generally been regarded as the centre for artistic creativity in the early decades of the twentieth century; in the case of poetry, London and Madrid were likewise important sites for artistic migration. What has been eclipsed in this Europe-centred narrative, however, as well as in the various nationalist alternatives, is the relationship between the avant-garde movements of Anglo America and Latin America. Because Latin American and Anglo American cultures came to be perceived by many as opposites in the early decades of the twentieth century, approaching activity from this time period from a hemispheric point of view can seem counter-intuitive – which is precisely why doing so is so important. Common sense is frequently ideological and this instance is no exception. In an examination of three figures, William Carlos Williams, the North American cultural historian and hispanophile, Waldo Frank and José Carlos Mariátegui, Archibald highlights ways in which the English and Spanish-speaking Americas intersected in the early decades of the twentieth century. No writer better illustrates the relationship between ideology and disciplinary definitions, and the power of the latter in general and literary modernism in particular, to circumscribe the production of knowledge and cultural imagination than Williams. As a Puerto-Rican-North American whose status as an Anglo American modernist has only recently come under question, her analysis of Williams disarticulates reified literary traditions that have obscured the dynamic and even baroque ways that identities, cultures and ideologies interact across the Americas. The second part of her essay deals with the complexities of Inter-American exchange through a consideration of the work, correspondence and friendship of Frank and Mariátegui. The fruitful dialogue produced by this somewhat unlikely alliance is particularly interesting in light of a key issue in contemporary Inter-American Studies, namely, the colonizing power of discourses associated with U.S. academe. By critiquing the Latin American and Anglo American dichotomy, as well as the false alternative between a worldly Paris and a provincial America, her essay makes a claim for specifically American forms of cosmopolitanism.

In 'From Anacaona we are born, through Défilée we remember: an Istwa (History/Story) of mourning and revolution', Natalie M. Léger explains how critical and literary renderings of the Haitian Revolution often focus on the exemplary masculine subject, specifically Toussaint L'Ouverture, Henri Christophe or Alexandre Sabès Pétion. Her paper critiques the normativity of this focus; it asks: where are the women and ultimately the unknowns in such accounts? Closely reading the manner in which Edwidge Danticat unveils the obscured to present alternative realities as well as histories of Haiti in the short story entitled, 'Nineteen Thirty-Seven', Palmer assesses how a move to gender the discourse of the Haitian Revolution, and, more broadly, Haitian history, induces the tragic, specifically a thematic and structural impulse conditioned by, what she terms, an aesthetics of mourning. This aesthetics memorializes the neglected, revolutionary figures like Dedee Bazile and Papa Boukman, and concurrently commemorates a community of subaltern women struggling towards greater collectivity. Such an aesthetics is at once a literary and political endeavour, where the art produced must and does as Danticat states 'stand-in for a life, a goal, a hope, a future.'[3] Danticat's stories ultimately reveal that despite

Haiti's bleak political reality there still remains, for the nation, the possibility of a future of difference, one embodied and fashioned by the unheralded and largely ignored woman in and of the mass.

1. DESIRE, ARENAS, AND COLD WAR DISCOURSE: REINALDO ARENAS AS PROTAGONIST IN JULIAN SCHNABEL'S *BEFORE NIGHT FALLS*

Stacey Van Dahm (Philadelphia University)

Julian Schnabel's 2000 film adaptation of Reinaldo Arenas' memoir, *Antes que anochezca* (1992), (*Before Night Falls*, 1993), offers a fascinating study of compromises. Artistically beautiful, it brought mainstream attention to the exiled Cuban writer with its moderate success in the box office, thus raising awareness of Arenas as a writer and bringing recognition to his work ten years after his death in 1990. This attention was merited; Arenas is one of the foremost Cuban writers of the twentieth century, and his work is recognized as a significant part of the Cuban canon despite the fact that he could not publish much of it in Cuba. But the film's success also depends upon framing Arenas such that the persecution he faced in Cuba for his homosexuality becomes more central to his exile than the censorship that plagued him. This takes the film on a course that purchases mainstream acceptance of homosexuality, defined in strictly U.S. cultural terms, at the cost of embedding the terms of this freedom in the binary discourses of the Cold War period that conflate the concepts of democracy and anti-communism. In so doing, the film underscores the ways that nationalist discourse shapes subjectivity. The film embraces Arenas while overlooking U.S. homophobia with its history of persecution of homosexuals under 'democracy,' and it limits homosexual desire to the national and cultural confines of U.S. identity politics. This is in contrast to the memoir in which Arenas' artistic endeavour works against this very process by suggesting desires and artistic beauty that thrive outside of nationalist discourses and may serve to undermine them. The goal of this essay is to highlight some of the facets of the film's construction that enact this appropriation of the Cuban author.

As a *Marielito*, one of the refugees in the chaotic third wave of Cuban emigration to the U.S. following the mob entry into the grounds of Havana's Peruvian embassy by those wanting to leave the country, Arenas was not as welcomed into the U.S. Cuban community as were earlier immigrants. The reasons for this mostly hinge on the make-up of this group. Unlike earlier waves of immigrants this group was made up of poorer classes and a greater percentage of them were non-white.[4] In addition, Castro took the Peruvian embassy debacle as an opportunity to empty prisons and asylums and offer passage to known homosexuals, thus further criminalizing those who wanted to leave by adding to their numbers those already marked as miscreants or insane in Cuban society. And the *Marielitos* were sometimes perceived as such by many Cubans already established in the U.S. Racism, fear of economic competition, homophobia, and concerns about criminality created a hostile environment. Despite the fact that in his memoir Arenas clearly positions himself as an 'outsider' to many U.S. groups with which he might have been affiliated, not just the Cuban community, and does so intentionally, this sense of not belonging contributed to his overall experience of hardship in exile, and it is one of the reasons he left Miami for New York City shortly after his arrival.

The entrenched *machismo* and homophobia of the U.S. Cuban *émigré* community was exacerbated by the conservative backlash of the 1980s, a movement which went hand-in-hand with a revival of anti-communist sentiment of the Reagan era. The 1970s paved the way for this with figures such as Harvey

Milk, tragically assassinated in 1978, and the disturbingly popular Anita Bryant. Bryant's rhetoric appealed to fears, and, similar to 1950s U.S. anti-communist discourse and the homophobic rhetoric of 1960s Cuba, children's safety was a key centrepiece. 'They can only recruit children, and this is what they want to do,' she warned Dade County parents. 'Some of the stories I could tell you of child recruitment and child abuse by homosexuals would turn your stomach'.[5] At the same time popular cultural forms like the hit film series, *Rambo*, worked for Reagan era mythologizing to revive the 1950s discursive manoeuvres that positioned homosexuals as threats to national security.[6] Overall, the 1980s saw a revival of anti-communist rhetoric that has contributed to the near impossibility of talking about Cuba and Castro without taking sides in an oppositional debate that is perniciously narrow and unproductive.

As an outspoken anti-Castro writer and a homosexual, Arenas entered the U.S. in a politically uncomfortable position during a time of turmoil for homosexuals. On the one hand, he stood for anti-communism in his experience of persecution under the Castro regime; on the other, he openly practised his same sex desires in a space where the dominant political stance had historically framed homosexuality as immoral and un-American. In a powerful but subtle shift from the 1950s lavender scare, the Cuban immigration issue became a site in the evolving discourse around homosexuality when, in 1990, the Board of Immigration Appeals upheld a verdict allowing asylum to one *Marielito*, Fidel Armando Toboso-Alfonso, because he was persecuted as a homosexual in Cuba.[7] This decision resulted in the removal of the 1965 provision to deny immigrants asylum for 'sexual deviation', and it demonstrates a quiet political prioritizing of anti-communism over homophobia. In the 1980s, Arenas entered and lived the contradictions of meagre progress in civil rights eclipsed by vehement anti-communist discourse of the era. The gay rights movement afforded him some affirmation, but this would be fraught with tension. Outside of the memoir we can find examples of the complicated nature of the author's position: his speaking against communism, but not homophobia, in the context of a conservative political panel consisting of figures like Senators Jesse Helms and John East;[8] his participation and promotion of the controversial 1984 film, *Improper Conduct*, a documentary about Cuban oppression of homosexuals and political dissidents which critics claim conflates socialism with homophobia and elides U.S. homophobia in the process.[9] In addition to this, the emergence of AIDS, before Arenas was ill with the disease, intensified pressure for gay rights groups and homosexuals in general, whose lives and politics were drastically altered by ignorance about the disease and lack of adequate political response to it.

The key effect of this social and political milieu for Arenas was a forced participation in identity politics of the era. Despite his clear intention to remain outside and separate, reinforced repeatedly in his memoir, Arenas' anti-Castro quest and his sexual desires forced him into the political fray of the gay rights movement which often framed gay rights in terms of minority rights, thus risking victimization. This position further corralled him into the gender and sexuality paradigms of the day, and did not account for his own self perception in terms of these complex categories. This is most aptly expressed by Arenas in his memoir when, after years of exile, he reflects on the sexual behaviour he and his friends engaged in while in Cuba where their reigning desire was to have passive sexual relations with *macho* men. After lamenting the nature of homosexual relations in the U.S., we can see in this passage that his U.S. negotiations with gender and sexuality have stymied his perception and even his language:

> Después, al llegar al exilio, he visto que las relaciones sexuales pueden ser tediosas e insatisfechas. Existe como una especie de categoría o división en el mundo homosexual; la loca se reúne con la loca y todo el mundo hace de todo. Por un rato, una persona mama y luego la otra persona se la mama al mamante. ¿Cómo puede haber satisfacción así? Si, precisamente, lo que uno busca es su contrario. La belleza de las relaciones de entonces era que encontrábamos a nuestros contrarios [...]. Aquí no es así o es difícil que sea así; todo se ha regularizado de tal modo que han creado grupos y sociedades donde es muy difícil para un homosexual encontrar un hombre; es decir, el verdadero objeto de su deseo. No sé cómo llamar a aquellos jóvenes cubanos de entonces; no sé si bugarrones o bisexuales.

> Lo cierto es que tenían sus novias y sus mujeres, y cuando iban con nosotros gozaban extraordinariamente....[10]

In this passage, Arenas ends with lamentable articulation of exilic confusion. He does not know how to identify the Cuban youth of the 60s, and the sexual terms that he uses here in his attempt – 'homosexuals in the male role', 'bisexuals' – demonstrate the sexual categorizing and labelling of people that the author encountered in the U.S.

Though Schnabel's biopic appeared in 2000, Arenas' appropriation into U.S. anti-communist and gay rights discourses during the 1980s, with their binary and cultural limitations, is evident in the film. The film purchases acceptance of homosexuality and Arenas by constructing him as a homosexual in U.S. sexual and gender terms and equating Cuban communism with homophobic persecution. Further, the film conveys a sense that this form of oppression continues in 2000 as it did in the 1960s and 70s, the period described by Arenas in his memoir. The film's construction of Arenas opens an avenue for the writer into the American imaginary, but to do so the energy of Arenas' memoir, found in its persistent sexual subversion against the Cuban regime, is dampened.

The advertisements and trailers for the film demonstrate the film's positioning in this tense terrain of U.S./Cuban politics and binary anti/communist rhetoric. They do this first by not framing Arenas as a gay writer or disclosing the film's political stance for or against Castro. Advertisements invited audiences to wonder about its position, but in doing so they belied the film's framing of Arenas as a persecuted homosexual whose freedom would come to depend on exile in the U.S. An advertisement of December 23, 2000 in the 'Arts and Ideas' section of the *New York Times* included a 'larger-than-life' image of Arenas and emphasized wordplay by including various statements of critical acclaim in different fonts and sizes. These words, however, reveal nothing about the film's content or Arenas' writing. The advertisement suggests that the film targeted either an audience already aware of who Arenas was or strove to attract its audience through critical acclaim and the popular actor Javier Bardem, who played Arenas, as well as cameo appearances by Johnny Depp, who is listed, unlike Sean Penn (also appearing in a cameo role), among the actors. The film most likely drew interest first as a non-mainstream production, appealing to artistic or intellectual interest, but it was fairly silent about its homosexual content.

The early Fine Line Features trailer reinforces this, but draws on interest in Cuba, thus appealing to the Cuban *émigré* crowd as well as scholars and others who are attuned to Cuban politics. It also avoids (or assumes) political identification by offering a series of scenes from the film put to music, depicting a rough chronology of moments and places in Arenas' life. Outside of critical acclaim only three key phrases are offered that allude to the content of the film: 'Cuba 1959', 'A Time of Great Promise' and 'Based on the Memoir of Exiled Cuban Novelist Reinaldo Arenas'. In this way, the trailer indicates that the film is an autobiography and draws on interest in the Cuban Revolution, without ever 'outing' Arenas as a homosexual writer or taking a direct political stance for or against Castro. The only overt framing here is the word 'exiled' which positions the viewer to be sympathetic with Arenas who probably was ostracized by the Cuban government. This suggests either a subtle appeal to anti-Castroism or an assumption that viewers already saw Cuba as an oppressive dictatorship. Interestingly, these advertisements appeared just months after Elián González was sent back to Cuba to live with his father. It seems that Schnabel's choice to open the question of Cuba and revolution with no other clear intentions might be even more appealing in the aftermath of the Elián story because it suggests the film might offer a perspective on Cuba that might help with the controversial question of where the child should finally settle. Further, its appeal might be its potential to bring light to the mysterious island nation. As Jacquelyn Loss points out, the film follows by just one year *The Buena Vista Social Club*, the 1999 Wim Wender and Ry Cooder film that similarly casts Cuba in a historicizing colour and mood.[11] This suggests that not only would the film deal with the larger political and philosophical questions of Castro's Cuba, but now viewers could see the 'real' Cuba.

This framing and the quality of the film was effective in drawing audiences. *Before Night Falls* quickly made it into mainstream movie theatres. It had moderate success, grossing $4.22 million dollars and ranking between other 2000 movies such as *Bread and Tulips* ($4.78 million) and *Quills* ($3.71 million), but it was a far cry from box office hits like *Cast Away* ($233.6 million) and *Miss Congeniality* ($106.8 million), released just a week earlier.[12] And among its other nominations and awards, Javier Bardem was nominated for an Oscar. Where the advertisements did not overtly suggest that the movie was about a gay Cuban writer, persecuted in large part for his sexuality, the movie and the reviews are not so shy about Arenas' sexuality. Max Kozloff for *Art in America* states, 'The film deals perfunctorily with Arenas' literary vocation, and at far greater length with his sex life'.[13] Indeed, in the movie reviews, the 'exiled Cuban novelist' of the trailer becomes the 'gay Cuban writer' (*New Internationalist*), 'gay Cuban novelist and dissident' (*New Statesman*), 'gay Cuban novelist and poet' (*Variety*), and the 'gay Cuban poet and novelist' (*The Gay & Lesbian Review Worldwide*).[14] Of course, this is not to suggest a streak of homophilia or homophobia running through a circle of film critics; rather, I emphasize that the film appealed to people based on Arenas' persecution as a homosexual, rather than as a writer. As such, it probably began to draw those interested in anti-Castro politics, Cuban scholars of all persuasion, and those interested in gay rights. Equally important, the film's success can also be linked to Schnabel's ability to capture the brutality of Castro's Cuba, therefore reinforcing prevailing conceptions about Cuba and communism that are packaged in mainstream American ideals about democracy.

Specific filmic choices reinforce this emphasis. In the DVD commentary Schnabel indicates that he chose colours and filters with the goal of setting the film in a specific time. 'If you're going to make a movie about Cuba, time has to stand still'. This choice helps to project a 1960s image of Cuba and the revolution's peculiar brand of homophobia into the 21st century. This mood is sustained by the inclusion of clips from both *Improper Conduct* and, during the rolling credits, *P.M.*, a film on Havana night life made by Guillermo Cabrera Infante's brother, Sabá, and banned in 1960.[15] Time has not stood still, but American anti-Castroism often depends on the notion that it has. But the taming of Arenas' sexuality and reframing it in U.S. terms is essential to the film's success as well. Not wishing to overlook the film's outstanding visual imagery nor its successful portrayal of many important aspects of Arenas' autobiography, I will briefly address these before returning to a discussion of how the film's depictions of Cuba and Arenas' sexuality serve U.S. national discourses.

The film effectively transforms the importance of Arenas' writing, as well as his sensual style, into vivid, tropical colours and lush landscapes that transmit Schnabel's painterly aesthetic. The film also includes excerpts from Arenas' poetry, and this inclusion of Arenas' texts is part of its homage to the author. Other important aspects of the autobiography are creatively depicted in the film, even if great liberties are taken by Schnabel, who conflates characters, events, and even fantasies in order to convey the spirit if not the historical facts of the autobiography.[16] Indeed, some of the film's power comes from Schnabel's ability to capture Arenas' style and passion for artistic expression through a medium quite different from writing. The film gives life to the lush rural countryside of Arenas' youth. It conveys the young Arenas' outcast position in his family and his tortured relationship with his mother. It suggests his emerging homoeroticism as an adolescent. It offers a glimpse of a colourful and tempestuous sexual revolution in Havana, and it implies Arenas' sexual voracity (though with calculated moderation). The film also offers a taste of both the brutality and absurdity of Arenas' time in prison and his constant persecution. And, finally, the film subtly illustrates the oppressive power structures of Cuba's gendered *machista* system under Castro (though, importantly, not their complexity). Schnabel's choices suggest a sincere loyalty to the author, or his idea of the author, something further reinforced by the fact that Arenas' long time friend, Lázaro Gómez Carriles, was one of the film's screenplay writers.[17]

Nevertheless, the framing of Arenas' sexuality, as I suggested above, produces familiar notions of homosexuality that are not complicated by Cuban cultural nuances, nor by the in-your-face, counter-revolutionary escapades offered by the hyper- and homo-sexualized Cuba of Arenas' memoir.[18] For Arenas, the writing of the memoir from the perspective of bicultural gender and sexuality paradigms allows him to show that, often, Cuban men who take the active or penetrative role in sex with other men are not stigmatized as homosexuals;[19] they are seen as *macho*, and this becomes essential to the memoir's anti-Castro agenda.[20] Schnabel attempts to capture the nuances of Cuban sexual power dynamics, but viewers unaware of this complexity will most likely miss the importance of Arenas' sexual life in relation to what he understood as his own rebellion. This aspect of the memoir brings us closer to understanding Arenas' lived experience. By having sex with society's *macho*s, the memoir suggests, Arenas enacted rebellion against the Cuban regime. Further, the film's simplification of sexual power dynamics allows the protagonist to become situated in U.S. national discourses that reify familiar conceptions about Castro's Cuba. Three overlapping areas in particular merit discussion: the taming of Arenas' sexual voracity, the simplification of Cuban gender and sexuality dynamics in relation to political power and oppression, and the omission of any sense of Arenas' sexual and romantic life, and the associated disappointments the author experienced, in the U.S.

In the memoir, Arenas claims 5,000 sexual encounters by his 25th year. Though this may very well be true, it is easy to attribute this to the author's penchant for hyperbole and humour. Still, a great deal of the memoir's energy and verve comes from narratives of sexual encounters, one after the other, and this is simply not found in the film. The film offers a glimpse of Arenas' frequent sexual activity, but it also subdues it, primarily through two scenes: when Arenas and his friends are found by the military recruits and they all laugh and play naked, exuberant, around a fire on the beach, and when Arenas narrates to Pepe his interpretation of the four categories of gays. The beach scene begins with tension and fear; military recruits approach Arenas and his friends as they sit around a campfire reading aloud. The two groups of men are characterized by their attire and demeanour: Arenas and his friends wear swimsuits, some are shirtless; they lounge with books and share laughter; the recruits wear full military garb and carry weapons, which they fire into the air as they march up to the '*maricones*'. The threat, marked by weaponry, ominous shadows cast by fire-light, hyper-masculine gestures, and verbal abuse is subdued by mockery, subservience, and seduction. Once the groups recognize their mutual interest in a sexual encounter, the mood changes. The scene is rendered safe through aesthetic distance with playful imagery that turns fear into frivolity. Indeed, it is reminiscent of Matisse's 'The Dance'. Men run around a beach fire at night; many are naked or nearly so, followed by or following other men in various stages of undress or military garb, some carrying guns, some running to jump on the back of the military truck, all of them laughing and indulging fully in the sensuality and pleasure of the moment. The painterly quality of the scene tames the orgiastic imagery, making it jubilant. The episode suggests the sexualized power dynamics of *machismo*, but fails to explain itself fully, conveying a sense of fantasy and surprise, but not the repression and rebellion involved for those involved.

Arenas' narration of the four categories of gays is similarly tamed through visual representation. Arenas (Bardem) himself, acts out the manners and behaviours he describes, self-reflexively presenting the various types of gays. In one case he narrates the characteristics of the 'closet gay', while having sex with him. This is depicted with a shot of the couple from the torso up. This filmic choice suggests a sense of frantic and furtive sex without being overly offensive to an American and global viewership not accustomed to explicit depictions of sex between men. In addition, the self-reflexive metanarration and the calm, sensual seaside setting of the conversation contain its sexual energy by making it satirical and humorous. What this scene cannot portray is the way that Arenas forgoes a critique or description of his own sexual desire in his categorization. In the larger context of the memoir, this becomes important to the way the author formulates a liberating sexual ideology based on his particular form of sexual desire for *macho* men. The film does not depict the memoir's sexual tension: the lines of men outside of Arenas' room, the recruits' clandestine turn to Arenas and his friends for sex and tenderness and then their return to their wives and *macho* personas. In both scenes potential punishment is linked to hidden or illicit sexual activities, suggesting that Arenas' persecution in Cuba will be due to his homosexuality rather than his writing and thus drawing audience sympathy to the protagonist as someone persecuted for his homosexuality and opening the way to a filmic depiction of Arenas as victim.

The taming of Arenas' sexual appetite and the lost opportunity to elucidate the *macho's* sexual power is almost overcome by the key scene in which the film attempts to depict the complexity of Cuban gender norms. Johnny Depp's second cameo appearance (after the compelling 'Bon Bon' episode) points to all the key elements of the regime's power. Depp, playing Lieutenant Victor, a state security officer responsible for coercing Arenas to rebuke his former life as a now 'reformed' homosexual and reject his published writing, takes on the role of the despondent Arenas' fantasized object of desire. The crisply uniformed official subtly strokes himself while moving back and forth between adoring looks at photographs of Che Guevara and Fidel Castro and hateful though seductive looks at Arenas. The office is dingy and stark, the Lieutenant's chair creaks and screeches, and we understand that power is the only resource the officer has. Arenas fantasizes of being comforted by the handsome man, but, in fact, Arenas angers the officer with a clever remark, and he responds by forcing his pistol into the terrified Arenas' mouth and pretending to fire. There are no bullets in the gun.

This scene carefully crafts and highlights the dynamic of *machismo* and oppression in revolutionary Cuba, but falls short of articulating the specifically gendered and sexual nature of social and political hierarchy. The Lieutenant is apparently turned on by Che and Fidel as symbols of power, and, further, his own power in relation to Arenas, a queered and imprisoned author who has provoked his anger. This links his show of force not only to *machismo* and homophobia, but to repression and anti-intellectualism as well. The phallus, stroked, forced as a gun into Arenas' mouth, present viscerally in the power dynamic of the scene, represents the New Man philosophy of the revolution. It is the ability and desire to penetrate that makes one a man and a part of Castro's revolution. As a passive homosexual, Arenas is not only disempowered, he perpetuates Lieutenant Victor's ability to be on top. My pun is intended, but its significance is missing from the film. Lieutenant Victor could choose to have sexual relations with Arenas while still maintaining his position of power, but the opposite will never be true for the emasculated Arenas. The sexual dynamics here reinforce Arenas' homosexual identity constructed in opposition to the violently heterosexist officer. In a mainstream imaginary the sexual fantasy marks Arenas' desire rather than articulating a specifically sexualized vector of power in Cuban society. Despite this effective scene, the film thus fixates on Cuban homophobia. By doing so it defines homosexuality and homophobia in terms familiar to a U.S. audience. Arenas desires men, marking him as homosexual; the officer treats him unjustly signalling a nationally structured system of homophobia that can be attributed to communism.

Further, the film suggests (as did the reviews mentioned earlier) that Arenas' imprisonment was more about his sexuality than his publishing abroad. Though the scene analysed above criminalizes Arenas for smuggling his work out of Cuba, the sexualized tones of the meeting and Arenas' forced confession and promise to reform and become a 'man illuminated by this revolution...' emphasize his persecution as a homosexual. The film is never overt about the passive-active sexual paradigm that Arenas takes up so productively (and with such *angst*) in the autobiography. Further, the film cannot convey to all audiences what was so rebellious about Arenas' role in the Cuban sexual revolution in the 1960s. Perhaps more importantly, it cannot convey the memoir's unique attempt to subvert that revolution by 'homosexualizing' the supposedly *macho* men, those like Lieutenant Victor, at its foundation. This problem is furthered by the film's refusal to address sexuality for Arenas in the U.S., where, according to the film but certainly not the memoir, there are no sexual or romantic relationships at all – even his relationship with Lázaro appears completely platonic – and the protagonist certainly never voices (as he does in the autobiography) criticism about the gay communities he encountered there.

Clearly, one reason for the taming of Arenas' sexual activity and the simplification of the gendered and sexualized power structure of *machismo* in the Cuban regime is that homosexuality is presented in the film for a predominantly American audience in terms familiar to that audience. Explicitly gay sex would either seem gratuitous or potentially offend many viewers; certainly it would preclude the film's entry into the mainstream (imaginary and box office). In addition, this portrayal of Arenas draws more sympathy than one depicting him engaging in rampant sex, or seeking out sex with *macho* figures whose desire for him might appear demeaning. Unlike the film, the memoir demonstrates Arenas' conflict with U.S. gender and sexuality norms. His assumption, carried with him from Cuban gender norms, that his desire feminizes or queers him, but not all men who engage in sex with men are problematized because in the U.S. gay sex is more homogenized. He is expected either to have sexual relations with those who are also 'passive' like himself, or to be 'active'. These encounters and practices demonstrate an affront to his ideas about his own sex and gender. Before, he laments, he encountered 'real men', 'aquel hombre, a aquel recluta poderoso',[21] 'powerful' and *macho* recruits who desperately wanted him. And he and his friends could find these men and have sex with them 'bajo los puentes, en los matorrales y en todas partes',[22] 'under bridges, in the bushes, everywhere'.[23] This lament about an unfulfilled desire for men who desired him for anonymous and fleeting sexual encounters is hardly one that could appeal to a wide viewership in the U.S. Without the context of sexual power relations in Cuba, the very hierarchy that Arenas subverts through exactly this kind of anonymous sex might frame the protagonist as desperate, passive, and even sexist and self-loathing.

The film's failure to depict Arenas' sexual life and disappointments in the U.S. significantly extends audience sympathy for the persecuted author. The film overlooks a large part of Arenas' life in New York as it is depicted in the memoir. As suggested above, the film does not convey Arenas' deep disappointment with the gay community, with what he deems its rigid categories and tedious practices. Nor does it share his positive sexual experiences in the U.S. In general, it foregoes his criticisms in the U.S., of the Cuban *émigré* community, of leftist academics, publishers, and alliances in general. It does not suggest that Arenas was ever politically involved in things like the plebiscite against Castro or the magazine, *Mariel*. Perhaps most sadly, it does not depict the ferocity with which Arenas wrote and struggled to keep writing his final novels before he was overtaken by AIDS, the hardly identifiable and unnamed disease that consumes the last portion of the film. Instead, the film emphasizes Arenas' poverty, illness, and loneliness. All of these choices draw sympathy for Arenas, even potentially from the Cuban *émigré* community he disdained during his life. He is the suffering protagonist, victim of persecution, example of Castro's oppression.

To conclude I will briefly discuss the directorial choices behind this depiction of Arenas. Schnabel's *Before Night Falls* presents a distinct separation between U.S. and Cuban treatment of homosexuals by framing the protagonist in terms of sexual identity. The film depicts Arenas as a homosexual – a familiar if not clear-cut identity category in the U.S. – persecuted and imprisoned, forced to confess, because of his homosexuality. This firmly plants Arenas as a figure in a gay rights discourse that risks victimizing him and moves the issue of homosexual identity and rights into the tug-of-war between the commonly opposed U.S. democracy and Cuban communism. Arenas becomes the centrepiece for that struggle. The question of sexuality is shifted away from the memoir's framework of sex as rebellion and into a framework in which the treatment of homosexuals is a question of democracy and individual rights. This move substantiates political discourses that minoritize and victimize homosexuals in the U.S. in the name of gaining those rights. That substantiation is bought with the currency of anti-communism, as the film indicts communist Cuba for its persecution of homosexuals. This manoeuvre is not new. It is not unlike Cuban ideologies that aligned homosexuality with capitalism in the 60s or American ideologies that aligned homosexuals with Communists in the 50s. And it is reinforced by the delicious scene in which Arenas and Lázaro enjoy the New York snow in the back of a convertible after their arrival to the U.S. Appearing after over an hour depicting Arenas' life in persecution, this feels like a celebration of specifically 'American' freedom.

Schnabel's motivations and perspective, as well as the reception and popularity of the film also speak to its political positioning. In addition to Schnabel's primarily artistic goals, mentioned earlier, the director makes it clear that he wanted to give Arenas a voice;[24] according to the DVD commentary, he saw him as 'a history of Cuba'. In doing so, the director and others involved in the process demonstrate an investment in giving due recognition to Arenas as a man and writer. Nevertheless, Schnabel claims that his goals are not political: 'I didn't set out to be a political film director'. 'I just wanted to make a movie about somebody whose words touched me'.[25] Indeed, Schnabel interestingly frames himself much like Arenas does – as an artist who is above politics: 'I don't know a damn thing about politics. I'm not on the right or the left, and I don't want to be used under any opportunistic labels'.[26] At the same time, he recognizes the political nature of his choices: 'By the nature of his mere existence, Reinaldo becomes a political figure'. 'By the nature of me deciding to tell his story, it becomes a political movie'. Despite this level of consciousness, Schnabel's views take on unwitting politicized tones – 'I'm somebody who's verifying that these things happened. It's a moment in history. Castro does control the newspaper and the television in Cuba. Many people who lived there don't believe there are forced labour camps'. Schnabel's choice to switch to the present verb tense in this last sentence – 'there *are* forced labour camps' – implies that the UMAP camps, closed in the late 1960s, were still open in 2000 at the time of this interview. Schnabel is clearly sympathetic with Arenas and critical of Castro, something which underscores the film's ability to freeze Cuba in the image of Castro's persecution during Arenas' coming of age. Of course, one sign of the film's success is that it has a life of its own, conveying meanings and being interpreted in ways that can never be accounted for by analysis of the director's and writers' apparent intentions. Nevertheless the film comes to reflect the political bind of taking any position in relation to Cuba. Dominant U.S. discourses shape the film beyond what Schnabel could have anticipated. This demonstrates the very problem, so productive for anti-communist discourse of the 50s and again in the 80s, of nationalist discourses shaping and limiting subjectivity.

Finally, to return to the troubling issue of compromises mentioned at the opening of this essay, it is important to note the film's ability to suggest an opening for the acceptance of homosexuality and rights for homosexuals in the U.S. By framing Arenas' persecution as a sign of oppressive communism, the film puts sympathetic American viewers in the position of embracing Arenas and homosexuality as a demonstration of support for democratic freedom. This illustrates a decisive shift from previous decades. The film contributes to a wedge between the communists and homosexuals and asks Americans to accept the latter at the expense of former. This is troubling, regardless of one's position on Castro, because it limits the perspective on these issues to the given binary nationalist paradigms. It only reverses the 1950s terms: 'communists are morally corrupt sexual perverts' becomes 'communists are morally corrupt persecutors of homosexuals.' One of the foreclosures enacted here is a critical look at the fact that the first part of this formulation existed. Still, on an optimistic note, this compromise has its appeals and it may have immeasurable affects by destabilizing, even minutely, the conventional notions of the national subject in relation to sexuality. The dialog that *Before Night Falls* opened up between mainstream viewers, artistic intellectuals, scholars, and more generally, political perceptions of Cuba and Castro, is productive. We discover that anti-Castro politics could offer a free pass to themes often rejected as high-brow or overly-liberal: homosexuality and human rights, non-traditional formations of gender and the social constructedness of gender, and assumptions about the inherent value in writing and art. In other words, these concepts are accepted as topics of discussion because they are tacked onto a bill of anti-Castro sale and sold in a popular film, regardless of how and in what form some would wish them to enter conversation.

Likewise, while the film compromises some of Arenas' apparent goals with the memoir, it successfully gives voice to his bitterness towards Castro's Cuba. It allows Arenas to speak, even perpetuating his voice beyond what could happen while he was still alive. That he wanted this opportunity is most poignantly demonstrated in his suicide letter, printed as the final pages of the memoir, which he sent to newspapers so that it would reach wider audiences. By making its way into mainstream imagination, the film won acclaim in many countries. Many viewers, made aware of a figure like Arenas and issues of oppression like those demonstrated in regards to Cuba, will find or even (re)value art as a source of new perspectives and knowledge, a form capable of raising awareness. Bourdieu's notions of taste and class suggest that for some, enjoying an 'artistic' film might be linked to rising awareness promoted by that film.[27] The new book cover for the memoir, now hosting an image of Javier Bardem as Arenas, and its increased sales, indicate such renewed interest. Where many of us might like to see a picture of the author on the cover and further problematize notions of gender, sexuality, desire, and national belonging, there is some pleasure in knowing that Arenas is now more widely recognized; this is the silver lining of compromise.

2. NO STRENGTH: FLACCIDITY AND RESONANCE IN THE FILMS OF LUCRECIA MARTEL

Dorian Lugo-Bertrán (University of Puerto Rico, Río Piedras)

The constitutive 'strangeness' of Latin American production is no secret. Many thinkers, from the early European 'cronistas' to later Latin American theorists, remarked that what was perceived as out of the ordinary by the 'outside' gaze was taken as day-to-day experience by the 'local' ones. It is not that Latin American production is, in essence, disquieting. More likely, instances of Latin American production unsettle fixed identity constructions, including the ethnic one. Outside of some cultural hegemonies, production from these poetic zones converges in motivation with traces of creole, diasporic, and populous elaborations, whether from a dependent or dominant geography. One could state that the more political instances of Latin American production stem from a creole subjectivity, staging liminal points of contact between things. From this very context, of strangeness and 'creolité', I wish to discuss the films of contemporary Argentinean director Lucrecia Martel.

As a matter of fact, 'strange' is one of the signifiers that surfaces most often by critics to describe Martel's films. With three feature films to her credit, this director's production does little, according to the general opinion of critics, to present a 'strong story-line'; to explain or justify fully her characters' motivations and liminalities, or even to expound any 'great truth' upon narrative conclusion. Queer theory will help in reading the historical and artistic specificities of these aspects of strangeness and 'creolité', there where fallogocentric tropes collapse one by one on these films' deliberately precarious grounds.

I intend a queer reading of Martel's production, partaking from the flaccidity and vibration tropes. The selection of tropes is not arbitrary. It shares intertextuality with what has become a commonplace in the criticism of the Argentinean director's films: the enunciation of the decadence of the middle and high sectors in provincial Argentina, and the consequent atmosphere of stagnancy and fatigue that permeates her works. Flaccidity, that is to say, the limits and possibilities created by the debilitation of the vertical axis in Martel's works, deserves attention in its own right.[28] No less is the case of the vibration trope.

Flaccidity and limpness open up the possibilities of the not-erect, not-standing. It also opens up the possibilities of reading the layered and the dense; even of an excess of mass or volume. There is, however, a simultaneous airiness, a forceless quality, in Martel's films that needs to be equally addressed: nothing, not even death, not even God, occupies the totality of the film's diegetic and cinematographic space. Nothing overwhelms it because everything is already overwhelmed.

The return of the real, or more so, the impossibility to ever traverse it; the given obstacles to fully suture, to fully heal, to fully imagine, or for that matter, to fully anything, are staged over and again in Martel's production.[29] The real is much too present; probably due to the characters' painstaking efforts to underwhelm it by a number of mechanisms, mechanisms which in psychoanalytic terminology could be referred to as repression, denial, projection, and introjection, among others, further fragmenting the real. The defence mechanisms make the real all the much stronger; it returns in the forms of phantoms,[30] partial objects,[31] opaque jouissance,[32] delirious fantasies, and somatisms. The leaks and cracks to the characters' imaginaries resonate all throughout the story and cinematography. The resonant effect and affect are hereby to be alluded to as 'vibration'.

This essay intends to follow closely the theorization of Deleuze and Guattari regarding the anti-Oedipal economies, the desiring machines,[33] where that which vibrates could ultimately be regarded as the suspension or *traversement*[34] of the scopic regime: the imaginary position of omnipotence, self-identity confirmation, and sub-alternization of the 'Other' through the believed power of the gaze. From this privileged standpoint, everything seen is either the self, or that which ratifies it or has the potential to do so: the unbridled fascination with identification. The debilitation of the vertical axis by the director in question is the condition of possibility, and not a limit to be exclusively denounced, although it is certainly not exempt of its fair dosage of subtle denunciation.

Vibration can, thereby, be read as the pronunciation of a horizontal-axis economy, an economy of desire that, displacing metonymically from partial object to partial object, offers resistance to scopic or totalitarian representation. It is no coincidence that Martel herself has claimed in more than one occasion that her craft is strongly sound-geared, sound being one of her films' most significant pieces of information. She also claims that sound is not a device to be used only in a realistic mode.[35] Not at all surprising, one must agree, in works where there's a striking prevalence of (a) minute, quotidian, off-frame, and acousmatic sounds;[36] (b) absence of non-diegetic music and narration; (c) unusual sound overlapping between sequences, and (d) extremely contrasted volume intensities, rhythms, and durations from shot to shot, from sequence to sequence.

Sound wave-lengths, vibration in general, regards that which is atmosphere-, and not narrative-, oriented. One could say along with the director that in Martel's films narrative and characterization are deliberately weak, concentrating instead on materiality: the signifying resistance to representation, to the vertically-inclined paradigmatic and metaphoric axis.[37] In said films, sounds are in fact indexical in that they point to something else; but they are also just sounds. Effect and affect have here a sedimentary not an additive-quality. They lead to nothing; they come from nothing. But they always resonate, as if a residual and ominous life would always linger around them. One is not sure what they reminisce or what they foreshadow, but it surely is not good – or at least, not totally so. (Is anything total in Martel's films?) In reading this director's production, one must be alert to the random characteristics of sound, a randomness which in and of itself could very well reveal the absence of fate or providence in the narrative. In fact, in referring to the characters of her film *La Ciénaga*, the director has stated that they are immersed in a sort of ('desamparo divino' ('divine abandonement').[38]

Queer Theory is indeed pertinent in the approach to her production, since as opposed to explicitly gendered takes on given objects of study, this theoretical framework allows gender and sexuality indeterminates to be read as such, as indeterminates. Whereas there are currents within Queer Theory that strongly pursue identity politics, equating for example Queer Theory with LGTB-minded thinking, this study is closer to those that rather, at times, delocalize the identity signifier, and, at others, traverse it, taking the signifier into account and at the same time going beyond it. It is not that identity politics does not fulfil a purpose; it is rather that to take identity as the *archē and telos* of the signifying process is not only delimiting but logo-centric. There are other instances to signification and reading than identity constructions.

Besides Deleuze and Guattari's post-human interests, we will read Martel's works by integrating Melanie Klein's, Jacques Lacan's, and Julia Kristeva's approaches to psychoanalysis; Laura Mulvey's elaborations on the cinematographic gaze; Luce Irigaray's post-feminist pondering, and, the most obvious to this endeavour, the necessary historicist reflection in the hands of Michel Foucault and Judith Butler. Ultimately, what will be of interest in this study is how the gender and sexuality questioning is one of the many questionings that Martel undertakes, among them and certainly not the least the representation questioning.

So far, Lucrecia Martel has directed three full-length features: *La Ciénaga* (2001), *La niña santa* ('The Holy Girl', 2004) and *La mujer sin cabeza* ('The Headless Woman', 2008). A fourth full-length feature is soon to be released.[39] She has also directed several short films; certainly worth mentioning is *Rey Muerto* (1995), winner of the Havana Film Festival Coral Award for Best Narrative Short Film. Martel has directed features as well for Argentinean TV. Her merits have instantly been recognized, earning various international film awards and nominations. The Argentinean director has been identified by critics as belonging to a generation of filmmakers in her country named *Nuevo Cine Argentino* (Argentinean New Cinema). There is considerable debate whether there is such a movement. In her interview for *La mujer sin cabeza* Martel herself has affirmed that she does not feel as belonging to a cinematographic generation.

Whatever the consensus, some critics have suggested that this generation of filmmakers started to produce and release their work around the nineties. Besides Martel, some of the other filmmakers are Pablo Trapero, Martín Rejtman, Bruno Stagnaro, and Adrián Caetano. Historically, they all share the development and aftermath of Argentinean governments' neo-liberal politics, culminating in the much-discussed and media-covered apex of the 'crisis' in 2001. For Alfredo Alfonso, the 'newness' of the generation is well-founded, if somewhat exaggerated, when compared with Argentina's previous film production. This generation's aesthetic is indeed innovative, not so much their insertion within the international market; their production values are equally innovative, not so much their thematics.[40]

Production-wise, the *Nuevo Cine Argentino* in general shares with a *bricoleur* mode of production the engagement in this process with the means at hand, as opposed to strictly state-sponsored or larger budgeted filmmaking, according to Alfonso.[41] Their aesthetics are not strictly anchored on narrative or character decisions; un-narrative and cinematographic ones take pre-eminence as well.[42] Within this context, of economic uncertainty and *bricolage* creativity, appears the indelible trace of Lucrecia Martel.

Rather than discussing each film one by one, my approach is comparative. The three films lend themselves well to a comparative approach, given that many experts have identified a thematic unity, almost as if with the last of them a trilogy would have culminated. A quick overview attests to the fact that the three films share an interest in portraying the life of the middle and high sectors in provincial Argentina, especially in the northwest province of Salto, the director's birthplace. But there is more to these films than meets the eye. As a matter of fact, there is more to these films that resists the eye. In this study, we shall start with a brief synopsis of each film. Then we will go on to mention some other signifiers that they share, outside of an interest in certain sectors of society. Lastly, we will go beyond signifiers and signifying economies, elaborating a reading on the flaccidity and vibration tropes.

La Ciénaga is a cinematographic production that takes place in the Argentinean northwest, alternating between a city by the name of the film's title and a country-house by the name of La Mandrágora. It is the story about two families with four children each, one of which lives in the city and the other, vacationing in the country-house. The mother of the family in the city and one of the main characters of the story is Tali (Mercedes Morán); the mother of the second family staying at La Mandrágora is Mecha (Graciela Borges). They are both cousins. Tali leads a warmer but overwhelmed life, undertaken by her many responsibilities, financial difficulties, and a somewhat domineering husband; Mecha leads an embittered life, swamped in alcohol, boredom, financial solvency, racial prejudice, and a deep-seeded resentment caused partly by a philandering husband. Not very serious accidents on both families bring them together in a hospital at the beginning of the story; a deadlier accident sheds some shadow on whether they will be torn apart at the end.

La niña santa is a film that takes place also in the Argentinean northwest, in a family-owned hotel at the time of a medical convention that overcrowds the business. The story revolves around Amalia, who is an adolescent girl with a mystical vocation, and daughter to Helenita, the co-owner of the hotel with her brother, Rafael. The two elders are divorced. Amalia is a friend of Josefina, who is the rather mischievous counter-part of the two. Amalia claims to be on a quest for a yet to be known God-sent mission, when all of a sudden a dubious physician, suggestively pressing himself against her in the midst of a crowded street performance, makes her realize that the mission has at last been announced to her. She decides to save him, much to his chagrin. Her haunting is sometimes with an erotic – or should we say mystical? – insinuation. Doom seems to lurk on the physician's fate towards the end of the story, while the two friends swim away in the solitary hotel pool, lilting a contemporary song.

Lastly, *La mujer sin cabeza* is the story about a female physician who supposedly kills a cyclist with her car, and leaves the scene. A sense of numbness on her part ensues, apparently made stronger the more both she and the complicit high sector around her, aware of what happened, cover it effectively. It is a ghost story, without spectres. Only here the ghost slowly begins to resemble the living, and the living slowly begins to resemble the ghost. Whether she killed a cyclist in fact at all is never entirely clear, since all we see as spectators is the remains of the 'mount' that has been run-over which could very well have been a dog, a tricycle, both, or none of the above. Inevitable allegorical readings of *La mujer sin cabeza* have followed. The entire episode of the main character bumping into 'something' could be read as the Real of Argentina's high, white, and conservative sector's reality: this is, the sense of ill-covered guilt for turning their backs on or being accountable for the well-known *desaparecidos* dictatorship incident, on the one hand, or its present-day oppressive relating with their own indigenous sector, on the other, as the film seems to indicate.

If we attempt to compare the three films, some signifiers recur. The most apparent ones are: (a) the race and class tension between the indigenous poor and the white higher sector; (b) the representation of life within fairly enclosed spaces; (c) the integration of horror movie effects, some of which go back to the eighteenth-century Gothic novel, Elizabethan tragedy, and cultural production *topoi* from Antiquity, such as the presence of lighting, thunder, and rain as ominous signs; (d) the considerable number of scenes that take place in/around pools or that make allusions to them; (e) the equally considerable number of scenes that take place with characters in bed, sometimes several of them, for non-erotic encounters or as a place for socialization; (f) the omission or *outside-of-cameraness* of dramatic moments or high points in the story: the spectator is either too late or too early, and s/he mostly gets reactions, metonymies; (g) sexual ambiguities in all aspects, including gyno-erotic, hetero-erotic, paedophilic, and consanguine; (h) adolescent sexuality; (i) catholic rituals and pieties, and sometimes mystical urges, and lastly, (j) family secrets, or suppressed or eschewed information.

Although said signifiers are often mentioned in criticism regarding Martel's work, sometimes as themes, more needs to be said in relation to the dismantling of signification. It is a problem to read the indeterminate in this very director's work as a transitive mechanism; there is something necessarily political to be said about engaging with the very mass of Martel's production. Critics in general have regarded the beginning of *La Ciénaga* as disclosing a kind of 'archaic' quality to it. Something telluric and way down deep is rotting in the state of Argentina, so much so, that saturation is out of the question, bringing all sorts of invaginations to the surface, the proliferation of open pores.

The archaic does come up often in the director's work. Above all, if by archaic we mean something similar to what Julia Kristeva understands by it: the revolt, the return of beginnings, of the not fully enclosed, the abject. Not subject, not object: abjection. That which by its very indeterminateness incites, to the very least, apprehension; to the very worst, horror, or even the death drive. Archaic as in *archē,* and thereby, as in archive, a sedimentation of information: half-living, half-dead, half-remembered, half-forgotten. Arcane. A ghostly resemblance. An apparition. The archaic as related to the mother's body or the *chorā,* economy of rhythms and drives.[43] Or if we use Melanie Klein and the English School of Psychoanalysis' terminology, the elaboration of the internal workings of the phantasy (the 'ph' intended),[44] with all that ghastly scenario of partial objects, gramenes,[45] rudiments, sadistic drives, and agony. Or if we use Jacques Lacan's terminology, and as mentioned before, the response of the real, or just simply the not entirely symbolized.

This prevalence of the kingdom of the archaic [(M)Other] comes as no surprise in a filmmaker's trajectory with a short film as *Rey Muerto*, mentioned before, as one of her first pieces. The very title translates to: 'Dead King', but what it leaves unsaid is that one cannot but think in Spanish of the proverb that says, if we translate roughly: 'Dead king, king rethroned' ('Rey muerto, rey puesto'). This film about domestic violence does punish in its own way an abusive male partner's transgressions towards its female companion, but he certainly does not end up dead, nor does she end up with another partner, as the proverb would suggest. In fact, in the story Rey Muerto is the name of a town, not at all clear if it is the one left behind or to be quested in order to start a new life. Rey Muerto is, if anything, a metaphor, not a signifier. We suggest it is an important metaphor in order to read Martel's work in general, and not only this specific short film: a work where stories mostly start with a state of numbness on the characters' part after the death of the king or the declining of the paternal function: weak or no fathers, young men as penises, if at all, bending rules or diffuse boundaries (for better and worse), ambiguities everywhere, little ideals or models, a general godlessness everywhere. Amidst this aftermath, it could be said that the spectator is just as lost as the characters: little markers, just a general sense of untold stories, to be reconstructed, if at all. In the end, all that remains is a future, equally unforeseen, for everyone, characters, spectators, without exception.

No beginning, no conclusion, no high or turning points. Peaks happen somewhere else; not in front of the spectator. The flaccid, the limp, are the politics of Martel, not the erect or the vertical. Characters take many naps; they sleep frequently, and they nap again, or just rest, or just converse lightly, also in bed. Sometimes they laugh, or cry, or yell, in bed. They rarely make love. The bed is a table, a chair, a coffin, maybe it is a car. The bed is de-loved, de-signified, de-bed-ed. Flaccidity to the point of no hope for the living dead, or, much to the contrary, to the point of all hope for the soon to be awakened people. A place where ideals could be reposited, or better yet, a place where just when little can be represented, because nothing stands (in its place), desire shows its face. For Deleuze and Guattari desire appears when representation falters. Desire, not Eros, seeks neither possession nor fetish. The films' gaze seeks not to sentence or condone; that would be appropriation. It prefers to stage the real in a society's and character's reality, or the partial object, in the phantasy. Maybe that is why even if quite opaque things do take place in Martel's work, and characters do not really fulfil their dreams at the end of the stories, one gets traces of a happy or possibly-happy futures. The characters' lives do seem confining, even suffocating; at times they do come across as repugnantly irresponsible. But there is always that space, that much space, which the films' gaze facilitates. If anything, that very space leaves air for not sentencing any life – for not closure.

Good or bad, due to the very indeterminateness of these lives' portraits, the gaze, our desire, is so alive. Good or bad, desire hereby vibrates, as if to stay in one place is impossible, or not all desirable, not true to desire. If desire aims not at given objects but at the lack, at that which is lacking, as Lacan indicates, in these moving pictures' gaze desire is anything but dead. Over and again, in these characters of *jouissance*, of addictive and painful practices, desire keeps lurking around them, as if too much tenderness, somewhere, is unable to fully close, to fully sentence the lives of any of them. It might even be their own desire, working on a molecular, not a molar, level, as Deleuze and Guattari would have elaborated it. Which might be why Martel herself has observed that ultimately she is always fascinated by how a 'little organism survives'.[46] This eye for the diminutive, the minorized, the anodyne, is alert. It might at times frame an image off-centre so that a background and un-related conversation acquires some prominence. However, the conversation is not a Greek Chorus; it keeps being un-related to the foreground, to the protagonist's life, but it resonates, it vibrates, in a way that it can easily travel from that moment to another further on, without ever making full sense, without ever vectorizing, without ever standing, without ever representing. After all, it is always just mumbling, noise at worst.

Sounds, little sounds and gestures, are everywhere. The microscopic workings of things alive, or half so. Is this Martel's version of hope, not in the grand, molar, gestures, but in the much too little to not be ignored? Is the debilitation of the vertical axis a sign of moral laxity, and just that, as some critics want to see in Martel's films? Or is that also a possibility? Is there a vibrating substitute? Is there a resonant prosthesis anywhere?

In a world such as hers, where all paradigms are down, it might be that vibration, not appropriation, is the survival strategy of the characters in these films. Another mode of travelling places, people, than to fully occupy them. The gyno-erotic logic of the feminine, for Irigaray, of touching, and letting go, if only to touch again.[47] As a matter of fact, these characters sometimes touch too much (And I am all for touching). The incidental moments of appropriation, of condensation, are most often metonymized. Brothers and sisters touch, sisters and sisters touch, mother and son touch, elderly men and younger girls touch, adult woman and adult woman touch, the indigenous and the white, in particular occasions, touch. It is a world of lingering fingers, but no slaps or fists. It is not ideal; it just goes unnoticed.

But maybe, just maybe, among so much flaccidity and pointless vibration, a girl will go to see a much-visited apparition of the Virgin, and upon her return state quite as-a-matter-of-fact that she did not see anything, as in the ending of *La Ciénaga*; or two girls will swim away lilting a song in a pool, one of them unaware that the other, without ill- meaning, betrayed her trust, exposing the fact that she had been sexually molested by the physician, and also quite unintentionally as well might end up doing some good, although they are both unaware of it, and so is the spectator, since the bomb and its effects are to explode sometime after the end of the story, as in the conclusion of *La niña santa*; or a woman who has seemingly killed a cyclist upon driving carelessly, and then leaving the scene, ends up unpunished after much tormenting guilt, the accidental murder carefully hidden by accomplices and herself, but... traces are everywhere: unrepaired car bumps, frustrated opportunities of philanthropy, mysterious pieces of a swimming pool that appear from underneath the home patio grounds, a sudden dye of hair from blonde to jet black on the part of the protagonist (as of a perpetual mourning perhaps, not to mention an untriumphant expression to her face by the end of the film, when accompanied by contemporary music in talking to some high sector friends at a party: not alienatingly happy (as one would expect in some Buñuel films), not sad: just untriumphant, as in the end of *La mujer sin cabeza*. The (irresponsible) living are to (keep on attempting to) live. They might even work hard at it, but among ghosts. Amidst all these sadness and mixed to opaque news. Maybe, just maybe, though no less sad, and against all evidence, there is hope.

3. YOUNG ARGENTINE FILMMAKERS: REMEMBERING THE PAST FROM A PRESENT OF CRISIS

Ana Ros (Binghamton University, SUNY)

In this essay, I reflect on the role of young filmmakers in the formation of the collective memory of the last Argentine dictatorship (1976-1983), proposing that their challenging approaches to the past are a crucial contribution to the current 'boom' of memory in Argentina.[48] Even though they are on the victims' side, their films question aspects of the human rights associations' narratives because they do not help them understand how so much violence was possible and how to prevent it from happening again.

Thereby, they open up the past to discussion, transcending the simplistic oppositional logic that equates a critical examination of the human rights associations' narrative with supporting the military's actions and views of the past. These directors encourage all the actors of the past who were adults back then to reflect on their experience: to examine what they did, or did not do, to contribute to the well-known tragic outcome of numerous cases of human rights violations. The point is not to create a new and extended list of actors to blame but, on the contrary, to try to understand collectively how so much horror was possible, while engaging in the construction of a more humane society in the present. In other words, the goal is to achieve a more inclusive and instructive collective memory of the dictatorship that allows all actors to learn from the past.

I argue that this step forward is possible because of the directors' position in relation to the past: They are close enough to feel the need of understanding what happened, yet have enough distance to identify fissures – gaps in the narrative which derive from fears and uneasiness.

The directors belong to a generation whose members were born in the years before and soon after the beginning of the dictatorships. Although too young to make sense of what was going on in the way adults did, they were deeply affected by the political situation. The children of bystander parents grew up in an environment of fear, distrust and isolation generated by the persecution of anyone suspected of supporting the army's enemies. Conversely, the children of activist parents faced several possible scenarios: some went underground during their early childhood while others went into exile or became orphans. For their parents, this past represents either traumatic memories that they are unable to evoke or painful experiences that they do not want to revisit. Therefore, they did not transmit a coherent personal narrative to their children and left the transmission of the past in the hands of institutional collective memories.

However, this transmission of the past was not unproblematic either. Typically, after a conflictive past, there are several collective memories with different interpretations of what happened, based on the experiences lived by the group which remembers and its goals. The promoters of these memories have priorities other than explaining the past to the younger generations: they are fighting to establish their truth in the public sphere in order to get governmental and legal recognition of their demands. In Argentina, the image of the recent past was fragmented by three narratives that assigned incompatible meanings to the events: the one supported by the army ('we waged a necessary war against subversion'), by the human rights associations ('the army committed crimes against helpless victims') and by the government which oversaw the transition to democracy ('we all went through a war between 'two demons': the guerrilla and the army'). The films I analyze are a response to this complex situation and show the younger generations' desire to know and understand the past in order to use it as a reference point for dealing with the conflicts in the present. Todorov refers to this as an 'exemplary' way of remembering.[49] I discuss *Diario argentino* by Guadalupe Pérez García (2007) and *Cordero de Dios* (2008) by Lucía Cedrón. As we will see throughout the essay, they represent the most advanced stages in the process of achieving a more inclusive and instructive collective memory.

I will start by briefly explaining the notion of collective memory I am using, central to this argument, as well as describing how the process of collective memory formation in Argentina is linked to historical and political context.

During the last Argentine dictatorship (1976-1983), an estimated 30.000 individuals 'disappeared'. They were mostly young people abducted by the army who suspected them of being involved in 'subversive activities.' They were tortured to death or murdered at illegal detention centres without a trial or contact with the outside world. In most cases, their families were denied information about their situation and, after it become obvious that they had died the army did not reveal the whereabouts of their remains. It is known, however, that some of them were sedated and thrown from planes into the sea, while others were buried in mass graves or cremated. The term 'disappeared' was, in fact, introduced by the dictator Jorge Rafael Videla in a press conference in response to the mothers' constant inquiries: 'It is a mystery, a disappeared, a nonentity, it is not here: they are neither dead nor alive, they disappeared'.[50]

In 1983, after the end of the dictatorship, the democratically elected president Raúl Alfonsín formed a commission to investigate the fate of the 'disappeared' prisoners. After hearing thousands of testimonies on abduction, torture, and executions from survivors and victims' families, the commission published a shocking report entitled *Never Again* (1984), and advised commencing trials against the army. The report's prologue, by the renowned writer Ernesto Sábato, presented an interpretation of the dictatorship and its actions different from the one promoted by the army, thereby introducing the idea of memory as part of social tensions and struggles. Argentine sociologist Elizabeth Jelin will later theorize memory in the same way.[51]

According to Jelin, collective memories are group narratives that assign meaning to the past in light of present circumstances and future goals; they are promoted by social actors through 'vehicles for memories' (books, museums, monuments, films or other forms of expression that incorporate the past performatively, such as mottos or demonstrations). Not all societal groups relate to the past in the same way, especially when the past is conflictive and involved confrontation and oppression, which implies having lived through radically different (political) experiences. Different groups typically interpret the past differently, not only in relation to what they lived through, but also in relation to their expectations of how to deal with the consequences of the conflict (for instance, whether or not the military crimes should be prosecuted). In a divided society, the act of assigning meaning or interpreting the past implies the possibility of shaping the collective present and future according to the interests of the most powerful group and against the others. For instance, the prosecution of military crimes benefits the victims to the detriment of the army's interests and vice versa.

As Jelin observes, 'controversies over the meaning of the past surface at the very moment when the events are taking place'.[52] During the dictatorship, the army presented the events as part of a long-term historical process in which they appeared as saviours of the nation from the 'Marxist threat': the military was fighting a war against 'subversives', 'bad' citizens who were corrupting the moral and physical integrity of the nation with their leftist ideologies. According to the army, the exceptional character of fighting 'internal enemies,' who could easily influence other people around them, justified their fighting a 'dirty war.' In other words, they claimed they had to fight a 'war' that would permanently discourage the 'subversives' from being politically active. This 'war' required special methods of repression, sometimes leading to 'mistakes' or 'excesses' regarding individuals' human rights. Prisoners were subjected to systematic sexual abuse, humiliation, physical torture (application of cattle prod, dry and wet submarine, mutilation and beating), psychological torture (fake executions, witnessing friends and families being raped or tortured) and ultimately 'disappearance.'

The army targeted 'subversion' as their main enemy, but was at the same time deliberately ambiguous about the sense of the term. According to their public statements, subversion was represented by the actions of the urban guerrilla movements but it also included endorsing and encouraging any left wing ideology, or any beliefs against what they claimed to be the traditional values of Christianity, family and private property.[53] Thereby, 'subversion' infiltrated the private sphere, including 'all kinds of social confrontation' such as 'the struggle between children and parents, parents and grandparents'.[54] Long after the urban guerrilla had been completely dismantled, the army continued to terrorize society as a whole in order to definitively eradicate 'subversion' and anti-establishment ideas or attitudes from Argentinean culture. On May 6th 1977, the Governor of the province of Buenos Aires, General Alfredo Oscar Saint-Jean, stated to the British newspaper *The Guardian*: 'We will first eliminate the subversives, then their accomplices, later their supporters and finally those who are indifferent'.[55] As a response to this state of terror, most bystanders naturalized the logic of repression by withdrawing into the private sphere and distrusting everybody. The popular expression 'surely there's a reason', when people learned about or witnessed a case of brutal repression, reflects the degree to which many actors disconnected from politics as a result of state terror.[56] When the public sphere reopened at the end of the dictatorship, previously censored memories emerged, expressing their own interpretations of the past. The human rights associations and the families of the 'disappeared' prisoners (represented by the Mothers of Plaza de Mayo) promoted a counter-official collective memory, summarized in the mottos 'never forget, never forgive', 'truth and justice' and 'never again.' These mottos indicate that the only way of remembering the past and preventing the repetition of state violence is by knowing the truth about the fate of 'the disappeared' and judging the military that perpetrated such crimes.

In the struggle for effectuating trials and sentences, the human rights narrative excluded any reference to the political activity of the victims because this could have been used by the army to corroborate their justification of the crimes as the result of a 'war' against internal political enemies. The human rights narrative, instead, focused on the image of the 'disappeared' as the ultimate expression of the military regime's inhumanity. Their image evoked the torment suffered by most of the prisoners, exacerbated by a tragic death, and the spectral nature of their impossible condition (neither dead nor alive). In this context, activism became a taboo topic to the point that the families of the 'disappeared' prisoners felt offended when asked if the victim had participated in any kind of political activity or belonged to any kind of armed organization.[57] In addition, in the testimonies of their surviving comrades who were reluctant to critically examine the years of activism – linked to feelings of pain for the losses suffered – the 'disappeared' became heroes of a 'sacralized past which, mystified, becomes untouchable'.[58] Hence, the 'disappeared' entered collective memory as victims of state terrorism, martyrs who offered their lives unselfishly or as heroes, yet detached from their revolutionary project of social change and from their historical context of great political awareness.

In 1985, the trials against the first three military juntas started, and were later extended to the other officers involved in human rights violations. However, within a few years, the military rose up against the sentences and, after meeting with the rebels, President Alfonsín restricted the scope of legal action. He established a deadline for pressing new charges and exonerated all those below the rank of colonel of responsibility. Thereby, and in spite of his intentions to avoid a new coup, Alfonsín was validating, on behalf of the State, the army's version of the recent events as a 'dirty war.' Nevertheless, the testimonies gathered in *Never Again* and heard at the public trials in 1985 had already changed the public interpretation of the past. The truth concealed by the army had been said. 'There was no doubt about the fact that there had not been a war but a systematic plan of extermination of those considered political enemies of the army'.[59]

As Jelin observes, the interpretation of the past is not fixed but varies according to changes in the political scene and the emergence of new political actors and generations. Even though President Menem in 1990 took impunity further than Alfonsín by pardoning the already reduced group of officers on trial, things were going to change only five years later. In 1995, Adolfo Scilingo, a retired navy officer, broke the 'pact of silence' kept by the army regarding the nature of the repressive actions used during the dictatorship: he publicly acknowledged the abduction, torture and murder of the so-called 'disappeared' and his own participation in the (until then denied) 'flights of death.' Although his confession was not driven by remorse but a way of expressing discontent about how promotions were handled between the army and the government, it produced a great commotion in the scenario of memory. Other officers followed in his footsteps, including the chairman of the Joint Chiefs of Staff, presenting a self-criticism on behalf of the institution and apologizing for their actions, no longer qualified as 'excesses' or simple 'mistakes.' In addition, the Mothers and Grandmothers of Plaza de Mayo found a way of resuming the trials against the army for having violated the right to identity by keeping the babies of the killed and 'disappeared' couples, pretending that they were their biological parents ('appropriation'). Suddenly, after a period of decline and stagnation following the Alfonsín and Menem pardons, the human rights narrative recovered a central position in the public sphere.

In this context, the group H.I.J.O.S. (Sons and Daughters for Identity and Justice against Oblivion and Silence) emerged and presented a new perspective on the image of the 'disappeared.' The members of H.I.J.O.S. are sons and daughters of 'disappeared', killed, imprisoned or exiled activists. They vindicate their parents' political activity as the main feature to be collectively remembered, constructing them as revolutionaries. They preferred to think of themselves as children of a generation that fought for a country more solidary and just, rather than as the children of victims of state terrorism.[60] Furthermore, they identify with their parents' struggles and choose to continue their fight in the present against the social problems of today, understood as a consequence of the economic policies implemented by the dictators. This sense of continuation between parents and children is expressed by the main motto of the group: 'We were born in their fight, they live on in ours' (H.I.J.O.S.).[61]

The films I analyze in this essay can be associated with the movement initiated by H.I.J.O.S. since they also express the need of going beyond the human rights narrative. However, the directors do not participate in H.I.J.O.S. and have concerns different from the group. The directors respond to the past by raising questions, critically analyzing the events and using the past to shed light on the present, and inform action. In an experimental documentary, *Diario argentino* (2007), Lupe Pérez García focuses on the so-called 'bystanders' – those who were neither activists nor perpetrators. She challenges their typical image as passive spectators in a war between 'two demons', introduced in Sábato's prologue of the *Never Again*,[62] and validates their role as political actors in the past and the present. Finally, in the feature film *Cordero de Dios* (2008), Lucía Cedrón, herself daughter of a 'disappeared' activist, proposes a way of taking the past as a guide for acting in present situations of hate and violence.

This documentary, directed by Lupe Pérez García in 2007, starts with a simple dilemma: she was never able to differentiate between her left and right hand. In order to elucidate this problem, she travels to Argentina, the country where she was born and lived in until the 2001 economic collapse: 'Tengo la sospecha de que mi problema no es ni físico ni neurológico: como todos los traumas, proviene de la infancia'.[63] Once in Argentina, she starts searching for clues by interviewing her family and other individuals close to her about historical events of which she cannot make sense through the political categories of left and right.

These events constitute central aspects of Argentine subjectivity and most of them are tragic episodes most people prefer not to remember: at the origin of her confusion lies the killing of left-wing supporters by right-wing supporters of the same political leader, Juan Domingo Perón. The list also includes the popularly supported Falklands War during the unpopular dictatorship; the contradiction between Carlos Saúl Menem's populist political affiliation and neoliberal policies, and the 2001 economic collapse as the reverse image of the 1970s political crisis. Typically, documentaries do not relate these moments, but Pérez García takes them as a continuum and focuses on the relations between them and with the present. She wants to understand how people relate to the past when making decisions in the present. The entire documentary is oriented by questions such as: Is it possible to learn from past mistakes and apply those lessons in what might seem a fundamentally different context? How do we come to make decisions in the present that might become regrettable episodes in future collective perception?

These questions structure her interviews, for instance those about the success of Menem in the 1989 elections. He was a candidate for the Peronist party and during his campaign gained popularity by linking his own image to Perón's, who is commonly perceived as a defender of the working class, the welfare state and national development. Once in office, Menem did just the opposite: privatization of national services and industries, increasing external debts and budget cuts in public health, education and retirement. These policies caused the 2001 economic collapse, followed by one of the largest waves of emigration since the dictatorship, which included the director of the film and her family:

DIRECTOR. Che Má... ¿Por qué vos votaste a Menem en el 89?
MOTHER. ¿Vos tenés un cuchillito para clavarme en el estómago?
DIRECTOR. No bueno, pero yo también lo vote.
MOTHER. Porque uno a veces cre en pelotudeces... Lo que es imperdonable con lo de Menem es la segunda vez, porque tropezar dos veces con la misma piedra no puede ser. Porque vos fijate que pasa a

ganar todas las elecciones y nadie puede decir que no las ganó honestamente, eh?
DIRECTOR. Pero la segunda vez no lo votamos, la primera vez lo votamos ¿Por qué votaste a Menem?
MOTHER. Y a quién ibas a votar.
STEPFATHER. Lo que pasa es que el peronismo es un movimiento; es un partido que es un movimiento multiclacista. Entonces gente que guardó en su recuerdo el peronismo lo voto a Menem pensando que Menem era peronsita pero Menem no era peronista, ese es el asunto
DIRECTOR. No sé lo que significa ser peronista porque si Menem es peronista yo creo que él debe pensar que es peronista, que él debe sentirlo así.
STEPFATHER. No Menem entregó todo el país a los poderes extranjeros a los monopolies extranjeros. Yo te entiendo a vos que para vos haya perdido sentido. Es que perdió sentido porque ya no está más el peronismo: se acabó en el 55.
DIRECTOR. Si el peronismo se acabó en el 55 porqué en el 89 mamá y yo votamos a Menem, esa es mi pregunta ¿Entendés? No entiendo por qué.
MOTHER. Porque no se votó a Menem, se votó a la idea que se tenía de lo que se podía hacer desde el peronismo como movimiento.
STEPFATHER: La gente necesita hacer su experiencia. Vos fijate cuantas luchas han pasado en la Argentina. La Argentina es un país muy castigado porque después de la caída de Perón tiene cuatro golpes militares, dos veces se descabezó la Universidad. Por todas esas desgracias vos tenés que irte a un país extranjero a trabajar porque acá no podés hacerlo.[64]

It is important to note the mother's comparing her questions to a 'little knife' with which the director stabs her, hostile questions. There is a resistance to analyzing the 'mistakes' of the past as if that meant taking the blame for the results – the opposite of a critical evaluation in which what matters is not finding scapegoats but understanding how the painful events were possible. Her mother first analyses why she cast her vote for Menem: she followed unquestioned beliefs. However, she then blames those who voted for Menem a second time in 1995.

Her stepfather, an ex-activist, offers a political analysis of the situation that does not fully account for why people kept responding to a political ideology linked to a long-gone political figure in a period of national glory. Instead, he establishes a circular logic: people vote for a political movement that no longer exists because they vote according to the positive memory of a political movement that used to exist. Next, he observes that people learn through experience, which at first seems to open a space for the analysis of the past, but then he limits himself to enumerating the catastrophes, including the ongoing crises, and the learning experience is postponed.

By asking these difficult questions about the past, Pérez García is actually focusing on the present: if her mother and stepfather can see themselves as actors of the past, with an impact on historical processes, they will also realize their impact in the construction of the present. This is linked to another exceptional feature of this documentary: its 'protagonists.' Unlike most artistic and academic works that aim to explain historical processes, she seeks to capture the perspective of 'ordinary people.'

For many years, only the survivors of the illegal detention centres and the families of 'disappeared' prisoners were entitled to interpret the dictatorial past. The undifferentiated 'rest of society' (those who were neither survivors nor perpetrators) were conceived as the passive audience of a fight between two political extremes who did not know much about the systematic human rights violations. *Diario argentino* chooses to focus on that segment of the 'rest of society', which happens to be her family: the people through which she received – more or less directly and coherently – a version of Argentine history. By interviewing them in front of a camera for a documentary, Pérez García restores their role as actors, asserting that nobody is foreign to the events of his or her times. In fact, during authoritarian and repressive periods, people's fear, distrust and isolation are instrumental to the success of the regime, as individuals start reproducing censorship and repression in their own circles.

Accepting one's active role in the construction of the present demands making decisions based on lessons from the past. This is the opposite of the three typical reactions expressed by the individuals interviewed in the documentary. Firstly, the preference for not revisiting sad episodes: when the director asks her mother about the killing of Perón's left-wing supporters at Ezeiza airport, she does not want to talk about it: '¿Por qué te estás acordando de todas esas cosas? Es una época muy triste que los argentinos tratamos de no repetirla, de no recordarla'.[65] Secondly, explaining decisions through tradition, in the sense of unquestioned habit: When Pérez García asks her mother why at the end of the dictatorship she voted for the Peronist candidate Luder – who supported the army's self-amnesty law – instead of for the radical candidate Raúl Alfonsín – who considered this law unconstitutional – her mother answers: 'Porque tradicionalmente uno siempre tuvo más simpatía por el peronismo que por el radicalismo, por generación anterior, por mis viejos'.[66] Finally, she explains decisions through lack of a better option, as we have seen above regarding Menem's first election, when her mother says: '¿Y a quién ibas a votar?'[67]

In addition to exploring the ideas of 'ordinary people', a group rarely taken into account, *Diario argentino* is also concerned with the transmission of the past. The younger generation's response to its present is based on the interpretation of the past received from their parents and from other adults who experienced it. For instance, in order to explain her decision to emigrate during the 2001 crisis, the director refers to these transmitted interpretations. We see images of hundreds of people out on the streets protesting against the government, attacking banks and ATMs, banging pans, burning tires, breaking into stores in order to steal food and firmly resisting the attacks of the army and the police. We hear the director's voice-over saying: 'Me gusta pensar una Argentina revolucionaria pero esa Argentina, por lo general, termina mal, pore so yo agarré el primer avión y me las tomé'.[68]

This direct link between social rebellion and failure results mainly from the prevalence of the 'punishment' (torture, prison, exile and death) over the passion and commitment that impelled the revolutionary political project in collective memory. As the formerly exiled activist Martín Caparrós observes: 'The memories of death covered up the memories of life [...] there was much suffering but there was also much happiness in doing what they thought that had to be done'.[69] This, in addition to the absence of an assessment of the 70s political movements' practices, produces the impression that all popular protests are primarily dangerous, as opposed to opportunities for finding an effective way of participating in politics.

Nevertheless, the discussion she had with her family about their reasons for acting one way or the other in the past already helps the director to start making her own history: she starts considering returning to Argentina for good. She expresses this idea visually through a metaphor. In a scene close to the end of the film, she goes to the cemetery to leave flowers on her father's grave and walks past Perón's grave: her initial impulse is to leave some flowers but then she hesitates, thinks, and continues her way.

Finally, it is worth mentioning that *Diario argentino* establishes a dialogue with Mariana Caviglia's journalistic investigation published as *Vivir a oscuras: escenas cotidianas durante la dictadura* (2006) and *Dictadura, vida cotidiana y clases medias: una sociedad fracturada* (2006). Caviglia, a member of the post-dictatorship generation (born in 1976) shares with the other authors and directors analyzed in this essay a concern about how the horror was possible. She looks for answers in her hometown, La Plata, among neighbours and family that belong to the group of so-called 'bystanders', focusing on their everyday life and routines during the dictatorship. She collected numerous testimonies about what people did in relation to the repression they witnessed (beatings in the streets, violent abductions from houses or public spaces, shootings between the army and people inside their houses). Many people suffered from the constant threat of being taken for a subversive and suffer the fate of the prisoners. Caviglia proposes that everyday life contributes to either reproduce or challenge the social order in which social actors live. A social order like the dictatorship can only materialize if social actors in everyday life behave according to the regime's expectations. She thinks that many of the factors that made the dictatorship possible were already present in society before. Conversely, the dictatorship impacted actors' thinking, ways of living and interacting, leaving a legacy that includes, for instance, a devaluation of life and death, distrust of collective initiatives, passive acceptance of conditions as given or inalterable and intolerance.

Similar to Pérez García, Caviglia's studies seek to promote an understanding of the past which challenges the notion of fixed conditions linked to a supposed incapacity of 'ordinary people' to be agents of history. In other ways, her work is an attempt to create a notion of historic agency that involves everybody.

If the 2001 crisis pushed Pérez García to leave the country, it had the opposite effect on Lucía Cedrón, director of *Cordero de Dios* (2008), who decided to return from France to live in Argentina. In 1976, when she was one year old, her mother and father had taken her with them into exile in France, where her grandfather was already living, also as a result of political persecution. Her grandfather, Saturnino Montero Ruiz, was a right-wing politician, and her father, Jorge Cedrón, a socially engaged filmmaker who supported the left-wing guerrilla group *Montoneros*. In 1980, when Lucía Cedrón was five years old, her grandfather was abducted in Paris. While her mother was testifying to the police about his 'disappearance', her husband was stabbed to death at the police station. A few hours later, Lucía's grandfather was released without ransom. The circumstances of Jorge Cedrón's murder were never elucidated.

When Lucía Cedrón was sixteen years old, her mother decided to return to Argentina, while she stayed in Paris where she had already a life with friends, studies and plans for the future. In 2001, when her grandfather Saturnino Montero Ruiz died in Argentina, she returned to comfort her mother and help her with paperwork. She encountered a city in chaos and rebellion: She saw the Mothers of the Plaza de Mayo chased by soldiers on horses using gases forbidden by international conventions, and witnessed the death of a man.[70] She immediately realized that this was the place she wanted to put her time, energy and work into: 'I am convinced that one affects one's context and is affected by it constantly'.[71] The money she was to receive as inheritance and planned to use to finance a film project was lost as her bank went bankrupt. But she had a story to tell and it was vital to do so: 'I realized I wasn't going to be able to shoot one more single photogram before facing the subjects that were really tormenting me. It was like turning the light on and lifting the ghost's sheet to see what it is made of'.[72]

Cordero de Dios is Lucía's response to her history, inspired by people and events from her life, in the form of a fiction. She refers to this relation as 'literal metaphors' since fiction is the result or the product of reality: 'It is not an autobiographical film. It departs from real facts to tell something else'.[73] What is that 'something else'? The film tells the story of Guillermina, a thirty-year old woman who lives in Buenos Aires. Her father (Paco) was a journalist and her mother (Teresa) a medical student, and they both supported their friends' political activism. Her maternal grandfather (Arturo) was a politician, owner of lands and pedigree horses. When Guillermina was five years old, her father 'disappeared' and she went into exile with her mother to France. Many years later she returned while her mother stayed. The fiction takes place in the context of the 2001 crisis. As it was common back then, ordinary criminals kidnapped Guillermina's grandfather and asked for an exorbitant ransom. Teresa returns from France to help her daughter, and also to testify in the trials against those who had kidnapped and tortured her during the dictatorship before she went into exile.

Nevertheless, Teresa seems reluctant to help her father: she does not want to sell the house, the only memory of her 'disappeared' husband, or accept the ransom money from a powerful military officer who tries to bribe her so that she will not testify in the trials. Guillermina cannot understand her mother's attitude and during one of the many arguments, she questions her principles and coherence as a former activist: '¿Para qué mierda les sirve tanta ideología si sos capaz de dejar morir a un tipo así nomás?'[74] After this, they separate for a few days and when they reunite, we learn that when Teresa was abducted, her father asked that same officer who tried to bribe her in the present for help, and agreed to release her only in exchange for her husband. Teresa and her father never talked directly about this because, like she explained, 'porque hay cosas que ni hablando se resuelven'.⁷⁵ But that meant the end of their relationship; she would never forgive her father for interfering with Pace's and her life and fate.

Teresa had never shared this story with Guillermina who felt cheated and deprived of her own history. But finally they empathize, sell the house, collect as much as money as they can for the ransom and manage to rescue Arturo. They pick him up, and the film finishes with an ambiguous shot – the most important, according to the director – of Arturo entering the car accompanied by Guillermina while Teresa looks inexpressively to the front. 'I always imagined the film as a big funnel of 90 minutes. My goal was to be able to give these three beings the chance of meeting once again, and then who knows what they'll do with their lives! It took me 90 minutes to bring the three of them together in the last shot (there are actually four people because in that car there was also one conspicuous by his absence); that family comes together again, and then, well, they will decide what to do'.⁷⁶

By creating this final ambiguity, the director sets the characters, but also the audience, free: we can now imagine the kind of reunion we think they should have. One could argue about whether or not the women forgave Arturo, but the director says that this is not a film about forgiveness but 'about the desire of putting oneself for a moment in the others' shoes to accompany them through the roads that life put in front of them and in the decisions – impossible decisions in many cases – they had to make'.⁷⁷ In this way, Cedrón proposes an approach to the political generation of the 70s guided by the desire of knowing and understanding their stories instead of judging them. Guillermina is more hurt about having been deprived of the possibility of understanding her mother's history and actions for so many years, than by the information about her own past (the exact circumstances of her father's death).

Just as in the film, the 70s generation has a legacy, but usually their stories are so difficult that it can be destabilizing for them to start talking. Cedrón observes that: 'the survivors have a tremendous burden as a generation, beyond their individual stories. I am grateful to them because, in the end, those who are no longer here cannot teach us anything: whatever we have to learn we will learn from the survivors'.[78] The role of the sons and daughters is, then, to open up spaces for encountering the history behind the pain, because their parents' generation did not envision a legacy of pain for the next generations: pain is paralyzing – they were thinking of movement, change and improvement. They were thinking of men and women relating to each other in a more humane way, engaged in achieving their own and others' wellbeing as inseparable matters. They were thinking of different ways of experiencing social relations, family, gender, work, etc., but those projects were brutally interrupted by the repression and could not be transmitted to the next generation, which, in addition, grew up in a world completely different from the one their parents knew during their youth. As Pilar Calveiro observes, the thirty years since the events of the 70s have witnessed not only 'new forms of accumulation and distribution of wealth' but 'a restructuration of societies, politics, imaginaries and the world as world of meaning'.[79]

For the younger generation to be able to identify their own project there has to be a transmission of the experience of feeling connected to others. As Lucía Cedrón shows in her film, for her parents' generation, exile was a tragedy because they did not want to separate from the community of young people, although it probably saved their lives. They saw themselves as part of something bigger: they were bringing about a change for a fairer and more solidary society – something they were already experiencing within their political movements. Conversely, when, thirty years later, in 2001, a severe economic crisis hit the country, the youth left the country as fast and soon as they could, without hesitating. Maybe if there had been a transmission of the importance of community for their parents, young people would have stayed, leading the initiatives to confront the crisis and reflecting on the social reasons for such a collapse.

Cedrón's case is different: She has thought about her parents' experience for many years and, for the film, she conducted exhaustive research on how young people lived and thought back then. *Cordero de Dios* is, in that respect, an act of inheriting the past, in Derrida's sense of knowing and knowing how to reaffirm what 'comes 'before us', which we therefore receive even before choosing, and to behave in this respect as a free subject'.[80] To reaffirm means, 'not simply accepting this heritage but relaunching it otherwise and keeping it alive'[81] and this is where freedom comes into play. In order to keep a heritage alive it is necessary to select, to filter, to interpret and therefore to transform in the present what has been received.[82] The director of *Cordero de Dios* affirms: 'The country we have today is the result of what has been done and what hasn't been done. That's my legacy. And my responsibility is not doing what my parents couldn't do but what I can do with the cards I have been dealt'.[83] For her, this means making a film that allows the audience to draw lessons from the painful events of the past to act in the present. This way of relating to the past coincides with what Tzvetan Todorov refers to as 'exemplary' memory. After recovering the painful event and without denying its singularity, the 'exemplary' way of remembering takes it as part of a more general category (generalization) and as a model to understand the new situation with different agents and components (analogy). Thereby, the past becomes an example that allows us to draw lessons for orienting our actions in the present. In that sense, a case of exemplary memory would be to 'take advantage of the lessons from the injustices suffered to fight against those happening nowadays'.[84]

Lucía Cedrón in her film proposes a reflection on the complexity of human relationships under dehumanizing conditions of fear and violence that do not allow judging actions in terms of right and wrong but require a certain degree of empathy. She creates two time frames, 1978 and 2001, connected by the repetition of a violent situation: an abduction that demanded a 'ransom' in exchange for the hostage's life. In the first scenario, a person dies to save the life of the hostage, in the second scenario, life becomes the priority, trumping ideas and even the past itself (represented by the house they finally sell and the conflict they put aside).

In the logic of the human rights associations' collective memory received by the post-dictatorship generation, exclusively focused on the preservation of the past, it would be unacceptable to compare the violent acts committed by the army to ordinary criminal acts. The army crimes were considered unique; any possible comparison was taken as an attempt to erase their specificity, and as facilitating their oblivion. Conversely, Lucía Cedrón manages to demonstrate that the comparison established in *Cordero de Dios* is a way of keeping the past alive: producing new meanings in the present that signal the never-ending work of the inheritors.

To conclude, the two films analyzed in this essay, Lucía Cedrón's *Cordero de Dios* (2008) and Lupe Pérez García's *Diario argentino* (2007), represent the most advanced stage in the collective process of elaborating the violent Argentinean past. The directors actively seek to know and understand the meaning of the events, either by interviewing its actors, as in Pérez García's case, or by researching that time, as Cedrón did in order to recreate the 70s environment in her film. In different ways, both films materialize an 'exemplary' memory in Todorov's terms, that is to say, a way of remembering which allows individuals to draw lessons from the past to orient decisions they make in the present. Both films make a connection between the dictatorial past and a present of economic crisis as two moments in Argentine history that invite reflection about transformative social practice.

4. BENEATH THE SURFACE: VIOLENT REPRESENTATIONS OF A COLLECTIVE TRAUMA IN *DOS VECES JUNIO* AND *GARAGE OLIMPO*

David Gregory (University of Notre Dame)

Aesthetics is an exercise in continuous tension with the public arena and its political discourses. In fact, there has been an extensive discussion about the political dimension of aesthetics and its possible uses as a political instrument, from Aristotle to the Frankfurt School. Following Adorno, I understand that aesthetics and art have a social role even in their apparent functionless. In fact, art is always political because it interacts in the public sphere or the *polis*, understanding that concept as the public interaction in a nation-state and the imaginary communities evoked under our modern political organization. However, the political dimension of art is more indirect than anything else and in different levels of this political dimension. It is an indirect relationship because, contrasting with political intervention, like marching, creating a grass-root movement and/or dealing with partisan politics, art can only respond to the *polis* from aesthetics or art itself, which has its own function (symbolic) in terms of the public-political arena. The function of art can only be symbolic because it is a sign whose function is representational. According to Corinne Enaudeau, the exercise of representation only tries to substitute something that is not there by giving some sort of presence that confirms this absence.[85] It is only from that space – as a substitute – that art tries to provoke reactions. The level of engagement depends on whether the aesthetic object presents itself as political or attempts not to engage with any theme that approaches in any way a political issue (*art pour l'art*). In the case of contemporary Argentina and the texts that I will be examining, both *Dos veces junio* and *Garage Olimpo* (1999) try to address, not only an historical trauma within the national psyche, but decisions made from the political arena, specifically, under the government that is now known as 'the last military junta' or 'last dictatorship'. In other words, both texts assume its political nature by engaging directly with the consequences of political affairs. At the same time, novel and film try to provoke, within fictional narrative, not only aesthetical and theoretical considerations, but political reactions as well.

Dos veces junio and *Garage Olimpo* assume their political dimension by responding to that specific period at the time of the military dictatorship.[86] The novel, written by Martin Kohan, reacts to events occurred under the dictatorship, specifically in 1978, placing the written word as a symbol to represent a past that was violently silenced. Marco Bechis's *Garage Olimpo*, on the other hand, builds an aesthetic language within the visual representation of film which also seems to take place in 1978.[87] The movie, like the novel, tries to revise the implications of a violent political policy that both marked a collective trauma and left many casualties as a result (both physically and psychologically). Taking into consideration that this trauma is shared within the limits of the nation and beyond, both aesthetical objects examine a wound that is part of that collective body of the community, a traumatized body that becomes a macro-symbol: one afflicted collective body in representation for that plurality of voices that were affected because of the last junta. The texts under consideration also represent a past which was silenced, providing then for symbols as a tool to break the silence and fill the void with the logical representational tools of each medium. However, these representations open up a series of questions between the symbolic space of art and the insistence of its use to respond to the *polis*. In other words, why art?

Taking into consideration that the dark secrets of the last dictatorship are already known by Argentineans, does it matter? How does aesthetics deal in this moment of time (more than thirty years later) with that repressed past and, given the contemporary political considerations on a (post?) global word, is it just a recreation of the past as a commodity or a real interest of poking the wound to create some new political responses?

Dos veces junio is a novel where everything that is happening is implied without being direct or obvious about what happens underneath the main events of the plot. Divided into small parts between each chapter, the novel mainly focuses on the experience of a conscript under his obligatory year of service for the military in June, 1978. The historical context of that time, besides the dictatorship, was the World Cup, celebrated in Argentina with total support of the militaries and no limits on the budget for its completion. The soldier is assigned to be the driver of an important Doctor, Captain Mesiano, and during the development of their relationship he gets involved indirectly with the crimes against humanity committed by the government in power. This plot is interrupted in a series of passages with a second narrative voice of a pregnant woman tortured in Quilmes, implying the Clandestine Detention Centre known as 'El Pozo'. There, she gives birth to a boy who, at the end, is revealed to be a child Dr. Mesiano gave to her sister, who was unable to give birth. However, no apparent resolution is given at the end. In the epilogue, both soldier and doctor meet again in 1982, at the end of the dictatorship. Dr. Mesiano does not pay for his crimes, although he keeps repeating that difficult times are ahead, and the former soldier goes to have the same dream he had with a prostitute the night he took Mesiano to acquire the child. The novel refuses to bring the 'criminals' to justice, preferring instead a fictional representation that leaves the reader to fill the blanks with the historical events that started to become public even since the last dictatorship in Argentina. For the writer, the representation of violence can only be achieved by leaving those blanks. Refusing to give graphic descriptions, the novel insists that the worse part of that violent past is that it was seized from the *polis*, leaving only a void to fill.

The representation of violence, that is, what tries to fill that absence, is precisely what motivates Kohan's writing. His approach is that of a revision, a *déjà vu*, a web of stories that are connected within the political (historic) imaginary of a nation. In fact, Kohan's characters are placed in a time and place that allows them to work as metaphors of the parties at stake during the dictatorship. All the characters working with the regime are metaphorical symbols of the system established by the junta: Sgt. Torres, Dr. Mesiano, Dr. Padilla and Corporal Leiva. Given that metaphorical meaning, it is no surprise that we have a nameless narrator, a symbol for an Argentina that just wanted to survive the dictatorship by following orders and not questioning the rules of the militaries. In a sense, he takes the place of the victims, which are also nameless, except for Guillermo, the son of the pregnant woman. From the mother who cannot escape the detention centre to the girl raped by four soldiers in the middle of nowhere, none of them have any possibility of escaping. Outnumbered and overpowered, they can only accept their unknown fates with resignation.

However, in contrast with the victims, the narrator renounces any action, while the former are robbed of any possibility of action. Thus, the nameless character becomes a victim of his luck (his time in the military was a result of a lottery), and a witness of a system that was using extreme violence to 'restore order'. His compliance opens the plot of the novel, when he is involved in the middle of a discussion about how to torture an 'enemy' and how young can one start torturing him. In fact, *Dos veces junio* begins with a simple question: '¿A partir de qué edad se puede empezar a torturar un niño?' (At which age can we begin to torture a child?).[88] To begin with such a question immediately sets the violent tone of the novel. The fact of considering *when* we can begin torturing a child aims to invoke the shock of a violent past on different levels. On the one hand, to place a 'child' into torture considerations is a complete game changer. The importance of the question lies, not only in the possibility of torturing another human being, but in the uneasy ambivalence of being witness to such a violent act as torturing a child, as if the act of torture or its consequences are not enough. The violent image that the question evokes puts its aesthetical representation at a level that, indirectly (always through art), tries to set the reader of the novel into a feeling of witnessing a torture, blending then the reader with the narrator's voice. In a sense, the novel opens by besieging the reader as an accomplice. Therefore, to read is to look at the symbolic presence of what is already absent. Idelber Avelar hints at that idea when he says that the past and its modern representation wait to be inserted in a metaphoric-substitutive operation.[89] Hence, to look is violent, not only in looking at the metaphor of a past that is already painful to look at, but in the act of being an imposition, a being forced to look at violence itself in its more crude and dehumanized form, without even daring to invoke it. Nonetheless, the imposition is evoked only by the symbol as a passing-for, in other words, the sign as a domesticated imitation.

The act of 'looking' to a symbolic past is also moved by the appearance or sensation of being looked at. The character explains that his transgressive act of reading through the question awakens a sensation of feeling observed, which also provokes a sense of guiltiness: 'Tal vez yo había obrado mal, y por eso me sentía observado. Era la impresión que me daba el sentido de culpa. Cuando uno obra mal se siente mirado, no importa cuán solo se encuentre'.[90] The desire to look back in *Dos veces junio* equals the uncomfortable feeling of being looked at in a closed society. In terms of that 'nostalgic return' (the painful journey to return 'home'), the written word mimics the moment of trauma in the past, when the modern logics of looking in order to discipline shaped the politics employed by the junta. According to Foucault, that modern logic or what he calls 'hierarchical observation' provides an instrument for discipline and coercion. The act of observation is an instrument of intimidation, and the dictatorship adhered to those principles.[91] For the junta, in order to repress the *demos*,[92] the state needed to enforce a repressive and powerful look to its citizens. In search of the oppositional forces, which represented a threat to the regime and order, everybody was a suspect, a possible subversive, blending subject and suspect into one menacing figure to look upon first, and then conceal. The symbolic image of an open notebook (where the question was written), the presence/identity of the kid, the act of torturing him, and the guilt provoked by that sensation of being looked at, serve as *deus ex machina* of, not only the story, but the response of art to that political situation, which still influences how the Argentinean society behaves politically. The fact that the narrator expresses a sensation of guilt serves as a parallel, not to the writer or his generation, but to the act of the 'nostalgic' revision, as if that guilt underlines the necessity of talking about what was silenced before.

In terms of the mimetical representation of the novel and beyond the early sensation of the narrator, the exhaustive look of the *polis* is translated into a lack of looking. Here we have the depiction of a society that does not want to see, does not want to question, and therefore, in contrast with the state, does not want to know. The World Cup of 1978 represents the maximum symbol of that social disconnection with the 'war underneath' or the so-called *la guerra sucia*. It is during the sporting event that the whole nation is more distracted from the oppressive hand of the government and the people disappearing. The novel depicts the night when Argentina lost to Italy as a desolate night, where the whole country stopped to watch the game. Even the narrator, who is waiting for Dr. Mesiano to finish watching the game, tries to know about the results on the street and radio, while there is a girl crying and running desperate on the streets, only to disappear into the shadows. It is also during that wait when the main character finds a ring on the floor, underlining his desire to ignore any micro-story behind the spectacle of the game:

> [...] un anillo. Un anillo dorado con una letra 'R' tallada en el anverso [...]. Y en el borde interior, en una letra tan pequeña que apenas si alcancé a leerla bajo la pobre luz de la calle, decía: 'Raúl y Susana', y un año: '1973'. [...] al anillo, no sé por qué, lo tiré en el arenero de la plaza y después lo tapé a patadas con arena, primero lo tapé y después revolví

todo con mis botas de soldado, hasta estar bien seguro de que no podría volver a encontrar ese anillo [...].[93]

This moment of 'not looking' serves as a parallel to the story of the tortured body of the mother. In fact, it is in her encounter with the narrator that the novel finds its climactic moment and where the main character's resolution of not doing anything that would challenge the political order is emphasized. Therefore, her encounter is about divulging the Argentina beneath the surface, what was real, but hidden, silenced, disappeared:

> Ella empezó a contar las cosas que estaban pasando [...]. La voz ronca me fue diciendo cada cosa que le habían hecho. En un momento no quise escuchar más y le dije: 'Callate, vos. Callate la boca'. Pero no me moví. No me moví porque si me movía capaz que sentía el tirón en el pulóver, de ella que me agarraba [...]. Yo no me moví y ella siguió hablando.[94]

The narrator's desire not to hear responds to a complete obedience to the law. His obedience followed his father's advice (an echo of authority), at the beginning of the novel, of not questioning anything. The authority, therefore, comes from the regime and is not to be questioned. These logics also follow a similar pattern of how the *polis* was organized for the Greeks. Rancière reminds us that there were clear divisions within the Greek *polis*. According to the philosopher, there was 'a particular disposition to act that is exercised upon a particular disposition to 'be acted upon'.[95] The people (*demos*) who did not have the right to act needed to know their place, follow those who had the power to act (*arkhêin*), and remain silent. The narrator follows a similar participation within the modern *polis* by following, remaining silent and knowing his place. For him, the law needs to be proclaimed by those with the authority to proclaim it. This levels the law with authority, which is then capable of being forced upon the subject, much as if it were a Kafka story. The law or the pretext of law creates a forced homogeneity which is permitted in contemporary politics with a state of exception, which declares an atypical empty space of force of law without law.[96] This means that what is supposed to be protected under the law does not apply and the acts unrecognized by law are imposed by force and recognized by the authority. In other words, the state of exception can be seen as an empty space which excludes all rights granted by law without renouncing to law itself or its authority within the *polis*. That suspension is always justified by an external threat (state of necessity) which habilitates a state of war. It is in that direction that violence is justified by the *polis* and it is in those terms that it is justified in the novel by Sergeant Torres:

> Dijo el sargento que las cosas habían que hacerlas con la mayor responsabilidad, que en los días que corrían los errores se pagaban muy caro; dijo que el enemigo estaba esperando cualquier distracción nuestra para golpear, y que en tiempos de guerra era imprescindible afrontar cada hecho con absoluta seriedad.[97]

The state of exception was then justified to pursue a national redefinition based, like all dictatorships, on a closed, authoritarian and homogeneous government.[98] The 'enemy' in this case is the citizen opposing the government, which immediately excludes him from his rights and from the *polis*. In fact, he is a proclaimed enemy as a result of the state of necessity which allows the state of exception and the war within the nation. Following Carl Von Clausewitz and developing her thoughts on violence, Hannah Arendt establishes that 'war is the continuation of politics by other means.'[99] In that sense, the state of exception not only justifies the suspension of law against an invisible threat – that of war – but imposes itself through that cycle (politics-state of necessity-state of exception-war-politics). In other words, the law is 'suspended' with the justification of war which, at the same time, consolidates the authority which proclaimed the suspension in the first place. War also expanded the political interest of the regime which was to facilitate the developing of the neoliberal project in the Southern Cone.

The external threat and state of exception is also what ignites the violence shown in *Garage Olimpo*. However, because the film uses a visual language in a contemporary world used to images, it can dispense of the 'child' figure to represent the violence of that past and the collective trauma shared by a national psyche torn down from within. The act of being 'forced to look' in the film turns into a graphic manifestation of violence, from the threat of being watched to the graphic torture as well, in an attempt to portray a nation 'at war' (following the narrative proclaimed by the regime) where all dissidence was to be more than silenced, erased. *Garage Olimpo* focuses its lens on the 'desaparecidos' (disappeared) themselves,[100] the graphic victims of the political regime and a common trait with other countries of the Southern Cone.[101]

The double layer of how Argentina was defined by the *polis* and what it was underneath the façade of the national discourse is also the approach Bechis uses to represent those years. *Garage Olimpo* focuses on the visual image of Buenos Aires from the very beginning. After the opening sequence of a close-up of river La Plata, we cut to a sequence filmed in an extreme-shot that provides a general view of the city while it plays a non-diegetic Argentinean pop-music from the seventies.[102] This opening places the viewer in a specific location (the Federal Capital) and moment in time. In that sense, the film uses media as an instrument to revise the past and what was not being told in that moment. Following Adorno, spectacle and entertainment (radio, pop-music) were instruments used by the political-economical system (what he called the Culture Industry) to distract the people from a government's oppressiveness and to undermine any resistance or critique.[103] In that sense, the distraction of the World Cup in *Dos veces junio* and the popular music in *Garage Olimpo* work as a form of distraction, an instrument to avoid the act of 'looking' at the horrors below the political discourses of a new, safe and prosperous nation.

It is no coincidence that the immediate following shot cuts to another specific moment in time: the terrorist attack of Ana María Gonzales – a member of the far left group 'montoneros' – who faked a friendship with General Cardozo's daughter in order to kill him by placing a bomb under his bed.[104] Therefore, the movie portrays a 'state of war' right from the beginning, starting with a reference to the far left groups which were used by the military to realize the coup and to justify the state of exception, which was as violent as the militaries. The choosing of this historical event and its use in the middle of the narrative underlines the idea of going beyond the regime's definition of the nation. The idea that the bomb was underneath the bed immediately stresses the importance of looking beneath the surface. What lies beneath in *Garage Olimpo* is always bursting or about to explode. Thus, Bechis insists on representing the idea of two nations: the one depicted by the political regime and the one underneath its political discourse, where tortures and murders were the norm of the day. This duality establishes a connection with Kohan's novel. In *Dos veces junio*, the World Cup is the event that unites 'all' the Argentineans under their hopes of national pride. *Garage Olimpo* uses that same idea without the image of the football. Not only does Bechis use pop music as a symbol of distraction, but the film itself uses a lot of aerial shots inserted between the narrative's plots. Those shots present a city moving as if everything were normal. At the same time, these aerial shots underline the double layer between what is seen at a first glance and what lies underneath. In fact, inspired by testimonies of survivors, *Garage Olimpo* even shows music radio coming from the sewers, while the city and its people continued with their lives on top of that.[105]

The film returns to the idea of what lies beneath at the end, when we see the airplane model Hercules C-130 in the air, ready to dispose of all the people kidnapped and soon to be disappeared, their bodies drugged to a state of unconsciousness and about to be dropped into the waters of the river La Plata. While 'La aurora' is set as non-diegetic music,[106] the plane, with the Argentinean flag on its wing,[107] opens its back doors as the audience get to see the shadow of María before being thrown to her death.[108] The final shot, which presents an image of the water as seen from a plane, links the end of the film with the opening shot, underlining the importance of that first sequence. The river is a watery grave and the final witness to the horrors committed during the military junta. The water therefore works as an oppositional icon that, instead of life, represents death. Its image also contradicts the happy music on the radio. As a result, image and sound oppose each other to symbolize an oppositional body that defies the homogeneous construction of the nation.

The dismantling of the national discourse allows an interaction between the imagined community and the space of aesthetics. In other words, not only is art always political because it deals with the modern *polis*, but the imaginary of the nation is also created and conceived (like art) and even when it represents and responds to the political or public realities of a community, it works on a symbolic level. The nation itself is a creation, used to artificially 'unite' the people.[109] As I have mentioned, that symbolic reality is imposed by force and in a unilateral direction in both *Garage Olimpo* and *Dos veces junio*, justified politically by the threat of 'war'. Consequently, the national construction meant a constant aggression from the state to its citizens. The symbol, therefore, becomes real through politics, defining that term as the actions of the political authority, which in Argentina meant affecting and ending the lives of thousands of people. The reality of that symbol is confirmed within film and novel through the representation of what is considered dear to the national identity of Argentina: the flag, the 'salute to the flag' (which invokes at the same time the flag and national pride), and the sport of soccer. That definition of the Argentinean community and their reassurance with national representations used by the 'National Reorganization Process'[110] can be traced even today. National pride remains strongly appreciated by Argentineans, especially after their last economical crisis in 2001. In fact, the use of flags, so well-described in *Dos veces junio* for the national holidays and/or world sport soccer events, remains as a popular custom. Today, in commemoration of their two-hundredth anniversary, thousands of Argentineans hang the national flags from their windows or balconies, using the colours of the flag for their clothing. At the same time, soccer and especially the World Cup, as in many other countries from Europe and Latin America, is so revered that the whole country stops during these events. In other words, those elements used by the regime to distract the people were powerful enough to achieve that intention, as they were and remain to be an important part of their definition as a nation. Their aesthetical representation serves as a link to connect the silenced past with present, working therefore as a reflectional tool of how the national imaginary and the discourses within the *polis* are built today. In that sense the representational symbol takes place of an absence (of sense) and gives meaning, becoming then a reality within the collective identity or the idea of the national.

In Argentina, that understanding has surpassed the mere elements of the spectacle. The nation is more than a flag, even though those elements are very much alive. Instead, the idea of a national identity is used as an ongoing project where the nation is understood as a visible space to work together. Usually, every time the idea of the nation in invoked it is in order to move certain politics forward for the common group of that community known as Argentina, economically, resourcefully and so on. That redefinition of the mere symbols, as used by the junta, has reshaped the understanding of politics, which is also an ongoing process in which the people are directly involved, especially in the past decade. Every little issue is reason enough to go to the streets and manifest in numbers. Along these manifestations there are different forms of aesthetics going hand in hand with the expressions in the street, in order to pressure those in charge. Music (*batucadas*), signs, popular songs and graffiti are necessary instruments for those manifestations. It is a situation which approaches the idea of Antonio Negri that, under the new conditions of capitalism, which implies a relationship in constant negotiation with the worker and his intelligence, the subject (multitude) opens his relationship with the sovereign.[111] In other words, to be part of the community is being able to interweave the relationships of power. In fact, Negri comments that in Argentina this political agency is noticeable. The end of the dictatorship, the lack of trust with the elected leaders after that, and the complexities of a global world that was not helping the specific situation of the country, only reshaped the dynamics and understanding of the nation. As a result, the demos have been actively inserted in the *polis* and art (or aesthetics) is one of the devices to negotiate within that *polis*.

At the same time, this political awareness is reflected in other artistic manifestations, such as film and literature, forming a continuum between art and the *polis*. On the one hand, the revision proposed by art and the texts at hand are a reflection of a collective psyche. On the other hand, art reinserts that awareness and promotes the discussion by its exposition within the *polis* (in the libraries, in the film theatres). This indicates that aesthetics seem to balance between being a reflection of a specific community and a popular instrument to resist any form of imposition from those in charge and the community. In any instance, artistic expressions refuse to settle to any imposition from those with the political authority. In fact, they are always a response from a subjectivity that takes a direct role within the *polis*, claiming a place in that collective imaginary.

The space that art demands for itself within the *polis* insists therefore on the inclusion of different possibilities for the reactions it wants to provoke, opening possibilities for other considerations that draw from the inventive of fictional representation. This is precisely how both texts reproduce the discussion of the disappeared, from fictional narratives that attempt to represent those voices or, in this case, bodies, that were ousted from that collective body. However, those bodies are even more important to Bechis, who seems to use his art to create an international awareness of Argentina's past.[112]

The disappeared are mainly symbolized in the film with the character of María (Antonella Costa), a teenager who was abducted by the militaries as a suspect of subversion, establishing a parallel with the nameless mother in *Dos veces junio* who also represents the body to be tortured. However, the whole experience of underlining the disappeared in *Garage Olimpo* moves back and forth within the identity of the victim (María), the torturer Félix (Carlos Echevarría), and the symbolized non-identity of the 'disappeared'. In other words, to be disappeared means to be a non-entity between the torturer and different levels of torture and victimization.

To represent the violence of being 'disappeared' as an act of torture, Bechis recreates the experience on two levels: the representation of the tortured body and the mimetic experience of the torture for the audience. The former is recreated with the representations of the bodies being tortured. Starting with the promotional poster, the movie evokes the figure of a tortured victim, from the picture of a person with their eyes covered (which was one of the most frequently used promotional posters), to that of a hostage down on his knees, held at gunpoint, and looking up towards the top-angle camera with an expression of resignation on his face. In fact, the image of the tortured victim is central to this film. *Garage Olimpo* not only presents the naked body of María to be sacrificed, but also of another presumed militant suffering through the process. These bodies are presented on the table of torture as naked bodies which are tools of information. At that table and in the centre of torture overall, the detainee is just something to dispose of, a number to extract information. The transgressive act starts by dehumanizing the prisoner, robbing all sense of identity to make them empty bodies, 'casualties of war'. In fact, *Dos veces junio* also uses this representation of the non-body in a state of exception. Talking about people captured 'in war', Doctor Masiano says: 'en una guerra los cuerpos ya tampoco son de nadie: son pura entrega, son puro darse [...] cuando en la guerra se acciona sobre un cuerpo, se está accionando sobre algo que ya no le pertenece a nadie'.[113] The insistence on this non-body in both texts follows the modern logics described by Foucault. In the case of an oppressive government in a state of exception, these logics become perverse. In that hole of the state of exception, the detainee ceases being a citizen; it does not belong to the national *polis* anymore, and therefore, is erased from all public life. That ousting echoes the image of the *Homo sacer* of Agamben, which was a political body who could be killed but not sacrificed, implying a sense of outlaw within the structure of society. In both film and novel, the body is discarded by the state (a non-citizen) and reclaimed by the state, becoming then a tool to extract information. This information, however, becomes symbolic, given that it was more an act of intimidation than a real effort to extract information. In fact, according to the testimony of Horacio Vivas, the torturers asked questions that did not make any sense, as if they were not sure what they were looking for. On the representational level of María, the character does not seem to have any real affiliation with the extreme left groups and is just shown as someone suspicious who taught poor uneducated people in the projects. In any case, the only thing she is asked for in the movie is to give 'some information', which leads her to reveal a point of encounter with her partners of an unknown resistance group. Nonetheless and besides that, they do not ask for anything in particular during the film, even when the torture goes on and on and she is still not set free. This reflects that the body of the victim was just a symbolic source of information. At the end, they were not looking for any information at all but kept looking for more bodies to torture.

On the other hand and as I mentioned earlier, *Garage Olimpo* uses the image to echo the experience of torture, though merely at the aesthetic level. The film is as much about showing the tortured body as well as a torture (or simulacra) to the spectator. To watch the torture places the audience, not only as a witness (as it happened in Kohan's novel), but in the position of the victim as well. In other words, because art can only interact with the *polis* through its role as art, its intention to be a film about torture itself can only work in terms of that. It will be a dishonour for the victims of the dictatorship to say that watching the film equals that experience, because, as with the disappeared victims, that experience cannot be expressed into words or images. The best art can do is to provoke the simulacra of a torture from a level of perception. As a result, we watch María, not only being tormented from the moment she is kidnapped, but also going through one form of torture to another, from a physical to a psychological level, in a situation that does not seem to have an end. María is trapped in a hopeless position where she is being robbed of every human right.

The emblematic moment for the character comes when she makes a desperate attempt to escape. In a moment of distraction by Texas (one of the most violent torturers at 'El Olimpo') while going outside, he leaves the door of the garage open. María makes her move then. However, it just takes fourteen seconds of the camera shooting at the empty garage door from the inside (without a new take) to see Texas dragging María back inside while yelling '¡Miren quién volvió! ¡La pajarita que quería volar!'[114] He ends up laying María on her knees and putting a gun to the back of her head. It is in that iconic image of the film that the constant suffering and the impossibility to return outside, that is, to rejoin the *polis*, is underlined. Even when Texas does not shoot her at the end of that sequence, one thing is clear, she would not escape and the torture, for the character and the audience, will continue. The body of the victim is reduced at that moment to the humiliation of being robbed of all sense of agency within the narrative, dehumanized, while the spectator is forced to look, feeling powerless to change what happened with those real voices that were silenced, to change the outcome of that imposition from the regime to its people. In other words, the audience is also robbed of its symbolic agency to change those events. The symbol, and the uneasiness of being forced to watch what any modern Argentinean now knows, is therefore a substitute for the absence of agency on a specific point in history, but aims to underline a collective knowledge in the modern *polis*. The intention is not to reveal any truth, to bring the torturers to justice, or to have this issue settled once and for all. Instead, art works as a sign for a past that works to preserve an uneasy memory into the present day. It insists on a memory that also needs to be recreated from the testimonies of survivors and relatives, from a political awareness created as a result of a collective trauma. In that sense, aesthetics, as well as the collective memory of a violent past, has to be invented to insist on the same political awareness that makes them possible in the first place. Only then can both re-creations challenge the strong artificiality of the nation, as described by the political regime in power.

Dos veces junio and *Garage Olimpo* assume then a political response that underlines a collective trauma that resists being forgotten or disappeared. At the same time, both texts aim to give a voice and image to those who had none and who were taken alive out of the *polis* in an exercise of power that pretended to deny them as citizens. However, their response only works as a symbolic figure. Even when both texts attempt to do a revision of the discourses imposed from the political arena, they both refuse to provide an absolute answer. On the one hand, such an act will echo the same absolutes proclaimed by the political regime, thus, the same violent imposition. On the other hand, these are aesthetic representations of those voices that were taken out and a reconstruction of them. Their involvement as aesthetic objects can only create sensations of what was real violence. In other words, their political involvement is as symbols that try to fill the void of the absence. However, even when those voices are gone forever, both texts provide another space to reincorporate them into the *polis* in the memory of them. They also try to provoke an awareness of the consequences imposed by absolute political positions and the trauma that survives that imposition, both for the victims, as for the ones that got to survive (the disconnected). In such a political response, their revision provides a tension within the *polis* and the concepts created from their political discourses (the nation, political ideologies to administrate, and so on). Art then opens the door for new interpretations of that national psyche, underlining the past in order to overcome those extreme manifestations in the present. In other words, these texts assume a political position in persisting on a certain level of engagement with the political arena, serving as cautionary tales to never repeat the brutality that traumatized the nation and that will remain as a dark stain on their collective imaginary.

5. THE MYTHICAL SOUTH: FROM MISSISSIPPI TO THE MAGDALENA AND INTO THE MAINSTREAM

Rubén Pelayo (Southern Connecticut State University)

I became aware that my adventure in reading *Ulysses* at the age of twenty, and later *The Sound and the Fury*, were premature audacities without a future. In effect, much of what had seemed pedantic or hermetic in Joyce and Faulkner was revealed to me then [at 23] with a terrifying beauty and simplicity. Gabriel García Márquez[115]

The 'mythical south' that frames my writing refers to the American Deep South and South America: Argentina's Borges, Cortázar, Puig, and Peronism immediately come to mind. *From Mississippi to the Magdalena*, on the other hand, makes an allusion to two large southern rivers, the former in the United States, and the latter in Colombia. This connects my writing with Nobel-prize winners William Faulkner and Gabriel García Márquez. The idea of 'into the mainstream' that closes the title makes reference to the 1940s and beyond, when Latin American writers, personalities, and political events came to world-wide awareness, and gave rise to a genuine sense of cosmopolitanism. My paper's core, however, brings forward two parallel lines: 1) Brief biographical accounts of Latin American figures, and 2) Confronting the traditional literary criticism that views Latin American writing of the second half of the twentieth century as an echo of either American or European authors as viewed by critics like Harold Bloom. My essay points out that while Faulkner can be traced in García Márquez's writing, among others, Cervantes is actually the one who can be credited as the more genuine influence. Thus what we have is a Spanish tradition, all along, as opposed to an English school of writing. I close my article with the observation that *One Hundred Years of Solitude* has much more of *Don Quixote* than there is of Faulkner's writing.

Shedding light on myth, whether in classical legend or regional belief, helps to shape man's thought. It makes us participants in the flow of nations or simply as members of our own community. As such, it carries strength and symbolism. The 'mythical south' that frames this essay refers to both the Deep South of the United States and the South of the Spanish Americas – mainly Argentina and García Márquez's Colombia. I have sketched names and personalities on the basis that 'everything incredible is true.' The biographical information of the people depicted seems rather impossible to believe (mythbuilding) and yet it is all true. *From the Mississippi to the Magdalena* makes an obvious allusion to two great southern rivers, the former in the United States, the latter in Colombia. Both rivers have prominence in several books by Faulkner and García Márquez. The idea of 'into the mainstream' that closes the title makes reference to the 1940s and beyond, when Latin American writers, personalities, and events beyond belief came to world-wide awareness. I have taken the expression 'into the mainstream' from the book title translation of *Los nuestros* (1966) by Luis Harss.[116] A text of interviews, *Into the Mainstream* is a pioneering text that introduced some of the leading names in Latin American literature to American readers and literary critics. Technically, the book was not supposed to include Gabriel García Márquez, but Carlos Fuentes convinced Harss, the interviewer, to do so. As incredible as it may sound today, Harss was in Mexico City in the mid-sixties to interview Carlos Fuentes and Juan Rulfo, and had never heard of the future author of *One Hundred Years of Solitude*, let alone read him:

At a dining table, I told a group of rather well-informed friends: listen to this, tell me whether you think this is true or false, history or fantasy. Her husband, when she died, wanted her embalmed. She was his second wife. Embalming, after all, has been practiced since ancient times. He, however, kept her opened casket in his villa and his third wife would comb the cadaver's hair. When he died, his tomb was exhumed, and someone cut the hands off his corpse. To date, neither the perpetrator nor the hands have been found. Does my account sound like a tall tale to you? Does that seem possible to you? To intensify my seemingly power of invention, I said let me add that the husband was a 3-time president of Argentina and the information is all true.[117]

What may sound as fantasy is actually part of history, chronicles we may ignore, but nevertheless factual whether fictionalized in literature or not. Most everything mythical or incredible, once turned into literature, becomes even less believable. By the time the public learns of it in books and magazines, television news, movies, and other forms of information, the individual sees it as pure fiction, as is often the case with the novels and short stories of William Faulkner depicting The Civil War and the Great Depression. A case in point is *The Sound and the Fury* (1929), the novel García Márquez had difficulty reading at the age of nineteen, and referred to in the epigraph of this writing. Faulkner's mythical South and his literary technique of multiple view points around a single plot inspired and steered Gabriel García Márquez's first novel, *Leaf Storm* (1955). To this extent, García Márquez himself wrote: 'I planned to diversify the monologue with voices of the entire town, like a narrative Greek chorus, in the style of [Faulkner's] *As I Lay Dying*.'[118] Some critics, however, have said that *Leaf Storm* is all Faulkner, as if such a pursuit in writing could be possible. Faulkner would have to be the Alpha of writing if that were the case. We know there is no orphan book; all books are related, interconnected. The aforementioned quotation makes a connection to a narrative Greek chorus, perhaps Sophocles' *Antigone*, whose central theme is indeed much the same as *Leaf Storm*'s proper burial, also the theme for *As I Lay Dying*. Rubén Darío, although not thinking about the writers we call modernists today, once said: 'The United States is grand and powerful.

Whenever it trembles, a profound shudder runs down the enormous backbone of the Andes. If it shouts, the sound is like the roar of a lion.'[119] No critic of Latin American literature has failed to point out the influence of Faulkner in García Márquez. How grand and powerful was Faulkner that his writing, in fact, was a profound jolt felt all the way down to Argentina. But Darío was actually criticizing the Mexican-American War and Roosevelt's imperialist moves. Literary critics as esteemed as Ángel Rama, on the other hand, have been writing as if with a colonized approach, as if Faulkner was the bearer of 'the know how' to write. Why ignore or put aside the Spanish tradition from Cervantes to Borges *et al*? I cannot help questioning whether this type of comparative literature is to some extent a form of colonizing thought.

By the time Gabriel García Márquez was twenty, in 1947, he was fascinated by Franz Kafka's *Metamorphosis*. That was Jorge Luis Borges' translation, as was the translation he read of *The Sound and the Fury*. By then one can only assume he had read Borges' own works, among many Hispanic authors, and no doubt the first modern novel: *Don Quixote*. The twelve years of publication between *Leaf Storm* and *One Hundred Years of Solitude* gave way to a large number of critics who fast and furiously made connections and found echoes of Faulkner, Kafka, Joyce, and Woolf in García Márquez but hardly anything from his own tradition, the one he knew best. One of the first critics to point this out was Ernesto Volkening. The commonalities between Faulkner and García Márquez blinded critics and readers alike: the invention of a physical place, Yoknapatawpha vs. Macondo; the constant repetition of characters: Colonel John Sartoris vs. Colonel Aureliano Buendia; the crumbling of the wealthy, aristocratic Sartoris family vs. the decay of the wealthy, titled Buendía family. Both authors depict a town after war and the fight between opposing political parties. The list of shared characteristics could go on, but like Volkening before me I would complain of a deep-rooted 'colonizing' way of thinking when an author is measured against parameters that do not include his or her own tradition, but only the literary movements of an English-speaking school of thought. By 1967 Volkening found similarities that tied together José Eustasio Rivera and Rómulo Gallegos. But Faulkner won the Nobel Prize for literature in 1949, a very 'attractive' connection for the critic who wanted 'to invent a venerable genealogical tree for García Márquez.'[120] It was truly a 'desirable' association for García Márquez himself.

Leaf Storm is a good attempt at what would eventually become *One Hundred Years of Solitude*, which in turn has much more of *Don Quixote* that we can find in Faulkner's writing. Take for example the treatment of the novel within the novel and the approach towards authorship. In *Don Quixote*, Cervantes plays with the concept of authorship by suggesting that he is translating the text from an original manuscript written in Arabic by one Cide Hemete Benengeli.[121] In *One Hundred Years of Solitude* García Márquez leads us to believe that we have been reading the translation of a Sanskrit manuscript written by some gipsy named Melquíades. The two authors take us for a ride, making us believe that the narrative voice is indeed someone else's, that they are editorial voices outside the text bringing forward someone else's tale. But the merit goes to Cervantes in the first place. García Márquez, as an attentive reader of the Spanish tradition, adopts the technique in *One Hundred Years of Solitude*. Ambiguity, as technique, allows both author and reader to have multiple points of view, in this instance, also first drawn in *Don Quixote*.

The literary techniques of Modernist writers like Faulkner, self-awareness and introspection, much attention to the unconscious mind of the character or shining a light on the darker side of the protagonists can be seen in *Don Quixote*. In an interview with Carlos Fuentes, Lewis MacAdams was quick to point out that Fuentes' *Christopher Unborn* was influenced by James Joyce. Fuentes added that if he thought so, then he would have to look then to Laurence Sterne, inferring he had influenced Joyce; if he did then he would have to consider *Tristram Shandy* and from there you go to Cervantes where you find the source of echoes and duplications of storytelling.[122] In García Márquez's Colombia, the incredible is often true. In Argentina, the lives of Eva Perón and Juan Domingo Perón surpass most fiction. On the other hand, the writings of Jorge Luis Borges, and the prose of both Manuel Puig and Julio Cortázar represent a large amount of reality without their necessarily being realist writers. In spite of that, Puig's allusions to gay-oppressed Molina were not simply a literary theme. Historians and journalists record facts; fiction writers take the whole story and create novels and short stories out of them. Juan Domingo Perón made the incredible seem ordinary. He was a military officer, a politician, an author of military history, a power-hungry man, a dictator, and a three-term President of Argentina. His life, like that of his second wife 'Evita,' is of mythical proportions. Unlike any other Argentine politician, his rule is identifiable with his own name: Peronism. Perón's social policies ran parallel to his anti-American, anti-British rule. While he confiscated assets owned by American and British business, he expanded the number of unionized workers and helped create the General Confederation of Labour. This form of strong nationalism, industrialization planning, and the nationalization of foreign-owned industries like the railway system and the telephone companies was dubbed *Peronism* by 1947.

A self-made man, Perón was the son of a farmer and a housewife. In 1944 he was elected Vice-President and Secretary of War under General Edelmiro Farrell, and forced to resign on October 9, 1945. Four days later he was arrested and imprisoned. Mass demonstrations organized by labour unions, the help from Evita (who had a radio program), and the support of some women's groups, demanded Perón's release from jail. He was freed on October 17 after eight days of confinement. Once released from incarceration, the popular military politician and the hopeful actress got married the day after in a civil ceremony on October 18, 1945. But this was not a rushed decision. Evita, as she would be known, had been his mistress for over a year. Theirs was a chancy marriage for Perón's political ambitions and the circles he frequented. Both, however, saw one another as the missing piece of the puzzle for each other's future success. On December 9 of the same year, they were married by the Church.

Perón, who was a widower, saw his first wife, Aurelia Tizón, die of cervical cancer, the same cause of Evita's death. 'Given what is now known about cancer of the cervix, the possibility exists that Peron infected both wives with a particularly aggressive variant of human papilloma virus, causing the cancer in both, or that his first wife infected him and he passed the infection along to Eva.'[123]

The unimaginable was only 'true' during the Perón years. Argentina was a leading haven, and heaven, for Nazi war criminals and Perón did nothing to oppose it. Among his good deeds, however, he promoted the tango, legalized prostitution, and resisted the military desire to persecute homosexuals. Perón won re-election for a second term in 1951. The national economy, high levels of corruption, and the conflict with the Catholic Church were out of control. He was overthrown by a military coup in 1955. Ousted and a widower (Evita had died in 1952) Perón first went to Paraguay, then to Panama where he met Isabel Martínez, his third wife and 35 years his junior, before settling in Madrid, Spain. Isabel Martínez was Perón's personal secretary before marrying him in 1961 in Madrid. In 1973 Perón returned to Argentina and to the dismay of many, paradoxically became president of Argentina for the third time with his wife as Vice-President. He died in office of heart failure on July 1, 1974 at the age of 79. Peron's death was mourned by many and celebrated by countless others – intellectuals, writers and artists, the upper middle classes, and university students with liberal ideals. Embalmed, he was buried in the Perón family tomb at the Chacarita Cemetery in Buenos Aires. In 1987 his crypt was defiled; his hands were cut off and stolen. To this day, the incident remains an unsolved mystery. No one has ever been charged and the hands were never recovered.

Best known in popular culture as *Evita,* she was born Eva María Duarte in Los Toldos, Province of Buenos Aires. Her life was short-lived; she was 33 years old when she died. The life she led as a young actress, an activist, and the second wife of Juan Domingo Perón was a reality of legendary magnitude. Her harshest attackers were members of the upper class, and among them her most famous detractor was Jorge Luis Borges. 'Eva Peron's impassioned devotion to social welfare earned her the love of the common people, while her ambition and vindictiveness made most others hate her. Some considered her a whore; others wanted her canonized.'[124] In the United States her image became most recognizable through the historically inaccurate 1978 Broadway musical *Evita*. Years later, the musical was taken to the silver screen in the 1996 film *Evita*, making her a recognizable symbol around the world. She was the fifth child of an unmarried couple. At the time of her birth, her father, Juan Duarte, managed a prosperous *estancia*, held a political office, and enjoyed certain prestige among conservatives. He died in a car accident before Evita turned seven. Her mother (Juan Duarte's mistress) had to provide for her large family working as a seamstress. When Evita was eleven years old her mother moved the family, 'the tribe' as she would tenderly call her children, to the nearby town of Junín. Evita's desire to be an actress started here. By 1935, at the age of sixteen, Evita moved to the capital city on her own. She was determined to pursue an acting career. Unlike the brown-skinned, black haired newcomers to Buenos Aires, she was white, a slender brunette with large brown eyes. But she felt closer to those brown skinned people called 'cabecitas negras' (black-haired ones) or '*descamisados*' (literally shirtless, the working class) than to the middle and upper classes who always made her feel uncomfortable for being not only of low birth but also illegitimate. In Buenos Aires she played small parts in vaudeville productions. A tenacious, ambitious young actress, she persevered and played roles in film, theatre, and the radio. During those years, few of these films were ever shown outside Argentina. In 1945 her role in 'La cabalgata del circo' (Circus Cavalcade), directed by Mario Soffici, exposed her for the first time to an international audience. It was a musical depicting the life of a travelling circus in the Argentine Pampa. Her part was minor. Her role demanded her to bleach her hair; thereafter she was forever blonde. On the radio her popularity grew strongly. By 1943 she had her own radio program on Radio Belgrano. Her show 'Biographies of Illustrious Women' continued through 1945. When she left her radio program it was to marry Colonel Juan Domingo Perón.

The two were illegitimate children. At the time of their marriage, she was 26 years old. He was 24 years her senior. Their marriage brought Eva fully into the limelight and the political arena. Elections for the Argentine presidency were held in February of 1946. Perón was the candidate for the Labour Party, the party of the *descamisados*. 'For the first time in history, a candidate's wife accompanied him. At each campaign stop, she handed out buttons and greeted the people personally.' Perón won the election. If her image is ambiguous to many, the bases for it are well-rooted in her personality. In her own words, as she went on to find the role she would like to play, she said, 'Perón had a double personality and I would need to have one also: I am Eva Perón, the wife of the President, whose work is simple and agreeable [...] and I am also Evita, the wife of the leader of a people who have deposited in him all their faith, hope and love.'[125] There was indeed a 'double' within the same person. *Evita* was the image she helped invent for herself and Eva Perón was simply the First Lady of Argentina, two different roles, as is the case in Borge's celebrated monologue 'Borges y yo' dealing with the duality of the self. The conflict was not on the basis of what is rational and what is not, but rather on the political and the emotional. Today we remember the Evita she wanted to be, not the First Lady she was. The two, however, as in 'Borges y yo,' were inseparable.

Her trip to Europe in 1947, the 'Rainbow Tour,' was under official government invitation. But she did not travel in the company of President Perón. She went with her brother Juan. In Spain she was received by fascist dictator Francisco Franco with all the pomp and circumstance befitting a queen. She was awarded the Great Cross of Isabel, the Catholic medal, the highest decoration conferred during Franco's dictatorship. In Italy, where fascism was out, she was not well received. Pope Pius XII met her at The Vatican for the customary half hour for wives of heads of state. In Italy she learned that the Queen of England would not receive her; therefore she cancelled her trip there. The French, like the Italians, were not gracious either; she cut her visit short and went to Switzerland. There, her car was stoned as she was driven from the Swiss airport and tomatoes were thrown at her when she tried to address a small crowd. She was viewed as a representative of a fascist government. The Second World War was over, but 'Perón had served as a military attaché in Italy just before the war, freely borrowed political ideas from Italian fascism, [and] openly admired Mussolini and the efficiency of the German army.'[126] Back in Argentina, Evita was instrumental in helping the movement for women's right to vote, enacted into law in 1947. The movement had begun at the turn of the century; it was indeed a milestone for Argentine women. With Peron's support, she created the Peronista Women's Party, with herself as their president. When Perón ran for re-election, the women's vote (for the first time a reality) was in his favour. The following year Evita created the Eva Perón Foundation to lead her social work contributions to aid the poor. This organization was disassembled when Perón was ousted in 1955 by a military coup. The foundation was instrumental in building hospitals, schools, housing, and orphanages, with the money taken from successful business owners. Many fortunes were destroyed as Evita ran her foundation. When Eva Perón died on July 26, 1952, the funeral ceremonies took two weeks, her body was embalmed and the government announced a 30-day official mourning. Her corpse was moved several times in Buenos Aires and then to a cemetery in Rome under a false name. From Italy it was moved to Spain and then back to Argentina. 'The body was exhumed from a small cemetery near Rome [some cite Milan] and transported in a silver coffin to Juan Perón's villa in Madrid. Italian and Spanish police officers accompanied the hearse. Perón kept the body in an open casket on the dining room table of his villa, where he later built a shrine for it in the attic. His third wife, Isabel, combed the corpse's hair in a daily devotion.'[127] Today her body is buried in *La Recoleta* cemetery, in Buenos Aires, in the Duarte family crypt beneath two bolts.

Although not a Nobel Prize winner, Borges is peerless in Argentina and certainly in Latin America. A shy person all his life, Borges wrote of courage, heroism, and the lack of love, among other themes. A ubiquitous name, a referent as ever-present as Gabriel García Márquez in literary circles, Borges still goes almost unread by the majority. He accepted honours in France and Italy, Israel and Mexico, Germany and Iceland; and in England Borges was selected to be a Knight of the British Empire by Queen Elizabeth. In 1980, as an 81-year-old, he shared Spain's Cervantes Prize with the innovative Spanish poet Gerardo Diego. His world-wide recognition was in great contrast to the obscurity of his earlier years in Latin America, particularly in his native Argentina. 'In Buenos Aires, his fiction and poetry [were] read by a few hundred readers at most, [and] praised by a handful of individuals many of whom were his friends and acquaintances'.[128] In 1941, *The Garden of Forking Paths* was released, one of his most widely read tales. Hard to believe, he married twice; the first time as a 68-year-old to Elsa Helena Astete Millán in 1967. The marriage was short-lived; three years later the couple separated. Sixteen years after, Borges was married to María Kodama, an Argentine writer forty-five years his junior. Kodama, the daughter of a Japanese father, had been a student of Borges in the 1960s at the University of Buenos Aires. At the time of their marriage Borges was 87 and completely blind. Their marriage took place in 1986, months before Borges' death. Before becoming his wife, Kodama had been his personal assistant, his secretary, literally his typist, and travelling companion around the world during the 1970s and 1980s. The marriage of Borges and Kodama was subject to much controversial criticism as to whether she was self-sacrificing or purely a gold-digger. Borges died on Saturday, June 14, 1986 of cancer of the liver. Maria Kodama was at his death-bed holding his hand. He is buried in Geneva, Switzerland, in the Plainpalais cemetery. His gravestone, marked with the number 735, reads in Old English 'And ne forhtedon na.' The phrase, from the Anglo-Saxon poem 'The Battle of Maldon' means 'And should not be afraid.'

'Ché' Guevara was born Ernesto Guevara de la Serna in Rosario, Argentina, on May 14, 1928. Like Eva Perón, he was also born under the sign of Taurus. Unlike Eva's lowly birth, however, he was the firstborn to Ernesto Guevara Lynch and Celia de la Serna, both from well-established aristocratic and liberal Argentine families. On his mother's side, the 'family bore a long line of pure Spanish noble heritage and owned extensive property. [His father] was an Argentine blue-blood with a fair amount of Irish ancestry and roots stretching back twelve generations.'[129] How ironic that Ché Guevara's main focuses in life were the troubles of the underprivileged people of the Spanish Americas and his belief in an armed revolution. No one ever knew 'Teté,' as he was called as a child, would become a medical doctor, a writer, a rebel, a consumer product, an iconic paradoxical figure of world-wide recognition, a symbol of rebellion, and a legend.

A combination of fact and popular myth, his life story was set in motion with a puzzling birth date. Most entries record 14 June 1928, but his actual birth was 14 May, 1928, making him a strong, decisive, and practical Taurus and not a confusing Gemini. The month difference may have changed his path according to the stars in the sky, but also helped cover his parents' reputation. His mother was three months pregnant on the day of her wedding: 'A doctor friend falsified the date of her baby's birth certificate, moving it forward by one month to help shield them from scandal.'[130] Rosario, his place of birth, was a mere accidental circumstance. The Guevara Serna family was travelling to Buenos Aires from Misiones when Ché was born. Soon after his birth, the baby contracted pneumonia. He recovered from the inflammation of the lungs, but later on developed asthma as a 2-year-old. He suffered this disease throughout his life. The asthma attacks kept him bedridden as a child, preventing him from attending school for long periods of time. It was then that his mother passed on to him her passion for reading. In elementary school he became interested in theatre, and his parents asked that he be excused from classes in religion. From his father's opinions regarding the Chaco War of 1932-35 between Bolivia and Paraguay and the Spanish Civil War of 1936-39, his political ideology began to take shape in his childhood. Nevertheless, 'Teté' was also interested in sports and made the rugby team when he was in high school. He also played golf and was an enthusiastic chess competitor. His audacious personality and his behaviour earned him the nickname 'El loco.' 'A propensity for pranks and recklessness took hold as he approached adulthood.'[131] Juan Domingo Perón took office as President of Argentina when Ché Guevara turned eighteen. The populist Perón and his beloved Evita, hated by some if not most of the upper and middle classes alike, did not seem to bother the future revolutionary who enrolled to study medicine at the University of Buenos Aires. The rebel with a cause was not born yet. He, in fact, dodged the military draft due to his asthma. The writer in him, on the other hand, gave way to founding *Tackle*, a sports magazine devoted to rugby. Sports and his own courses in the school of medicine were his concern, not politics. His indifference to fashion combined with his poor hygiene earned him yet another nickname, only this time less flattering: 'El chancho' (The Pig). It was as if he would insist on being contradictory; he bragged about the number of days he would wear the same clothes without changing. His obsessive will to travel began in his childhood, but he started to document his journeys, the diaries we know today, in 1950. Of those diaries, the one he wrote while travelling with friend Alberto Granado, in 1952, was turned into a motion picture – 'The Motorcycle Diaries.' Ernesto Ché Guevara wrote constantly. His first book, *Guerrilla Warfare,* was published in April of 1960, followed by *Reminiscences of the Cuban Revolutionary War* in 1963. While these books were meant to be published, his diaries were not. He also wrote about socialism in Cuba, Cuban foreign relations, his revolutionary experience in Congo, his viewpoint on Vietnam, and a world-wide revolution. He wrote essays on a myriad of topics and on salient historical figures. Among other subjects, the list includes his position on Cuban economics, the role of the doctor in Latin America (a book he never finished), poetry, and a significant epistolary. The acts of reading and writing were thoroughly related to his everyday existence. A considerable number of his works have been published posthumously. His oeuvre is a living legacy, an object of analysis, study and constant assessment. His intellectual ability to write was equal to his physical involvement in Castro's '26th of July Movement' that led to the triumph of the Cuban revolution first and then in the newly found administration. He was a soldier, an industrialist, a banker, a diplomat, a statesman, but above all a warrior, a revolutionary of his own making.

However, the Ché Guevara that readers around the globe came to know was the revolutionary 'Ché' (slang for *buddy*, mainly in Argentina) alongside Fidel Castro. He is the iconic figure of a bearded young man wearing a black beret with a single gold star on it. They first met in Mexico City in July of 1955. If there is in fact a marriage of ideals, theirs was one: they believed that change in Latin America could only be achieved through armed warfare, not elections. He abandoned his wife and daughter to follow Fidel Castro and engaged in combat as a rebel against Fulgencio Batista's army. He was proud to be a member of Castro's '26th of July Movement.' Some researchers seem to agree that he was not seeking power, but change in the unjust Latin American world he had seen time and again in his travels, in the copper mines of Chile, the leper colonies in Peru, the extreme poverty he saw everywhere he went. Not even fatherhood would make him change his mind. The struggles and killings at Sierra Maestra on behalf of the Cuban Revolution against Batista were his ultimate goal. The objective became a reality. On New Year's Eve 1958 Batista fled Cuba. The event, depicting the ongoing corruption in Cuba, is recreated in the 1974 film *The Godfather: Part II*.

On January 8, 1959, Castro's rebel army and Ché rolled victorious into Havana. Ché is often quoted saying 'We've won the war. The revolution begins now.'[132] Those words may seem metaphorical, but we have come to realize that his words were prophetic *ab initio*. His role as a diplomat in the new Cuba began in June of 1959; his 'Good Will Tour' started in late June and ended in early September. Then he worked as the Minister of the Department of Industry. As if he were all-knowing, he was subsequently elected director of Cuba's National Bank.

As immersed and obsessed with the revolution as he was, Ché Guevara found time to find love. In Guatemala he met a woman altogether different than the aristocratic, green-eyed, María del Cármen Ferreyra portrayed in the film 'The

Motorcycle Diaries.' Hilda Gadea was 'a short, plump woman with Chinese-Indian features;'[133] he married her and fathered his first child, Hilda Beatriz 'Hildita.' Gadea was an exiled Marxist Peruvian living in Guatemala. Readers and biographers alike may question if this was a marriage of love or one of Guevara's self-interest. She brought him closer to high-level members of the newly elected revolutionary Guatemalan government under President Jacobo Arbenz, who allowed the Communist Party to organize and operate. In 1954, Guevara moved to Mexico and soon after his wife joined him. Their daughter Hildita was born there in February of 1956. In November of the same year, mother and daughter returned to Peru. They would not see him until 1959. In June of the same year, a few months after getting a divorce from his first wife, Guevara married Aleida March. Aleida was a white upper-middle class Cuban revolutionary who had been his assistant all along. She bore him four children. The last was a boy the couple named Ernesto after him. As he did to his first family, he left his second wife and children for yet another uprising, this time in Africa. A hero at the Bay of Pigs conflict between the U.S. and Cuba and a key player of the Cuban Missile Crisis of 1962, Ché Guevara left the island in 1965. He thought the Congo was ready for an armed revolution. He was wrong. He met defeat in Congo and left Africa after seven months of failed attempts to train the troops. In 1967 he was betrayed in Bolivia organizing his last guerrilla war and writing his last diary. He found no support from the peasant people; he was captured and killed. On 9 October 1967 he was shot to death by Mario Terán, an obscure Bolivian sergeant trained and armed by U.S. Green Beret and CIA operatives. His hands were amputated, to prove it was he who had been killed. He was buried in a mass grave in Vallegrande, Bolivia, until 1997. In October of the same year his remains were returned to Cuba and given a hero's funeral. He was laid to rest in a mausoleum in Santa Clara. After Ernesto 'Ché' Guevara's death, Jean Paul Sartre 'was widely quoted as saying *Che was the most complete human being of our age.*'[134]

Manuel Puig was born Juan Manuel Puig Delledonne in General Villegas, in the treeless, flat, grassy plains (the Pampa) of the Province of Buenos Aires,

Argentina. He was the firstborn to Baldomero Puig and María Elena Delledonne. On his mother's side of the family he was of northern Italian descent. The surname Delledonne means 'of or about women.' In his father's genealogy, the name Puig is Catalan. A college dropout, the gay Argentine novelist, short story writer, scriptwriter, and playwright published his first novel, *Betrayed by Rita Hayworth* (*La traición de Rita Hayworth*) in 1968: 'No biography can resurrect more vividly the world of Manuel Puig's childhood than *Betrayed by Rita Hayworth*.'[135] Puig's oeuvre is not plentiful; nevertheless, he left a deep imprint in Latin American letters of the twentieth century. His exploration of gay sexuality and gay issues is not what made him famous, but rather delayed his first publication. He authored eight novels, wrote seven plays and screenplays combined, and about ten essays. Not all his works are translated to English, but his novels are. His passage to immortality was through *Kiss of the Spider Woman* (1976; *El beso de la mujer araña*), a novel turned to film (Puig's biggest passion in life), and then adapted as a Broadway musical. *Kiss of the Spider Woman* reached colossal audiences of readers and viewers around the world. 'More than simply loving the movies, [Puig] wanted to live in them; he would have liked to be a diva like Norma Shearer, but more than that, he wanted to be the character she played.'[136] Before he became an author, he worked as a Spanish tutor and translator in Rome, a dishwasher in London, a receptionist in Paris, clerk at the Kennedy Airport Air France counter, and even waited tables at a restaurant in New York. While Julio Cortázar's mother provided her son with books at an early age in Argentina, Manuel Puig's mother would take her son to the movies. Puig's true love for the fantasy world of celluloid stories began as a 4-year-old in 1936. Going to the movies, almost every day, was a way to escape the monotonous, claustrophobic life of the town where he was born and where he finished his elementary education in 1946. The following year, as a 13-year-old, he was sent to a boarding school in Buenos Aires. After high school he entered the University of Buenos Aires to study architecture, but did not finish his freshman year and decided to study philosophy instead. He could not get interested in either subject and dropped out in 1952. He then studied in private language schools, mainly French, English, and Italian. Around that time, he came in contact with Borges, as a student. He took a course from him on the detective novel at the Argentine Association for English Culture. Their paths, however, never crossed again.[137] In 1955, when Juan Domingo Perón was ousted, Puig won a scholarship to study in Italy. He was twenty three; he had dreams of becoming a movie director. He travelled to Italy with a scholarship to study cinema at the *Centro Sperimentale di Cinematografia* in Rome. The experience contributed to his fiction writing, but he never directed a film. Puig wanted to be a screenwriter; he kept trying to make a career in film, to no avail. He moved to New York City in 1963, his first time in the city. He got a green card and began writing *Betrayed by Rita Hayworth*. Working for Air France in NYC provided Puig the opportunity to travel more than before and above all to travel with his mother, the only constant love in his life. In February 1965 he finished the manuscript for the book. It was eventually published in Spain, France, and Italy, but not without censorship problems in Spain. Argentina, however, published it first in 1968. The French translation came out the following year; *Le Monde* selected it as one of the best novels of 1968-69. Meanwhile, the same year, *Heartbreak Tango* (*Boquitas pintadas*) was published in Spanish. By 1970 *Betrayed by Rita Hayworth* was a best-seller in Argentina, and Seix Barral wanted to publish it in Spain. The English translation did not come out until 1971 and *Heartbreak Tango* in 1973.

In 1973 he published his third novel, *The Buenos Aires Affair*, and in September of the same year, after life-threatening phone calls and being followed by secret police, he left Argentina and moved to Mexico City. As an established writer, Puig adapted *Heartbreak Tango* as a movie script and the film was awarded *The Golden Pen* (*Pluma de Oro*) prize for best script, at the San Sebastián Film Festival of 1974 in Spain. Four years later, at the same film festival, Puig won *The Golden Pen* award for his film adaptation of *Hell Has No Limits* (*El lugar sin límites*.) In 1976 he published in Spanish his fourth and most significant novel: *Kiss of the Spider Woman* (*El beso de la mujer araña*). The

English translation was released three years later. Puig's fame was international and his friends and acquaintances were famous too, but he lived in a small studio apartment in New York's Greenwich Village. *Kiss of the Spider Woman* was released as an Oscar-winning film in 1985. By February of the following year it was nominated for four academy awards; it won one. The Oscar for best actor was awarded to William Hurt, who played Puig's alter ego. The play version of *Kiss of the Spider Woman* opened first in Paris, Toronto, London, Los Angeles, several other cities and then in New York in 1993. Unfortunately Puig did not witness its great success: winner of seven Tony awards as a Broadway musical. The accolades, the rave reviews and the awards were homage to a writer who was more interested in movies than in literature. The musical played in cities around the globe. It was a post-mortem success: Manuel Puig had died on July 22, 1990 in Cuernavaca, Mexico. He was cremated; the urn was given to his mother, who was living with him at the time. The rumour was that he died of AIDS or perhaps that he had been HIV-positive. Neither was confirmed: he died of complications from gallbladder surgery. He survived the operation, but succumbed two days after. Contrary to the New York Times obituary, the Argentine novelist left no descendants.

It is hard to think of Julio Cortázar by any other name. But there was a time when he was Julio Denis. He was born Julio Florencio Cortázar in Brussels, Belgium, on August 26, 1914. The Cortázar family returned to Argentina when Julio was a 4-year-old, in 1918, and settled in Banfield, a suburb of Buenos Aires. His father, about whom he spoke very little, was a businessman with ties to the Argentine Embassy in Belgium at the time of his birth. There is a veil of speculative vagueness surrounding Cortázar's biography, whether about which magazine published his first works, when, and why his father abandoned the family, the cause of his death, and even about the number of wives he had. His father abandoned him in 1916, when Cortázar was 6. There were no male figures in his childhood. He was raised by his mother, his grandmother, an aunt, and the company of his sister, a year his junior. His mother awoke in him the love for reading and his predilection as a child for Jules Verne. An asthmatic boy, this sickly condition was also conducive to reading. His passion for writing, on the other hand, began when he was nine. He left for Paris in 1951, took French citizenship thirty years later, but kept his Argentine nationality as well. He lived in Paris until his death in 1984. He is considered one of the great masters of postmodernism. His writing is known for its experimental technique and his dialogue with the anguish and ambiguity of the individual's existence. His passion for the cinema, photography, and jazz can also be observed in his oeuvre. Several of his works have been successfully turned into film.

In 1938 he published *Presence* (*Presencia*), his first book. It was a thin volume of poetry he signed as Julio Denis. Unlike Ché Guevara, he was affected by the Peronist administration, the dominant political party at the time. A school teacher by profession, he was later certified as translator in both English and French. The novella *The Kings* (*Los Reyes*), his second book, was the first to appear under his own name. The text, written in the form of a play dealing with the Greek mythological figure of the Minotaur, received little attention.

His first major short story, 'House Taken Over' ('Casa tomada') was published by Jorge Luis Borges, editor-in-chief, in *Annals of Buenos Aires* magazine, and later in *Bestiary* (*Bestiario*) in 1951, his first book of short stories.[138] 'The mingling of bisexual fact and sublime fantasy is absolute in the wonderful 'Bestiary,' which condenses a novella into just twenty pages.'[139] It was then, at age thirty seven, that Cortázar moved to Paris. His departure from Argentina, however, was not as a political exile: he left with a 10-month scholarship from the French Government to enhance his profession as translator. Among the most familiar authors he translated into Spanish are Daniel Defoe and Edgar Allan Poe; of the former he translated the complete works. In 1953 he married Aurora Bernárdez, an Argentine writer, translator, and member of the upper class. They were divorced in 1967. During the years of his first marriage, Cortázar published some of his signature works, mainly *The End of the Game and Other Stories*, *Blow Up and Other Stories* and *Around the Day in Eighty Worlds*.

His genuine interest in the Cuban Revolution allowed him to travel there several times. Unlike many Latin American intellectuals who gave up on the ideals of the Cuban uprising by the early 1970s, Cortázar never did. In 1963 he made his first trip to Cuba; the same year he published *Hopscotch* (*Rayuela*), considered by many his magnum opus. It was acclaimed for its experimental structure, for its open-endedness, its multilayered viewpoints, and the prescribed alternative plot development for reading it, other than the traditional chapter-by-chapter format. Its translation by Gregory Rabassa won The National Book Award in 1967. 'While Garcia Marquez's *Cien años de soledad* (*One Hundred Years of Solitude*) has been a more popular book, there is little doubt that the work of greatest literary significance among those of the Boom period – and quite possibly the most significant novel ever to come out of Spanish America – is Cortazár's *Hopscotch* (*Rayuela*, 1963).'[140] It was followed by *62: A Model Kit* (*62 Modelo para armar*, 1968) and *A Manual for Manuel* (*Libro de Manuel*, 1973). In 1974, France awarded him the Prix Médicis Étranger (for non-French authors) for *A Manual for Manuel*.

In 1967 he married his second wife, Lithuanian-born Ugné Karvelis. As was the case with his first wife, Ugné worked as a writer and translator. She was an intellectual who contributed to Cortazar's publishing and political orientation. In 1978 Cortázar married Carol Dunlop, a photographer and writer, 32 years his junior. The marriage lasted until her death from leukaemia in 1982[141]. All three wives contributed to Cortazar's writing, but only Dunlop as co-author in *The Autonauts of the Cosmoroute* (*Autonautas de la cosmopista*, 1983). In the United States, Cortázar was a lecturer at the University of Oklahoma in 1975 and at Barnard College in New York in 1980. His approach to literature helped revolutionize the structure and the uses of language within the text in Spanish; his impact was also felt in the cinema, i.e., Michelangelo Antonioni's 'Blowup,' 1966; and Jean-Luc Godard's 'Weekend,' 1967, among other adaptations. The life of Julio Cortázar was never in the public domain as was the case with other members of the Latin American Boom of the 1960s, mainly García Márquez, Carlos Fuentes and Vargas Llosa, all of whom were friends of his.

He died of leukaemia on February 12, 1984 at Saint Lazare Hospital in Paris. He was 69 years old. His remains, in Montparnasse Cemetery in Paris, are in the same tomb as his wife's, Carol Dunlop. Cortázar left no descendants. His memory is much alive in the consciousness of world readers, but in Buenos Aires one can actually visit the Plaza Julio Cortázar in the Old Palermo neighbourhood of the city. Surrounded by clubs, restaurants, bookstores, and art galleries, the city dwellers call the neighbourhood Palermo Soho. As is often the case with famous authors, several of his works have been published posthumously.

The world of literature, often associated with fantasy and myth, is repeatedly rooted in facts, cold hard truths. When we read that the hands of Juan Domingo Perón were cut off and stolen in 1987 after his tomb was desecrated, and neither the perpetrator nor the hands had been found, one gulps in disbelief. The same happens when one learns of the fate of Evita's corpse. Tomas Eloy Martínez, among the many authors who have written about the life, myth, and biography of both Perón and his wife Evita, is known for a fiction that 'mingled journalistic and novelistic techniques to conjure an Argentina more authentically strange and elusive than either fact or fiction alone might allow.'[142] Ché Guevara had little or nothing to do with Peronism, but his hands were also severed. The circumstances were not alike, yet the fact that both lost their hands is a coincidence hard to believe. Ché Guevara's hands were severed from his corpse for identification, although a single finger would have been enough. When his body was found, 30 years after his assassination, his hands were not. As is the case with the Perón couple, the literature about Ché Guevara is copious. Unlike the Perón couple, Ché was also a writer; and like Julio Cortázar, he was asthmatic too. However, Cortázar was never disenfranchised from the Cuban Revolution; Ché Guevara was. At the turn of the 21st-century, knowing what we know today, it is difficult to see Guevara as 'the most complete human being of our age,' as Jean Paul Sartre saw him. To some people, in fact, he is a war criminal. Was he ruled by egocentricity and heartlessness? How could anyone accept to be minister of industry, president of the national bank, and commander-in-chief of the armed forces and expect to do a just job in such dissimilar venues? Furthermore, he left both his first and second wives and children. One can assume Ché must have fallen victim to self-grandiosity. He continues to be revered by thousands, some of whom know very little or nothing about him. Borges, the *memorioso*, the shy and introverted writer also astonishes us when we learn of his private life; although it is his *oeuvre*, and the impact he had on twentieth-century writing which amazes us most.

The names depicted in this essay are of my personal preference. I believe their imprint in the American consciousness is both mythical and mainstream in certain circles. While the influence in García Márquez, most say, is heavily Faulknerian, I insist the 'influence' comes from Cervantes. One can trace Faulkner, Joyce, and Kafka, but there are also traces of Rabelais' *Gargantua and Pantagruel* and Swift's *Gulliver's Travels*. The theme of the double and the usage of circular time, on the other hand, are rather salient in Borges, whose writings were available in Spanish. Such themes, although not necessarily Borgesian, are found in *One Hundred Years of Solitude*. The selection of names in this essay may appear as mixing apples and oranges but my reasoning was to group them to follow my quest in proving that 'everything incredible is often true.' *One Hundred Years of Solitude* portrays Colombian civil wars, neo-colonialism, political violence, corruption, sexuality, death, and solitude in the midst of other dominant themes. However, these concerns are treated through myth and fantasy with a magic realist format that leaves many readers unaware of the historical, political, and ideological content of the novel's background.[143] It can be considered the magic realist novel *par excellence*, but at the expense of simplifying it. In defence of his own *Christopher Unborn*, Carlos Fuentes traces his influence back to Cervantes. García Márquez, on the other hand, is always fond of citing Faulkner as his master; yet Faulkner 'reread *Don Quixote* yearly to sustain himself as a writer.'[144] The literary techniques of Modernist writers like

Faulkner, Joyce, Kafka, and as far back as Laurence Sterne, such as self-awareness and introspection, humour, much attention to the unconscious mind of the character, and shining a light on the darker side of the protagonists can be seen in *Don Quixote*. Those literary techniques, plus the source of duplications of storytelling observed in García Márquez are first found in Cervantes. The road from Mississippi certainly leads to the Magdalena and into the mainstream since it carries along the echoes of *Don Quixote*.

6. FRATERNAL DIALOGUE BETWEEN JOSÉ MANUEL PRIETO AND FERNANDO DEL PASO'S FICTION WORKS

Itzá A. Zavala-Garrett (Morehead State University)

José Manuel Prieto, reveals himself as a postmodernist[145] accent writer through his novel *Rex* (2007), which forms part of the trilogy including: *Encyclopedia of a Life in Russia* (1997) and *Nocturnal Butterflies of the Russian Empire/Livadia* (1999). In these and many of his other fictional works we are reminded of Del Paso's novels, especially *Palinuro de México* (1977). Both authors, Del Paso and Prieto use intertextual displays and the fine arts to expose the reader to a total renovation of language including similes, metaphors and kinaesthetic descriptions that are used in intricate ways. In addition, they make us aware of contemporary topics such as social movements, political ideological breakdowns, cosmopolitanisms and interdisciplinary fields.

The purpose of this research is to connect the aesthetic perspectives of these writers accentuating Del Paso's playful and encyclopaedic style and Prieto's intercultural and new baroque style. Both literary styles of Del Paso and Prieto develop a similar dialogue that is essential to the analysis of the tradition of magical realism in Latin American literature. While both incorporate magical realism in their works, the situations differ due to the inversion of space, which in turn inverts the perspective. Europe is described as an exotic and magical continent where Mexico and Cuba are no longer the chaotic and mad locations that contemporary readers expect. For example in Del Paso's *Noticias del imperio* (1987) concerning the emperors of Mexico, Charlotte and Maximilian, in 1864, the first chapter introduces a magical realistic description of Vienna:

> Viena prefirió, y también le enseñó al mundo, las delicias de la música de Johann Strauss, de la música mecánica que parecía salir de la nada cada vez que los relojes indicaban las medias horas con minués o con gavotas los cuartos de hora [...]. También los burgueses ricos de Viena, que cada ocho días recibían a domicilio una tina de agua caliente para bañarse, colgaban de los arboles de sus jardines arpas eólicas que tenía el viento de los Alpes.[146]

Similarly, in Prieto's trilogy we discover exotic sceneries such as Istanbul, Marbella and Livadia near Yalta.

The famous short story written by Jorge Luis Borges 'Pierre Menard, autor del *Quijote*' and his metaphysical works remind us of Del Paso and Prieto because their writing belongs to Borges' literary tradition that works with literary forgery: apocryphal elements, plagiarism, invented chain of events, false encyclopaedias, and where knowledge defines how the stories work. When we analyze Del Paso and Prieto's literature it is like opening a Chinese box or a Matroska doll because as readers we must pay attention to each direct and indirect reference to other writers, high culture, and popular culture's statements. Everything becomes like an interactive chain connecting different disciplines, topics and styles.

This chapter focuses mainly on the ways in which Del Paso's novel reflects Prieto's more representative novels. In *Palinuro de México* the main character is a young medical student who becomes involved in the riots of 1968 at a stage where he is still enjoying life, but at the same time, he is motivated by the idealistic perspectives of the sixties and his desire to do something relevant. Palinuro dies tragicomically during the military's repression led by Gustavo Díaz Ordaz (1964-70). This novel consists of several speeches, stories, myths, genres and voices. It is practically a world mosaic of artistic and thematic diversities and can consequently be read under a wide range of perspectives: as a political novel, stylistic, historical, and mythical, with baroque surrealistic enumerations, testimonials and allegorical references. The transcendent, the everyday and the eschatological merge without conflict to uplift culture and knowledge.

The novelistic parameters of Bakhtin are instrumental in the analysis of *Palinuro de México* and Prieto's works, specifically his theories about heteroglossia in the genre of the novel. These works represent the coexistence of social and ideological contradictions between the present and past, between different socio-ideological groups in the present, between tendencies, schools, and literary circles, all affected by an aesthetic form.

Palinuro de México is a monumental novel thematically and technically, and a symbolic space where Fernando del Paso describes a genealogy of male heroism in the wars of French intervention in the Mexican Revolution and during the student movement. This writer enriches the narrative through multiple literary devices such as the use of intertextual references, homage to other writers (James Joyce, Lewis Carroll, Ambrose Bierce, among others), while mimicking their styles in his writing. One of the sources that inspired this novel was obviously Homer's *Ulysses* and *The Unquiet Grave* (1944) by Cyril Connolly where Palinuro embodies the idea of the modern Western man, who is bankrupt and without direction. This novel differs from the *Aeneid* where Ulysses' boat pilot Palinuro is a victim of fate but for Connolly, Palinuro deserts his post. In both cases, the myth of this hero is not found in the shipwreck, but in posterior disorientation experienced due to crossing the stream of Styx souls where as a result of having been buried it is not necessary to wait for another hundred years.[147]

In Del Paso's novel, the merry and anonymous student Palinuro becomes Palinuro of Mexico, an icon of the sacrifice of students, when he dies as a result of repression in the main square (Zócalo in Mexico City). In this regard [according to Álvarez Lobato] the author notes:

> Aprendí [...] que el mito era el símbolo de hombre... que se deja arrastar por sus sueños, y a causa de ellos muere. De esta manera, la identidad individual se transforma en identidad nacional vía el idealismo, el sacrificio y el arte. Sin embargo, la identidad que reconstruye el autor, no es, en absoluto, única y acabada, sino una visión caleidoscópica, a veces monstruosa, producto del *collage* de la diversidad de planos, textos, puntos de vista, fragmentos culturas y disciplinas humanas que habitan la novela.[148]

The protagonist represents the idea of *carpe diem* proposed by the youth of the late sixties and early seventies through the ideal of sexual freedom by living an incestuous relationship with his cousin Estefanía and spending each day engaged with his eccentric cousin Walter and his friends. His rejection of conventional life and his satirical view of humanity mean that the society they live in is less healthy and has no meaning in contrast to the strange world of creative language with which the characters interact.

Both Palinuro and the rest of the subjects represented are developed in a context where social norms are broken and reversed. Their eccentric behaviour is projected into the incest, masturbation, flatulence contests, interpreting the world upside down, long nonsensical talks, and random sex. Although these actions are considered by mainstream society as a kind of mental asylum, Mikhail Bakhtin uses the term 'grotesque realism' to refer to the body as a positive element that connects man with his world. The body under grotesque realism is not a closed unit, but transgresses its own limits. Bakhtin emphasizes that the body parts are open to the outside world and are susceptible to the penetration of the universe. Life is viewed as a contradictory process, as the symbol of incompleteness. Both images of the body as a literary work make an open unit and therefore contradict and transgress its own limits. The body is constantly changing so that death in the novel is shown as the end of a cycle that facilitates the initiation of another. In this way, the sacrifice and resurrection of Palinuro is in play.

Palinuro de México is a tragicomic reinterpretation of events from 1968 designed to attack power through the symbolic space of Tlatelolco[149] and a subversive youth that rails against authority. In addition, this novel, like others in

Del Paso's collection, is self-referential and intertextual. In this regard, Ángel Rama argues that the heterogeneous composition and the mixing of genres in such novels are conducive to a smooth integration of literary forms with the reporting of precise situations, specifically when dealing with political repression.

Some of the chapters that manifest these attributes are: 'Estefanía in Wonderland', 'Cousin Walter's Erudition and Tristram Shandy's Apples', and 'The Tragicomic Sense of Life'. These scenes are taken from works of Carroll, Sterne and Unamuno, respectively. Furthermore we detect direct and indirect references to writers like Joyce, Twain, Cervantes and Quevedo. In the last chapter there are keys that refer to figures in literature, film and comics when he presents his condolences over the death of Palinuro in the student revolt of 1968. Although the plot is claimed Palinuro will be reborn as a fictional character.

In his various articles on the influence of Joyce in *Palinuro of Mexico*, Robin W. Fiddian argues that medicine, the body and sexuality, the use of myths and archetypes, and their attitude to language are three basic concerns that connect Fernando del Paso and James Joyce. According to Fiddian, the role of language is to establish control and supremacy over man. Human intelligence is related to the ways in which memory affects words (Aristotelian idea). When language suffers a renovation in speech or writing it is not accurate and does not necessarily satisfy human communication. In this way, the arbitrariness of the linguistic sign is an issue in the creative use of writing in this novel.

The use of jokes and outlandish language are recurrent in the characters of Palinuro. By using problematic language found in the novel *Tres tristes tigres* (1997) by Guillermo Cabrera Infante, *Paradiso* (1968) by Lezama Lima and Carpentier's work, readers run into a collage of rhetorical and satirical situations. In this respect, Severo Sarduy comments that the neo-baroque in Latin American literature is a way of writing that satirizes the functionality and simplicity as they did in their time and intellectual modernist artists like Joyce, Magritte and Foucault, ridicule those who question the conventional ties between words and images (signifiers) and things (meanings). Samuel Arriarán studied the presence of the baroque and neo-baroque characteristics in writers like Borges, Piglia, Bolaño and Fuentes, among others. As stated by Arriarán, Fernando del Paso is within this group of authors who use criticism, irony, parody, far from an apology to the man to show other realities such as the recovery of popular speech, the use of carnivalization and encyclopaedic knowledge through the accumulation of references in which ideas such as love, sex and death converge. In the words of Arriarán: 'no se trata de una simple adición sino de una construcción nueva del mestizaje cultural en el contexto de la posmodernidad'.[150] However, this critic prefers to use the term 'otra modernidad' or 'neobarroco' instead of postmodernism in referring to the positive interaction between cultural practices, images and symbols of Western modernity and local Latin American cultural traditions as we have seen in Del Paso and Prieto's writing.

An important chapter to understand the perspective of the antihero in Palinuro is 'The Brotherhood of the Flaming Fart' (Chapter 23). In this section the narrator criticizes the government and politicians for their corruption and hypocrisy; the monuments and symbols for witnessing the injustice and repression to society for supporting the government, the Olympics for being a modernization project at the expense of poverty of the country; and student traitors for accepting their part in the political system in power. That representative collage is handled under a tragicomic tone:

> Nada de nada todavía. Estamos en espera de la respuesta. Los verdaderos agitadores son la miseria, la ignorancia y el hambre. Los estudiantes nos estamos organizando para acabar con ellos. Las estatuas, como es de esperarse en caso de apuro, han sido testigos [...]. Por la levita y la peluca de circunstancias del Licenciado Verdad, siempre de pie en el paseo de la Reforma y el Río Neva, pasaron ciertas ondas hertzianas en busca de un continente: era la respuesta, que estaba todavía en el aire, confundida con los derechos flotantes, en tanto que algunos licenciaditos en derecho, provistos de plumeros tricolores, remueven el polvo de viejas constituciones y otras vastas necrópolis y eligen las leyes más ventiladas para hacer un ramo con ellas y regalárselo a los jueces en suspensión de garantías. Eso quiere decir que nos tienen miedo: los gobernantes conversos, los limosneros que mendigan un poco de unto presidencial, los

escritores cenizos que ahogan en el tintero su sed de martirologio y con ellos los banqueros expertos en negocios churriguerescos, los ministros tumefactos, los diputados y los senadores siempre de pie como órganos domesticados [...]. Haremos una nueva manifestación, vaciaremos el entusiasmo de quinientos mil corazones en la Plaza Mayor [...].[151]

Mikhail Bakhtin[152] explains that the stools are the way that man has to establish an exchange with the world. *Palinuro de México* contains a joycean-rabelaisian essence by being against Western tradition that is characterized by its puritanical repression inherited from St. Augustine. This means, Del Paso's style combines satire, grotesque, scatological jokes and commentaries, and anarchism against the established authority, imitating and immolating at the same time the styles of Rabelais and Joyce. For this reason, the intellectual subject represented mainly by Palinuro and Walter tries to save the legitimacy of the body through its mention of all those bodily parts or functions that have often been censored with euphemisms. Other resources used are the parody of political rhetoric and the carnival atmosphere,[153] especially in the chapter 'Palinuro on the Stairs or the Art of Comedy' (Chapter 24) a play style of Rabelais. This section refers to President Diaz Ordaz's speech on television in which he explains how to deal with the rebels and 'save the honor and peace of Mexico.'[154]

The student movement occurs via a weak Palinuro as a knight fighting against the presence of hidden characters in masks and costumes that are moving into a bloody carnival. Del Paso, through various linguistic registers of his characters, represents classes ranging from bureaucrats to the president of the nation, ending in the tragicomic death of Palinuro, in order to show a country raped and pillaged by the system in power. Based on true events recorded in the press and testimonials, Del Paso re-creates a play that takes place in a residential building in Tlatelolco, in parallel, Palinuro, Estefanía, the omniscient narrator and a doctor. In addition to individuals who represent different social extracts: a policeman, a neighbour, a bureaucrat and a postman, a play is performed whose characters are based on the tradition of *Commedia dell'Arte*. Let us remember the party's scene in *Rex* where the main character J., his guests and the beautiful

Nelly are described under a magical realism technique but at the same time the narrator ridiculed himself and the absurd plan of the Russian family to restore the monarchy in their country under the leadership of Vasily as a new czar:

> Abrió su boca el pájaro, se balanceó un segundo sobre el borde, dejó que por su pecho rodara hacia abajo, sin esfuerzo en los músculos, una primera nota, un suspiro prolongado que fluyó larga e inconteniblemente, al tiempo que intentaba abrir las manos que habían quedado atrapadas, adelgazadas y frágiles, en los huesos de sus alas [...]. [E]mpujé un poco más la puerta para verla mejor. Cruzó mi mano arriba las teselas del piso abajo, espié las ventanas, barrí con la vista el suelo por si veía la capsula o el generador de aquella imagen, de la mujer, del pájaro (no la encontré). [...] ¡Era Nelly! Porque también, y acto seguido, lo supe por el collar que rodeaba el cuello del pájaro [...]. Radiando ahora desde su cuello al tiempo que cantaba y movía lentamente la cabeza, de modo que los rayos que salían de las piedras iban moteando las paredes, los vitrales, el piso, con puntos multicolores.[155]

At the end of *Palinuro de México* the reader is facing a microcosm, a limitless world within the fiction, described as a carnival that involves a constant exchange with other texts, a state of confusion and a unique blend of genres and stylistic categories. By joining violent acts with a carnivalesque atmosphere, the writer creates an intertextual system comprised of popular items, but of elaborate artistic quality at the same time advocating a critical understanding of the historical component. Moreover, the coexistence of different aesthetic and genre resources emphasizes the carnivalesque atmosphere which stresses violent acts that symbolize repression but also resistance. The purpose of this style is to expose and challenge the functioning of the repressive government officials and the falsity of the justification for their actions against civil society. In this novel, Del Paso uses a multiplicity of narrative perspectives orchestrated by the same intellectual subject to emphasize the playful nature of the novel while analyzing the problems of 1968 under an absurd context. The author connects the form and content to express the ambivalence of the human condition which is as contradictory and difficult to categorize as are the various aesthetic styles, eras and generations of literary writers. At the same time, this novel is also a tribute to all of these styles, periods and writers who have contributed to world literature as Prieto does through his works.

Just as Del Paso's writing is, Prieto's too has been influenced and is at the same time a tribute to Nabokov, Kafka, Borges, García Márquez and Kundera's works. As one begins to familiarize oneself with Prieto's fictional works at first, one assumes passages are mistakes in translation. We are not sure whether certain metaphors are badly written, poorly translated or delivered in an absurd manner. The narrator of the trilogy is the first person to mistrust everything because he is part of the characterization of the protagonist. He is an adventurer engaged in smuggling out and selling various articles to be found in Russia and the old Iron Curtain zone, such as 'cut-rate antiquities' from Kraków, the loot of 'liquidation sales' in Berlin, and night-vision glasses from a bankrupt Red Army. Further, we learn that J.'s native language is Spanish that he is Cuban and his mother lives in Havana. The protagonist also is an 'apprentice writer' and we can deduce that he is also a great reader. *The Tale of Genji*, and works by Conrad, Chekhov, Poe, Dostoevsky, Ovid, Raymond Chandler, Pushkin, Aldous Huxley, and Oscar Wilde are mentioned as if they are old friends or other literary presences like Borges and Proust in *Livadia*. According to Heather Clark:

> Prieto's inexhaustible current works reflect his ability to understand every language in the world, for he has glossolalia (the gift of tongues). Perhaps this is why he tells his story from 'a thousand angles, circling around it'. Implicit in this defiance of linguistic boundaries is an attempt to undermine the totalitarian state, indeed the beautiful but elusive yazikus is a symbol of political liberation. Post-Communist life, however, is not glamorized: its miseries are reflected by a heightened sense of disorientation and darkness. Yet, as much as the book *Nocturnal Butterflies of the Russian Empire* is freighted by the nocturnal, it also possesses the grace and delicacy of a nocturne. Despite its gritty edge, this novel is a celebration of desire: a love letter exquisitely patterned as a butterfly's wing'.[156]

Del Paso employs similar use of the language, using it is a malleable material in order to create fantastic worlds to express love, hate and a socio-political critique. Besides beings a writer, Del Paso is also an artist who uses plastic assembly techniques (incorporation of drawings, paintings and employing of diverse objects, confined to small boxes of wood and glass). Pastiche, kitsch, high and popular cultures coexist in Prieto and Del Paso's fictional works. For example, *Rex* is a Proustian pastiche and a commentary on Proust at the same time. Even though the novel is not from the 1990s, Prieto's writing and circumstances reflect a similar literary style to the generation of Cuban writers from that era. Like them, he is marked by the collapse of the Soviet bloc of communist countries after 1989, and the hope for a Cuban perestroika as well as the stagnation that ensued. As previously mentioned before, *Rex* is the last novel of a trilogy conceived in the 1990s, including *Encyclopedia of a Life in Russia* and *Livadia*. It is a case in point of a neo-modernist work dedicated to the discussion of its literary predecessors, especially Proust. Prieto's gesture emphasizes pastiche, not parody like Del Paso's *Palinuro de México*. Anke Birkenmaier affirms that:

> The pastiche in Prieto's narrative is more playful, the writer of a novel equally pays homage, willingly or unwillingly, to his predecessors. The Proustian difference between pastiche and novel would be then a matter of acknowledgment, and indeed of tone. Situated in the confines of the copy or the counterfeit, the pastiche presents the tension in the relationship between one author and his or her predecessor more openly, and turns it into 'gaieté', fun; the novel in contrast glides over this intention.[157]

Prieto's novels consist of a kind of digressive drift; a cubist shattering of experience into shards of recollected fragments. This writer calls his method 'creating a pattern like a delicate construction of reeds'[158] and this imposes a taxing weight on the narrative pace. As with Del Paso, Prieto's works are love stories, part international thriller, part New Age phantasm, part erudite literary anthology, part musical score (Mozart's *Die Entführung aus dem Serail* (*Abduction From the Seraglio*), and part epistolary satire as we read in *Livadia*. Besides the use of parody Del Paso enjoys pastiche as does Prieto. Both authors invite us to participate in their intraliterary and metaliterary works but at the same time, they observe and analyze their sceneries, their actors and actresses as part of Latin American literature's tradition in connection with other literary universes and cultures, and incorporating different disciplines in their own art productions.

7. THE BORDERING OF IDENTITIES WITHIN GLORIA ANZALDÚA'S *BORDERLANDS/LA FRONTERA: THE NEW MESTIZA* AND AUDRE LORDE'S 'AGE, RACE, CLASS AND SEX'

Briah Luther (San Francisco State University)

An identity contained within the confines of one label or specific trait loses the possibility for a person's entire persona to be seen. By allowing stereotypes and the hegemonic patriarchal system to create the identities, anyone outside the heteronormative societal norm automatically becomes an out-casted 'Other', branded by parts of who they are. Gloria Anzaldúa and Audre Lorde picked up this battle in an attempt to urge those with multiple aspects outside the norm to embrace all of who they are, as well as to encourage those within the safety of these boundaries to step up and claim responsibility in an attempt to close the gap between inequalities. If those with multiple aspects of their identity which fall outside the norm embrace all of who they are and encourage those within the safety of these boundaries to step up and claim responsibility for the unequal system, then we will shift the social paradigm rather than create superficial change.

Gloria Anzaldúa wrote *La Frontera/Borderlands* with a vision that was not within the typical binary guidelines. She expresses her current position before delving into the concept of identity, and how it relates to her, by defining the borderland as 'a vague and undetermined place created by the emotional residue of an unnatural boundary. It is in a constant state of transition. The prohibited and forbidden are its inhabitants.'[159] She furthers the idea of this unnatural boundary, within the concept of identity, as the physical place in which one can inhabit, the mental place one inhabits, as well as the spiritual realm that one inhabits.

Within this undetermined place is where many people who cannot be placed into the binary normative box reside. Anzaldúa describes these people not as abnormalities, but as the key to showing how the system is flawed, by stating:

> Contrary to some psychiatric tenets, half and halfs are not suffering from a confusion of sexual identity, or even a confusion of gender. What we are suffering from is an absolute despot duality that says we are able to be only one or the other. It claims that human nature is limited and cannot evolve into something better. But, I, like other queer people, am two in one body, both male and female. I am the embodiment of the *hieros gamos*: the coming together of opposite qualities within. (GA 41)

By being forced into a constricted identity, many people are left limited, because they do not fit into either extreme of the binary system. Once one is pushed out of the system, which is deemed normative, it is easier to exploit their differences and keep them from obtaining actual equality or power within the system. The *hieros gamos*, however, allows a person to fluidly connect to both male and female. Being both female and male, and not feeling constricted to choose one aspect of the gender binary, starts the process of ending, breaking down our limited foundation that keeps us from finding common equal ground.

Groundbreaking poet and activist, Audre Lorde, also tackles the subject of bordering identities. She struggled to fight against the binary terms that have displaced those who do not fit into the proper places, as well those who become exploited because of the places defining them. In 'Age, Race, Class and Sex,' she openly acknowledges this exploitation:

Much of Western European history conditions us to see human differences in simplistic opposition to each other: dominant/subordinate, good/bad, up/down, superior/inferior. In a society where the good is defined in terms of profit rather than in terms of human need, there must always be some group of people who, through systemized oppression, can be made to feel surplus, to occupy the place of the dehumanized inferior. Within this society, that group is made up of Black and Third World people, working-class people, older people, and women.[160]

Lorde conveys her belief that this is not a means at an attempt to understand someone who is different, but a blatant use of a faulty system to subjugate those differences in order for the dominant to remain in power. By basing a system on profit rather than human need, there will always be this conflict of struggle occurring within society, because everyone is focused on personal gain rather than humanistic needs. Once we become conscious of this fact, we can break free from reinforcing the system and begin building one with a more humanistic approach.

No stranger to the feelings of this subjugation, Anzaldúa constantly finds many parts of her identity being placed into the negative binary status. She addresses this when she says, 'Woman does not feel safe when her own culture, and white culture, are critical of her; when the males of all races hunt her as prey' (GA 42). As a lesbian, Chicana woman, Anzaldúa feels hunted by the dominant culture, as well as by the males within her own. Because of this lack of safety, she expresses how she had to feel competent enough on the outside and secure enough on the inside in order to live life on her own terms (GA 43). This confidence of all her selves, not just the parts accepted by the majority, is essential to the breaking down of the binary system. By acknowledging there are multiple aspects of a self, while simultaneously feeling equally good about each piece, it shows that one should not feel confined to accepting the self that is accepted within the system. This new acceptance opens an opportunity to resist the shaming and denial of the multiple selves that often gets displaced into the negative binary space.

This hunt is shown as part of everyday culture, when Lorde communicates, 'In order to survive, those of us for whom oppression is as American as apple pie have always had to be watchers, to become familiar with the language and manners of the oppressor, even sometimes adopting them for some illusion of protection. Whenever the need for some pretense of communication arises, those who profit from our oppression call upon us to share our knowledge with them. In other words, it is the responsibility of the oppressed to teach the oppressors their mistakes' (AL 114). This illusive protection is meant to shame and force all the negative parts of your 'selves' into the dominant portion of the binary system. It pressures one to feel as if those aspects make you an outsider and urge the assimilation that is necessary for survival. Not only does Lorde feel that this oppression is a part of her American experience, but she also describes in detail the struggles of being the sole administrator responsible for fixing it. Rather than closing the dominance gap by taking the initiative themselves, the oppressors rely on the oppressed to educate them. This responsibility may bring education to those who are unfamiliar, but it also reinforces the power structure. In order to stop this superficial change, the oppressors would need to step outside their dominant position and allow the education to be on an equal foundation. If both the oppressor and the oppressed were not bound by their positions, then they would not be reinforcing the roles that help stabilize the inequality within the system.

Anzaldúa is hauntingly aware of this job that has been plurally placed upon her shoulders. However, she creates a new concept that gives her some freedom and provides an opportunity for those who are already free within the system to make an effort in her direction. She explains, 'What I want is an accounting with all three cultures – white, Mexican, Indian. I want the freedom to chisel my own face, to staunch the bleeding with ashes, to fashion my own gods out of my entrails. And if going home is denied me then I will have to stand and claim my space, making a new culture – *una cultura mestiza* – with my own lumber, my own bricks and mortar and my own feminist architecture' (GA 44).

All three cultures are facets of her whole identity. She is neither white, Mexican, nor just Indian. She is a mixture of all three. By already being outside the dual system, she has the ability to recognize the need for creating a new culture that openly accepts people who do not find themselves on just one extreme of the binary system. This *una cultura mestiza* embodies the need to be heard and the right to be seen for everyone who participates, because it is not a part of the dominant or minor groups within the duality, but a hybrid creation from the two. This provides the dialogue of a new beginning. Once others allow themselves to break free from the dual system and begin using the hybrid language, then both parties are making genuine efforts upon the same foundation. This shows the oppressed that the oppressive majority does not want to continue working within the imbalanced system, as well as providing an opportunity for education of one another's cultures to occur without simultaneously reinforcing the old system.

Lorde feels the confines of the system, but offers an approach that centres on accountability. Expressing the need for those in the powerful aspect of the binary to recognize and own up to the responsibility for their capabilities, she states, 'Certainly there are very real differences between us of race, age, and sex. But it is not those differences between us that are separating us. It is rather our refusal to recognize those differences, and to examine the distortions which result from our misnaming them and their effects upon human behavior and expectation' (AL 115). Similar to Anzaldúa, Lorde does not want to be the sole educator and remain an inferior to the dominant culture. Instead, she wants those within the dominant culture who are sympathetic to a harsh system to take responsibility for their power within the system and learn how it affects others. Lorde is aware that if one forgets the important task of recognizing differences, then one automatically displaces any responsibility for changing the negative aspects that occur. Furthering this problem is the idea that we only examine the issues once they have caused a negative result to a specific minority within the community, thus setting up the imbalanced task of the minority having to educate. However, by acknowledging the distortions that have occurred because of our refusal to recognize it, we can begin chiselling away all the excess that has been the negative effects of those efforts. To Lorde, we must not only be aware, but have the accountability and desire to work together to begin fixing the aftermath if we are to move forward and create genuine social change.

Alongside the need for the dominant culture to claim responsibility, Anzaldúa is also urging for a shift in focus within the system to take place. She articulates this shift:

> There is another quality to the mirror and that is the act of seeing. Seeing and being seen. Subject and object, I and she. The eye pins down the object of its gaze, scrutinizes it, judges it. A glance can freeze us in place; it can 'possess' us. It can erect a barrier against the world. But in a glance also lies awareness, knowledge. These seemingly contradictory aspects – the act of being seen, held immobilized by a glance, and 'seeing through' an experience – are symbolized by the underground aspects of *Coatlicue*, *Cihuacoatl*, and *Tlazolteotl* which cluster in what I call the *Coatlicue* state.
> (GA 64)

Anzaldúa uses the imagery of a mirror and her Indian culture as a way to urge this shift of focus. Her Indian culture consists of goddesses of fertility (*Coatlicue*), purification from vice and diseases (*Cihuacoatl*), and a patron for women who die in childbirth (*Tlazolteotl*). Instead of everyone being fixated on the gaze of the subject and feeling frozen by its ability in a negative space, she offers an empowering way to look at this experience of possessive judgment. She is not so naïve as to think that changing the focus will eliminate the negativity surrounding the subject. Instead, she becomes the patron who absorbs the gaze and all of its positive and negative judgments. Then, she calls upon the concept of purification as a means to cleanse herself of the negative subjectivity. Once she feels purification, she walks away with the ability to see the entire process with a clarity that allows her to teach someone else these vital tools.

Similarly, Lorde does not want these experiences to solely have a negative focus. Lorde provides an explanation for why the focus remains penetrative, when she protests, 'Either way, we do not develop tools for using human difference as a springboard for creative change within our lives. We speak not of human difference, but of human deviance' (AL 115-16). Like Anzaldúa, she sees frozen, anti-creative realities, which occur because of these experiences. Rather than looking at differences as deviant, we can begin seeing difference as a way to express oneself uniquely. By creatively accessing oneself – with a shift in the focus for those going through these events – one can begin looking at the human differences in a positive light, rather than solely feeling the callous negativity that hinders the possibility of change. It is with this hybrid change of reflecting upon the experiences that have occurred, shifting the gaze, and creatively utilizing the process of overcoming these experiences to build a foundational bridge that connects us all in positive ways.

Within the concept of using experiences positively to create change, Anzaldúa dives deeper into the background of *una nueva mestiza*. She encompasses this by educating, 'But Chicano Spanish is a border tongue which developed naturally. Change, *evolución, enriquecimiento de palabras nuevas por invención o adopción* have created variants of Chicano Spanish, *un nuevo lenguage. Un lenguage que corresponde a un modo de vivir.* Chicano Spanish is not incorrect, it is a living language' (GA 77). For Anzaldúa, having a living language, which is a hybridization of the duality she is encased in, allows for the possibility of these invented words to evolve into change. Rather than trying to assimilate into the dominant culture, or hold onto one's own culture and allow the domination to take place, she urges for unification between the two that can set up a new foundation where both parts are found equally within the communicative system. Once unification takes place, people can be consciously aware that one can successfully step away from the binary system and find positive change upon common ground.

Along these lines of change, Lorde uncovers the problematic issues that help keep the inequality firmly in place. She writes, 'We find ourselves having to repeat and relearn the same old lessons over and over that our mothers did because we did not pass on what we have learned, or because we are unable to listen' (AL 117). It is not sufficient to create a new perspective, which can become a catalyst for revolutionary change. One must also learn from past lessons in order not to repeat the exact same previous mistakes. Going a step further, once a perspective that allows for change is successfully implemented, we must be diligent in keeping it alive by passing it onto others. This will help bind together past and present efforts, as well as allow better synthesis for future catalytic thinkers to continue bettering our society on a humanistic level without feeling the restrictiveness of the dualistic system.

This unification (which can become the product of a successful attempt at creating an equal platform) can become consuming if the oppressed is the only person working towards the creative and educative aspects of the process. Although Anzaldúa acknowledges this drain, she also positively conveys an alternative focus, 'We are a synergy of two cultures with various degrees of Mexicanness or Angloness. I have so internalized the borderland conflict that sometimes I feel like one cancels out the other and we are zero, nothing, no one. *A veces no soy nada ni nadie. Pero hasta cuando no lo soy, lo soy*' (GA 85). By expressing the negativity in English ('I feel like one cancels out the other and we are zero, nothing, no one'), but allowing for the possibility of positivity to become the focus within the Spanish (*'Pero hasta cuando no lo soy, lo soy'*), Anzaldúa has successfully bridged the gap for those who have taken the initiative to understand both languages. She sees the negative focus as a dangerous, dominant focal point within the struggle, but shows her hope for overcoming this danger through the marginalized voice of her ancestor's culture. By using the non-dominant language to express a hope within the struggle, she succeeds in bridging the gap between the cultures by fusing them both together with a positive outlook.

Likewise, Lorde is very much aware of positive and negative focal points to the continual conflict that is immediate to her multiple identities. She sheds light on the disadvantages that come with losing sight of either focus, when she says, 'Therefore, for Black women, it is necessary at all times to separate the needs of the oppressor from our own legitimate conflicts within our communities

[…]. Black women and men have shared racist oppression and still share it, although in different ways […]. On the other hand, white women face the pitfall of being seduced into joining the oppressor under the pretense of sharing power' (AL 118). Lorde is not undervaluing the struggle of white women, but cautioning them to be wary of leaving her Black sisters behind for an elusive partnership with the dominant oppressor (in this case, the upper class white male). Lorde shows just how dangerous focusing on the positive and losing sight of the negative can become for those apart of the oppressed group. She realizes it is not enough to just hope these gaps will get bridged. However, by using Anzaldúa's *una nueva mestiza* that requires cooperative effort from the dominant and oppressed, there is a necessary step forward in an effort to providing awareness to the situation. This cooperative effort, combined with the awareness of possible pitfalls that can occur, help create a more intelligent united front.

All this is not possible until there is a cohesive understanding and belief of one's entire self. Anzaldúa expresses just how important it is to embrace all of one's identity while fighting for common goals, when she says, 'To write, to be a writer, I have to trust and believe in myself as a speaker, as a voice for the images. I have to believe that I can communicate with images and words and that I can do it well. A lack of belief in my creative self is a lack of belief in my total self and vice versa – I cannot separate my writing from any part of my life. It is all one' (GA 95). For Anzaldúa, her ability to write and communicate within the system is not separate from her identity. This creative self is Anzaldúa's outlet that comes from the turmoil of the hegemonic system, but has the ability to bring beauty and strength to rise above it. By allowing her creative self to flourish, she has the opportunity to create something within the restrictive boundaries in a way that is universally understandable. The ability to become the writer she is and the wish to use her creative aspects of writing for a common goal of equality is all part of who she is, as well as her place of origin.

Lorde concurrently speaks of this necessity of having an awareness of all the identities, but furthers it by adding that this as an inclusive integrative process.

She declares, 'As a Black feminist comfortable with the many different ingredients of my identity, and a woman committed to racial and sexual freedom from oppression, I find I am constantly being encouraged to pluck out some one aspect of myself and present this as the meaningful whole, eclipsing or denying the other parts of self. But this is a destructive and fragmenting way to live. My fullest concentration of energy is available to me only when I integrate all the parts of who I am, openly, allowing power from particular sources of my living to flow back and forth freely through all my different selves, without the restrictions of externally imposed definitions' (AL 120-21). Lorde is mindful that it is too easy to allow one aspect of the self to remain hidden when dealing with multiple struggles. However, she is insistent that leaving any aspect of the self out of the process will only serve as a destructive tool against that which is meant to be accomplished. Rather than allow pieces of your self to disappear and passively fall into the destructive aspects of the system, she encourages the reader to keep all the selves that makes one whole. This utilization of a whole, creative being dynamically harnesses the power found within and results in a free-flowing integrative identity. Taking this a step further, by harnessing the power meant to be squelched, we can successfully fight the system and prove that all aspects of the self are important and should not be discarded in order to live safely within the binary system.

Anzaldúa further acknowledges the capability for exclusionary possibilities by examining the reasoning behind this taking place. She gives the example within the context of her Indian identity when she writes, 'Those who are pushed out of the tribe for being different are likely to become more sensitized (when not brutalized into insensitivity). Those who do not feel psychologically or physically safe in the world are more apt to develop this sense. Those who are pounced on the most have it the strongest – the females, the homosexuals of all races, the darkskinned, the outcast, the persecuted, the marginalized, the foreign' (GA 60). Once again, Anzaldúa makes a point to show how this marginalization can produce more than the negative subjugation. This experience allows for these others to become more sensitized and consciously aware of how this subjugation can affect someone else. Taking this reasoning behind the marginalization of those not within the confines of the hegemony a step further, her concept of the *new mestiza* allows for these groups to speak freely once the complacency of the conflicting agents – which originally define power – are no longer holding them back. It is this opportunity that creates a new organic infrastructure to a system that allows for education and positive alternatives to come from negative circumstances.

Along the same lines, Lorde conveys the necessity for unification, to forge a *lenguage* and utilize all these differences in order to obtain true equality from the hegemonic force. She empowers, 'But our future survival is predicated upon our ability to relate within equality. As women, we must root out internalized patterns of oppression within ourselves if we are to move beyond the most superficial aspects of social change. Now we must recognize differences among women who are equals, neither inferior nor superior, and devise ways to use each others' difference to enrich our visions and our joint struggles' (AL 122). Once women have moved past the want of superficial social change, which has previously only given a deceptive product to white women at the expense of 'Othering' those not within the dominant racial binary, they can use their differences together to impact change for all. Lorde expresses how essential it is to relate to one another within the realm of equality for not belonging. Once we can create a mutual understanding of one another's differences without discrediting individual experiences, we can begin to appreciate the qualities and start using them to break down the superficial aspects of change and replace them with a substantial version that is inclusionary.

Anzaldúa analogously calls to women to unite all that is separate through a *mestiza* consciousness, when she writes, 'It is the possibility of uniting all that is separate. This assembly is not one where severed or separated pieces merely come together. Nor is it a balancing of opposing powers. In attempting to work out a synthesis, the self has added a third element which is greater than the sum of its severed parts. That third element is a new consciousness – a *mestiza* consciousness – and through it is a source of intense pain, its energy comes from a continual creative motion that keeps breaking down the unitary aspect of each new paradigm' (GA 101-2). Since there are multiple identities, Anzaldúa is aware of the need for a unitary attempt to create a change through all of them. This can only be done by uniting what is separate, as Lorde states, as well as creating an equal place, such as the *mestiza*, for this unity to take place. By allowing a third element to take place, one no longer abides by the binary and can use this creative force, known as the new *mestiza*, as a platform for others to stand in solidarity for a system that is open to more than just duality or binary options.

Although Lorde does not come up with her own system as Anzaldúa has, she is in agreement with the inspiration of something not built solely by the dominant groups. This is shown when she says, 'For we have, built into all of us, old blueprints of expectation and response, old structures of oppression, and these must be altered at the same time as we alter the living conditions which are a result of those structures. For the master's tools will never dismantle the master's house' (AL 123). By stepping outside the basic boundaries of utilizing only what the master gives within his house, one has an actual possibility of breaking away from the illusive and obtaining concrete change. When combining this internal progression with Anzaldúa's hybridization of cultures and language, a plausible path to use within women's grasp to make these conceptualized hopes a reality becomes more obtainable for all.

Even with this equal platform for women to unite and work towards common goals, Anzaldúa argues that they should not leave out those who have a common interest solely because they are among the dominant groups. She sympathizes with the males who stray from the dominant norm, when she describes, 'Lumping the males who deviate from the general norm with man, the oppressor, is a gross injustice' (GA 106). Anzaldúa does not want to continue the exclusionary process, which has put the marginalized groups in the situations they find themselves presently constricted within. Rather, she calls for an open-arm-to-action policy that allows those with similar goals to become part of the process. By creating a space where everyone who deviates is accepted equally and can help create positive social change, she has already begun the process of shattering the basic misconceptions of difference that allow for the binary system to perpetuate itself. She believes that men and women can co-exist equally and work for unequivocal change together rather than forcing one or the other to completely assimilate into the dominant or marginalized paradigms.

Lorde proceeds to sympathize with the painful part of this process that each person will face when fighting the injustice of the hegemonic binary system. Even though she is aware of the hardship, she focuses on the positive, when she addresses, 'Change means growth, and growth can be painful. But we can sharpen self-definition by exposing the self in work and struggle together with those whom we define as different from ourselves, although sharing the same goals. For black and white, old and young, lesbian and heterosexual women alike, this can mean new paths to our survival' (AL 123). Lorde does not want anyone to give up an aspect of who they are, nor does she want those differences to hinder the ability for everyone to co-exist equally and work towards a common goal. By acknowledging these differences, and choosing to work together, she feels that this painful struggle can achieve new heights that were not seen when working separately or against one another.

This ability to recognize differences, while it creates a place where these differences can co-exist equally and unites all to work towards a common goal, is not stated to be an easy road for any of the people involved in the struggle towards true equality. Both Anzaldúa and Lorde are aware of the problematic issues, the possible contradictions which could occur, and the overall difficulty of building and educating everyone of something new and foreign to their current beliefs. Despite all of these potential dangers that can occur within the struggle, they continued to show both the positive and negative aspects, while choosing to change the focal point to the positive outcome. When combining both of their theories and conscious awareness, the resulting chance can lead to acceptance of differences and unification towards a common goal, as well as provide a plausible solution when combining all this with *the new mestiza*.

8. URBAN (AS) FLÂNEUR: NARRATOR AND CITY IN *THE LAMENTABLE JOURNEY OF OMAHA BIGELOW INTO THE IMPENETRABLE LOISAIDA JUNGLE*

Hilarie Ashton (New York University)

Edgardo Vega Yunqué's fiction, broadly drawn, uses humour, irony, and elements of magic to illuminate the lives of Puerto Rican American characters as they intersect with (largely) white culture in a highly specified subset of the quintessential urban American environment: the East Village neighbourhood of New York City. In a more extreme fashion than classic and more often examined exemplars of the magical realist genre like García Márquez, Morrison, and Vargas Llosa, Yunqué's novel *The Lamentable Journey of Omaha Bigelow Into The Impenetrable Loisaida Jungle* explodes its locale out of the realm of setting and pushes it toward the realm of character by casting place as an intensely motive force, amplifying the typical role assigned to it in a novel. Duality of meaning, inescapable and sometimes inexplicable, and parsable in the most reliably Saussurean sense, is an issue that both frames and destabilizes my project here.

Of the key words that inform and inspire my analysis of Yunqué's text, for instance, several have at least one meaning that is descended from action: perhaps most importantly, author (the noun), hidden inside the verb authorize, making the verb form take on an additional, action-based meaning that, for me, merges to write, to fictionalize, and to create and adopt a writer-persona. (Also noteworthy in this context are act, meaning to do something as well as to play a role; and cast, as in to place in a role and perhaps to be in the business of spells, as well as the verb of motion associated with lines). In line with these multiple meanings, *The Lamentable Journey of Omaha Bigelow Into The Impenetrable Loisaida Jungle* exists within a postmodern tradition in which such ambiguities are decidedly at home. They are also, perhaps, an indispensable part of the overall project of moving away from – and at the same time chronicling the move away from – modernism.

While it is certainly plausible to imagine a city literally brought to life in the context of a magical realist novel, Yunqué's project is subtler: he blurs the lines between reality and fictional characterology, both with his expanded setting function as well as when he inserts himself into the novel in character form.[161] Embedded squarely in the tension that exists between city-as-environment and city-as-character and then again between each of the former and author-as-character, Yunqué's novel twists and expands Walter Benjamin's theory of the *flâneur* in 'Some Motifs on Baudelaire,' updating it to the specifics of a new century and a different city, as well as to an expanded typology of place and person.

From Omaha Bigelow's first lines, Yunqué makes it clear that in what follows, he will be delineating a very specific narratological relationship to a city: he tells the reader exactly where Omaha Bigelow, his eponymous protagonist, is walking, giving a commentary on the buildings, streets, and people that make up the scenery, and mapping out when Bigelow turns and when he pauses. With this detailed approach, Yunqué ultimately makes it possible for a close reader to sketch a mental map of the neighbourhood that is taking shape within the text. Even in places where the landmarks that Yunqué references have been effaced and/or replaced by others as the (actual) city evolves, it would be easy for a local (or New York-located) reader to trace the fictional walks through a real landscape. Yunqué's intensely close attention to the details that complexly differentiate and blur together different sectors of his setting marks the area both in the mind of the reader and in the evolving, broader role which I posit that the city takes on.

For the purposes of specifying a kind of 'personality' for his setting, it is noteworthy that Yunqué begins the novel by immediately drawing a complex distinction between the East Village and the Lower East Side, marking the place on Allen Street where the 'East Village esthetic' had 'seeped' into the neighbourhood below Houston Street.[162] In doing this, he defines his setting geographically and also limits it to a real set of boundaries that can be (at least partially) verified and that are actually lived in real-life New York. Yunqué very clearly wants the feminine reader to know exactly where she is located within his story, both geographically and culturally (and needs her to recognize that she is entering a real set of intertwined neighbourhoods at a real moment, in both History with a capital H, and local, lowercase history). Yunqué lets the reader know all this in the first few pages, even before the reader has had a real chance to delve into his text.

The detailed, rapid-fire naming of places, then, situates us very specifically in the setting. If the reader does not know what they are, of course, her readerly interaction with them will be different, but nonetheless, Yunqué is letting her know that this is not a place that she is free to imagine for herself. This exertion of control may also be an effect of (authorial) intervention into fiction: by taking on a more readerly role as well as a more fictional one, the combined author/narrator figure is limiting the amount of freedom (at least, to construct the text) held by the reader. Yunqué takes a similar tack with the ways in which he places the novel in the magical realist tradition, starting with the introduction of a 'friggin late July blizzard' and its follow-up on the same page: 'On Sixth Street a polar bear asked [Omaha] for the time. It's obvious that polar bears and penguins don't exist on the same pole, but there were gaps in Omaha's education and this was his mind' (Y 13).

These phrases, and Omaha's ensuing dialogue with the polar bear, could easily be chalked up to Omaha's earlier consumption of hallucinogenic mushrooms, but Yunqué refuses to give the reader clarity on that front. The drugs are a less plausible explanation, for example, for a phrase like the following: 'Maruquita Salsipuedes left Tompkins Square Park, turned into a chihuahua, barked at a few people, saw a pitbull coming, changed into a cat, and scurried down the stairs to a basement, saw a rat, had an urge to catch it, but concentrated and put it out of her mind' (Y 28). Maruquita's use of magic such as this recurs again and again in the book, to such a degree that the reader would be hard-pressed to come up with a non-magical explanation.

True to quixotic, unpredictable form, Yunqué turns this explanation on its head later in the book, using the comparison 'like some kind of derivative Gabriel García Márquez magical-realism crap' (Y 98). He makes a similar denialist move later on, exhorting the reader to let him 'totally disintegrate the fourth wall, step forward and address the audience directly' (Y 157), a disingenuous request, since he already has done so, in the asking itself. Later still, he reverses the direction of his magical realist rejection, saying, 'By the way, if you see animals in New York City and they seem a little crazed and out of sorts, it's very likely they're Puerto Rican witches in disguise. Be careful around them. Oh, very funny. No, we don't do roaches and rats. Watch it! Maybe you do! Yeah? Your mother! *Tu madre, pendejo*' (Y 229). Such refusals to (consistently) define, and, more importantly, refusals to play along with readerly expectations, even when founded, is, as we shall see, fairly typical of Yunqué's style, and it plays a strong role in making his prose so interesting to read, and so unexpected in its direction. Such twists and turns merge with his descriptions of the city, allowing him to construct and reflect a setting for his narrative just as he is constructing (and perhaps reflecting) a certain persona for himself.

Overall, the depth and breadth of Yunqué's descriptions of the city, magical or realist, give an immediate signal that this is no ordinary setting; the 'personality' of the city that is taking shape cannot be easily substituted for any other location. Hannah Arendt, in her introduction to Benjamin's *Illuminations*, connects the figure of the *flâneur* to the Angel of History,[163] and Yunqué shores up this comparison: the past is everywhere in his depiction of the city, blurring with the present just as past and present do in the real East Village. Although certainly other settings in other novels are affected in a similar way by the inexorable tension between past and present, Yunqué's foregrounding of the play of temporal influences serves as a constituting factor for the setting, laying bare the neighbourhood's genealogy through its shifting composition.

Since Benjamin's definition of the *flâneur*, drawn primarily from his readings of Baudelaire and Poe, is both complex and intensely well-known, I would like to briefly set out selected elements of the *flâneur*'s figuration that are most fitted to interact with the version of urbanity in Yunqué's text. The way in which Benjamin delineates the 'personality' of the *flâneur* aligns in specificity with Yunqué's initial personalization of the city. Using the aforementioned texts as a kind of case study, Benjamin paints a picture of an identifiable character, bracketed as upper class – or at least, as Benjamin puts it, 'unwilling to forego the life of a gentleman of leisure'[164] – who is free both physically and economically to move about the city and observe the activity of the masses. Mapping this character onto Yunqué's city initially distances it from Benjamin's analysis even before allowing Yunqué's narrative space to play with the figure: for Manhattan's people-packed streets – and the narrow blocks of the East Village – make it harder to keep separate from one's surroundings in the way that seems possible in Baudelaire's Paris or Poe's London.

By now you will have noticed, particularly if you have not read Yunqué's novel, that I have barely gestured toward what the book is about, beyond the very general summary with which I began. This is because it is not comprised of events, in the traditional conception of the term, a characteristic that is central to my analysis. The city affects the characters' actions to such a degree that without its influence, one could actually accuse this novel of verging on the plotless: that is, the events that it does contain are, for the most part, instantiated by locations in the city and the characters' interactions with them (and with other characters) rather than by monumental events. (Richard Lester's semi-biographical Beatles film *A Hard Day's Night* is an instructive parallel here, at least insofar as it is driven by dialogue and interpersonal chemistry rather than momentous 'things' – a piling-up of small actions rather than set-pieces). The melding of setting description and narrative voice that I described above takes part in this dynamic, reacting so vivaciously in front of – and directed toward – the reader who barely misses the plot in the digressive or magical moments in which it might escape him/her.

Lamentable Journey's absence of events is foregrounded by the increased role the city plays in the narrative: the characters spend the majority of the book interwoven with the city, whether outside in the streets or in the bars and clubs of their neighbourhood. This palpable, ebbing and flowing absence of action is supported by Yunqué's narrative style – he writes conversationally, letting his attention wander away from his immediate purpose by something occurring out of a character's eye, or something that occurs to him as narrator (on which more to come). He does map out a skeleton plot, giving the reader characters to get to know and elements of their situations to unpack that seem as though they might engender an event. Stylistically, then, Yunqué lets the reader know what might be on the verge of happening, and then sits back to watch, and to comment.

A brief caveat to all of this is the common difficulty of separating this personalized city from the people who live in it. People, after all, literally make up the living fabric of the place in which they live: the intensity of Yunqué's description and its preliminary plot function, as I have glossed them above, emphasize the extent to which this is true. A narratological difference, however, is that in Yunqué the trope of the *flâneur* widens to accommodate more than one character, each of whom acts as a *flâneur*-like focal point as well as a focalizer for the reader. Although much of the story is filtered through the titular protagonist's perspective, his vivacious and literally magical girlfriend Maruquita Salsipuedes takes over at a quickly increasing rate, prompting Yunqué (as narrator) at one point to express incredulity at the extent to which an initially secondary character has taken over the narrative. One might even posit that Yunqué unites himself with her perspective to some extent, as when he promises, 'I'll do my best to wind this up now and I hope you will forgive my excesses and Maruquita's youthful exuberance, her political involvement, and her overactive sense of justice' (Y 348).

Maruquita embodies a secondary aspect of the city's impact on the narration, namely, what I would like to call the literalization of motion in the extra importance that Yunqué places on where the characters go and how, directionally, they get there. In the several instances when Maruquita moves about the city in the guise of a bird, giving the reader a panoramic, pulled-out view of her surroundings as she experiences them, she embodies the novel's personification of the city itself, moving across personalized space and highlighting, with the help of the narrator, the places that mean something to her human self. In this way, Maruquita is of the neighbourhood in a highly familiarized (and literally, occult familiar) way that Omaha is not, and, in line with my argument above, in Yunqué's hands the motion of the characters becomes a quasi-event in itself.

The character of Omaha Bigelow is similarly sharply sketched, although with a different valence of personality. In contrast to the vivid and unmistakable setting in which he finds himself, Omaha is a cipher-like pivot around which the decidedly more exotic characters and locations coalesce within the narrative. The fact that Yunqué has Omaha grow up in Kansas and that he names him after a quintessentially middle American city puts even more of a focus on the urban neighbourhood in which the novel lands him: along the lines of Barthes' cultural codes, Yunqué's selections of places with which his (American) readers (at least) will be familiar makes certain oblique comments about the very different setting with which he is actually dealing. Omaha's move to the big city parallels the re-imagining of New York through 'smart magazines' that Catherine Keyser cites in her study of the interplay between New York women writers and the magazines in which they published: she writes, 'New York was imagined as a place where behaviors could be audacious, chic commodities and lifestyles could be easily obtained, and small town identities and constrictions could be abandoned'.[165] Yunqué's move also gestures toward certain culturally and geographically-based assumptions that are literalized in Omaha's visit home, when he brings his Midwestern mother in direct and uncomfortable contact with his urban Latina girlfriend (Y 145-6); I will examine these assumptions below in my reading of this scene.

In Yunqué's hands, then, Omaha Bigelow is purposely blank and verging on boring, outflanked in intrigue by the unexpected convergence of his first and last names, which evoke an out-of-the ordinariness that falsely signals (and only superficially could even denote) an attention-grabbing individual. Omaha is not particularly interesting and only pedantically articulate (as when he corrects Maruquita's English grammar errors). His blandness and chameleon-like malleability is visually marked by the fact that he has to dye his hair when he moves into the projects (Y 148) in order to blend in. Neither is he ambitious, talented, or handsome enough to justify the extreme interest that he inspires among the women of the East Village as Yunqué writes them. Taken on its own, this latter phenomenon could be written off as an expression of (some sort of) narrative irony, but Yunqué both simplifies and complicates it by tracing it across racial and cultural lines. Simply put, this boring white boy is of supreme interest to the (actually fascinating) white and Latina females who populate the novel. In this sense, Omaha's function as an object of affection for all of them makes him a uniting factor in line with the neighbourhood itself; everyone wants to connect to him, for reasons that Yunqué unapologetically casts as sexual. Omaha gives the lie, ultimately, to the intriguing promises of the title, unless we take the adjective 'lamentable' to be a commentary on his blandness, in contrast with the more interesting situations of other characters.

Even if we take Omaha's boring nature as a given, his very presence in the novel problematizes certain aspects of the situations in which he finds himself. For example, the 'culture clash' scenario of the Midwestern visit, as I defined it above, is loaded, and deserves a brief examination. For one, the notion of a culture clash itself is rarely as simply realized as the one that Yunqué's scenario lays out. Omaha Bigelow himself is evidence for this, since, although he does represent the gringo white boy better than anyone else in the novel, he also problematizes the 'gringo'/ 'person of colour' dichotomy just by being there; in a sense, he throws Latino (and maybe even New York City urban) cultures into relief just by standing next to them, and then affects them further with the aspects that he tries to take on (most obviously, the Spanish language). Somewhat simplistically, one could say that he makes the setting look different just by being in it, and he makes others look differently at their surroundings. This forceful role, however, still has very little to do with who he is, and everything to do with the mere fact that he is different.

The culture clash scene also foregrounds the simultaneous importance and lack of importance of birth (or ancestral) identity to the novel. Maruquita's mother is an interesting example here, since she has raised two extremely different children, one who speaks in the general vernacular of her culture and her city, and one who speaks the correct language of the dominant culture that surrounds him. Maruquita, the former child, lives in an unfiltered, natural (to what she knows) way, whereas Samuel Beckett Salsipuedes literally embodies a dual cultural existence, one that is encapsulated in his very name. By dyeing his hair, Omaha Bigelow is making a version of the same move, i.e. unification, but in a way that ends up (literally) obscuring part of his roots.

Complicating matters is the fact that Maruquita herself will give the lie to this division later in the novel, when she (temporarily, at least) sheds her stereotypically Latina-ized background to attend Harvard. (Even this comparison that I have just made is a problematic one, since neither advanced nor top tier academic study necessarily obviate the use of natural language as opposed to Standard English, even though the latter is more often used (and perhaps adopted) than the former. In fact, tension between the academic (or the 'correct') and the colloquial is threaded throughout this book, in part through comments that the characters make on each other's language, but also in the form of the words Yunqué himself uses. His style marks himself as educated, but he very vocally supports those who are not. Despite these linguistic and cultural issues, the basic distinction that he initially draws between Maruquita and Omaha's mother in the Kansas scene, via their differing ethnic and cultural backgrounds, still holds.

Yunqué's choice of setting is particularly interesting as a method of dramatizing ethnic/cultural difference. In the Kansas visit scene to which I alluded above, the fact that he takes Maruquita out of her comfort zone and puts her in one that, stereotypically at least, is much less accepting of difference, is an interesting move. It takes on even more significance in the context of the importance, to this novel, of a highly specific setting: by taking one of his main characters out of it, Yunqué highlights the things about her that are so conditioned by the setting to which she is accustomed, including her ways of speaking and her lack of familiarity with many places other than her immediate environs.

Boring attributes aside, Omaha Bigelow is still useful in himself to Yunqué's project, as a new kind of *flâneur*. He wanders as part of his daily routine (a necessity for many – or most – city-dwellers, to be sure), yet the primary difference from Benjamin's figure is that Yunqué puts the focus more on what happens to Omaha rather than what he does, emphasizing his stand-in blandness in yet another way, and circling back to the 'event-free' nature of this text. More by being who he is than by virtue of anything that he does, then, Omaha actually unites and divides simultaneously, complicating my above assertion – he is a shared object of desire who engenders animosity within a relatively closely-knit social group. Although Yunqué seems to indicate that his protagonist is never fully aware of the impact or implications of his actions, Omaha links Loisaida, the original Latino neighbourhood of the East Village, with the newer gentrifying one west of Avenue A (in his historical moment, the dividing line past which the neighbourhood's largely white and upper class residents rarely ventured). Ultimately and not without some contradiction, as I have described, Omaha serves as a connector through both his shifting identity and through his duelling romantic relationships, one with Maruquita, very clearly a Latina, and one with a very obviously white (and definitely stereotypical) blueblood, Winnifred Buckley. (It should be noted that Maruquita, too, is a new kind of *flâneur*, with her power to move about the city in any of several different guises, as quoted above. Her motions force the reader to look at the city in a different way – from the air, as a bird, or from the sidewalk, as a mouse, to give two examples).

The way in which Benjamin describes the *flâneur* imbricates it in the particulars of certain time periods, but more important for my analysis, within a certain class and a certain culture. The primary representative of the upper class in Yunqué's novel is the aforementioned Ms. Buckley – who is, perhaps without accident, also the novel's primary representation of whiteness other than Omaha himself. Winnifred, referred to often by her narrator as a WASP, comes from old New England money and presents a very direct challenge to the Latina women who also covet Omaha: she is both interpersonally abrasive and willing to be one of several women in a way that the more possessive Maruquita is not. The differences in their socioeconomic statuses are almost constantly foregrounded. In this, Yunqué makes it clear that his sympathies lie much more with Maruquita than with Winnifred, yet he shies away from casting her completely as a villain in multiple ways, including the bestowal of a parallel magical power on Winnifred as well as Maruquita.

Yunqué (as narrator) is open with the vector of his narrative project, saying 'We're left now with a triangular plot in which Maruquita Salsipuedes and Winnifred Buckley will vie for the affection and control of Omaha Bigelow. There is no need to try to figure out what these three characters represent. I don't even think they're archetypes for anything, unless you want to drive yourself nuts trying to attach symbolism to them' (Y 228). These types of phrases are characteristic of Yunqué's style: he very often directly addresses the reader, and almost as often comments on the reader's own interpretative experience in a way that could either be meant to discourage or to satirize it, as above. Brian

Richardson claims that the use of 'you' in narrative engenders 'a continuous dialectic of identification and distancing [...], as the reader is alternately drawn closer to and further away from the protagonist. This *you* is inherently unstable, constantly threatening to merge with the narratee, a character, the reader, or even with another grammatical person'.[166] Richardson places much of the power with the *you*, whereas it seems to me that what Yunqué is attempting is even more transgressive: he wants to pull the reader herself into the plot of his novel.

In a comment like Yunqué's archetypes denial above, I am primarily interested in the way in which it bumps up against his appearance as Vega, as he calls himself in his character role, and how the combination fits in with the fictionality of the city that he is creating. Several of Richardson's points interact interestingly with Yunque's enactment of this project. Yunqué's use of himself as material for his own text fills in the gaps where an evental plotline is absent, as I argued earlier; he puts himself in the action less directly than a writer like Philip Roth tends to do, instead letting his narratorial interjections and his characterological appearances speak for themselves. Richardson introduces the related idea of the 'transparent voices phenomenon' – 'in which the most unreliable internal narrator can readily (and, more importantly, incontrovertibly) articulate the ideas of the author',[167] but what Yunqué is doing is, it seems to me, much more subversive; that is, writing oneself into a fictional text bumps up against the oft practised notion in fiction that the author-persona is to stay behind the text, distinct from the narrator. Finally, Richardson also writes that 'the author speaks directly and sometimes incongruously through that character's mouth'.[168] While this notion is clearly related to the project that Yunqué is undertaking, his refusal to meld himself completely with a character marks his originality, as well as contributing to the effects outlined above.

With his first reference to himself as Ed Vega (Y 45), Yunqué inserts himself directly into his own narrative on two levels, the first via direct, first-person address, in which he straddles the line between narrator and character, as in the following remark to the reader: 'I'm not a mean-spirited person who will leave things unanswered and make readers search all over trying to find significance and symbolism in narrative.' He continues this thought by saying, 'But I don't want to be accused of using the novel as a political platform and of pamphleteering or of some sort of diluted form of socialist realism. Well, maybe' (Y 156). The obliqueness of these entrances into the narrative gets sharpened in the several places where Yunqué does make his commentary explicit.

This is particularly interesting as part of a novel that treats a rapidly changing – and, more specifically, rapidly gentrifying – neighbourhood, and Yunqué is not shy about expressing his distaste for them, as when he comments, 'By the way, the East Village grows more staid and conservative as more and more rich people invade the neighbourhood to live a pseudo-exciting bohemian life' (Y 239). Such opinions, with their left-wing glosses, put another, finer point on Yunqué's use of a white and interloping protagonist. By virtue of class and economic birthright, Omaha Bigelow is a gentrifier too, literally changing the city around him just by being there. The other function of the insertion of authorial opinion in the way that Yunqué performs it is to shape the reader's perception of the city through Yunqué's own experience of it. His political comments come, after all, from his own experience of the neighbourhood about which he is writing. He thus broadens the city's function in yet another way, using it as a way in which to enter the politics of class and race, and, however oblique in tone, exhorting his readers to involve themselves in it.

Yunqué also inserts himself into the text on the level of actual presence, as a fictive creation also named Ed Vega who interacts directly with other characters, for instance, in the two places in the text when he carries on phone conversations with Maruquita (Y 265-71 and 340-47). The complication here, which makes my separable naming convention of Vega and Yunqué difficult to defend, is that even as a character, Vega is still performing as the narrator/creator figure in relation to the other characters, and they know it. In this respect, his own fictionality as a character is problematized and problematic. His interactions with his characters are all that definitively prevents him from being part of the real in this moment – and yet it is an open question whether (again as with Philip Roth) the biography of a writer from a certain neighbourhood who then writes about that neighbourhood should play a larger role in any interpretation of the work. By fictionalizing himself, at least, Yunqué implicitly invites readers to examine what they know of his authorial self. In this respect, he himself could be considered a *flâneur*, wandering as he does through the fictional text as a melded narrator/author/character figure. As such, in this text, he is always already Edgardo Vega Yunqué, no matter how he or I might refer to him – a combination of writer and character.

Although the city as portrayed in *The Lamentable Journey of Omaha Bigelow Into The Impenetrable Loisaida Jungle* derives a great deal of additional force from its author's structure and plot (or lack of plot) choices, it turns out that the author himself is just as intriguing a figure as the version of the *flâneur* that his protagonist or his location enacts. The degree to which the combination of his incarnations shapes the text aligns him even more closely with his text's version of the *flâneur*, distinct from Benjamin's original form. In contrast to Benjamin's emphasis on the category of 'the masses' in Baudelaire,[169] Yunqué gives a smaller, more personal look at a city for both the characters and the reader to move about in. He interweaves his own persona with the fiction he creates, and pulls out social and political elements in an evasive yet direct way that manages to avoid hewing itself too closely to fictional convention and keeps his narrative voice unique even among the more well-known members of his magical realist cohort.

9. 'WHAT WILL WE DO WITH OUR BEAST?': REVERSING THE SPECTACLE IN EDWIDGE DANTICAT'S *THE DEW BREAKER*

Ghazala F. Hashmi (J. Sargeant Reynolds Community College)

In the title story of *The Dew Breaker*, which serves also as its concluding chapter, Edwidge Danticat returns to the Haiti of the Duvalier past; it is the site from which the inexorable ghosts of her characters' haunted lives arose. In this last chapter, Danticat reveals the full story of the Dew Breaker's ignoble history. The notorious *ton ton macoute* and torturer both confronts his final victim, the preacher who will not be silenced, and attempts to find a fragmented redemption through exile and a complicated marriage to Anne, a woman who both knows and does not know how to read the violent calligraphy etched across his face by her lost stepbrother. Danticat resurrects this past so that she may give flesh to Ka's father and mother, people whose lives had been otherwise shaped falsely into being by Ka's imagination and by their own lies and silences.

Throughout his exiled life in New York, Ka's father, the Dew Breaker himself, has sought to escape the gaze of others whose too-inquisitive glances, he fears, would reawaken, or at the very least reaffirm, the brutal man he once was and whose sins he can never fully expiate. Ironically, his fears are not unfounded. All about him, in Little Haiti, are the gazes of the internally damaged and the psychologically wounded. Whether or not they are his immediate victims, they are haunted by a history in which he played a direct and immutable role. Even in his own basement apartment, he unknowingly harbours a tenant, Dany, who suspects him as the murderer of his parents.

This fear of the gaze of the tortured and the imprisoned is an ironic reversal of Foucault's argument in *Discipline and Punish*. While governments, dictators, and torturers such as the Dew Breaker possess the powers of Bentham's panopticon, Danticat appears to be positing – as she does in much of her writing – that the power of memory, testimony, and storytelling emerges as a resistant and resilient response to the punishing controls of such authority. In her novel, the gaze upon the abused and the condemned prisoner is reversed, and the various shards of the mirror of memory turn their focus upon the torturer and the abusers. The hope of such reversal is that the panoptic gaze actually brings greater accountability to abusive power and that it paradoxically turns about the 'panoptic schema [which] makes any apparatus of power more intense.'[170] More invasive, direct, and visceral than the collective records of a formal history (housed within legal documents, academic papers, and reports), the gaze of the abused and the fragments of memories offered by the survivors reverse the spectacle itself. The torturer is the one who cannot escape the panoptic vision that begins to surround him, emerging as it does through the stories of his various direct and indirect victims, gathering together slowly within *The Dew Breaker*. Adding to that gaze is the scrutiny of the reader who is given the task to piece together the true narrative of the torturer's past.

Thus it is fitting that the Dew Breaker must wear his now-legible scar upon his cheek, a scar whose ambiguous hieroglyphic was so easy to misread without the proper code for its interpretation. It is also fitting that the sculpture, carved lovingly by Ka in honour of a false father, lies bloated and bastardized at the bottom of a lake. It is a grim baptism from which the real father, the Dew Breaker himself, must emerge. He rises, reconstituted, in his final chapter, 'The Dew Breaker.' Ironically, he is the central figure of coherence among the various short stories whose connections otherwise are not immediately clear; his presence brings a thread of unity to the text as, one way or another, the narratives of all the other characters' lives are developed in reaction to, or because of, him.

Throughout the final story, the narrative voice draws subtle but frequent attention to the presence of observers from the United States and Europe who record and comment upon the local conditions in Port-au-Prince but who are ultimately ineffectual and anonymous actors upon the scene. A journalist from *Life* magazine describes the filthy conditions of the Bel Air neighbourhood but simultaneously mourns the fact that this degenerated environment has wasted its 'enviable view of the cobalt sea of Port-au-Prince harbor'.[171] As part of his investigation of the final crime committed by the torturer, a reporter from *Le Monde* interviews the young boy who bought cigarettes for the Dew Breaker on the fateful day that he stalked the preacher (DB 195). International human rights observers are also present, and they too record the testimony of those who witnessed the blatant abuses of the despised Dew Breaker (DB 184). These observers document and disseminate abroad the chronicles of the suffering, but to what effect? Their presence reminds one of the complicit and often-tacit natures of abuse, corruption, and betrayal: the United States and Western European actors have played no small role in fostering and bolstering dictators when political and economic expediencies have required it. This complicity is further magnified with the nuanced reminders within *The Dew Breaker* that the rule of law and constitutional democracies still remain vulnerable to the abuse of power and that they too harbour torturers: in the story 'Seven,' the cases of Abner Louima and Patrick Dorismond, both victims of American police brutality, are mentioned as tragic examples of this terrible capacity for authoritarian violence (DB 38, 45).

Further, outside observers' efforts at turning the panoptic gaze upon the 'prison wardens' are at best inadequate or distorted, and at worst, they are deliberately obscuring or false. While these formal records and testimonial files become a part of a broader archive of collective memory, the visceral record of trauma cannot be fully comprehended until the torturer and the tortured gather the pieces of memory together themselves and create a valid space within that formal record for the terrors of nightmares (as experienced by Dany), for grief over a child that will never be born (and who is mourned daily by Nadine), and for the rippling effects of violence and suffering. As Cathy Caruth points out, the private reactions to trauma 'occur in the often delayed, uncontrolled repetitive appearance of hallucinations and other intrusive phenomena'.[172] The private re-enactment of trauma is an intimate and psychological process between victim and torturer, reminding us that 'the condemned man and the executioner [...] are in a sense twin brothers'.[173]

In many ways, Danticat's short stories of *The Dew Breaker* replicate the direct recording of political abuse victims' testimonies. Their presentation imitates a history that is often relayed in a disjointed manner to those who transcribe testimony as evidence. However, as a creative work, this narrative collection transcends the limitations of factual records, opening up the introspective and elusive realms of memory that need a proper translation for the observing world. Danticat speaks of similar experiences from her childhood when she served as the literal voice for her beloved uncle who lost his own in a laryngectomy and as the transcriber of personal letters for those bound by the barriers of illiteracy: 'When I was a girl in Haiti I wrote letters for people who couldn't read or write. And that was an act of translation too [...]. I guess it's a way of stealing people's stories. They see you as a vessel for their voice and you do the best you can.'[174] For the characters who were once the victims of the Dew Breaker, Danticat serves as vessel and voice. These fragmented versions of the trauma create, then, the interwoven tales of *The Dew Breaker*.

In *That the World May Know: Bearing Witness to Atrocity*, a study of the observation and testimony about human rights abuse and genocide, James Dawes addresses crucial questions raised by one of the reviewers of his own book. The reviewer points to the paradoxical situation of those who are paid to expose human rights violations: 'Who nominates you to publicize pain and suffering that you can walk away from? How does one avoid the trap of commodifying intense suffering to elicit maximum effect (or career advantage)?'[175] Interestingly, Ka herself confronts this same dilemma within the first story of the collection: she has commodified her father's imagined victimization in the figure of the statue that she is now preparing to sell. Her unprovoked journey towards the discovery of her father's real past begins literally as a car trip to sell and profit from his false narrative of suffering.

Dawes pursues these questions even further: 'How do you resolve the paradox that your audiences hunger for these images and stories of calamity both because they want to understand their world and their moral responsibilities in it, and because they are narrowly voyeuristic?'[176] Boundaries distinguishing moral outrage from mere titillation are often difficult to identify. Dawes explores the dilemma of terrible choices often borne by those witnesses who have sought to turn the observing lens upon the abusers. Executions and brutalities are sometimes committed because of the stagecraft offered by the recording cameras; the abusers appropriate the lens to embolden their exercise of power. The recording observers grapple with the dilemma of personal involvement and objectivity. Further, the stories that they tell, whether through photo, video, or print, sometimes receive accolades and are rewarded monetarily. Singularly disturbing is the implied promise that is made between the abused and the storytellers: the promise to listen, report, and perhaps serve as the conduit for transformative action. As one photojournalist explains to Dawes:

> We have this idea that the simple act of bearing witness is what matters to survivors, but it's far more complicated than that. When you come and interview them, their hope is that their lives are going to improve, that they're going to be helped by this in some tangible way. So they tell you their stories, these painful stories, and you listen knowing that you're almost certainly not going to help them. It's not deception, but sometimes it comes close to feeling like it.[177]

Those who testify and those who record that testimony are bound together by what has been witnessed, experienced, and what must be shared.

While one might consider fictional texts about human rights abuses to be exempt from the expectations of journalistic reporting, fiction too suffers from similar dilemmas. The linearity of the fictional narrative form, which compels itself towards an appropriate closure, becomes a challenge for writers in this genre of the 'human rights novel'.[178] Being true to reality often places the writer at odds with the instinctual narrative desire: 'The basic narrative pull of so many of the novels that take human rights violations as their central plot concern [...] is hope. What draws readers through the landscapes of ruined bodies is the hope of a just conclusion'.[179] Struggling between the narrative impulse towards meaningful resolution and the grim reality that is its subject matter, this genre of writing navigates a delicate balance of truthful representation and artistic desire.

The fiction writer of trauma struggles with questions of audience (to whom and for whom is one truly writing), a similar dilemma of receiving public recognition for a body of work based upon graphic violations of human dignity, and questions about the purpose of the text. As Peter Brooks argues in *Reading for the Plot*, 'Narratives portray the motors of desire that drive and consume their plots, and they also lay bare the nature of narration as a form of human desire: the need to tell as a primary human drive that seeks to seduce and subjugate the listener [...]. [T]hese different yet convergent vectors of desire suggest the need to explore more fully [...] the dynamics of exchange and transmission, the roles of tellers and listeners'.[180] When political and social purpose is added to this 'dynamic of exchange and transmission,' the desire of the plot moves toward the need for retribution, compensation, and salvation.

I suggest, however, that Danticat in *The Dew Breaker* is able to transcend this difficulty of the narrative desire for 'just' resolution because she deliberately replicates the ways in which most testimony of trauma reveals itself: it is inscribed within scars; it is pushed forth by shattered psyches; it is shrouded in whispers or in lies; it is spoken only at night and through the prod of nightmares. The private narratives of abuse exist separately, but just as legitimately, from the public narrative that is made official in legal documents, journalists' accounts, and historical summations. In this novel, the story of the Dew Breaker himself unfolds through the fragmented and fragile memories of those who suffered his abuse directly or inherited that trauma from his victims. In 'The Ethics and Aesthetics of Representing Trauma,' Jo Collins argues that the reader is given the responsibility 'to construct a weave of narrative connections and this implies a therapeutic model, where the traumatic event is reconstructed in dialogue between therapist and survivor, or here between reader and text'.[181] The desire of this genre is partly fulfilled through the act itself of speaking the pain.

As Danticat disrupts the chronology of the Dew Breaker's story, she also disrupts this narrative impulse towards hope or the reclamation of a private peace. What we move towards, instead, is the vacillation which replicates Anne's metaphorical pendulum which sways 'between regret and forgiveness' as she contemplates the effort that it takes to love her husband, the Dew Breaker (DB 242). Danticat provides her reader with the opportunity to understand the Dew Breaker's own traumatized childhood, but she also:

> precludes the appropriation of the trauma by problematizing the accessibility of traumatic events to the audience. Rather than testimony, there is a textual politics of distancing and indirection, so a reader must work to reconstruct Haitian history and the possible relations between the characters. We are not given moral guidelines from which to judge the Dew Breaker: we see fragments of his perspective, the brutalization of his family by François Duvalier's regime, and the suffering of his victims. We do not have *access* to his feelings or trauma any more than we can *access* the other characters that we fleetingly encounter in the text's episodes.[182]

If the movement of Danticat's text swings between forgiveness and regret, a panoptic vision encompassing the torturer is entirely necessary; otherwise, we cannot understand his private tale. We may not have full access to his history, but we have access to the contradictory elements that compel him: 'Unlike most trauma theorists, Danticat is a bit more reluctant to mark a clear division between victimizer and victimized, since all of them seem to be burdened by a history in which they have been pawns of forces they could not really control'.[183] As the

Dew Breaker, the torturer's actions are reprehensible; as Ka's father, he is a different man.

Brooks suggests that '[t]here can be a range of reasons for telling a story, from the self-interested to the altruistic'.[184] In the example of Joseph Conrad's Kurtz, we find that '[a]t the end of the journey lies, not ivory, gold, or a fountain of youth, but the capacity to turn experience into language: a voice'.[185] The broader journey of the storytelling, the discovery of voice is also a search for meaning which 'will never lie in the summing-up but only in transmission: in the passing-on of the 'horror,' the taint of knowledge gained. Meaning is hence dialogic in nature, located in the interstices of story and frame, born of the relationship between tellers and listeners'.[186]

As readers, our journey into the Dew Breaker's story is similar to his daughter Ka's own traumatic introduction to it. In 'The Book of the Dead,' the first story of the collection, Ka's father, the man she loved, respected, and towards whom she bent all of her creative impulses as a sculptor, disappears both literally and figuratively. She wakes in a Florida motel room to find her father inexplicably vanished, along with her car and the sculpture that she is in the process of transporting to her buyer, the Haitian-American television actress, Gabrielle Fontaneau. The father that she thought she knew now lies submerged in the lake: the Dew Breaker has deliberately drowned the sculpture because he cannot confront the lie that the wooden figure represents. When her father returns to confess himself to her, Ka imagines the submerged work of art at the lake's bottom, the wood split apart as the water takes its inevitable toll upon the piece. It is, she realizes, an artifice, a construction of imagination, a false memory. Like histories illegitimately conceived or national narratives deliberately generated as propaganda, the statue's wooden cracks, which she once treasured for their beauty and organic purity, are now more truly emblematic of the porous lies that always surround such fictions.

The man that returns from the lake that day is no longer Ka's father; he is the Dew Breaker. As he now confesses, he was the hunter and not the prey, and he is most certainly not the noble sufferer who has held Ka's artistic imagination and love. Just as she confronts her misreading of his scar, she confronts also the fundamental betrayal of a life constructed by the deliberate silences of both her parents.

As her mother Anne tries to explain her own ambivalence and past deceptions, Ka hangs up the phone 'in mid-conversation,' not knowing whether she will resume it 'in a few minutes, a few hours, a few days, even a few years' (DB 26). This terrible silence between mother and daughter completes the cyclical construction of the text, linking the beginning of *The Dew Breaker* to its ending, for we encounter the same silence again on the final page, this time from Anne's perception:

> She had hoped to close the call by saying something tender and affectionate to her daughter, something like, 'You are mine and I love you.' Or maybe she would reach for a now useless cliché, one that she had been reciting to herself all these years, that atonement, reparation, was possible and available for everyone. Or maybe she would think of some unrelated anecdote, a parable, another miracle story, or even some pleasantry, a joke. Anything to keep them both talking. But her daughter was already gone, lost, accidentally or purposely, in the hum of the dial tone. (DB 242)

The mechanical hum of the disconnected call, replacing words that are simultaneously laden with meaning and utterly meaningless, echoes the stark mechanisms by which trauma is so frequently defined and displayed: on television screens, in news reports, and in legalistic language. Danticat offers little relief herself in the course of her text, recognizing that the conversation of trauma is often elusive, cut off at its very roots, or unutterable:

> Traumatic events are rendered incompletely and without the possibility of closure. Examples of this are Beatrice's partial account of her torture and her belief that the Dew Breaker continues to pursue her (which it transpires is false), and Dany's attempt to elicit his aunt's testimony about his parents' murder, which is thwarted because she dies before she can disclose her version of events. This then problematizes the possibility of

empathy, and demonstrates Danticat's textual politics of dissociation, as the audience cannot fully access these accounts and experiences.[187]

Anne herself recognizes her attempts at explanation as being hackneyed and clichéd, especially in the context of her husband whose atonement for his past crimes is not readily apparent. His flight from Haiti, his concealment of his identity, and his false narrative to his own daughter have all served to protect him from a real expiation of his crimes. The victims' desires for revenge is both driven and hampered by history. As Martin Munro argues:

> Haiti, with a spectacular history of anticolonial retribution, is perhaps the postcolonial state most starkly and unequivocally founded on revenge [...]. [I]n Haiti, the notion of righteous revenge was inscribed directly into the 1804 Proclamation of Independence, which declared that the spirits of the dead who had died at the hands of the French 'barbarians' demanded revenge, and liberty had to be protected from them.[188]

Dany, the tenant who has the greatest opportunity to enact revenge upon the Dew Breaker by either murdering him or exposing him, is caught in indecision reminiscent of Hamlet. Munro suggests that '[t]he historical images of the merciful Toussaint and the vengeful Dessalines have to some extent been insinuated into modes of behavior in post-independence Haiti, most recognizably in politics'.[189] Although Dany's inaction may not be equivalent to the granting of clemency itself, others in the novel – most notably Anne – have moved beyond vengeance.

Still, the Dew Breaker has the responsibility to face his crimes, and his own silence on matters so dark and brutal makes exposition of the broader nature of state-sponsored criminality all the more necessary. Silence pursues a dark course through the various short stories of *The Dew Breaker*: we see it in Nadine's patients who suffer the pain of laryngectomies and in people like Dany and his aunt who can speak their trauma only when asleep. Most significant is the silence of the disappeared.

The Dew Breaker's final victim, the preacher, Anne's stepbrother, is among those who are disappeared; his story is told only at the end when Anne is forced to confront her complicity in the silence that now shrouds his memory. The Dew Breaker's first contact with the preacher is a literal attempt to cut off his voice. The preacher's sermon is an act of testimony as he tells his congregation the story of his own wife's recent murder by those who seek to intimidate him. This testimony is silenced when the torturer, escorted by his gang of volunteers, forces his way into the church and '[grabs] the preacher's neck, wrapping his long, plump fingers around the preacher's Adam's apple, putting extra pressure on the preacher's voice box to keep him from speaking' (DB 211). The preacher had long anticipated his fate:

> He'd dreamed his own death so many times that he was no longer afraid of it. He'd imagined himself being pushed off the highest mountain peak [...], forced to drink a gallon of bleach, burned at the stake like Joan of Arc, beheaded like John the Baptist. In all his dreams, however, he always saw himself being resurrected [...]. When he was decapitated like John the Baptist, he bent down to the floor, picked up his own head, and fitted it back on as though he were a plastic doll (DB 201).

When the preacher disappears into the prison and marks the Dew Breaker forever with his terrible scar, his voice is silenced by the official lie disseminated about him, that 'he had set his body on fire in the prison yard at dawn, leaving behind no corpse to bury, no trace of himself at all' (DB 242). The preacher goes into the prison; and, ironically, the wounded man who emerges from it, collides into Anne, and takes on the role of the tortured victim is the torturer himself: the preacher and the Dew Breaker have switched places, and the torturer has both silenced his voice and stolen his story. The preacher never conceived that his resurrection would be through the body of the Dew Breaker.

In this act of 'doubling' that occurs between the preacher and the Dew Breaker, Danticat re-enacts a literary device with which she is familiar. Speaking about *Breath, Eyes, Memory,* Danticat states, 'I started thinking about [doubling] because I had often heard the story of our heroes, like Jean-Jacques Dessaline

[...]. In the folkloric explanation, he was such a strong individual because he was really two people: one part of him could be at home and the other on the battlefield [...]. The idea is that someone is doubly a person but really one person – as opposed to the twins who are really two people'.[190] In *The Dew Breaker*, Ka is meant to be her father's double, the talisman and his good angel who is to balance the evil of his past life. As he explains to her, 'A ka is a double of the body, [...] the body's companion through life and after life. It guides the body through the kingdom of the dead' (DB 17). However, the preacher too becomes the double of the Dew Breaker in the final story when the torturer emerges from the prison and is sheltered by Anne. Victimizer and victimized are both caught in a history not necessarily of their own making.

The narrative desire of *The Dew Breaker* is not toward hope; nor is it toward reconciliation. The narrative moves toward coherence as it flings tenuous strands from one fragmented life to another, demonstrating that private memory and collective history may be lost, damaged, or preserved, but both are surely worthy of attempts at reclamation. As the speaker of Eliot's *The Waste Land* concludes, the arc of history may be a downward spiral into chaos and sterility, but the broken bits of the past can be brought together to create some semblance of narrative that still retains meaning and purpose: 'These fragments I have shored against my ruin.' The fragmented memories contained in *The Dew Breaker* shore against the ruin of memory's loss and history's sweep. The search for private and collective history, even if it is scattered, in fragments, or transcribed in the most unusual places, such as the brutally scarred feet of the seamstress tortured by the Dew Breaker, must be gathered together to shore against the ruins.

The preacher is targeted, pursued, and disappeared because he raised the question, 'What will we do with our beast?' But what exactly is the beast? The emaciated corpus of Jesus Christ hangs above the door of the preacher's Baptist Church of the Angels in stark contrast to the corpulent body of the Dew Breaker who has become the most visible symbol of the rapacious beast which is the Duvalier regime and the grim history that has led to it. The images of angels and the beast haunt the final story. However, as is to be expected, Danticat resists the easy dichotomy of good and evil, God and the devil, and heaven and hell. The Dew Breaker emerges from the prison carrying a vicious slash on his face that may be read either as the mark of the beast or as the wound of his salvation. He was the Dew Breaker; he is to become Ka's father, a man who equates himself to the broken Ancient Egyptian statues in the Brooklyn Museum that are missing parts of their bodies, parts of their being. When Ka looks upon the statues as a child, she sees only what is missing and not what remains. Like Isis seeking to reconstruct the dismembered Osiris, both Ka and the narrative impulse of the novel seek to re-constitute the fragmented body of a story that is both individual and collective. I suggest that the beast is not, even in the eyes of the preacher, merely the abusers of power but the spectacle that remains and that distorts our perception when we see only what is missing or only what is visible. For the picture to be complete, both need to be brought together and into conversation with one another. History and memory are surrendered up in fragments; the telling of stories in varied genres and artefacts is the necessary path of preserving, testifying, and reclaiming.

10. LIBERATING BORDERS: EDWIDGE DANTICAT'S POETICS OF HAITI'S 'VULNERABILITY' IN *THE FARMING OF BONES*

Marika Preziuso (Virginia Foundation for the Humanities)

'At every border there are rigid wires and fallen wires'. - Nestor Garcia Canclini[191]

This article defines the border, as seen in Haitian-American author Edwidge Danticat's *The Farming of Bones*, as a spatial trope, generative at a number of levels. In the novel, the border refers to a geographical space and also a projected one, both of which echo the issues of identity and representation that are relevant not only to Haitians and Haitian-Americans but to the Caribbean region as a whole. This concept of the border suggests a way of looking at the world that is intrinsic to the complex texture of contemporary Caribbean spatiality.

The article argues that Danticat's novel uses the border as a trope, along with its dynamics of border-crossing, in order to challenge the concepts of and the assumptions made around the post-colonial Caribbean nation. My article, then, sets out from the following question: What dynamics of recognition and rejection are at work between two officially independent Caribbean nation-states that are contained within a single geographical entity, but are kept apart specifically through vehement nationalistic discourses?

Haiti and the Dominican Republic constitute the two halves of the island once called La Hispaniola. From the Dominican side, the border was, from the beginning of the twentieth century, sanctioned by the aggressive national rhetoric of Rafaél Léonida Trujillo, who was responsible for one of the longest (1930-61) and most repressive dictatorships of the Caribbean and Latin America.

Haiti, on the other hand, despite being the epitome of both national – and transnational – freedom as the first black republic in history, founded in 1804, has recently been left by many of its people in search of work, security and freedom elsewhere. I will argue here that the tensions that exist within both Haiti and the Dominican Republic have been affected by their individual relationship with the inter-island border in terms of how each of these two states perceived, imagined and used it discursively and politically. The specificity of this border lies in the fact that while it has been defined by the two nations it has also defined them. As an historical and symbolic marker, the border exemplifies the ambivalences of Caribbean post-coloniality. In line with Shalini Puri's argument against the 'non-threatening hybridities' that are canonized by post-colonial nationalisms,[192] the Caribbean nation often revolves around the bonding narratives of 'one people out of many' and of 'unity in difference'.

Edwidge Danticat narrativizes precisely these tensions between the 'national' and the 'post-colonial', and between individual freedom and national unity, by presenting the border between Haiti and the Dominican Republic as a specific trope, a 'chronotope'. As a literary trope first defined by Mikhail Bakhtin, a chronotope is the product of the collision of temporal and spatial dynamics, neither linear nor definite. Bakhtin observes:

> In the literary artistic chronotope, spatial and temporal indicators are fused into one carefully thought out, concrete whole. Time, as it were, thickens, takes on flesh, becomes artistically visible; likewise, space becomes charged and responsive to the movements of time, plot and history.[193]

In this respect, the chronotope of the border in *The Farming of Bones*[194] sets up 'questions of context, temporality, historicity and space'.[195] It will not only reveal the ideological borders that existed – and still exist – in the representation of Haiti, but it will also challenge those borders that impede a constructive attitude to difference, both within and outside the Caribbean region. Most importantly, it will link the discursive use of the border with the lived reality of it in contemporary Haiti, thus bridging, in literature, the abstractness of symbols and the materiality of space – in the chronotope. At the same time, through my journey across the discursive language of border and its lived reality, I aim to prove how literature is in a privileged position to mediate the words of abstraction (discourse) and of what we conventionally call 'reality'. This is done by Danticat showing to her readers that certain symbols of colonial origins are not static but change across time and can be resignified differently, and equally that material places can be foundational to people's identity, relating especially to those people whose vulnerability resonates with their mobile and restless existence.

Edwidge Danticat was born in Port-au-Prince in 1969, at the height of the Duvalier dictatorship,[196] and at the age of twelve she fled to the United States to join her family there. Her novels are often concerned with the forms of 'spectacular' marginalisation that add to the racist practices exerted on Haitians living overseas – especially in the United States, where, as Anthea Morrison explains, Haitians are the epitome of 'the black Caribbean migrants from a country known of late more for its political turmoil than for its glorious past'.[197] Danticat has based some of her reflections on her own experience as an immigrant child in Brooklyn, where racism and marginalisation were 'like lashes from a whip, a constant reminder of who we were, and how the children at school thought of us'.[198]

Considering her public declarations of her affective attachment to Haiti and her admiration for its people's spiritual strength in the face of adversity, I was surprised when, during a 2004 interview with *The Guardian*, the author affirmed, 'My people are vulnerable: not able to live behind high walls.'[199] I was intrigued by her use of the word 'vulnerable', which sounded as if it contradicted the ideas of resilience that the image of Haiti conjures up in our minds, especially as a counterpoint to its political unrest since its independence. In *The Farming of Bones*, I argue that Danticat underlines her association of Haiti with vulnerability by making the latter the counterpoint to the discourses that conceptualize Haitian people through the problematic category of authenticity.

Historically, the Haitians' inability to 'live behind high walls' was in fact due to their sense of justice and freedom that led them to react to foreign powers, whether France or, later, the United States. It was Saint Domingue's watershed act of defiance in 1791, the start of the slaves' revolution, which led to the overthrowing of the French colonial regime and transformed the 'jewel of the French Crown' into the independent *Ayiti*[200] in 1804.

Prior to that action, which became known as the Haitian Revolution, the ideals of universal freedom, equality and democracy proclaimed by the French Revolution had conveniently been banned from France's colonies; colonial capitalism had thrived on the racial stigmatisation of slaves, on the grounds of their 'biological inferiority'. This justified the lack of the most basic rights for the slaves, in turn allowing the colonial economy to flourish and underpin the capitalist system of the West. But the acquiescence of France – and indeed of Europe in general – to the injustices of slavery was brought to halt by the Haitian Revolution. The shift of political power not only diverted the focus of international interest from Europe to the colonies in the Caribbean, but also, as Susan Buck-Morss argues:

> [It] gave proof that the French Revolution was not simply a European phenomenon but world-historical in its implications [...]. The Haitian Revolution was the crucible, the trial by fire, for the ideals of the French Enlightenment.[201]

The fact that the ideals underpinning the French Revolution were intrinsic in the creation of the Haitian nation is a truth that if not denied could have contributed to the recognition of the world-historical implications of the Haitian enterprise and its interdependency with French – and European – history.

Jean Jacques Dessalines, the first ruler of independent Haiti, did indeed realize Haiti's project to create a modern and free nation and to end slavery throughout the Caribbean, and he did this partly by the re-naming of its people.[202]

In his 1805 Republican Haitian Constitution he declared, 'Haitians will all be addressed as black', by means of which he was attempting to 'legislate away the categories of mulatto and various gradients of interraciality'.[203] Haitian citizenship, along with the designation of blackness, was bestowed on anyone, irrespective of their race, nationality and ethnicity, who had contributed to the country's independence; this was part of the project of the Haitian Revolution, intended to reach the heart and mind of every slave in the Americas and empower them to claim their freedom.

However, the colonial powers launched an attack against Haiti's political project, which was in line with their definition of it as 'the blackest island in the Caribbean'. Haiti's 'revolutionary modernity',[204] as Michael Dash aptly calls it, unsettled the French and the other colonial powers, who were convinced that Haiti's republican model would infiltrate the colonial *status quo* in the Caribbean and disrupt it. Consequently, they strategically downplayed the transnational dynamic of Haiti's revolutionary project by linking the image of the maroon/revolutionary slave to an almost-mythical – and essentially backward – 'blackness'. Hence, the reference to Haiti's blackness became synonymous with the country's deprecated closeness to Africa, and 'authenticity' became in turn the ontological badge that turned the Haitians' revolutionary spirit into an ethnic mark of shame.

The contradictory outcome of Haiti's independence – the discursive bridge that was created between the nobility of its project and the way in which it came to be represented and was then made to crash financially[205] – has also justified the chasm that other Caribbean islands have created between themselves and Haiti, a chasm intensified by the French departmentalisation of Martinique and Guadeloupe in 1946. With reference to Haiti's isolation, for instance, Édouard Glissant has commented, 'The favourite argument that those in charge of the system in the French Caribbean used in order to pity Haiti, was: 'See where independence leads to!''[206] Even when positive emphasis was laid on Haitians' strength as a distinctive mark of their collective personality as a people, for instance in the comment below by George Lamming, this contributed to the reinforcement of the trope of its authenticity:

> It is a curious irony that the poorest of all Caribbean territories is also the richest and most secure in its collective sense of identity. There is no Caribbean territory where this is stronger or more *authentic*.[207]

Such an image resonates in the representation of Haiti in contemporary media through what Haitian journalist Joel Dreyfuss calls 'the cage of words'. Dreyfuss specifically focuses on the caption 'the poorest nation in the Western hemisphere' that is used almost any time Haiti is mentioned in the international media.[208] This caption is easily identified yet rarely investigated, and ultimately makes Haiti the site of an 'irreversible' destiny, turning it into a receptacle for all the fears of invasion and contamination by 'others' that haunt the West. Dreyfuss sees a specific reason for the existence of the caption and its working like a 'border': 'keeping the veil over the island [is] easier than trying to understand factions and divisions and mistrust and history', which are, then, according to the paradigm of authenticity, left unexamined, as a 'spectacle'.

In *The Farming of Bones*, Danticat challenges both the internalisation and the celebration of the borders that takes place every time paradigms of authenticity are reinforced in social, cultural or political discourses. Her novel reveals the ambivalences and limits – indeed, the borders – of the narratives of identity and origins, by testing them against the experience of 'vulnerability' of the Haitians living within the Dominican border region.

I argue that what makes Danticat's border a chronotope is that it is a space of freedom, with an explosive potential, which resonates and touches on the reality of contemporary Haiti. It literally puts on the map the tensions and dialogues that Glissant articulates as necessary in the Caribbean: these are what he sums up as 'relation'.[209] Glissant has argued that the foundation of any relation is that each protagonist 'must face the density of the other. The more the other resists in his thickness or fluidity, […] the more fruitful the interrelating'.[210]

In this respect, Danticat's text challenges the Dominican discourse of *Indigenismo* that claimed to dissolve the borders between classes, races and ethnicities within the Dominican national space. Trujillo sanctioned the term *Indio* – referring to the Tainos, the native Indians of the region – to delineate its people's mixed-race identity. His plan was primarily to offer Dominicans a lineage that was effective in detaching them from the physical and symbolic 'blackness' of their neighbouring nation, Haiti. Given that the Spanish *conquistadores* had exterminated most Tainos on the island as a whole, it was doubly ironic that the discourse of Indigenismo forged a mythical Indian origin to become the perceived authentic foundation of the Dominican identity and, furthermore, had it peacefully coexisting with the Spanish ancestry of its people. The Dominicans were reassured on the one hand of their rightful claim to the space of the island by the narrative of their 'native' Taino lineage, while on the other, by virtue of their Spanish blood, they were enabled to perceive themselves as more civilized than the Haitians.

Since the border had historically been the site where most power relations between the two countries had been negotiated – a 'porous frontier', according to sociologist Lauren Derby – Trujillo in his endorsement of the 'Dominican nation' transformed its material and discursive significance into 'the skin of Dominican body politic'.[211] Through his discourse, Trujillo made Haitians appear as an infectious virus that needed to be at least contained, and possibly destroyed, to ensure the survival of the Dominican people.

Since Haitians crossed the border – mostly to work as *braceros* on the Dominican plantations – and thus 'invaded' the Dominican nation, the latter came to be defined by the constant policing of its neighbour, to avoid contamination by it. Consequently, Dominican-ness was materially and discursively contained by Trujillo's politics just as much as he intended to contain the invasive Haitian presence on his side of the border. In other words, the discourse of *Indigenismo* worked as a spectacle not only of Haitian but also of Dominican identity. Trujillo's celebration of his people's unique racial origin lacked any consideration of the history of his country, which is visible in the highly varied Dominican cultures, races and ethnicities. Trujillo's obsession with Haiti's 'blackness' was therefore a smokescreen concealing his concerns about the reality of his people obviously being not only racially and ethnically mixed, but also presenting internal class differences aggravated by the disastrous economy for which Trujillo himself was in the main responsible. He specifically channelled the concerns and unrest of the poorer Dominicans, most of whom constituted the majority of the country's darkest population, towards two places: first, the imagined *Quisquey*a, the Taino name for the Dominican Republic that represented the ideal of the nation embodied by Trujillo himself; and second the border with Haiti, beyond which lay what he presented as the ultimate threat to national security.[212]

Amabelle, Danticat's protagonist in *The Farming of Bones*, and her lover Sebastien, are two *Haitianos* living in the Dominican border region. Sebastien is a cane cutter, and Amabelle is housekeeper to the wealthy Dominican Señora Valencia, who is married to Pico, a colonel who is devoted to Trujillo – and indeed we see Pico promoted to general after his service during the 1937 massacre of around 20,000 Haitians at the border. Amabelle's adoption by Valencia's family after the death of her parents, who had drowned in the border river when she was only six, has granted her a privileged condition, particularly in comparison to the work in the fields that most border-Haitians, including Sebastien, are forced to do.

However, Amabelle's apparent privilege is denied her by the Massacre. One of the most telling moments, in which we perceive the vulnerability of her position, is when, after Sebastien has disappeared on the first night of the Massacre, and we see her desperate for memories, recollections and reconciliation: 'A border is a *veil* not many people can wear' (FB 364). Veils and borders can be attached to and signified by discourses of ethnic and cultural belonging, yet they can be also naturalized into part of one's identity, in ways that allow its crossing and make it more than solely a marker of religious or ethnic identity. A veil may be simultaneously perceived as a visual proof of cultural or religious beliefs, and appreciated simply as a beautiful ornament. Its 'opacity' of interpretation allows it to be 'crossed' and transgressed.

In his seminal book *The Wretched of the Earth* (1961) Franz Fanon explained the symbolic significance of the veil in the colonial context. The time-space coordinates in which Fanon locates his analysis are provided by the Algerian war of independence, in which he participated by joining the FLN (*Front de Libération Nationale*) while he was working as a psychiatrist at Blida-Joinville Psychiatric Hospital.

Algerian women are shrouded in a veil that engages ambivalently with the colonial gaze. The veil makes the women invisible as individuals and visible only as the embodiment of a traditional culture that colonial France both condemns as 'other' and yet of which it believes itself to possess full knowledge. To Fanon, however, the veiled woman challenges these colonial assumptions that in his book are embodied by the French officer who 'sees' her. Since the colonial gaze does not register the presence of the veil as a threat but perceives it merely as an authentic signifier of female submission in Islamic culture, the veil becomes a useful place under which to hide weapons and documents to be smuggled by the National Front organising the resistance.

Importantly for my discussion, the discursive 'vulnerability' of the veil suggested by Fanon's reading of it indicates that the strategic use of the veil by Algerian women disrupts the acquiescence of the French to its supposed 'authenticity', detaching it from its association to female submission. The veil blurs the distinction between the 'native' (i.e. Algerian) culture and the strategic practices of anti-colonialism that play on the coloniser's cultural barriers preventing him from perceiving the other accurately.

To wear one's own border as a veil is, I argue, also in line with the project that the Republic of Haiti had set out since its birth: to resignify its 'otherness', from a marker of inferiority into what Michael Dash calls the New World's first composite culture.[213]

The vulnerability inherent in the history of the Haitian Revolution is echoed in the contemporary reality of Haitians' border-crossing as explored by Danticat in *The Farming of Bones*. Both events remind us that the machine of colonialism with its paradigms of domination and exploitation often permits the possibility of circumventing authority. The plantation was a system geared toward the containment of any subversion against colonial authority, but it was also a space where spectacular contradictions and slippages of control took place; due to the constant intermixing of peoples, the Hegelian division between slave and master was necessarily diffused into multiple subject positions that were neither clearly defined nor vertically hierarchical. It was a multifaceted palimpsest that possessed a material and discursive power both to engulf differences and to generate them.

The Farming of Bones, in its questioning of a single form of absolute authority, digs deep into the plantation as another trope of vulnerability. Despite Amabelle's gratitude and loyalty to her mistress, Señora Valencia, the two women have always been 'dangling between being strangers and being friends' (FB 300). As Amabelle lucidly observes: 'Nearly everything I had was something Señora Valencia had once owned and no longer wanted. Everything except Sebastien' (FB 45). Amabelle's vulnerability is signified by her increasing awareness of the unbridgeable difference between her world, which includes Sebastien, and that of Valencia, which is filled with the presence of Pico and the national rhetoric of Trujillo. Her shifting is also mapped in the novel visually, as she constantly walks in and out between the security of the walls of Valencia's house, where she is valued as a loyal domestic, and Sebastien's precarious world of the cane fields, peopled with *vwayajés*. It is in the latter that she is confronted with the first 'real' border: she is asked to prove her loyalty to only one of these worlds: 'Who are these people for you?' [...] Sebastien asks her. 'Do you think they are your family?' (FB 110) Amabelle's somewhat ambiguous reply ('The señora and her family are the closest to kin I have.') is indicative of the friction between her conflicting personal desires that creates the fragility in her sense of belonging: 'And me?' he asked. 'You too', I said, wanting to announce that he came first.

'We'll see', he said' (FB 110). Sebastien's rejoinder turns out to be an omen of their eventual separation: in order to attend to her mistress, ill after giving birth, Amabelle misses her appointment with Sebastien in the church – and he is then captured by troops during their first anti-Haitian raid, and taken away.

Nevertheless, Danticat seems to suggest that despite Sebastien's refusal to cross the 'border' the relationship between Amabelle and Valencia points in a different direction. Overriding but not dismissive of the borders of race, class and history, the uneasy bond between the two women provides an illustration of the existence of forms of interdependency between Haitians and Dominicans that not only have resonance in their own lives but also symbolically represent the border as a trope, a physical space and a figurative site of change and 'relation' *à la* Glissant. The two women are the representatives of two classes and races that are kept apart less by the economy of the plantation than by the policy of ethnic containment exerted by the Dominican male-centred nationalist discourse. Danticat's insights into their relationship thus allow it to disrupt the Dominicans' assumption of the inferiority of the Haitians, but without neglecting the many differences that characterize the two people. In this way, Danticat still acknowledges the borders of history, geography and race that are all informing Valencia and Amabelle's place in the plantation society. However, the writer also makes it possible for them to cross this border thanks to the fact that they become more and more conscious of their interdependency. Such awareness is also what differentiates their relationship from the hatred and violence that characterize the relationship between the Dominican men and the Haitian cane cutters.

One instance of crossing of the border in the novel is found in the use of language, through which Danticat contradicts the discourse of Dominican *indigenismo*. For example, Valencia's reaction to her babies being born with different racial features reveals the Dominicans' constant racial preoccupation that lies beneath Trujillo's official denial of race as a concern of the nation. Although Valencia renames her children 'my Spanish prince and my Indian princess' (FB 29), reproducing the discourse of Dominican *indigenismo*, Danticat uses the scene of the twins' birth to reveal the contradictions beneath Trujillo's colour-blind discourse. As Shemak reminds us, 'in Haitian vodou twins are considered powerful and dangerous [...] associated with transitional spaces such as thresholds'.[214]

Another episode in the novel in which the language belies the idiosyncratic nature of racial definitions which runs deep underneath the veneer of 'Dominican nation' is when baby Rosalinda's apparently European birthright is questioned by doctor Javier: '[she] has a little charcoal behind her ears'. Interestingly, Danticat uses the title of a famous *decima*[215] by the Dominican poet Juan Antonio Alix (1833-1918), entitled 'El Negro tras de la Oreja' ('The Black behind the Ear'). The poem mocks the concerns of the light-skinned Dominican élite about the increasing presence of the darker population in the country, which has brought them to assert their whiteness. This attitude is ridiculed in the poem, where Alix repeats that such concerns have no place on Dominican soil, where 'a little charcoal is indeed in fashion'.[216]

The 'little charcoal' in Danticat's novel and in Alix's poem serves the same purpose, denouncing the contradictory attitude of the Dominicans toward the issue of race.[217] Yet whereas Alix does so by way of mocking it, Danticat makes the Dominican racial denial erupt in the most intimate and yet vulnerable location: the family household. Danticat unveils these contradictions by proving that once the 'little charcoal' invades the borders of the Dominican white upper-class household it is no longer tolerated as a fashionable trait of exotic difference, but is openly branded as a threat. In fact, Doctor Javier's comment on Rosalinda's 'charcoal' is taken as an unacceptable offence by Valencia's father, who is quick to remind him that his family's bloodline 'traces itself back to the *conquistador* – Christopher Columbus' (FB 18).

The 'little charcoal' loses its exotic allure once it materializes into a 'real' racial marker, and one that can channel what Trujillo fears most: interactions between Haitians and Dominicans. It is precisely at the border that the 'little charcoal' is viewed as at its most threatening to the Dominican national identity, since the border region is a space where official racial divides and paper certificates of 'Dominicanness' no longer grant a definitive identity. The 'little charcoal' echoes in Danticat's idea of the border as a veil, in that it makes explicit the racialization of the border on the Haitian side to the racial denial displayed on the Dominican side.

By revealing to what extent the lived dynamics of people and space can challenge the Dominican discourse of *indigenismo*, Danticat's 'little charcoal' finally shows the discourses of racial stigmatization and denial as interdependent.

In this respect, the first night of the Massacre brings home to Amabelle an awareness of the true effect of the Dominican politics of containment of Haitians. This episode represents the watershed when the Dominicans' seeming tolerance of Haitian cane cutters gives way to their explosion of racist violence. Although at this stage Amabelle has not been physically touched by that violence, the first night of the Massacre enters her life like a thunderbolt, from rhetoric to bodily violence, annihilating her previous efforts to straddle the geographical and emotional border between the cane fields and her mistress's house. Initially, the young Amabelle had not questioned her status in Valencia's family, making her blind to the danger that was developing at the border. Retrospectively, however, she admits that part of her inability to recognize the danger came from her sense of security inside the walls of Valencia's house. She was convinced of Sebastien's and her own safe status in the plantation, on the grounds that they provided labour and were therefore needed by Dominicans:

> I was never naïve, or blind. I knew. I knew that the death of many was coming. I knew that the streams and rivers would run with blood [...]. But it must be known that I understood, I saw things too. I just thought they would not see me. I just thought they would not find me [...]. The Dominicans needed the sugar from the cane for their cafecitos and dulce de leche. (FB 140)

The pivotal moment, which contains the indication of her change of perspective, is when Amabelle, anxious to meet Sebastien at the border but committed to her duty to Valencia, dumps her dilemma onto Valencia, testing her loyalty:

> Help me Señora, I wanted to say, but what could she do? How much did she know? Would she be brave enough to stand between me and her husband if she had to? (FB 140)

Valencia will indeed eventually 'stand between' Amabelle and Pico, but only in a way that will not threaten her role as a dutiful Dominican wife and mother. Valencia's situation prevents her from crossing the political and ideological borders set by Trujillo (and shared by many Dominicans) to meet Haitians; any contact that she initiates with them – such as her closeness to Amabelle as well as her genuinely well-meaning encounter with the cane cutters – is doomed to failure in a wider context, as it does not challenge the *status quo* in substantial ways.

In contrast to the compliance of Valencia with the Dominican conceptions of 'national' womanhood, the language of Amabelle and Sebastien's romance transgresses the gendered conventions and expectations of the colonial space; it materially and symbolically locates itself precariously across different places so that their desire can claim its own legitimacy. By focusing on the vulnerability of Amabelle and Sebastien's love, Danticat cuts clean across the vertical power structure that the plantation at least formally reproduces, thus making their romance in itself a potentially anti-colonial strategy.

Since their romance is marked by the hardships of their life in the plantation, where it cannot exist freely, Amabelle and Sebastien's passion is permeated with unsaid words and unexpressed tenderness. Nevertheless, the secret level of communication they adopt – involving 'the simple flutter of a smile' to communicate 'all those things we could not say because there was the cane to curse, the harvest to dread, the future to fear' (FB 131) – already locates the couple outside the conventional, gender-constrictive code of expectations that most couples of the Dominican élite – the backbone of the impeccable moral standards of the nation – must comply with. As Amabelle admits, passion is, to her, less like 'the gift of a ring in a church ceremony' and more like the desire itself, as expressed in 'a smile I couldn't help, tugging at the sides of my face'. Danticat relishes exploring her protagonists' 'bashful, undeserving, almost ashamed' attitude towards each other as unconventional expressions of desire (FB 130).

I argue that what makes Amabelle and Sebastien's romance transgressive in the structure of the plantation is precisely their 'vulnerability'. This is, however, portrayed as strength, in that it makes them malleable but also opaque, as they build their happiness in the interstices of the system whose contradictions they also expose.

Ironically, both Sebastien and Amabelle have survived thus far thanks to the plantation system they loathe, as this has granted them sustenance and a home of sorts after they have suffered terrible familial losses.[218] Their ability to carve out their own niche by accommodating themselves across the fissures in the control system of the plantation accounts for their transgressive identity. They exceed, then, any identification with the figure of the maroon slave, synonymous with the 'authenticity' of Haitian identity. Since Danticat shows the couple as constantly negotiating with the limitations that are inherent in their life at the border, yet also unable finally to either defend themselves or resist the hurricanes of history, Amabelle and Sebastien come across as failing the standards of the Haitian heroism so familiar to the discourse of authenticity that has been the double-edged sword in the representation of Haiti.

Instead, the lovers are the representatives of what Tobias Döring has called 'the poetics of passages, of cross-cultural connectedness and spatial relocation',[219] a poetics that is in my view closer to the actual configuration of the contemporary Caribbean. They embody Danticat's antidote to the Haitian myth of authenticity that ignores individuals like them, whose vulnerability is expressed also in cultural and linguistic terms, as they are always caught 'on the narrow ridge between two nearly native tongues' (FB 69).

Water becomes the spatial equivalent of the affective bond between them that is realized despite the harshness of the plantation. A waterfall is the place where Amabelle and Sebastien first make love; rather as the geographical border of the Massacre River is used by Trujillo to release the tensions between races, classes and nationalities yet connect the two countries, so the waterfall is an ambivalent trope that symbolizes both dangerous aggression and optimistic regeneration. To the couple, it is an idyllic place of safety that protects them from the rest of the world and that can keep time at a standstill (the secret cave at the bottom of the waterfall 'holds on to some memory of the sun so that you do not realize when night comes', FB 100) – but it is at the same time a dangerous place, subject to the unpredictable violence of nature and, as we will see, to the inevitable passage of time. And against both nature and time, humans are powerless.

When, upon her return to Alegría twenty years later, Amabelle cannot recognize anything familiar around her, she looks for the waterfall. Once she finds it, she still remains dissatisfied with her discovery:

> The drop was much larger and the pool deeper than the one I remember. Perhaps time had destroyed any sense of proportion and possibilities. Or perhaps this was another fall altogether. (FB 302)

Doubting the reality of her recollections, Amabelle is left with the choice of making Sebastien become the only site of memory and belonging, her absent homeland:

> His absence is my shadow, his breath my dream [...]. I wish at least that he was part of the air on this side of the river, a tiny morsel in the breeze that passes through my room in the night. I wish at least that some of the dust of his bones could trail me in the wind. (FB 281)

Having survived, Amabelle, by identifying her home with where her heart belongs – Sebastien – becomes living proof that one's sense of location can exceed both geography and ethnic identification. Valencia, on the other hand – and perhaps reluctantly – chooses to remain in the family home, to stand at her husband's side.

The complexity of border crossings is shown in the final meeting between Amabelle and Valencia, twenty years after the Massacre. As well as the debris of regret, loss and physical disfiguration with which it has bespattered Amabelle, the Massacre also has bestowed on her the freedom from her belief that life in servitude is the only option available to her. Thus she can revisit her condition of submission and loyalty to Valencia's family in the light of her new free status that has come with her losses. So while Amabelle discovers a freedom that materializes in her dual physical crossing of the border (from Alegría to Haiti, and from Haiti back to Alegría again), Valencia in contrast remains symbolically and physically entangled in the discourse of the Dominican nation that she constantly tries to accommodate within herself, yet within which she finds herself inadequate.

Language is also finally exposed in the novel through Trujillo's use of Spanish against Haitians; Trujillo's henchmen imposed an *ad hoc* language test on the people they caught at the border. Assuming that Haitians could pronounce neither the Spanish rolled 'r' or the *jota*, they would ask anyone with dark skin to identify a sprig of parsley; the Spanish word for this is *perejil*, which includes both consonants.

Like the other tropes in the novel, 'parsley' – the word and the herb – lends itself to ambivalent significations, both figurative and real. Amabelle's condemnation of Trujillo's use of the Spanish *perejil* has little to do with her privileging the Kreyòl word *pèsi* as her claim to Haitian authenticity. Rather, she sees something outrageous in choosing a mundane word denoting an everyday herb as a tool for the perpetuation of sanctioned violence targeting innocent people:

> *Que diga amor?* Love? Hate? Speak to me of things the world has yet to truly understand, of the instant meaning of each bird's call, of a child's secret thoughts in her mother's womb, of the measured rhythmical time of every man and woman's breath [...] of the larger miracles in small things,

the deeper mysteries. But parsley? Was it because it was so used, so commonplace, so abundantly at hand that everyone who desired a sprig could find one? We used parsley for our food, our teas, our baths, to cleanse our insides as well as our outsides. Perhaps the Generalissimo in some larger order was trying to do the same for his country. (FB 203)

If it is precisely its commonality and translatability that makes 'parsley' the perfect linguistic border to be resignified by Trujillo as the linguistic equivalent of his power over the Haitians, Danticat ultimately restores the deep spiritual and symbolic significance to the Kreyòl *pèsi*, through Amabelle's detaching the word from its identification with the physical and spiritual violation of Haitian people's lives. In the beautiful monologue above, while she tries to find a meaning for the use of parsley as a tool of the Massacre, she recovers, re-members, the Haitian context of the term by attaching it to the life-world of the people she knows, whether living in the border region or in Haiti proper. She tries to re-connect the image of parsley to the everyday life of Haitians, who would use it to clean babies, to savour their food, to cleanse 'our insides and outsides […] and a corpse's remains one final time' (FB 62). Rooting parsley back within the local, familiar space of the border region, means liberating it from being identified primarily with the violence and the trauma of the Massacre.

The conclusion of *The Farming of Bones* confirms the border as an explosive threshold. We see Amabelle slowly submerging herself in the Massacre River in search of reconciliation and healing within its waters, but also apparently letting herself drown in its depths, as so many have done before her.

Amabelle's form of farewell seemingly suggests that she has chosen the river as the cathartic and empowering threshold from which she will bid adieu to the world of the living. And yet her departure is neither a fluid nor conciliatory border-crossing: 'Breath, like glass, is always in danger' (FB 283) she reminds us; in danger of the sudden intrusion of history against which one cannot always build 'high walls', but neither to which one can simply surrender. As April Shemak remarks, Amabelle's bathing 'evokes contradictory images: the attempted ethnic cleansing of the Massacre, the image of parsley as a symbol of loss of speech, death, but also renewal'.[220]

Whatever interpretation we might care to give to the final pages of *The Farming of Bones*, I argue that Danticat's message remains optimistic: perhaps one day the Haitians of the border region will have the chance to proudly wear their own selves as a border-veil, as a real and imaginative foundation upon which to build and express their sense of self. The sense of self that Danticat has in mind is opaque enough to avoid the reproducing of Haitian authenticity; at the same time, it is a sense of identity that is also flexible enough to permit them not just to come to terms with, but actually to overcome the opposing narratives that present Haiti as either the model of freedom or the violent setting of the worst nightmares in contemporary times.

In the title of this article, I have called the specific strategies in the novel with what I call Danticat's 'poetics of the border'. Such poetics evokes the tension that still exists between diasporic Haitians and those who have remained in the island, a tension felt at a very personal level by Danticat and reflected in the reception that the authors from the Caribbean diaspora like her often experience back on the island.

The choice of language is also in line with the author's understanding of the act of writing as itself a form of re-translation: 'When I write', Danticat argues, 'I am transferring an image in my head onto the page. Add to this the fact that my native language is not the one I am writing in and you also have another kind of translation. It is always a challenge, but personally I love it.'[221]

Similarly, the novel translates the official history of the Massacre promoted by Trujillo in support of his national project, by diffusing this history through the various memories of the survivors. As Sara Ahmed affirms, usually for migrants 'the community comes to life through the collective act of remembering in the absence of a common terrain'.[222] The fragmented stories that surviving *vwayajés* tell each other in the novel, to try and bridge the distance with their beloved ones murdered in the Massacre on the far side of the border, are an attempt to create an imaginary common terrain, which is, however, frustrated in history due to their experience of historical trauma and physical uprooting.

Indeed, as the novel demonstrates, given the paucity of evidence available to the Haitians that crossed the border and made it safely back to Haiti during the Massacre, testifying to the event is for them a hard task that inevitably involves some degree of reinvention, of re-membering, especially if the aim is to heal them of their trauma:

> At times you could sit for a whole evening with such individuals, just listening to their existence unfold, from the house where they were born to the hill where they wanted to be buried [...]. This was how people left imprints of themselves in each other's memory so that if you left first and went back to the common village, you could carry, if not a letter, a piece of treasured clothing, some message to their loved ones that their place was still among the living. (FB 73)

Lacking adequate information, survivors of the Massacre perforce rely on ephemeral traces, a valid way of translating the stories that are available to them in their vulnerable condition. These stories of lived memories constitute alternatives to the official memory imposed by the Dominican regime (as in Trujillo's speeches celebrating the unspecified 'liberators of the nation'). The national memory sanctioned by the government, which in fact also involved collective denials and forgetting, was based on a mythical past that was to a great extent disembodied in the sense of having no real bearing on Dominicans' actual ethnic constitution or on the lived interactions of Dominicans with Haitians.

Stories – told or written – seem to be the ultimate 'border-veil': a suggestive space where we can perceive the transforming power of language, its potential to translate and retranslate across space and worlds, and by doing so to bridge silences and erasure and making the past more bearable, by revisiting and questioning it. In this respect, by choosing the space that contains the shared history of Hispaniola in her final gesture of reconjunction with the river, Amabelle epitomizes Danticat's belief in the possibility that literature can constitute a valid testimonial. Indeed, it reveals the global potential of an event that is in itself ambivalently 'real'. If it is irremediably engraved in the body and mind of border-Haitians as well as in the local space of the border, the Massacre is also suspended in the limbo between the two countries, since neither the Dominican nor the Haitian government has formally accepted responsibility for it, nor has either of them done anything to acknowledge the individual testimonials of the survivors.

The Farming of Bones, both in its themes and as the product of the author's writing talent and imaginary, marks the explosive potential of the tensions both within the national space and within the discourse that supports it. It not only examines the effects that the contradictions between the nation's rhetoric of freedom and its narratives of unity have on human lives, but more generally, it alerts us to the multiple points of encounter, and the interdependence between the lived and imagined that make up who we are. It was due to the tensions between the myths superimposed by the Dominicans upon the Haitians and the true vulnerability of those Haitians that the violence of the Massacre can be understood in its complexity and taken as a lesson for the present.

11. WHAT'S IN A NAME? READING TRANSFORMATIVE FARCE IN CÉSAIRE'S *LA TRAGÉDIE DU ROI CHRISTOPHE* AND NAJMAN'S 'ROYAL BONBON'

Mariana Past (Dickinson College)

In Haiti, as elsewhere in the Afro-Caribbean, the cultural landscape abounds with a wide range of names. It is common for men to be called 'Charlemagne' or 'Dante', for example. And in literary works such as Michel-Rolph Trouillot's *Ti difè boulè sou istoua Ayiti*, children may have monikers like 'Sèdènyè', 'That's the last one' or 'Asefi', 'Enough girls'. On the street *tap-taps*, or popular buses, sport multi-lingual slogans like 'Sagesse et effort' ('Wisdom and effort'), 'Muchas gracias' ('Thank you very much'), or, simply, 'I Love You Jesus'. (Even Michel Martelly, Haiti's newly-elected president, was widely known for years by his stage name, 'Sweet Micky'). In short, a multiplicity of registers, languages, and identities constitute daily realities in a place which inspired Alejo Carpentier's concept of the 'real maravilloso', or 'marvellous real' in the mid-twentieth century, shaping new perceptions of Latin America as fundamentally distinct from Europe.

For readers of Aimé Césaire's dramatic text *La tragédie du roi Christophe* (1963),[223] the court scene wherein a host of seemingly farcical titles of nobility (such as 'Duke of Marmelade') are conferred upon a group of ex-slaves will likely stand out. That famous episode is closely replicated, with some interesting twists, in Charles Najman's film 'Royal bonbon' (2002), which also depicts the spectacular rise and fall of Haiti's first king. This apparent parody in both literary and visual texts underscores the importance of names, and the process of naming, not only in Haiti, but the Afro-Caribbean overall, in an historical context that many consider 'post-colonial'. Curiously, although scholars have explored a wide range of questions related to Césaire's play in particular –such as the aspects of Greek tragedy it manifests, or the author's approach to nation-building and decolonization – no one has addressed the problem of the onomastics in the court scene, which speaks volumes about the articulation of Haitian history and the fact that it is often misunderstood. Before putting into dialogue the respective cultural productions of the Martinican writer and statesman and the French-Polish cinematographer, I offer two brief examples which help illustrate both the profound power of names in Haiti, and the significance of new names being bestowed on black subjects in the world's first black republic.

On January 1, 1804, after a turbulent 13-year revolution, the republic of Haiti came into existence through an intentionally extreme change of names. Earlier, Columbus had dubbed the island 'La Española', and the French called their eventual colony (and crown jewel) 'Saint-Domingue'. In an article called 'The Naming of Haiti' the prominent historian David Geggus observes that the transformation of the western part of the island into 'Haïti', which is the indigenous Taíno term for 'rugged' or 'mountainous', is the sole example of 'a Caribbean colony undergoing a radical change of name on achieving independence'.[224] Geggus explores why Jean-Jacques Dessalines and other revolutionary leaders gave the new nation an Amerindian name immediately following their declaration of independence, though 'its population was overwhelmingly African and Afro-American, and it had been ruled by Europeans for three centuries'.[225] Taking a name that evoked the island's aboriginal population,[226] which was rapidly and almost completely wiped out, but not without violently resisting European imperialism, was a way to transcend the problematical colonial period and make a symbolic break with Europe. Amerindian symbolism thus served to unify a heterogeneous population, whose mixed-race leaders rejected both African culture and European control. Geggus concludes that Haiti's new name provided 'a legitimizing link with the pre-Columbian American past, of which all Haitians could approve and which resonated with people of all social levels'.[227] I contend later in this analysis that the figure of King Christophe as represented by Césaire and Najman also taps into the mythical pre-Columbian past to help shape the Haitian people's imaginary; what is surprising is that no one has noticed.

Conversely, and much more recently, Haitians found themselves unified by the inability to find an appropriate name for a collectively catastrophic experience: the January 2010 earthquake. In the aftermath of the devastating event, the renowned Haitian-American writer and storyteller Edwidge Danticat pointed out that 'natural disasters in Haiti usually have nicknames, [but] no native name exists for earthquakes, and that lack of a linguistic reference in this case was not only unsettling for people, but 'reinforces the uncertainty of everyday life, and how every waking moment should not be taken for granted.'' Danticat assured her audience that 'a measure of comfort [could] be found in the reality that every Haitian, either at home or abroad, had felt some impact from the tragedy, which was popularly referred to as 'bagay,' or 'thing,' for lack of a better word, because its impact and scope were monstrously unimaginable [...]'.[228] For Haitians, the incapacity to name, or find meaning through assigning a name, here seems to signify as much as the process of naming itself. With this in mind I will consider the intricate court scene in the main texts at hand, but not before further contextualizing both works.

Césaire's *La tragédie du roi Christophe* is arguably the most canonical work of fiction to address the Haitian Revolution in the twentieth century; it is certainly the best-known of his trilogy of anti-colonialist plays.[229] The *Tragédie* participates in a new wave of Francophone Caribbean political theatre, where activists aim 'to use drama as a tool to raise awareness and campaign for independence' from France, as Bridget Jones observes.[230] At the same time, many critics propose, Césaire's notorious Christophe serves as a warning for revolutionary leaders in the era of African Independences; this notion has been somewhat controversial. A. James Arnold calls for grounding Césaire in a more local, Antillean, context, for example, and Maximilien Laroche, a prominent Haitian critic, disputes the notion of tragedy associated with Césaire's protagonist. He maintains that the Haitian worldview does not include such a concept, because death is popularly understood as a transitional phase before the deceased rejoin their ancestors in the spirit world 'anba dlo', or under the water; the excesses of Christophe's reign represent not a tragedy, therefore, but a link in a chain of events involving unfinished revolutionary business.

Nearly four decades later, Charles Najman produces 'Royal bonbon', his very first film, which won the Prix Jean Vigo. With 2004, the bicentenary of the Haitian Revolution, looming large on the horizon as a floating signifier that competing groups seek to pin down, Najman seizes the opportunity to interrogate Christophe's notorious *devise*: 'Je renais de mes cendres'.[231] Through a literal example of postcolonial 'folie', Najman's film appears to question the usefulness of (reflexively) reviving Haitian history again and again. Specifically, 'Royal bonbon' sharply critiques the impulse towards hero-worship, nostalgia for a glorious, distant past, and the tendency to idealize or expect too much of one's leaders, which together embody a particular kind of 'folie', and are unproductive.[232] The aspects of 'madness' involved in Najman's representation of Christophe's chapter in Haitian history will be subsequently discussed in more detail.

Both Césaire's and Najman's texts successfully invade and redefine what Hertzberger calls 'the safe zone of myth',[233] simultaneously challenging historical legends and re-articulating, or reinforcing them. This study proposes that the nuanced treatment of geographical names in Césaire's play simultaneously highlights and obscures the history of the Haitian Revolution, altering the image of the world's first black republic for twentieth-century readers in an awkward, if perhaps inadvertent, way. Najman's film contains an abbreviated, distorted echo of Césaire's parodic scene, as 'Royal bonbon' revives not just the figure of Christophe, but a legendary local impersonator of the king, known as 'wa kaka'. I do not wish to suggest that either the literary or cinematographic re-enactment of Christophe's courtly endeavours represents an endless rehashing of historical occurrences, however, and the conclusion of both works (particularly Najman's) remains open to multiple interpretations. To borrow from Walter Benjamin, these texts bring to light moments in a 'revolutionary process' instead of being mere thematic repetition; this is largely due to their insistence on the act of naming.

La tragédie du roi Christophe has a traditional structure, consisting of three acts that are separated by interludes and introduced by a Prologue.[234] The Prologue features a cock fight – a play within a play – whose contestants are named (Alexandre) Pétion and (Henri) Christophe, the two leaders struggling for control of the new Haitian state. 'La foule', or the crowd, is obviously the embodiment of the Haitian people. The victory of Christophe brings his rule a certain legitimacy, both at home and abroad; implied in the scene is that the Western world is intently watching the cocks fight, and the winner has everything to prove. Unquestionably, Césaire's *Tragédie* is full of irony and incongruity. Written almost entirely in French, the dramatic text emphasizes the Kreyòl language and *vodou* religion as authentic pillars of Haitian culture in a not-quite-binary opposition to King Christophe's mimicry of European courtly customs. In Act I, for instance, a chorus dedicates a hymn to Shango (AC 40), the Yoruba god of thunder and lightning;[235] also, during an interlude, one of the labourers lifts up a conch shell and blows (AC 67), which is a direct reference to the mythical vodou ceremony of Bois-Caïman in 1791 that signalled the beginning of the Haitian Revolution and the overthrow of French rule. The play shows how Christophe effectively re-enslaves his people by forcing them to construct the massive *Citadelle*, a European-style fortress towering over the tropical forest, designed to protect Haiti from future French incursions. In a near-final scene the king hears a distinct African drumbeat in the distance and cries, 'Les salauds! Ils battent le mandoucouman!' (AC 139)[236] He realizes that his fate has been sealed: 'Cela signifie qu'il est temps pour le vieux roi d'aller dormir' (AC 140).[237] Soon thereafter Mme. Christophe, the more perceptive queen, begins singing to the god Damballah in Kreyòl, declaring 'Moin cé moun l'Afric' ('I am African') (AC 141-43); in a final piece of irony, the jester Hugonin transforms himself into Baron Samedi, the *lwa* or god of the dead (AC 149). Vodou traditions prevail over Christophe's obsession with Catholicism, and Kreyòl (provisionally, at least) attains a more elevated status on the lips of the queen. Thus for Césaire, the tragedy of Christophe is that he denied his African roots and religion, maintained European models of domination, and was ultimately unable to blend past and present. But his intentions were good, as Césaire also allows: through purposeful replication of French examples, onomastic and otherwise, the self-appointed king seeks to transform Haiti's ex-slaves into a civilized body. I make the case that in the *Tragédie* Christophe's vision for the new republic – as evidenced through the titles distributed in the court scene – is anchored in nothing less than the heroic Amerindian narrative that gave Haiti its name. And this complex set of realities humanizes the infamous king to a greater degree than most have imagined.

My reading of the court scene, which is a microcosm of cultural and political tensions, takes into account the underlying significance of names in post-colonial Haiti. Obvious at this point is that Christophe and his advisors are acutely concerned with the opinion of France and the rest of the Western world regarding the (newly-named) Republic of Haiti, with nothing less at stake than the dignity of the black race and the stability of the new nation. Accordingly, a European *maître de cérémonies* sent by the TESCO (Technical, Educational, Scientific Cooperation Organization), which provides technical assistance for developing nations (AC 30), is organizing a royal spectacle. As the ceremonial rehearsal is clownishly and awkwardly carried out, one participant expresses fear that the French will mock everyone's new titles:

DEUXIEME COURTISAN: Avec nos titres ronflants, duc de la Limonade, duc de la Marmelade, comte de Trou Bonbon, nous avons bonne mine! [...]. Les Français s'en tiennent les côtes![238]

But Christophe's sycophantic secretary Vastey assures everyone:

VASTEY, ironique: [...]. Le rire des Français ne me gêne pas! Marmelade, pourquoi pas? Pourquoi pas Limonade? Ce sont des noms à vous remplir la bouche! [...]. Après tout les Français ont bien le duc de Foix et le duc de Bouillon! [...]. Il y a des précédents, vous voyez! [...]. Avez-vous remarqué qui l'Europe nous a envoyé quand nous avons sollicité l'aide de l'Assistance technique internationale? Pas un ingénieur. [...]. Pas un professeur. Un maître de cérémonies! La forme, c'est ça, mon cher, la civilisation![239]

The master of ceremonies figure in the *Tragédie* has been regarded by many as 'entirely satirical', as Roxanna Curto notes in a recently-published article.[240] She goes on to argue that, in a post-colonial context, theatre is development, though, and an emphasis on performance represents a necessary type of technological innovation for building a new nation and participating in a global media culture. Surely Césaire was aware of that, as his Martinican motherland struggled with self-definition in the mid-twentieth century. In any case, in the above lines the names 'Marmelade' and 'Limonade' are bandied about in jest by Haitians themselves, and can very easily be glossed over by readers. The scene's climax has yet to come, however. Christophe arrives at last, and the master of ceremonies recites the register of newly-assigned names:

LE MAITRE DE CEREMONIES, apercevant Christophe: Messieurs un peu de silence. Je vais faire l'appel des noms:

Sa Grandeur Monseigneur le duc de la Limonade
Sa Grandeur Monseigneur le duc de Plaisance
Son Altesse Sérénissime le Marquis de l'Avalasse
Sa Grandeur Monseigneur le duc de Dondon
Sa Grandeur Monseigneur le duc de la Marmelade
Monsieur le Comte de Trou Bonbon
Monsieur le Comte de Sale-Trou
Monsieur le Comte de la Bande du Nord
[...] Allez-y Messieurs![241]

For decades, critics have deemed this amusing list to be strictly 'verbal silliness',[242] or, alternatively, 'farcical', 'parodic', 'hilarious', 'ridiculous', or 'fantastic'. But can this apparently ridiculous naming ritual be appropriately understood as mere servile imitation, defying the revolutionary triumph of Haiti that ultimately transformed, or 'tropicalized'[243] Enlightenment ideals? And does Césaire hereby imply that Christophe's reign – an embodiment of the perils of neo-colonialism – leaves the fledgling Haitian republic open to ridicule? I am convinced that there is much more than farce here at play.

The fundamental reason why Christophe's tragi-comedic court is not a complete farce is because the Haitian reality is present in the geographical details. Not only are 'Limonade' and 'Marmelade' actual provinces in the northern region of Haiti, but all the other ostensibly satirical titles refer to real places. Even a cursory glance at a map of the republic reveals the names of the provinces of 'Limonade' and 'Marmelade'. There are also areas called Dondon, Plaisance, Caracol, Le Borgne, Pignon and Phaéton, referenced in the *Tragédie*.[244] However farcical the names may sound, through this gesture of re-naming his subjects Césaire's king Christophe is in effect redistributing the land in the former colony of Saint Domingue to the people, which is equivalent to granting them their freedom. After all, in the wake of the Haitian Revolution, freedom was broadly comprehended as the ability to own and cultivate one's own land. But even more significant is that Dondon and Limonade are central locations in Haiti's struggle for independence, and specifically for the process of baptizing the new nation with an indigenous Taíno term. Just after the Revolution, Moreau de Saint-Méry notes an abundance of Amerindian physical remains visible in these sites: 'rock carvings, tombs, earthen mounds, and artefacts that were strewn on the ground'.[245] Geggus surmises that 'slaves who worked the land and hunted in the woods could hardly have ignored them. Dessalines, born on the border of Dondon parish, must have known of its caverns with their petroglyphs and burials, fetishes and axe heads. Of Limonade parish, in the plains below, Moreau wrote that 'Every step you take, there are the remains of Indian utensils'.[246] So beyond the fact that Dondon and Limonade are real locations in the northwest of Haiti, they constitute the geographic heart of the fledgling republic, where independence itself was declared (in Gonaïves). The notion that Césaire was not aware of these historical circumstances, after spending many months in Haiti himself, is unlikely.

Why have so many failed to notice that Limonade, Dondon, etc. are not just jokes? This is a potentially serious misunderstanding, and reveals a lack of comprehension of part of Césaire's anti-colonial project. How can this tendency be explained? An overly simplistic answer would be that too few are familiar with the actual geography of Haiti. It might also be tempting to assume that – as reflected by some of the excesses of Henri Christophe – Haitian history and culture are grounded in imitation. After all, even contemporary Haitian naming practices include references to European heroes and historical figures, as we have seen (this phenomenon will subsequently be discussed at greater length). And so the veracity of the place names in Césaire's *Tragédie* is lost, and no one bothers to look beyond the layer of farce. In any case, the effect of this blending of the authentic and the false through Césaire's use of surprising yet accurate geographic details, serves to reflect the chaos and uncertainty characteristic of the post-revolutionary period in the Haitian republic. It is just lost on many readers, unfortunately, who interpret the farce straightforwardly.

Playing with names, and the idea of being transformed by the naming process, has long been characteristic of Afro-Caribbean cultures. At the risk of seeming deterministic in this analysis, I want to consider some recent scholarship on Caribbean naming patterns, particularly slave-naming patterns, because it seems both relevant and instructive. In an article called 'Names and Naming in Afro-Caribbean Cultures' Richard Burton writes, 'Hilarious though its results often are to outsiders, [playing with names] is part and parcel of the 'deep play' that is Afro-Caribbean culture in general'.[247] The use of playful names (for both slaves and ex-slaves) suggests a 'kind of magical nominalism whereby the substance of a person is believed to inhere in his or her name', and names do 'not merely echo but actively embody the moral and other qualities of the person so designated'. Simply put, to take on a new name is to assume a new power, at least symbolically;[248] given that a name makes a person, name changes are thus often desirable. Trevor Burnard, another scholar, disagrees as to the degree of choice slaves had in assuming new names, but his study concurs with Burton's in general that names were crucial aspects of identity. Burnard notes that 'slave owners knew that the giving of a name was neither a casual affair nor a matter suited to levity[...]. Colored owners were more conscious of the psychological need for freed slaves to change their name than white owners were'.[249] By extension, then, Césaire's king Christophe 'gets it' better than most, in spite of his tyrannical inclinations. The court scene shows his profound understanding of the power to be transformed through a name, and he has poignant motivations for the allocation of new titles:

> CHRISTOPHE: Ces noms nouveaux, ces titres de noblesse, ce couronnement! Jadis on nous vola nos noms! Notre fierté! Notre noblesse, on, je dis ON nous les vola! Pierre, Paul, Jacques, Toussaint! Voilà les estampilles humiliantes dont on oblitéra nos noms de vérité.[250]

Christophe then admits to not knowing his own real name – the truest tragedy of the play – and he fully realizes the importance of renaming his subjects, whom he intends to personally deliver from 'la raque de l'histoire' ('the refuse of History') albeit through forced labour.

In colonial history, changing one's name through baptism yielded tangible benefits to slaves. Catholic planters in Saint-Domingue frequently baptized their slaves, and this transformation was largely welcomed and sought after. Being bestowed with new names in this process allowed them to obtain godparents and thus form new relationships between one another.[251] Whether consanguineous or fictive, these kinship ties were extremely important. Burton notes that baptism, and the 'change or modification of name it entailed, represented in the first instance a means of broadening and strengthening the slave's network of non-biological kin, an essential prerequisite for survival on the plantation. It further represented an authentic *rite de passage,* not so much from heathendom into Christendom, as from African-ness into West Indian-ness; in a word, as lived by the slaves, baptism into the White Man's religion enacted and figured not their Europeanization, but rather their effective *creolization;* the name of the Other is less an obliteration or alienation, than it is a transmutation or renewal, of identity'. Although the rites in the *Tragédie*'s court scene are not religious, the underlying gravity of the apparently farcical name changing process seems clear: Christophe's newly-named subjects are now part of a network which affords them an improved, collective status in the young republic (which they ultimately exploit to overthrow the tyrannical king), even if they did not choose their own names.

For centuries, the transmission of names in the Afro-Caribbean has been an imaginative process. Césaire must have known something about the 1848 organization of 'registres d'individualité' in his home of Martinique, wherein white registrars assigned surnames 'on the spot' to 150,000 newly-freed blacks. New names, 'dreamed up on the spur of the moment', included many references to classical literature and history, both ancient and modern; moral qualities (like Patience); anagrams; matronyms; days of the week; and special events (such as a girl named Fetnat, for 'Fête Nationale'). For Burton, in present-day Martinique, the 'improbable gamut of names' that is the heritage of emancipation represents nothing short of a 'triumph of créolité', an affirmation of one's Antillean status, or Americanness.[252] In the contemporary Afro-Caribbean space, the practice of inventing names remains important. Patrick Chamoiseau considers nicknames to be a kind of 'onomastic marronnage', a 'petit' marronnage representing the 'multiplication of identities and a limited, ambivalent freedom'. Burton concludes his study by asking, as do I, 'What's in a name?' His answer is that, for Afro-Caribbean people, it is 'the whole *servitude* and *grandeur* of their history, its *splendeur* and *misère* [...]'. As we have seen in the case of the Dukes of Limonade, Marmelade, Dondon, etc., much more than farce is at play.

Charles Najman's film 'Royal bonbon' (2002) fascinatingly re-enacts a page of Haitian revolutionary history in the present day, almost entirely in Kreyòl, with an oneiric montage of images featuring *vodou* rituals, dances and pantomimes, as well as some stunningly beautiful landscapes. The protagonist is a vagabond (whose name is unknown) who declares himself to be Henri Christophe; he wanders through the streets pushing a wheelbarrow, laughing uncontrollably, and announcing to the bewildered people, 'You're slaves. I'm king!' He wears a makeshift crown adorned by a broken compass, which suggests not only that he does not know where he is going, but possibly serves as a critique of Haitian leaders today. As parades of children chant 'wa kaka', he makes his way up the mountain to the ruins of the Palais Sans-Souci, which houses an old desk chair (serving as a throne) and a larger-than-life white marble bust of a European female. The king then organizes a 'court' under the shade of a tree and distributes official titles to his earnest 'followers', promising them the world. They are a group of elderly people who are obviously poor, but neatly and formally dressed, and are thoroughly intrigued by his actions; they solemnly accept the noble names he bestows, as if in a trance. (A notable difference between the court scene in 'Royal bonbon' and the *Tragédie* is that no one in the film seems remotely worried about Europe).

Disillusionment ensues, when 'Henri' becomes despotic towards his followers, and the king is ultimately killed. But through his oft-repeated *devise*, 'je renais de mes cendres', Najman implies that Haiti's history and its heroes can never die. The king's final realization is that 'Life has condemned me to be a slave. All my life, I believed in my dream: 'The kingdom is not of this world' (this directly alludes to Carpentier's novel). Translated very loosely, freedom is illusory in Haiti, and dreams are mere madness. The only hint of optimism comes from Timothée, the young boy who has been a constant presence at the crazy man's side. As 'Henri' dies, the boy's words suggest that the mad man, known as 'wa kaka', was a father-figure to him, and is now at peace, 'anba dlo' or 'under the water' with the spirits. Through his symbolic acceptance of his problematic heritage, the child attains a new and forward-looking subject position. The king's body remains visible on the empty, rocky plain, with a wide-open sky in the background; though difficult to interpret precisely, one could read the scene as a kind of purging of the excesses of past leaders, ushering in a new, transparent chapter in government. Is the 'folie' thus exorcized? I am not convinced of this, and I find support for this view in Najman's 2004 documentary film 'Haïti: la fin des chimères?', which critically chronicles Aristide's first year in office, and surveys two centuries of political strife. Like 'Royal bonbon', this film laments the heavy weight of Haitian history, and the tendency to place too much stock in one's leaders – even Aristide – while literal 'Chimères', or armed gangs, rule the streets.

'Royal bonbon' has received scant critical attention aside from Gilbert Doho's important article.[253] This silence is probably due to the film's limited distribution, or the possibility that metropolitan film critics have less than complete familiarity with Haiti's history; however, there is also the fact that its emphasis goes against the grain of official discourse in France, wherein the former colony is oft likened to a 'petit frère' ('little brother'), with emphasis on the 'petit'. In any case, I agree with much of Doho's analysis: drawing from the work of Fanon, he addresses the problem of 'folie' in post-independent Africa and Haiti, and critically reads 'Royal bonbon' alongside Césaire's *Tragédie*. Doho proposes to deconstruct the myths that have seemed to stymie both Haiti and Africa, using as a lens the perspective of crazy people themselves in order to understand the schizophrenia that characterizes the period of post-independence. The upshot is that, in a context where everyone perpetually seeks to be Other, the impossibility of filling this gap renders violence inevitable, and death banal. Doho suggests that through the marginalized, or the 'fous', hope can be reborn, and the rereading of history (beginning with Christophe) can be restorative. Fully understanding Christophe's poor management of his heritage requires a return to historical origins; not only can this recalibrate a people on the road of nation-building, it can cure the crazy and exorcise the realm of madness. Though in many respects Doho's argument is compelling, I find his reading of 'Royal bonbon' to be overly optimistic. He concludes that Najman affords viewers a 'euphoric' re-reading of the Revolution, which is not a 'long, sad saga'. Instead, the re-reading is an 'act of regeneration, and a willing correction of a poor choice.'[254]

To my mind, Najman's film shows that the poor choice is something inevitable, which people consistently choose. Instead of demystifying the myths and mistakes of Haitian history, then, 'Royal bonbon' illustrates how people voluntarily remain mystified, under the spell of false hopes. Najman's film leaves viewers with many more questions than answers. Might the film represent a call to action? This could be appealing. If people have historically allowed themselves to be deluded, they can nevertheless one day choose to act. But will they? But does not Najman show that searching for meaning in history is futile, an empty gesture? Will the cycles of violence in Haiti forever repeat themselves? Are people so desperate that they will go along with whomever seems to incarnate great things, crazy though that leader may seem? Is another revolution necessary? The latter seems painfully true, if unlikely at the present moment.

But there is another problem at the heart of 'Royal bonbon', as was the case with Césaire's *Tragédie*. Although both texts take on Christophe and his mimicry of European traditions, the layer of farce proves to be an unfortunate mask, for embedded beneath the veneer of the ridiculous there are present some undeniable truths. 'Royal bonbon' is based upon the story of 'Wa kaka', a phenomenon that occurred during the mid-twentieth century in the northern city of Cap Haitien, and which has been transmitted to date through the oral tradition. A colleague recommended that I contact the linguist Jacques Pierre, who teaches courses in Haitian Kreyòl at Duke University, about the legend of 'wa kaka', since he hails from that northern city. He responded, 'I do not know too much about the history [of 'wa kaka'] based on what is documented. However, I recall when I was a child there was a man with mental health issues who was in his forties who wandered around the streets of Cap-Haitien with a crown on his head and acted like a king to emulate the former Haitian Northern king named Henri Christophe. Kids as well as adults in the town nicknamed the man 'wa kaka' and other names'. According to Pierre, in Kreyòl 'wa kaka' means, literally, 'the king of shit'. Alternatively, the phrase 'w a kaka' means 'you will never be a king'. He writes, 'In the latter case the 'a' is a tense marker for a hypothetical future. People regularly use 'w a kaka' to tell others that they will never be able to achieve a particular thing or get what they are seeking, as in: A. 'M pral jwenn lajan nan men gouvènman an pou m rezoud pwoblèm nan'. ('I will get money from the government to solve this issue'.) B. 'W a kaka'. ('Never in a million years!')' This heretofore undocumented historical phenomenon, which pertains to the rich oral tradition of Haiti, obviously merits future investigation. That the nickname for the impersonator of the notorious king Christophe still exists in the contemporary Haitian lexicon underscores the multiple layers of realities, past and present, which constitute Haiti and its history.

The ostensible parody of geographical names in the *Tragédie*'s court scene, closely replicated in 'Royal bonbon', simultaneously highlights and obscures aspects of Haitian history and ultimately alters understandings of the world's first black republic in an awkward, if perhaps inadvertent way. Part of the notion of tragedy surrounding Césaire's *Tragédie* – however controversial it may be – is that too few are aware of either the history of Haiti, or its significance for the rest of the world. Do these texts represent statements of possibility, or, on the other hand, a more ominous decree for Haiti – a condemnation to endless cycles of violence? Personally, I am persuaded by Jean Guion's positive reading of the *Tragédie* (if not his entire argument): 'Ici, le Phénix ne se contente pas de renaître de ses cendres: il est capable de s'améliorer, d'apprendre afin de transformer ses défaites passées en victoires futures'.[255] But as Président de l'Alliance Francophone, it is of course in Guion's interest to speak prophetically about the agency of Caribbean people. It is interesting that his work neatly reflects Carpentier's pronouncement in his experimental novel *El reino de este mundo* (1949), where the writer declares that it is the duty of man to improve himself by carrying out constructive projects, thus realizing his own greatness in the kingdom of this world.

As for 'Royal bonbon', differences of opinion regarding its implications are inevitable; as we have seen, the film's historical density is downplayed – as in the court scene, a distant echo of Césaire's parody, based upon a legend which remains obscure to the average viewer. As Manon Dumais remarks, 'Le destin du roi despote est si rapidement évacué que ceux qui sont peu familiers avec l'histoire d'Haïti n'y verront là qu'un conte naïf à saveur folklorique'.[256] Once again, historic specificity is suppressed, and the ridiculous reigns. Is the 'rebirth' of Christophe through 'Royal bonbon' to be seen as ironic, tragic, cathartic, or hegemonic? In truth, I think that any one of these arguments can be made. As for whether the lens of 'folie' is productive, that is entirely another matter; in the film about 'wa kaka', it is difficult to see what underlies the charade.

In a broader framework, the history of Haiti within the Caribbean space represents a vital, recurring narrative that informs both daily life and larger cultural processes. The Haitian Revolution is reclaimed again and again, filling in the gaps and silences of official, or Western, history, and 'working-through' difficult or uncertain circumstances, past and present. Commemorative moments such as the Bicentenary provide useful points of departure to propose innovative ideas and settle historical scores – but also deform them. Given the willingness of outsiders to make assumptions about the character(s) of Haitian history/culture, and of Haitians to glorify their own history, understandings of Haitianness have been sadly, if not tragically, deformed through repeated re-readings of Césaire's famous scene. Victor Figueroa proposes that Haitian history is 'a Caribbean embodiment of the colonial condition, with its multiple possibilities and contradictions'.[257] Will Afro-Caribbean cultures remain oppositional, inherently defined and divided by the pressures that they resist, which Burton and Burnard appear to believe, or can true freedom from the colonial past eventually be achieved? What seems evident is that one should avoid the reflexive use of labels like 'hilarious', 'crazy', and so on, because inventiveness, playfulness, and spontaneity are necessary parts of the long process of decolonization. At a recent conference called 'Haiti and the Americas: Histories, Cultures, Imaginations', the well-known Caribbean scholar J. Michael Dash suggested that a potential starting point would be for Haitians to reconfigure their national imaginary, allowing for multiple Haitian realities and locations to be embraced: first, the nation's Guinean, or African, origins; second, 'lot bo dlo', or Haitians living abroad, in the diaspora; and third, 'moun an deyò', people outside urban centres of privilege.[258] Simply put, the collective notion of what is 'Haitian' needs to change.

For Haitians today, the Revolution remains a complex presence, and an entirely unfinished process. But instead of healing a post-colonial population through demystifying one of its legendary leaders, Césaire and Najman make these contradictions abundantly clear. To be fair: one must acknowledge that of all the Haitian Revolutionary leaders, Christophe was saddled with the most monumental task – that of governing the new nation – given that the internationally celebrated general Toussaint L'Ouverture and the nationally loved 'Papa' Dessalines died long before he. Césaire's Christophe was not the comedian many have thought him to be; to a greater degree than many realize, he, too, was attempting to rewrite the nation's history by evoking the original legends behind the national narrative (based upon 'Ayiti') and the long-established ritual of re-naming. And for his part, 'Wa kaka' evidences the ongoing process of unfinished revolutionary business being carried out.

12. GASTRONOMICAL METAPHORS: THEIR PRESENCE WITHIN THE SEXUAL AND SOCIO-POLITICAL CONTEXT OF HAITIAN CULTURE

Patrick Sylvain (Brown University)

The indisputable existence of metaphorical patterns in Haitian speech provides an interdisciplinary blueprint for a culture that is heavily influenced by agricultural activities and a language pregnant with food attributive metaphors. The metaphors used in Haitian reflect the overall disposition of the people and an acceptance of certain views that are represented through speech and text. The 'Woman as Food' metaphor is a consequence of the patriarchal nature of Haitian society; the overall permeation of gastronomical metaphors in the language is a product of a culture that has a strong preoccupation with food. The predominance of these gastronomical metaphors that are couched in cultural analogies proves that language is not only reflective, but it is also constitutive of social realities. My objective is to demonstrate that Haitian consumptive language is the manifestation of the conscious in a state of non-escape that consumes time, being and material condition. Here, in the act of consumption, to 'devour' another becomes a potent metaphor because of the exploitative totality in which the speaker exists. In Haitian, not only does hunger carry its own symbolisms, but also the act of eating (*manje*, to eat) often serves as the metaphorical 'container' to embed the suggested meaning. In Haitian Creole, the verb *manje* may have various connotations (sexual, political, competitive, sacred, symbolic), but it is at the same time a gastronomical act. What is operating at the core of the culture is an obsession with eating, while giving special consideration to the constructive and destructive properties of food. This obsession, what I refer to as a psychology of consumption, in reality represents a fear of being consumed:

> 'I wake each morning to a canvas by Paul Théaud of a woman, with no body as we understand a human form, walking in a lime green ocean; she is strolling by a lovely, living coral fish. But there on the shore is a young boy whose stomach is missing, simply not there. His face is scrambled with confusion. There is a fish alive, a woman with no body walking in the sea, and he is on shore with no tummy. What does this mean?'[259]

I begin this paper by prefacing it with Shange's description of Théaud's surreal painting and its symbolic message of hunger, which acts as driving force, a primordial fear of need and of the importance of food in Haitian society. Subliminally, in the painting, there is a message of consumption: consume or be consumed. I will further elaborate on those two dualities in order to illustrate how certain cultural concepts are imbedded in polarities and consequently form a specific *lingua* and cultural understanding in a set domain. Here, the domain of concern is food and all of its attributes/functions. This domain will serve as a guide to identify and deconstruct certain polarities that operate as normalcy within the cultural construct. Those polarities are: Food and Women, Food and Politics. Through the usage of metaphors in the cultural context and the acceptance and constant recurrences of those metaphors, those polarities are no longer perceived as polarities.

To help in mapping-out this metaphorical concept of gastronomical metaphors, I will draw primarily upon Helen Haste's work, 'The Sexual Metaphor' (1994); George Lakoff and Mark Johnson's work, 'Metaphors We live by' (1980); Sidney Mintz's 'Tasting Food, Tasting Freedom' (1996), and that of other scholars who have written on figurative language and metaphors. Unfortunately, the well-known Haitian critic, Maximilien Laroche, has flirted with metaphors but did not develop a theory, or a deep structural study of metaphors. His literary works however have had a profound influence on my approach to cultural criticism, especially the ways in which he deciphered the symbolism, or metaphors of wood and the father figure in seminal texts such as those of Moreau de Saint-Méry, Christian Werleigh and Jacques Stephen Aléxis. As Laroche studied the diffusion of certain images from the culture that became solid national metaphors, he noted 'the image of the strong and virtuous tree that one of the founding fathers, Toussaint L'Ouverture, alluded to when he was captured by the French. [This] offers an inter-textual paradigm, materials that are extremely rich to the Haitian artist who really wants to push the language, in that sense, Aléxis did not miss that opportunity.'[260] With the absence of Haitian scholars in the discipline of 'discourse analysis' and metaphorical studies specifically, I am obliged to primarily reference other scholars who have engaged in in-depth studies in the field. However limited, symbolic and idiomatic usages of Haitian Creole's proverbs in politics have in the 1990s been subject to scholarly study.[261]

To unpack gastronomical metaphors, I have gathered a battery of references from the folk culture and from the 'creative' culture (oral and written). Given Haiti's high rate of illiteracy, my references from the written-cultural-production model will be limited; although, our literary tradition is among the richest in the Caribbean. I will be drawing heavily from the folk-cultural-expression model and from the popular-oral-production model, namely music. Each of these models differs vastly from the other and carries its own aesthetic, biases and messages. As I will demonstrate, each of these models is continually interacting with another to form a Haitian-Patriarchal construct of naming. This act of naming manifests itself via the metaphors produced by anonymous individuals within the folk culture and permeates throughout the collective/national culture: 'Metaphors, as we have seen, are conceptual in nature.

They are among our principle vehicles for understanding. And they play a central role in the construction of social and political reality.'[262] By choosing to analyze and categorize food as metaphor, I have identified several domains where this metaphor appears and draws upon a wealth of pre-existing symbols. Thus, by phrasing and enlarging this existing metaphor onto other domains (sexual and socio-political), I have synthesized it into one larger domain, namely 'gastronomical.' Gastronomical becomes the master container, for it encapsulates all forms and manners of consumption.

My approach in unpacking and mapping out this concept (gastronomical metaphors) will be heavily cultural and socio-political. Undoubtedly, just because these constructs or conceptualizations are cultural does not necessarily mean that they are independent of psychological consequences and analysis. Given my multi-disciplinary approach, I have developed an historical associative sensibility to culture. Meaning that, in my view, one must not interact with culture only in the present tense, since from such an optic only a superficial template can be produced. One must enter the labyrinth of the past in order to formulate a proper understanding. In other words, culture is not a spontaneous creation: there are always associative elements that help in shaping new constructs. My argument here is in tandem with Mintz who wrote: '[s]uch linkages can be studied historically, and many anthropologists have learned from social historians how they can reveal the political and economic significance of past events connected to food.'[263] Food is not just food as a singular entity, there are social institutions, social uses, a type of pragmatism, and thus histories attached to it as well. In a sense, the socio-cultural permutations and articulations through gastronomical metaphors are embodied with a cultural consciousness of consumptive representation.

Haiti, a tropical country, shares the infamous island of Hispaniola with Santo-Domingo (Dominican Republic) where Christopher Columbus accidentally anchored in 1492 as he searched for the gold and spices of India and Japan. After the subsequent discovery of gold on the Island, approximately ten years later, most of the Taino and Awarak people were wiped out. When the amounts of gold in the mines were thought to be insufficient and too costly for the Spanish Crown, the colonists changed their production focus from gold to sugar. The introduction of African slaves replaced the dying native inhabitants of the Island. Following Spain's rapid growth and expansion in the 'New World,' most of the European countries joined the race to conquer land, resources and even people. As a result, nearly 130 years after Spain's conquest, in 1625, the French challenged Spain's dominion over Hispaniola, and by 1697, France had obtained control of the western part of the island.

The French established an extremely lucrative colony based on slavery, the production of coffee, indigo, cocoa, cotton and above all, sugar. By the mid 1700s, France became one of the richest nations in Europe, and the number one importer/producer of sugar. In Saint-Domingue alone, in what is now Haiti, France had built close to 600 plantations, producing more goods than all of the English Caribbean colonies.[264] The economic system that reigned on that part of the island was a predatory one based on the systematic and inhumane exploitation of slave labour. The outnumbered plantation owners, living in perpetual fear, invented through the 'Black Code' the most atrocious system of torture for even the slightest infractions: 'The slaves received the whip with more certainty and regularity than they received food'.[265] It was said that Saint-Domingue was a mill for crushing Negroes as much as it was a mill for crushing cane. Thus, the relationship between slaves and owners was one of hatred. Consequently, the slaves also hated their relation to the plantations. During the bloody and merciless revolution of 1791 to 1804, the slaves adopted a 'slash and burn' policy, as the idea of continuing to work on the plantations was unthinkable. Unfortunately, due to historical trauma and the lack of an alternative system of production, many Haitians became agricultural workers and subsistence farmers. Although Haiti broke with the French, it was and still has been impossible for it to break from the earth and its resources. Hence, a great portion of our metaphors, symbolism, metonyms and idioms are *agronocentric* – the earth and its elements are the source.

Due to many years of mismanagement, corruption, class divisions and occupations by external powers such as Spain, France, and the United States, Haiti has experienced rapid economic degradation and arable land scarcity. The dense population of the country has increased the existing pressure on available land, leading to hunger and uncontrolled deforestation. The deforestation, which amounts to an irreversible ecological catastrophe, has had an unquantifiable effect on the nation as a whole: from prostitution to corruption, famine to over consumption, and from massive accumulation of wealth to landlessness. With the existence of these conflicting polarities and the need to survive and to sustain life, Haitians' language and mannerisms reflect the condition of the patriarchal and imbalanced nation. I should stress that despite the patriarchal nature of the society, women are very independent and are in control, for the most part, of the informal agricultural sector; they are financially independent and are quite often the *de facto* head of household, whether there is a male present or absent. However, the status of women is largely devalued and subpar: 'They [women] pretend to wear the pants, but we gave them the privileges to rejoice while we are unsatisfied'.[266] To some, it is a contradiction to have women as being strong and even financially independent, and yet their status/value as person is less than that of men. The answer is simple: Haiti is submerged in contradictions and polarities, and whoever has the power of naming and creating myth, is eventually the most powerful.

Since this paper has its focus on the subject of metaphors and not politics or economy, I will focus on food as the basis for constructing the concept of 'Gastronomical Metaphor' as it fits into Lakoff and Johnson's theory of 'conceptual metaphors [that] are grounded in *correlations* within our experience.'[267] For, our experience with food or the notion of consumption occurs within a cultural framework that presupposes that you either consume or be consumed.

In almost all cultures, novelists, writers, 'filmmakers, poets and songwriters take common advantage of the fact that food and sexuality lie close together,'[268] and the symbolic meaning that arises will be dictated or influenced by those with power of naming. The power of naming is essentially a natural process of symbolization in human speech; however, the target or the object of the symbolic process of naming becomes by default a subject-object. And with the global rise of patriarchy through colonialism, naming has become a patriarchal domain of structural imposition, with women being the subject of desire. A desire to control often results in the restriction of her (a woman's) sexuality prior to marriage by her family, to 'have her hand' is a form of conquest, and a desire to consume her sexually satisfies a carnal hunger: 'Nourishment, a basic biological need, becomes something else we humans transform it symbolically into a system of meaning for much more than itself.'[269] It must be emphasized, however, that although Haiti is contaminated by patriarchy, which has in turn influenced our symbolic languages, and it must also be clear that 'Men as Food' metaphors are also prevalent. As the well-known novelist Edwidge Danticat writes in her book *Farming of Bones*, 'I can still feel his lips, the eggplant-violet gums that taste of greasy goat milk boiled to candied sweetness with mustard-colored potatoes.'[270] The edibility of the other becomes a site of mutual desirability and not simply an act of objectification of the other.

Emeline Michel, our national singer and star par excellence, also uses gastronomical metaphors to illustrate desirability through a form of symbolic consumption or desire to consume. In her CD *Rhum & Flamme*, she personified Haiti as a man and said: 'like he flows in my blood/ hides underneath my ebony skin/ his aroma of citronella mixed with cinnamon/ his tiny taste of caramel'.[271] Through Emeline's song, Haiti becomes irresistible due to his lush, consumptive gastronomical essence. Generally, the term or use of the verb *'manje'* (food, or to eat) remains gender neutral, even though the object of most publicly sexualized discourse is about women.

Manje, to eat, just as in English, offers multiple meanings and is not conditioned by the scarcity or abundance of food. When an American says that he or she is going to make another person 'eat his/her words'; or commands for another to 'eat me' or 'bite me' it is not reflective of a *gourmand,* or food deprived culture. However, in the case of Haiti, a unique socio-political history imparts a particular language and perspective in relation to the way that the people experience consumption, and thus, several levels can be explored:

(1) From the slaves thrown overboard being subsequently consumed by the seas as in 'lanmè a manje yo,' to the various forms of consumption that occurred on the plantations: from the lives lost to the hardships of slavery, to the food provided for consumption or lack thereof. Such metaphors do carry certain elements of residual fear that are manifested through the symbolic magnitude of the hunger, or the need to escape it. 'Eskalavaj *manje* anpil moun' (slavery *consumed* a lot of people); 'se *devore* yo te konn devore esklav ak kout rigwaz' (they used to *devour* the slaves with the whip).

(2) By the time of the start of the major Haitian slave revolt in 1791, the language of consumption shifted camps; the slaves began *devouring* the whites, not cannibalistically, but figuratively as in the destruction of the power structure through the act of rebelling. Of course, many whites lost their lives, as was necessary for freedom to occur in 1804.

(3) The various dictatorships that were instituted after the nation was established consumed many lives in order to maintain power. Thus, from our genesis, political 'cannibalism,' or the politics of destruction, which is the politics of dictatorship, became a part of our political culture. Hence the saying, '*politik manje* anpil moun' (politics devoured a lot of people).

(4) From 1915 to 1934, the politics of consumption entered a new phase during the U.S. occupation of Haiti. Not only were people's lives 'consumed' by the attacks of the marines but the companies that were established and subsequently exploited the workers and the land brought new metaphors into the culture. With the establishment of the Haitian-American Sugar Company (HASCO) and its

infamous trains that trekked the south littoral coast, songs and figurative speeches developed and mimicked the locomotive sounds that corresponded with social events and the loss of limbs. '*Ban m'janm pran kann*' (give me legs take canes) became a popular refrain as kids used to run alongside the train cars to pull sugarcane out. Furthermore, the HASCO workers, up until the 1980s, used to say that the company devoured them or sucked them dry. To say that one is devoured by the train or the company it is to say that the speaker(s) feel(s) to be in a state of non-escape that consumes his time, being and material condition. Thus, the act of consumption, to be devoured becomes a potent metaphor because of the exploitative totality that the speaker is in.

(5) Sexually, the richest field for 'Gastronomical Metaphors' is found in the music, particularly during Rara and Carnival seasons that take place in February and March, and in the Vodoun festivities especially during the month of November when the Gédés are celebrated. It is through these realms that agriculture and sexuality are fused to produce some of the best sexual metaphors. René Depestre entitled one of his books *Alléluia pour une Femme-Jardin* (Hallélujah for a Woman-Garden), which won him considerable praise as well as a few negative epithets. In Lyonel Trouillot's short story *Holy Mary, Mother of God*, he writes about this young girl who did not wish to be pregnant and felt so embarrassed by her pregnancy that she referred to herself as 'Amelia, swelled-up calabash'.[272] As the 1979 popular carnival song by the group DP Express demonstrated, the nexus of sexuality and food or food machinery is really narrow: '*Pilon rale-monte glise-desann, manch pilon mete pou yo*' (the pestle goes up and down, the pestle gave it to them). In Haiti, various types and sizes of mortar and pestle are used in order to grind grains, nuts and other food products that need to be minced. In the above song, *pilon* (pestle) becomes a metaphor for penis in the sexual act.

In René Depestre's mosaic novella *Alléluia pour une Femme-Jardin*, he pushed his symbolic language into the realm of agronomic discourse with the result of having his socio-cultural and linguistic consciousness represented in a creative act of representation so that he became the embodiment of the articulator's or the protagonist's intentions. In describing his various encounters in his travelogue, the protagonist labels his journey 'geological libertinage', the ultimate non-violent form of conquest and consumptive freedom. He writes: 'Ukraine produced a high quality vanilla. Sugar cane grew feverishly. Norway and Greece, coffee lands, were not too far from Brazil's production, whereas cereal, the wheat of the Congo, yielded as great a value as the Canadians' wheat. The honey of Cambodia was in demand everywhere. But, it did not have the monopoly. One could find excellent honey on all of my continent.'[273] Using geological libertinage as a kind of protagonist he enters the perfect nexus between sexuality and food, but uses the symbolic process of codifying his intention. In a later passage, Depestre or his protagonist becomes obsessed with the consumptive abundance that Paris offered as an imperial centre and he claims that 'Paris, round, fertile, promised me to infinity new lands to till. Paris offered me the spectacle of her roundness, mother of all exotic roundness, fertile, that thrashed its waves against the hull of my absolute thirst.'[274] As a colonial subject who was deprived of the power to freely consume on his dictatorial and relatively homogeneous terrain, he had to move to one of the centres of colonial power in order to find opulence, diversity and fertility, illustrating this capacity of replenishing the consumptive field. As an astute writer, Depestre properly transposed his symbolic field in order to feed his creative needs.

Although this paper is far from being a critique of Alta Mae Stevens' paper 'Manje in Haitian Culture: The Symbolic Significance of Manje in Haitian Culture', published in 1995 in the *Journal Haitian Studies*, I must nevertheless remark on some fundamental points that she addressed in her intellectual interpretation of certain cultural nuances that are specifically Haitian, and which accordingly necessitate a deep understanding of the culture to decipher. Her paper purports to describe the symbolic uses of the verb '*manje*' (to eat), and through this description, attempts to outline various cultural connotations as she examines the symbolic and substantive functioning of *manje*. Her general premise at the start of her essay is correct when she writes: '*manje* is used either as a noun (meaning generic food, *manje aswè*, for example, meaning supper), or as a verb with both an active and passive form. In its active form it means to eat or to feed (another). In its passive form, it means to be eaten. Used positively as a noun or verb, *manje* connotes *abundance, friendship, sex* and above all *power*.'[275] I, however, would argue that she confuses the symbolic uses of *manje* for literal meaning, when they are clearly parabolic. Furthermore, she confuses *manje* as a state of desire with *manje* as a state of consumption. '*M' anvi manje ou*' connotes sexual desirability, just as in English, *I want to eat you up*. Eating here is not synonymous with the cannibalistic act of actual consumption of the other. She refers to the rites of those 'who will not share [...] *gro voras* (greedy)',[276] however, there are better translations for selfish people, *egoyis*, *mesken*, or *chichadò*.

One must beware of the facile construction of socio-historicism by professional social scientists that have amassed power to interpret while intending to influence readers though intellectual discourse that is semi-prescriptive. Being an intellectual means to belong to a privileged category of authoritative experts, thus having certain powers of interpretation and propagation. However, as Thomas McLaughlin reminds us, 'there is no 'proper' meaning, only arbitrarily 'assigned' meaning.'[277] As certain social scientists assign meaning to certain cultural nuances they seem to negate the fact that language is a powerful entity and it 'is part of the fabric of social and political life. It shapes our perceptions, but it also is shaped by its social context. That is, because of its strategic role in perception, language must be shaped to serve the needs of dominant groups.'[278] The quintessential soft power resides in the hands of those who are responsible for naming and interpreting.

Although language is representative of the cultural ethos, knowing the historicity of the language allows for better interpretation of its symbols and figurative aspects. Not being a native speaker, Stevens made too many general statements and relied upon the references of a sensationalist anthropologist such as Melville Herskovits who was inaccurate in his reading of a great part of the Haitian culture. Since metaphor, as McLaughlin explains, 'involves a transfer of meaning from the word that properly possesses it to another word which belongs to some shared category of meaning. A metaphor is therefore a compressed analogy.'[279] Thus the complexity lies in the unpacking of metaphors that are culturally embedded. In Joan Dayan's book, *Haiti, History, and the Gods*, she illustrates very well, although indirectly, the problem of interpretation by providing the reader with an interview transcript conducted by Drexel Woodson, an American Anthropologist doing fieldwork in Northern Haiti and who interviewed Erosmène Delva:

> Damn! What the fuck is wrong with you, Foreigner? How can you have such a big head and still be so stupid [sucks teeth]?
> Your thing, Right! [Stands and grabs her crotch.] This!
> They say every woman has a *karo* of land [between her thighs]. If I let a man feel my twat, he's got to give me land. There are women in the city of Cap-Haitien who say it's sweetness for sweetness [i.e., a direct exchange of sexual pleasure]. That's a pretty good way to look at it.[280]

'What is most instructive about the way Erosmène thinks through her relationship with the La Guille landowner and the other men in her life, whom she calls "comrade friends" (*zanmi kanmarad*), is her mode of representation. Quite artful in her own schemes of commodification, Erosmène not only confirms the metaphor of garden-woman but also embodies and particularizes it.'[281] Any superficial reading of the present cultural template can only lead to misinterpretation, as Erosmène's frustration demonstrated. In an attempt to establish her authority on the culture, Stevens appears to be misinformed when she writes 'in truth there is no equivalent word in Creole for meal.'[282] As a native speaker I know that we use terms such as *kolasyon*, *repa*, *goute*, *konsonmen*, and *dine* for meal. Here the verb *goute* means to taste and reflects a state of desire, as in *anvi manje* (wanting to eat), or the sexual consumption of the other. Unlike the 'food for thought' metaphor in English, in Haitian, food becomes a body of consumption, thus the body becomes a 'container and conduit metaphor.' We are astutely reminded by Lakoff and Johnson that 'each culture must provide a more or less successful way of dealing with its environment, both adapting to it and changing it. Moreover, each culture must define a social reality within which people have roles that make sense to them and in terms of which they can function socially. Not surprisingly, the social reality defined by a culture affects its conception of physical reality.'[283]

Land (garden), water and food are nothing more than manifestations of natural energy that humans utilize for biological needs, but they are also captured and contained for social domination. Although those elements are natural, once 'domesticated,' they form a social function: 'underlying the rich symbolic universe that food and eating always represent, however, there is the animal reality of our living existence. It is not separate from our humanity, but is an integral part of it.'[284] In the Haitian culture, food must not be wasted and eating is not only a biological act, it is also sacred, for the soul must be fed. It is also sexual. Food revitalizes, it gives one *Jèvrin*, sexual potency, especially in the eating of conch or bull/goat testicles. Supposedly, such delicacies are only reserved for men. It is believed that a woman who indulges herself in such a 'feast' will be too wild, sexually out of control. 'Out of control' here can be interpreted as a need for men to control women's desire from wanting more; women's insatiable appetite to consume might lead to the demise of men. The idiom that warns about certain women with an insatiable appetite is *Fanm sa a ta souse mwèl ou* (this woman will suck the marrow out of you) and it expresses a sure male demise, hence there is a need for men to consume sexually potent foods. In Edwidge Danticat's *Breath, Eyes, Memory*, the protagonist, Sophie, upon her return to Haiti is publicly courted by a taxi driver who says: 'I would crawl under your dress and live there. I can feed on your beauty like a leech feeds on blood. I would live and die for you.'[285] Here the protagonist is voluntarily offering himself as a *gourmand* who would die feasting on his favourite gastronomical dish that represents not only his last dwelling place but his ultimate site of consumption.

Biological needs are worrisomely joined by sexual delight/ appetite; with women being the constant subject of desire, the ultimate *plat* for the *gastronome* minded individual who not only seeks to satisfy his palate, but is also looking to be sexually stimulated. Women are either metaphorically the main course (lovemaking and sex) or the dessert (just sex). Food and women are constantly constructed as permanent 'subjects' of desire. Illustrative of that discourse is one of the passages taken from the Marcelin brothers' 1941 novel, *The Beast of the Haitian Hill*, which was translated into English in 1946. Here, the narrator describes the main protagonist's consumptive desirability for his maid: 'She was an attractive Negress. Clean, tall, carved with vigor, she had provocative breasts and buttocks, and her lips were plump and violet like the skin of a ripe fig.'[286] While men's discourse about women prevails; women's usage of gastronomical metaphors to express desire is also present. *M' ta manje ti piti sa a* (I'd consume that little one) expresses a woman's sense of sexual prowess over a man she deems small yet consumable. Or yet, one hears of a woman's desire to *manje yon kann kale* (eat a peeled sugarcane), in reality, one does not eat a sugarcane; one chews and sucks its juices. Using sugarcane as a metaphor for the penis, a woman expresses a specifically sought pleasure that cannot be culturally misunderstood. Gastronomical metaphors are widespread, but they express varied sexual and socio-political symbols that are often coded and if wrongly interpreted can carry completely different cultural meanings.

The two polarities women and food are now one entity: Usually, men are the consumers and they consume the consumable. A man who is materially wealthy and has a large appetite does not only excessively consume food, but may also indulge himself by having more than one woman for partner. Paradoxically, it is commonly believed that poor people tend to overeat because of the lack of assurance that food would always be available. This same behaviour manifests in men's interaction with women and women are ready to be consumed because of their comestible qualities: *Tout fanm dous* = All women are sweet; *Fanm se mandarin* = Women are mandarins. Consequently, in the folk-cultural model of symbolizing, women are turned into a non-interactive, but yet consumable object as in: *fanm se kokoye, li gen twa je men li pa wè nan youn* = A woman is like a coconut, she has three eyes (openings) and she cannot see in any of them: 'Ingestion and sexuality, both intimate manifestations of our nature as living creatures, and equally remote in our case from their roles in the lives of other species, stand in different but parallel relationships to our human consciousness.'[287] The nexus of food and carnal appetite creates a unique interface for our species.

Given the scarcity of and the manifestation of a fixation with food; Haiti can rightfully be categorized as a hungry nation with a strong culture and a pocketful of people who are malnourished. One of Jacques Stephen Aléxis' novels, *Compère General Soleil*, presents a man (Hilarion) who is hallucinating as a result of torrid hunger and is also wanted by the police for an alleged killing. 'In his belly, his tripe tied in numerous snake's knots [...]. In his head, no more rational thoughts. When one is hungry, the sensation of the imagined and the real are the same. A strange hallucination cradles, shakes the body [...].'[288] Not only does hunger carry its own symbolisms, but the act of eating or the verb to eat, *manje*, can be viewed as a 'container' which contains its own metaphorical concepts. In Haitian, *manje* (eating/consuming) is a multifunctional metaphor, it is at the same time a gastronomical act (a), a sexual act (b), a political act (c), a competitive act (d), a sacred act (e), it is a symbolic act (f), and sometimes it is an act of self-reliance and communal sharing (g).

> a) ***Manje*** *anpil pa vle di byen dijere* = Eating a great deal doesn't mean you digest well.
> b) (i) *Mwen ta **manje** fanm sa a. Or, Fanm sa a renmen **manje** bwa* = I could eat/devour (wanting to have sex) this woman. Or, this woman loves to have sex.
> (ii) *Fanm se **plat manje**, jan ou ban mwen l' m'ap pran l'* = Women are culinary dishes, however you feed them to me, I'll eat them.
> c) (i) *Se pa de moun Duvalier yo **manje**! Or, yo **manje** misye nan prizon an*. The Duvaliers have killed lots of people. Or, they killed him while in jail.

(ii) *Dan pouri gen fòs sou bannann mi* = Rotten teeth take advantage on ripe bananas.
d) (i) *Match sa a se chyen-**manje**-chyen.* = This match is dog-eat-dog (to each its own).
(ii) *Fanm jalou pa janm gra* = Jealous women are never voluptuous.
(iii) *Dan griyen pa bwè soup* = A laughing mouth cannot drink soup
e) (i) *Manje sa yo se **manje-lwa**.* = These foods belonged to, or are reserved for, the spirits (food for the gods).
(ii) *Lwa ou yo febli, ou pa ba yo **manje*** = Your spirits are weakened, you've not fed them.
f) (i) ***Manje** se rasin kò. Or, **manje** ki bon konn tiye mèt li.* = Nourishment is the source of life. Or, the food that tastes good can kill its master.
(ii) *Lè ou pa gen manman ou **tete** grann* = A motherless child suckles his grandmother.
g) (i) *Yon sèl dwèt pa **manje** kalalou* = You cannot eat gumbo (okra) with one finger.
(ii) *Se grès kochon ki kuit kochon* = A pork is cooked in its own fat.

The multiple usage and implications of the verb/noun 'manje' in the Haitian lexicon has no correlation to the availability, nor the voluminocity of descriptors in the language. What is operating at the core of the culture is a subconscious psychological obsession with eating and food's constructive as well as destructive properties. This obsession, what I refer to as a psychology of consumption, is really the fear of being consumed. After all, there is the myth of the 'Lougawou,' the werewolf, in the general culture. The Marcelin brothers' novel is rich in cultural parodies and myths like this. For example, the only midwife in the town of Musseau was summoned a bit late to assist with Madame Horace's labour. When the delivery was proven difficult, she said to the Sheriff in an emphatic voice: 'I could have done what was necessary to save the child. Now it is too late. The werewolves have completely devoured the infant in its mother's womb.'[289] When a healthy person dies, particularly a child, it is usually believed that: '*Logwood manje li*' (the werewolf /the devil has eaten it). Madame Horace, who was married to a devout Christian and relatively educated individual, during her moment of labour-pain, yelled to her husband: 'Oh, Horace! They have stolen my baby from me! They have devoured it alive in my womb.'[290] The psychology of consumption and an entrenched belief in supernatural elements become the perfect paradigm of a unity of polarities and of symbolisms. The women as food and the werewolf as supreme invisible consumer metaphors can be viewed as conscientious and accepted cultural constructs.

In Haitian, metaphorically speaking, women have been transformed to women-garden and women-fruit. As the former, they produce consumable goods, and as the latter they are ripe to be eaten. Thus, women are: peaches, mangoes, quinepas, mandarins, and so on. They are also fertile gardens. Haitian poets and writers, regardless of class status, have written and referred to their 'women' as oranges, or as possessing breasts of oranges. In 1925, the young Emile Roumer, in keeping with the national trope, the psychological-consumptive-obsession with women-gardens, wrote in the poem Areytos: 'Your brown body perfumed within my arms lies, / With the scent of flower-vines which dressed your bed, / And your lips the taste of the apricot dyes.'[291] Roumer's poem offers a transparent connection between the symbolic world and his experiential world. Again, the poet-writer and essayist, René Depestre, demonstrates this point in *Alléluia pour une femme-jardin* when the sixteen year-old male narrator, Olivier, becomes infatuated with his preferred aunt Zaza, whose body captivated his teenage mind: 'Looking at Zaza's elegant way of walking as if rolling in sensual waves under the sun, the fruit-like plumpness of her flesh, the roundness of her posterior reminded of good earth to be labored, I thought of the terror and the pitiful shame that religion has placed upon sexual organs of women.'[292] In this passage, not only is the male narrator a labourer who must till the metaphorical fertile soil, but he will do so with care, for the final reward is the consumption of a perceived copious meal despite the aberrant desirability of one's aunt. The insatiable male appetite through Olivier becomes limitless because women remain as food.

Haitian culture is so heavily influenced by agricultural activity that the language is pregnant with food attributive metaphors. As Bell Hooks observes, the 'commodification of Otherness has been so successful because it is offered as a new delight, more intense, more satisfying than normal ways of doing and feeling.'[293] Although Hooks is referring to the consumption of the Other by

Whites, her observation is still pertinent for the fact that Haiti, as a supposedly Catholic country, on the one hand tries to suppress sexuality and desire from the public realm. And on the other, interestingly so, the popular culture follows the Gédé (Vodun entity) ethos which is more of a libertine attitude toward sex and sexuality. Furthermore, our carnival culture, which is highly sexualized, subverts the restrictive norms that the patriarchal church tries to impose through pseudo-aristocratic norms. The gastronomical metaphors used are not limited to cooks and peasants but also are a part of ordinary speech in daily use, and in some ways, are simply subversive. Our proximate environment is experienced in a multimodal way and offers multisensory stimulation. It can be touched, smelled, tasted, heard and seen. In our daily interaction with nature and with others we refer to the familiar to explain the new. Sometimes, we purposely line or integrate polar opposites to construct dualistic mental images. This synaesthetic tendency, the ability of a stimulated sense to evoke a mood associated with another mode of perception, is commonplace and is the ground, the conduit through which metaphors emerge. It is an evocative and transformative capacity which language (in humans) allows. Such transformative capacity rests in the intentional structure of metaphors that permits the mind to intercept and link the vehicle and the tenor. In literature and in music, our composers have managed to run the gamut with such a tool where the intended term is unstated and conveniently located between A and B. The listener can create a synthesis based on what already exists within the popular imagination.

In the Haitian pop culture, Gesner Henry a.k.a. Coupe-Cloue and Michel Martelly a.k.a. Sweet Micky, are two of the most well known icons that are famous for lyrics that are loaded with sexual metaphors, especially gastronomical metaphors. Coupe-Cloue went so far as to label his albums with an explicit language parental advisory well before the practice became established in the U.S. in the late 1980s. In 1974, he placed on one of his album covers, *Saint-Antoine # 2*, 'interdit aux mineurs' (not permitted for minors). Many of his most loved lyrics had to do with coded sexual themes; he had mastered the *double-entendre* to the point that people used to skilfully defend his lyrics by asking listeners to provide evidence of the uttered profanity. Of course, we all knew what Coupe-Cloue's lyrics were expressing, but his delivery and artistic skills made him the darling of popular culture and the nightmare of conservative parents. Growing up in a respectable catholic household, we were not allowed to listen to Coupe-Cloue, especially after his 1976 hit song 'Sociss' (hot-dog) that became a catchy metaphor for penis. The narrative drive of the song rests on the fact that a major accident occurred between the driver of a Haitian-American Meat Company (HAMCO) and an anonymous driver. The crescendo of the song occurs when one of the large hot dogs flew from the HAMCO truck and landed on a blind woman's chest who proceeded to carry out a tactile examination of the item and finally uttered 'if everyone is not dead, I am certain that the driver died.' The intention of the singer/articulator was to articulate a new symbol or sign that could be easily grafted onto the cultural linguistic field and become instantly operational as a metaphor. From the late 1980s to the early 2000s, Sweet Micky, much younger and more vulgar than Coupe-Cloue, represented the more libertine side of the culture, blunt and relatively direct with live albums that were explicit in nature. What was unstated between A and B was no longer necessary.

As Haste pointedly remarks in her book, *The Sexual Metaphors*, the 'mapping of gender metaphors on to other domains has been particularly interesting in the history of ideas about the human being's relationship to the natural world.'[294] In Haiti, what we have done with the mapping of gender onto the natural world is beyond interesting; it is at times bizarre yet it follows the patriarchal model of gender and class hierarchy.

Sweet Micky's 1997 self-titled album '*Aloufa*' (greedy), in which he displays an array of foods and fruits as he happily sprawls in his tropical garden, proves to be a crucial album for this study. Not only does one find visual metaphors with the picnic-style display of foods, and his childlike expression. This symbolically indicates the possession of wealth and the joy felt in the act of consumption. '*Aloufa*' therefore, becomes the metaphor for the well consumed and the wealthy. In the Haitian body of symbolism, a well-fed body signifies *'social* transcendence of the laboring, striving 'economic' body.'[295] Additionally, *'Aloufa'* comes to symbolize sexual satisfaction through the visual metaphor that more is better. Thus, Micky's diverse display of food types becomes an architecture of desire that one wants to satisfy oneself and others through sheer opulence. Subsequently, one of the album's songs is entitled 'Pigeon' to correspond with the food as a sexual metaphorical concept: *'Chak samdi w'ale nan mache, kòmsi w'ap regle yon bagay serye, Pijon an limenm li poko menm manje'* (every Saturday you go to the market, pretending to be busy, meanwhile the pigeon has not eaten).[296] *Pijon*, another name for penis in Haitian, becomes not only a *double entendre* but also a metaphor for consumption of the body. The *pijon* then becomes a body that needs to be fed. Poetic and artistic awareness of the conceptual system of language and environment becomes the resonance factor for metaphorical language.

The Haitian writer Pierre Clitandre in his celebrated novel *La Catedral du mois D'aout* (*The Cathedral of the August Heat*) is governed by the iconography of hunger and monumentally connects the characters' history, mortality, and destiny by the threat of eradication not only through the oppressive dictatorship apparatus, but also through the lack of food: 'The poor people held out their calabash bowls, and chicken legs, chunks of beef, and great spoonfuls of rice descended into them like manna from heaven. They tore the meat apart with ravenous teeth, wounding their lips and gums.'[297] The use of hunger in its raw state articulates a relational power of signs and the symbolic process. The essence of articulation becomes a complex and artful construction that seeks to elicit a visceral response. In a later passage, after the assassination of Dimonbien's wife, the protagonist, he writes: 'She had lost her voice again, and was shaken by shuddering fits. She ground her yellowed teeth. Then she bit deep into the battered flesh of her husband's corpse, in the chest as if she wanted to devour his uncorrupted heart. But her teeth were blocked by the ribs. She rose to her feet, her face smeared with blood, and disappeared once again among the smoking ruins, a beast looking for its hole.'[298] Such a viscerally descriptive narrative not only echoes the fears of a population once gripped by dictatorship as they wish not to be consumed by its oppressive apparatus; but, it also reinforces the cannibalistic myth of the gluttonous subject that turns beastly in order to consume other subjects as consumptive objects. Here, the verb *manje* moves from the metaphorical realm into the physical where A denotes A. In the case of Dimonbien, as his name connotes, the wife wanted to consume his good-hearted self through the consumption of his heart so that the military would not further destroy his body and soul.

In the passage below, although Leslie Casimir is not describing the act of eating as part of the metaphorical or metonymic field of consumption, she is bringing gastronomical items and commodities that are Haiti-related and serve as symbolic reminders or visual and sensory metaphors that rekindle memories of a time past. Here, the time past connotes hardship as it relates to memories that are deep-seated and only uprooted by the aroma or the flavour of brought-food-items:

> 'The only time I could get people in my family to speak freely about their past was when a relative would come back from Haiti, bearing gifts. I don't remember when I came to realize how important it was to receive these items: food, liquor, embroidered cotton bed sheets, even a pair of plastic slippers. But I now know those things helped to remember where they came from, to relive their cherished memories. For it was through those items that I was able to catch glimpses of a sweet and bitter Haiti, of my grandmother and parents. The bites of molasses candy packed with cashews, the sip of egg yolk liquor, the spices, loosened their tongues and they would speak about hunting for pheasants, horseback riding, and summers spent on family farms. My parents would tell fragmented stories from their childhoods. Pasts that were broken in tiny pieces just like the jars that carried the pickled peppers and fine-shredded cabbage soaked in white distilled vinegar, the fiery odor clinging to the gift-bearers' shirts. Of my father's father abandoning his five children to start another family in neighboring Santo Domingo or Havana, Cuba. No one is really certain where he ended up. Only thing that is for sure is that he came back to Haiti, dying of cancer, so that his children, the ones who made it to America, could bury him. It was as if the odors wafting from the soaked, rickety suitcase brought to our home stirred memories in my parents' minds that were otherwise kept buried deep.'[299]

Food then becomes metonymic for memory, and carries with it a packed sensory-related metaphorical and symbolic field that is culturally specific. The food items hold a container of memories that can be accessed through the vehicle of food. Food as a cultural vehicle moves between realms of selves that embody fears, shame, happiness, sadness and a familial identity that is tied to the land of one's birth where daily engagements with the environment/society give birth to metaphors and symbols.

It is commonly believed that children tend to be more synaesthetic than adults. Due to limited words in their language repertoire, they have a tendency to make objects vivid by constantly referring to other objects. In doing so, they make the act of remembering easier. Thus, their metaphorical use or creation is more perceptual than ideational as in the case of poets. In Helen Haste's view, metaphors must not be regarded as 'peripheral linguistic frills' that are used by poets, they: 'provide analogies, models for explanation, and therefore facilitate innovative thought. New scientific ideas, for example, frequently arise as a result of a shift to a new metaphor. Metaphors are a bridge in communication; because speaker and audience share a common culture, a metaphor from one domain can enlarge meaning in another. And by using a familiar metaphor, we can communicate novel concepts.'[300]

Language is saturated with quiescent metaphors, and people using them are often unaware of the ways in which they enrich meaning, or the subliminal effect they have on perception and action. Those metaphors (with multisensory qualities) are conduits; they enable a new way of seeing, feeling, understanding and projection. In Haitian, frequently, metaphors carry environmental epithets (animal and food). Those epithets are usually very reductionist and loaded. In Haitian, for example, '*jouman*,' connotes a severe insult towards a type of personality or a criticism of a certain kind of behaviour. People are usually referred to as a 'pig' for being filthy or lazy; a 'dog,' for having a lack of self-respect; a 'monkey,' for being ugly; a 'donkey,' for being a brute; and a 'cat,' which carries multiple meanings (sneaky and thieving, but also used in reference to a woman's vagina). In the case of the latter, the cat (black) is usually very furry, docile and always ready to be stroked. Certain metaphors, regardless of affect, appeal to something deep inside of us and have assiduous effects.

A metaphor, though clearly a product of someone's mind, reaches backward into synaesthesia and forward into symbol. In one direction, it becomes an automatic response and in the other, it becomes a product of culture, an act of the 'collective' imagination. At the centre of metaphoric production, regardless of the 'metaphorical concept,' culture is the operant core. Hence, I am in agreement with Haste that they 'are important, therefore, both in an individual's own interpretation and in communication with others; shared metaphors, symbols and images are crucial for the effective negotiation of meaning.'[301] Accordingly, the metaphors we use reflect the overall disposition and acceptance of certain views that are represented metaphorically. The 'women as food' metaphor is a consequence of the patriarchal nature of the Haitian society; and the overall permeation of gastronomical metaphors in the culture is a product of a society that has a strong preoccupation with food. Hence, when the well-known Haitian novelist, Dany Laferrière, entitled his fourth novel '*Le goût des jeunes filles*' (The Flavor of Young Girls), his readers and critics were not surprised given the literary exotic slant of his previous works. This coming of age novel, with its protagonist discovering poetry and the taste of women while hiding from Duvalier's Macoutes, has become an important yet touching literary work that contributes to the overall tapestry of Haitian culture.

As Gauguin metaphorically and literally fused sexuality with food in both his actions and his art while in Tahiti, Laferrière creatively and symbolically uses one of Gauguin's colourful paintings, (which features two girls, one of which is bare-breasted and holding a pail of red fruits), as the backdrop for a room where one of the girls in the novel gets dressed and the young protagonist secretly enjoys the view from his room in the house across the street. Conscious of the voyeuristic symbolism as well as the metaphorical rapprochement of the milieus, he writes after a short description of the girls' breasts and beauty that: 'there is always a confusion between Haiti and Tahiti.'[302] As Gauguin created his own 'paradise' in Tahiti, Laferrière through 'Le goût des jeunes filles' creates his paradise as the *Macoutes* were destroying life around him. Through their arts, both Gauguin and Laferrière used the body of the other as food, thus a metaphorical 'container.'

As we have seen, the predominance of the gastronomical metaphors that are couched in cultural analogies proves that language is not only reflective, but it is also constitutive of social realities. Grammatical construction and meaning alone are insufficient to penetrate cultural and philosophical intentions that are embedded through metaphorical constructions unless contextual linkages are found in the modalities of the cultural edifice of meaning where memories, histories, habits, metonymies and tropes reside. The metaphors of war that are prevalent in the United States are not translatable, for the most part, into Haitian because of the historical and social-relational nature of language development that is environmentally and culturally specific. The Haitian gastronomical metaphors that I have categorized are for the most part specific to Haiti and arose out of an agricultural environment that is labour intensive and a cultural environment that is undemocratic and where needs are immediate. Thus the cultural coping mechanisms as well as the distinctions employed have helped to inform the metaphorical parameters in ways that are culturally specific and can only be methodically decoded by an expert native, or an outsider with comparative native knowledge. Hence, the verb/noun '*manje*' used in metaphorical terms can be difficult to grasp given the socio-cultural underpinnings.

In the mid-1990s, the metaphor 'Granmanjè' (big eater), comprised of an adjective and a noun, became compounded to form at times a noun, or an adjective describing a noun. For example, '*politisyen granmanjè*' is a voracious politician; the term denotes either corruption or corrupted politicians. The emergence of this new metaphor evolved in the continuance of gastronomical metaphors where food as a celebrated cultural and biological form of sustenance can be transposed into the political realm where it becomes either exclusive or inclusive. In Haiti's political culture where the people are always excluded from the realm of power and development, they created the ultimate expression for the corruptible politicians who consume without sharing: '*Granmanjè*'.

Given Haiti's history of slavery, dictatorship and deprivation, making the consumptive potentiality of the other is central to the cultural prowess of absorption, and the ingestive mode of dominance is a pillar within the gastronomic equation of representation. Symbolically, the relational of power and dominance is rested on the possibility of subject-object consumption: '*mwen ka manje ou*' (I can eat you), followed by a defiant response: '*ou pa ka manje mwen*' (you cannot eat me). Such consumptive parlance within the metaphorical realm provides a cultural system of knowledge that enables social scientists to analyze metaphors across multiple disciplines and are as a result, infinitely important to an understanding that lies beyond semantic and lexical meanings. As Linda Olds explains: 'because of its special status and relevance to all forms of human inquiry, it has the potential for facilitating communication between fields.'[303] Not only is the study of metaphor crucial to interdisciplinary understandings, it, especially in the Haitian context, allows one to fully grasp the common experiences within the culture that grounds its metaphors.

13. RECIPES FOR DISASTER?: THE KITCHEN AS CREATIVE SPACE IN LATIN AMERICAN WOMEN'S FICTION

Alexandra Fitts (University of Alaska Fairbanks)

More than three hundred years ago (1691), Mexican nun, poet, and playwright Sor Juana Inés de la Cruz clearly elaborated the links between women, cooking, and literary creation:

> Pues ¿qué os pudiera contar, Señora, de los secretos naturales que he descubierto estando guisando? Veo que un huevo se une y fríe en la manteca o aceite y, por contrario, se despedaza en el almíbar [...]. Por no cansaros con tales frialdades, que sólo refiero por daros entera noticia de mi natural y creo que os causará risa; pero, señora, ¿qué podemos saber las mujeres sino filosofías de cocina? Bien dijo Lupercio Leonardo, que bien se puede filosofar y aderezar la cena. Y yo suelo decir viendo estas cosillas: Si Aristóteles hubiera guisado, mucho más hubiera escrito.[304]

Sor Juana lays forth the key elements of the issue: women are so often confined to the domestic sphere that the kitchen becomes their only locus of knowledge and creation, but the 'philosophies of the kitchen' may be as valid and as valuable as knowledge generated in the public, masculine arena. In fact, there may be a particular kind of creation that happens in the feminine sphere from which men may have been excluded. By addressing herself to a female reader ('my lady') she also establishes a community of women who might learn from each other's kitchen experiments. While women may have been confined to the kitchen by patriarchal forces, they can find power by transforming that prison into a schoolroom and learning from the resources at hand. On the other hand, the fact that the 'lady' addressed in this passage is no lady at all, but rather a male bishop who had criticized Sor Juana for overstepping the reach of both her vocation and her gender makes Sor Juana's *faux* humility more biting while further problematizing the dichotomy between male power and female marginalization.

The connection that Sor Juana makes between the knowledge generated through the science of the kitchen and the creative process of writing is one that continues to echo today in Latin American women's and Latina writing. While Virginia Woolf may not have been thinking of the kitchen as 'the room of one's own' that would be necessary in order for women to engage in literary activity, it can be argued that the kitchen has long served as the site of women's power and production. Women writers of the twentieth and twenty-first centuries have alternately rejected that supremely domestic space and embraced it as a source of creativity, community, and empowerment. But while the kitchen may be the locus of women's creative power, it also serves as a strong symbol of subservience and oppression, making it a particularly fraught literary setting. The eroticism of food is undeniable, with the mix of smell, taste, and touch that a good meal provides, but it is impossible to ignore the heavily loaded connection that is too often made between women, sex, and food.

Mexican writer Rosario Castellanos' classic story, 'Lección de cocina (Cooking Lesson),' published in 1971, clearly reflects the feminist awareness of its time and of Castellanos herself. For the narrator, the kitchen is a place of confinement that serves to limit her access to the professional and public spheres. Castellanos challenges the essentialist notion of women's innate ties to cooking, and by extension, to nurturing. The formerly competent woman in the story finds herself dumbstruck by the task of preparing the first meal for her new husband, for she has no innate connection to the kitchen or instinctive sense for cooking. Still, she states, 'Mi lugar está aquí. Desde el principio de los tiempos he estado aquí', realizing that as wife, she has been removed from the public world and must accept, if not embrace, her new position.[305] A writer, she attempts a fruitless literary analysis of her cookbooks and calls in vain on the community of women that she wishes could help her with this seemingly impossible chore: 'Cómo podría llevar al cabo labor tan ímproba sin la colaboración de la sociedad, de la historia entera [...]. Qué me aconseja usted para la comida de hoy, experimentada ama de casa, inspiración de las madres presentes y ausentes, voz de la tradición?'[306] She views domesticity as a code, or a secret, and no one has given her the key; she seems as excluded from the science of the kitchen as were the men Sor Juana wrote about. Very aware that her new role is precisely that (she hopes that she will get a different part in her 'next movie') she still sees no alternative but to accept it. She contemplates her metamorphosis from professional, independent woman to dependent wife as she watches the burning steak transform into a charred mass of flesh.

Castellanos offers no redemption of the domestic – the narrator refers to herself as an unpaid servant. The kitchen is not a space of production, be it culinary, literary, or personal, but of destruction. The meal is a disaster, her autonomous identity is disappearing as quickly as the shrivelling meat, and the marriage is clearly doomed from the outset. Already, she reflects on their courtship and honeymoon with nostalgia, as she wonders whether she can use the burnt meat as a tool to manipulate her husband into taking her to a restaurant (and back into public, albeit in a limited way). The comparison is obvious when she discusses her own sunburned flesh on her seaside honeymoon and the charred, unrecognizable meat: 'Aparece, primero el trozo de carne con un color, una forma, un tamaño. Luego cambia y se pone más bonita y se siente una muy contenta. Luego vuelve a cambiar y ya no está tan bonita. Y sigue cambiando y cambiando y cambiando y lo que uno no atina es cuándo pararle el alto'.[307] But she actually envies the meat because 'A esta carne su mamá no le enseñó que era carne y que debería comportarse con conducta'.[308] In a sense, the meat is just fulfilling its destiny, but she cannot accept the 'destiny' that is being artificially, but inescapably, forced upon her.

About a decade after Castellanos, Rosario Ferré evokes a theoretical connection between the productivity of cooking and writing in 'La cocina de la escritura':

> Lo importante es aplicar esa lección fundamental que aprendimos de nuestras madres, las primeras, después de todo, a enseñarnos a bregar con fuego: el secreto de la escritura, como el de la buena cocina, no tiene absolutamente nada que ver con el sexo, sino con la sabiduría con la que se combinan los ingredientes.[309]

For Ferré, writing, like cooking, is about transforming one thing to create another and of bringing together disparate ingredients in the crafting of something new. Castellanos, however, sees the kitchen as an arid, infertile place, one more of destruction than any kind of creation. The room is described in terms that seem more appropriate to an operating room than a warm centre of creativity and feminine power – it is white, spotless, clean, impeccable, For her, the room that has been deemed her own is solitary confinement, and antithetical to the kind of literary creativity and freedom that she had experienced in the world outside the kitchen. Nor does the kitchen provide the solace of female community or of knowledge passed from woman to woman that Ferré celebrates. Castellanos' narrator never mentions her own mother, but it is obvious that she has not been taught to cook. The 'experienced housewife' that she invokes is as distant to her as Dear Abby, whom she also considers as a last resort. In any case, the sarcastic tone with which she addresses this invisible 'señora' implies that any domestic or maternal advice would probably be unwelcome and unheeded as she chafes against the role that she has been cast into. Castellanos' story serves as a seething (sizzling?) criticism of the institution of a 1970s marriage and of the Mexican ideal of the obedient wife who will sacrifice herself to serve her husband and family.

Laura Esquivel's 1990 novel, *Como agua para chocolate* (*Like Water for Chocolate*) is probably the best known and most analyzed example of Latin American writing that combines cooking with fiction, and was also the basis for a highly successful film. The novel is subtitled 'Novela de entregas mensuales con recetas, amores y remedios caseros' (A Novel in Monthly Installments with Recipes, Romances, and Home Remedies) and the narrative is interspersed with recipes, purposely blurring the lines between the culinary and the literary. In the story, which takes place during the Mexican Revolution, Tita is the youngest daughter of the family and her prescribed destiny is to remain unmarried so that she can take care of her aging (and thoroughly domineering) mother. Sadly, Tita is wildly in love with Pedro, who marries her unpleasant sister Rosaura so that he can be near his true love, Tita. For the most part, Tita is confined to the house, and primarily to the kitchen, where she learns about cooking and nurturing from the indigenous cook, Nacha. Tita's emotional connection to her cooking is so strong that the emotions that she feels when she prepares the food are transferred to those who eat the meal. As she makes the feast for Pedro and Rosaura's wedding reception, the tears that fall into the cake cause all of the guests to burst into uncontrollable sobs even as they try to celebrate. Like the narrator of 'Cooking Lesson,' Tita accepts the role that she has been given (though much more passively), and she and Pedro only unite when both Tita's mother and Pedro's wife have died, but their joy is short-lived, as the erotic spark produced by their lovemaking causes Pedro to die of a heart attack and the bed to literally go up in flames.

Like Water for Chocolate celebrates the space of the kitchen as the locus of feminine power and creativity. Esquivel's work puts a positive spin on the possibilities for women's gastronomic creativity as Tita finds her power in the kitchen and its strong links with Mexico's nurturing feminine and indigenous past. Starting with the epigraph of the novel 'a la mesa y a la cama una sola vez se llama' (to the table or to bed you must come when you are bid) it also makes explicit the link between cooking, eating, and sex. For these reasons, many readers, viewers, and critics praised what seemed to be progress from Castellanos' militant rejection of the kitchen.[310] Rather than cast aside a source of women's creativity and empowerment, Esquivel embraces the kitchen and finds in it a female community to contest patriarchal power, thus continuing the legacy of Sor Juana's kitchen philosophy. Cecilia Lawless writes that 'Tita participates in a reconstruction of the kitchen and its tools as a positive site for change'[311] and movie reviewers praised the film's tasty mix of magic, sex, and spice. For film critic Roger Ebert, '*Like Water for Chocolate* creates its own intense world of passion and romance, and adds a little comedy and a lot of quail, garlic, honey, chiles, mole, cilantro, rose petals and corn meal.'[312] It reigned as the highest earning foreign film in U.S. history for about a decade.

However, upon examination, it is difficult to classify the novel or the movie as empowering of women given its essentialist portrayals of the ideal woman as a simultaneous nurturer and sexual object. In some ways, the novel may seem to offer alternative sources of authority for women, but in fact it actually serves to reinforce stereotypes: good women, and Latin American women in particular, are seen as confined to the domestic space, and above all, as belonging there. In contrast to Rosario Castellanos' repudiation of the essentialist linking of women and cooking, in *Like Water for Chocolate* Tita's connection to the kitchen is a natural, almost biological one. She was, in fact, born on the kitchen table. Throughout the novel, Tita virtually never leaves the kitchen, unless she is serving meals or acting as a sexual object. And she is very much an object of desire, rather than an agent. In one scene, Tita is grinding grain on the stone floor of the kitchen:

> Bajo su blusa sus senos se meneaban libremente pues ella nunca usó sostén alguno. De su cuello escurrían gotas de sudor que rodaban hacia abajo siguiendo el surco de piel entre sus pechos redondos y duros. Pedro, no pudiendo resistir los olores que emanaban de la cocina, se dirigió hacia ella, quedando petrificado en la puerta ante; a sensual postura en que se encontró a Tita. Tita levantó la vista sin dejar de moverse y sus ojos se encontraron con los de Pedro. Inmediatamente, sus miradas enardecidas se

fundieron de tal manera que quien los hubiera visto sólo habría notado una sola mirada, un solo movimiento rítmico y sensual, una sola respiración agitada y un mismo deseo.[313]

The maleness of the erotic gaze here is unquestionable, as is the sensual equation of food/ smell/ kitchen/ woman/ sex. It is, after all, Pedro who finds the scene 'erotic.' We get little sense of what our protagonist is feeling, or what produces her 'passionate gaze.' Particularly problematic is the way that this scene ignores the physicality of real food production. I have never done it, but I am willing to bet that most women grinding meal on their knees on a stone floor would not be glorying in the eroticism of their heaving braless breasts. In this scene and throughout the novel Tita's sexuality is objectified, subservient, and maternal. She is the nurturer, providing food for the family in all ways. When her sister is unable to nurse her and Pedro's baby, Tita somehow manages to do it, though she has never been pregnant. Maite Zubiaurre discusses Tita's strange positioning as a sexual object who at the same time exhibits little sexual desire herself, and is in fact a virgin through most of the novel: 'the more able and caring mothers in *Like Water for Chocolate* are unmarried, presumably virgins, and of course, extraordinarily talented and experienced cooks'.[314] The biological mothers in the novel are fairy-tale caricatures of spite and neglect, but kind, pure, self-sacrificing Tita proves to be the real maternal figure. She is, in fact, precisely the model of selfless Mexican womanhood that Rosario Castellanos railed against two decades earlier.

Janice Jaffe states that *Like Water for Chocolate* establishes a community of intergenerational, multi-ethnic women that 'defies the norms' of Mexican culture by creating a female community.[315] However, it is difficult to see exactly how this novel and film defy norms: The only particularly nurturing relationship that Tita has is with Nacha, the indigenous cook and nanny. Being cared for by the earthy native servant rather than the frigid, white mother is not particularly groundbreaking. As Zubiaurre points out, in *Like Water for Chocolate*, 'the kitchen mirrors an authoritarian and segregationist society; instead of fostering an alternative sense of community, solidarity, and equalitarian justice among women'.[316] The racial messages of the book may actually be more objectionable than its portrayal of women – it is only Tita's sister Gertrudis who revels in unashamed rebellious sexuality, but her natural sensuality and rhythm are later explained by the revelation that the father of Gertrudis was a mulatto.

The celebration of women's traditional work – cooking, quilting, sewing, as artistry and power is potentially empowering, but that is not the effect of Esquivel's novel. Instead, it reifies the stereotype of the Latin woman as simultaneously submissive, maternal, and sexy. I think of an old perfume commercial where the woman boasted that she could 'bring home the bacon, fry it up in a pan, and never let you forget you're a man' except Tita is not even allowed into the public sphere to bring home the bacon.[317] Any power that Tita possesses is directly tied to her position as surrogate mother and object of impossible desire.

Perhaps due to the commercial success of *Like Water for Chocolate*, the 1990s saw a spate of books by and for women that intertwined storytelling with recipes. Among them is Chilean Isabel Allende's 1997 *Afrodita: Cuentos, Recetas y Otros Afrodisíacos* (*Aphrodite: a Memoir of the Senses*). Part memoir, part natural history, part cookbook, and part erotic manual, Allende's book is difficult to categorize, and maybe for that reason it has not received an enormous amount of attention, and critical reviews were mixed. Still, many readers were thrilled to find what they have come to expect from Allende – lively storytelling with a dollop of sex and a sprinkling of magic. It is made up of mini-chapters with titles like 'En la variedad está el sabor' (The Spice is in Variety), 'Pecados de la carne' (Sins of the Flesh), and 'Con la punta de la lengua' (With the Tip of the Tongue). Allende refers to it as 'un viaje sin mapa por las regions sensuales', implying the groundbreaking nature of the enterprise.[318] As a contrast to the creatively stifling kitchen in Castellanos, Allende celebrates the connections between not just sex and food, but also writing. She states:

Hacia el final, cuando los colaboradores de este proyecto creíamos haber terminado y estábamos en las últimas revisiones, comprendimos que entre tantos afrodisíacos, desde mariscos con hierbas y especias, hasta camisas de encaje, luces rosadas y sales aromáticas para el baño, había uno, el más poderoso de todos, que no habíamos incluido: los cuentos.[319]

Although in some ways Allende treads the familiar ground of *Like Water for Chocolate*, she goes a step further by taking the woman out of the kitchen and to the bedroom. While the book contains recipes, the primary focus is on women as consumers of both food and sex. Allende recognizes that it is the subversion of expectations that is erotic: a man who knows his way around a kitchen is sexy, though a woman is not necessarily so (in spite of the sweating, freely moving breasts). Likewise, a man who indulges in gluttony may not be seen as desirable, but a woman who freely indulges her appetites is. Indeed, the women of this book are not the passive Tita-type. Allende herself and the other women she writes about actively seek out desire, pleasure, and romance. There is an obvious difference between preparing food and eating it, just as there is between being an object and an agent of desire. The image of the voracious woman is both liberating and unsettling in a world where women have been taught to rigidly control appetites of all sorts. A woman who consumes rather than being passively consumed is threatening, harkening back to the *vagina dentata*, but it is also an image that is exciting in its transgressive possibilities.

Maite Zubiaurre makes a distinction between 'kitchen tales' where women are merely preparers of food, and 'table narratives' where 'women appear at the other end of the food production line, namely as 'real' consumers, and not as producers, endowed with magical skills, of culinary delicacies'.[320] In some ways, this transition is represented in the contrast between Esquivel's Tita, who prepares and serves but almost never consumes, and Allende's avid women who consume food and sexual adventure with equal gusto. Allende does indeed take women out of the kitchen and to the table, but food is presented more as a component of eroticism and sensuality than a pleasure unto itself. For example, she proclaims that 'nada hay tan afrodisíaco como la *mousse au chocolate* sobre la piel' but goes on to counsel that the mousse should be on your skin rather than your partner's because you would have to lick it off 'y contiene muchas calorías'.[321] In other passages, she describes voluptuous, full-figured women who presumably care less than she about calories, but they too are presented as sexual objects: in one case, the woman is fed delicacies by her professor in a failed attempt at seduction. So while Allende's women do eat, their consumption of food is mediated by its effect on a male lover and with an eye to the waistline.

While Allende includes writing as an important aphrodisiac, it seems in many ways that the eroticism of story-telling which Allende discusses is more linked to cooking than to eating: the spark comes from the effect that the finished product has on others more than from the process itself. The consumer, or viewer, or reader, or eater is still generally meant to be someone else. Joy Logan points out the other-focused nature of the book's eroticism: 'Allende equates the eroticism of storytelling with the erotic gaze. Being told, being observed, is being eroticized or enhancing the desire of an other desiring agency.'[322] She also discusses the preponderance of female nudes in the book's illustrations (not to mention the ever evocative half-opened flower buds) and the lack of corresponding males to serve as the object of the desiring gaze. So, while Allende does fulfil Zubiaurre's definition of a 'table narrative' by taking the woman out of the kitchen and to the table and the bed, ultimately it is a male who is meant to be the consumer of the food, the paintings, and the stories. The celebration of a woman who takes sexual pleasure in providing for a man is certainly a step beyond Tita's subservience, but the continued connection between women, food, and sex is not necessarily groundbreaking.

While *Como agua para chocolate* and *Afrodita* were written in Spanish, they were both popular among U.S. English-language audiences. Esquivel's novel had more success, probably due to the popularity of the film, but Allende remains among the most-read Latin American writers in the U.S. The popularity of these works reflects the trendiness of the novel or memoir cum cookbook that also relies on stereotypes about exoticism and otherness. One of the most salient facts about recipe/ cooking/ fiction narratives à la Allende in the United States is that they are almost invariably written by women – a pretty clear indication that cooking is still women's work – and very often by women from minority and foreign cultures. A recent article listed 14 such works, 13 by women and 1 by a man. Furthermore, 3 were from and about mainstream white U.S. culture, while the other 11 were by Latina, Indian, African, Jewish, and Chinese-American women writers.[323]

The facile linking of spicy food and spicy woman in these books allows for a sort of sensual armchair tourism and colonialist consumption of the exotic while reinforcing ethnic and gendered stereotypes. Writing about the U.S. interest in ethnic cooking and cookbooks, Lisa Heldke identifies what she refers to as 'cultural food colonialism', the impulse to 'collect cultural artefacts from another culture without thinking about the appropriateness of removing them from their cultural setting'.[324] In Heldke's case, the cultural artefacts in question are recipes, and she describes the process by which consumers of ethnic recipes seek to increase their own 'novelty' and exoticism by sampling the Other. Such an enterprise is always gendered in nature: as with the cooking novel or memoir, the cookbook reader is overwhelmingly female and she is able to enhance her own imagined sexual appeal by her proximity to the stereotypical exotic woman who 'provides just the right touch of beauty, mystery, and servility to get us Western gals into the spirit of imagining ourselves as the heroines of this colonialist culinary tale'.[325] Much the same could be said of the reader or viewer of Esquivel or Allende's works – it is all too easy to enter into the romanticism of the earthy Latin woman who is indelibly connected to food and sex. Writing about *Like Water for Chocolate*, Miguel Segovia challenges 'the implications of women as food and food as metonym for Mexican and Chicana/o identity within Latin American and popular U.S. culture'.[326] For him, U.S. audiences accept the authority of the narrator (and presumably of the Mexican writer) and do not recognize the essentialist and racist overtones of the novel and film: 'Anglos fail to question these representations due to stereotypes of Mexican women and patriarchal views of cultural domesticity'.[327] The stereotype of the Latin woman as a 'hot tamale' is a difficult one to combat.

'STUFF' a play by Coco Fusco and Nao Bustamante (first performed in 1996) is a pointed response to cultural tourism, food colonialism, and sexual exploitation. Fusco, Cuban-American, and Bustamante, a Chicana, wrote the play to 'look at the cultural myths that link Latin women and food to the erotic in the Western imagination'.[328] To them, 'if food serves as a metaphor for sex, then eating represents consumption in its crudest form'.[329] They are particularly concerned with the kind of tourism (literal or metaphorical) that equates exoticism with sex and erases the difference between the consumption of food and of women. The play follows Blanca and Rosa, representatives of the 'Institute for Southern Hemispheric Wholeness'. The 'Institute' mixes New-Age mumbo jumbo with 'authentic food and music' and lovely women for those travellers who wish to avoid the 'tropical storms, masked bandits, parasites, and poverty' that might mar a Latin American vacation.[330] The women describe the drudgery of food production and sex work and another character, Judy, a 'Spanish-speaking transvestite', makes the connection between sex and food clear, as she knows that bringing home a man will also mean bringing home some food for her hungry family. The clients of the Institute are parodies of the Western consumer and traveller, as they learn only enough Spanish words to order margaritas and the appropriate lines to pick up women as sexual partners (who suggest that they could use some 'financial support'). One client complains about having paid too much:

> They said the camote was an aphrodisiac, so I ate five and all they gave me was the runs. I was hoping to get a little more – you know what I mean. And those girls weren't exactly spring chickens. I thought it would be more like those kinds of places – it's like the way everybody moves, the way they let you know things with their hands.[331]

The disillusioned client imagined an experience where he would not have had to communicate with the women, who would have let him know things 'with their hands'. Maybe the few pick-up lines in Spanish were too much to learn. 'STUFF' challenges the very assumptions made by *Like Water for Chocolate* and *Aphrodite*. For Fusco and Bustamante, food preparation and service can be neither empowering nor erotic as long as stereotype, essentialism, and differentials of power enter into the equation.

In 'Mimesis and Metaphor: Food Imagery in Twentieth Century Women's Writing', Harriet Blodgett states that 'observably, men are more inclined to link food with sexuality than women, who attach it rather to female roles and status in their writing.'[332] In part, my questioning of Esquivel's and Allende's reframing of the kitchen as erotic and empowering is based on precisely this distinction: it is easier to see the sensuality of food preparation if one has not been historically confined and constrained by it. She recognizes that some women writers focus on the 'life-enhancing abilities' of the woman as cook, others are more inclined to 'object to her domestic servitude' and that third-world writers are more likely to fall into the latter category, presumably given their greater familiarity with the strictures of poverty and patriarchy.[333] Blodgett goes on to ponder whether women are enslaved or empowered by their roles as 'food givers' and says that 'feminism since the 1960s has [...] inspired vociferous complaints about women's traditional role as purveyor of food'.[334] Some critics cast 'feminists' into the role of backward-looking complainer, suggesting that Castellanos wrote 'in a different time' and that in this post-feminist era it is possible to move beyond a view of food and the kitchen as symbols of oppression.[335] I fear, however, that we have not progressed into nearly such a post-feminist division of domestic labour, particularly when we think about Latin America. Women still are responsible for food preparation to a much greater degree than are men, even in the United States. A 2008 NSF study reports that childless married women in the U.S. do an average of 10 hours per week more housework than their husbands (17 hours to the man's 7 hours), while married women with children spend 28 hours a week on household work while their husbands put in 10 hours.[336] Meanwhile, a 2007 Norwegian report found that, of 34 countries studied, Chilean women logged the most housework in the world at 38 hours a week.[337] And an Organization for Economic Cooperation and Development (OECD) study of 29 countries found that the highest unpaid labour differential between men and women was in Mexico, where women worked more than four hours a day more than men and where 'tasks that have traditionally been thought of 'women's work' (e.g. cooking and cleaning) continue to be primarily performed by women'.[338] The notion that we have left behind the era of Sor Juana, Rosario Castellanos, or 'STUFF', where the kitchen is a space that limits women's freedom seems an idealized one. I see both Esquivel and Allende as presenting a romanticized notion of cooking and food that too often ignores not only the realities of domestic labour but also the damaging conflation of women, sex, and food. It seems that too little has changed since the times of Castellanos or even of Sor Juana to easily celebrate the power of the kitchen or the eroticism of cooking.

14. AMERICAN FRIENDSHIPS AND HEMISPHERIC DISCOURSE

Priscilla Archibald (Roosevelt University)

American avant-garde movements are often contextualized in an international arena. Paris is generally cited as the centre for artistic creativity in the early decades of the twentieth century; in the case of poetry, London and Madrid were likewise important sites for artistic migration. What has been eclipsed in this Europe-centred narrative, however, as well as in the various nationalist alternatives, is the relationship between the avant-garde movements of Anglo-America and Latin America. Narratives that emerged at the end of the nineteenth century, which contrast a pragmatic and puritanical Anglo-American culture with a spiritually rich if economically challenged Hispanic American culture, and which oppose the provincial Americas with a cosmopolitan Paris, have made it difficult for scholars to appreciate the hemispheric cosmopolitanism of a number of writers and literary cultures in the first half of the twentieth century. While many well-known figures in North and South American literary circles in the 1920s, 30s and 40s were inclined to look toward Europe rather than to each other, there was also a thriving trans-American intellectual community at this time. Through an analysis of the work and ideas of William Carlos Williams, a Puerto Rican-American poet long canonized as a white Anglo-American modernist, the first part of my essay examines the mono-cultural norms which circumscribed American identities in the first half of the twentieth century, as well as 'knowledge' about the Americas. The second part of this essay examines the intellectual friendship and collaboration between U.S. cultural critic, Waldo Frank and Peruvian Marxist José Carlos Mariátegui that flourished in spite of the Hispanic-Anglo divide. This hemispheric relationship brings the difficulties and possibilities of trans-American exchange into sharp relief.

The two North Americans examined in this essay represent a study in opposites. Nothing could be further from Williams' emphasis on form or the 'mathematics' of poetic language than Frank's personalized metaphysics and 'over-ripe' prose, as one critic described it.[339] The anti-metaphysical and non-symbolic poetry which Williams produced almost from the start characterized the work of many modernists, but most arrived at this point only after a lifetime of poetic experimentation. If Williams disappears on the page, Frank looms large. In his spiritual agenda, the Americas are assigned the task of restoring 'wholeness' to the world, and Frank, one cannot help but conclude, is ultimately the prophet of this messianic proposal.[340] In contrast to Williams, who was at the forefront of modernist experimentation, Frank was not concerned with Latin American artistic innovation; he gravitated toward regionalism, and showed little interest in the Latin American avant-garde. If Frank's tendency to prioritize content at the complete expense of formal issues is predictable enough from an ideological point of view – the plentiful South offering refuge from a modernizing North – everything about Frank's intellectual life prior to his discovery of the Hispanic world would lead one to expect a very different type of engagement with Latin American culture. Frank was one of the co-founders and editors of the journal *The Seven Arts*, which during its short life-span was an important forum for artistic experimentation, and a member of the circle of avant-garde artists and writers which took shape around the studio of Alfred Stieglitz, a key promoter of artistic innovation.

However different their world views, sensibilities, and styles, the two writers shared a similar if idiosyncratic passion. Spain held tremendous appeal for both. According to Frank, Spanish culture at one time was the highest expression, and still possessed remnants of a 'wholeness', which he believed Europe had not known since the Middle Ages. As Frank saw it, the spiritual Hispanic tradition which Spain bequeathed to Latin America was part of what would make the latter a primary protagonist in the world's regeneration. For his part, Williams identified characteristics in a local Spanish literary tradition which he regarded as a more appropriate model for a genuinely American poetic language than the English poetic tradition represented by T.S. Eliot; the latter, he contended, would ultimately be detrimental to cultural creativity. In a rich and highly original analysis of a variety of Spanish literary figures, among them Federico García Lorca and Luis de Góngora, Williams identified the same local and 'non-literary' (Góngora!) qualities he was trying to cultivate in his own poetry.[341] This admiration for Spain was far from common. The loss of Puerto Rico and Cuba to the United States in 1898 – the definitive end of the Spanish empire – for most people meant that Spain's glory belonged wholly to the past. It represented the opposite of the modernizing impulse of the twenties, and was not where most looked to find the key to the future. At the time, particularly in the United States, pan-Americanism was not universally regarded as inconsistent with pan-Hispanism. This view was not exclusive to scholars in the United States, however. José Vasconcelos, for example, whose idiosyncratic coupling of Mexican nationalist sentiment with a celebration of Hispanic cultural traditions conforms to this point of view as well.[342]

Williams and Frank shared a loathing for the Puritanical traditions which they regarded the very core of U.S. culture. Considered responsible for a host of social ills, among them, utilitarianism, economic imperialism, and cultural sterility, it would be difficult to overstate either writer's conviction about the perniciousness of the protestant legacy. As Steven Bercovitch points out, the effectiveness of this critique was limited in so far as it left the structural roots of the culture it would expunge intact.[343] The anti-puritanical critique common to many if not most intellectuals of the day was more than simply ineffectual, however. While it may have possessed some counter-cultural force, it also reinforced an emerging U.S. hegemony in so far as it catered to a cultural myth which defined U.S. identity, however negatively, as white, Anglo and protestant. As a consequence, the conflictive heterogeneity that has always characterized U.S. society disappears from view, unavailable as a creative or contestatory resource. According to Williams, only African-American culture represents an alternative tradition. Like many writers of the time, he was influenced by the primitivism then in vogue:

> Only the negro, with a keen necessity to find an equivalent, for the voodooism, the mystery of his African jungles, where one cannot see far, has been able to make a vital thing of our religion. For *the rest of us* the influence is degenerative. It is largely a persistence of the stasis of early beliefs, together with their vigor.[344]

Contextualized as it is in the binary of us-them, this highly problematic fantasy about African-American culture reinforces the dominance of the protestant culture ostensibly under critique. Even more to the point, where does this description place Williams, the poet of Puerto-Rican origin whose first language was Spanish? Beyond the one authentic African-American Other, there is only 'the rest of us'. Frank shared Williams' conviction about the pervasive protestant psychology of the United States. The fact that both writers were ethnic Americans – in Williams' case Caribbean American and in the case of Frank, Jewish American – points to the homogenizing social logic which informed thinking at the time. Neither Frank nor Williams regarded themselves as exceptions that disproved the rule, but rather their exceptional status was rendered, if not invisible, at the very least inconsequential with respect to a larger social description.[345]

If this erasure of his own difference ('the rest of us') suggests that Williams is not without some responsibility for his canonization as a white Anglo-American writer, at other times his work explicitly contests the mono-cultural logic which came to inform approaches to the Americas. Nothing could seem further from the essentializing impulse evident in this stereotype of a uniformly protestant culture than William's classic text, *In the American Grain*. *In the American Grain* is an unconventional history of the Americas, where, as Vera Kutzinsky observes, Williams 'penetrate[s] the 'dead layer' of cultural consensus and touch[es] the very roots of New World history'[346] – something that could well be said of Williams' poetry as well. In this text, Williams writes about the French Jesuit, Père Sebastian Rasles, who in the early eighteenth century lived among the Abnaki Indians in the disputed border ground of Maine, learned their language, and was accepted and even loved by them. Père Rasles is as an exemplary illustration of the 'New World' spirit Williams has in mind. According to Williams, Rasles was 'a new spirit in the New World', 'rich, blossoming, generous, able to give and to receive, full of taste, a nose, a tongue, a laugh, enduring, self-forgetful in beneficence.'[347] Among that which Williams highlights about Rasles is his ability 'to create, to hybridize, to crosspollenize',[348] qualities present in the poet's own text, if only by virtue of the fact that the Spanish, French, and Anglo Americas are dealt with in a single volume. Williams contrasts this cultural cross-pollination with the 'fear of touch' he associates with the Puritan tradition, a fear which he implies is ultimately motivated by racism: 'Do not serve another for you might have to touch him and he might be a Jew or a nigger.'[349] (Or 'a bastard from the Caribbean', to quote Ezra Pound's one-time epithet for Williams).[350]

Marjorie Perloff is certainly right when she observes that Williams' poetic work was 'far ahead of his time'.[351] His anti-interpretative writing, and belief that – quoting Poe – 'the highest order of the imaginative intellect is always pre-eminently mathematical',[352] has made him particularly attractive in the post-structuralist age,[353] as has his celebration of inter-cultural malleability. At the same time, Williams does not fulfil contemporary expectations with the consistency or to the degree that he is sometimes credited with doing. He was not a prophet all the time, and sometimes not even when he most seemed to be. Whatever Williams' celebration of cultural cross-pollination, or certain messiness with respect to human interaction, his essay on Père Sebastian Rasles is structured around an unyielding dichotomy: the Catholic versus the Protestant, the Spanish versus the Anglo. The warmth, physicality and generosity of Catholicism – 'the Spaniard gave magnificently, with a generous sweep'[354] – is paired against the meagreness of the Puritan pioneer – 'It is their littleness that explains their admirable courage [...]. Their sureness which you praise is of their tight tied littleness [...].'[355] Williams limits himself to an either/or option so that the 'new' in this case can only be the old. In a bit of eccentricity that seems worthy of Waldo Frank, Williams predicts a singular religious future for the Americas and that future will be Catholic: 'Catholicism gains in that it offers us alleviation from the dullness, the lack of touch [...].'[356] 'Alleviation' is the key word here. While modernists did not fabricate the alienation that is one of the conditions of modernity out of whole cloth, the mono-cultural myth they fostered at the expense of the multiple and competing cultural traditions that, to be accurate, did indeed exist, paradoxically reinforced the same psychic oppression they complained of.

Williams may well be able to celebrate Catholicism's sensuality, and overlook its history of oppression – particularly in Iberian America, because as a world power, it is at this point but a shadow of its former self, and comparatively almost innocuous. It is less easy, however, to explain away Williams' more explicitly anti-democratic comments: 'Let everybody be rich and so equal. What a farce! But what a tragedy!'[357] (Nor, for that matter, can one explain away the reflexive Eurocentricism where the French rather than the Native Americans are the heroes of an exemplary borderland experience). Who is speaking in this instance – the critic of North American culture, who would demystify the doctrine of social equality, less because theory does not extend to practice, but rather because he understands it to be one and the same with cultural sterility? Or, is it the Caribbean-American, whose identification with an aristocratic Spanish heritage makes him more comfortable with social privilege than he otherwise might have been? This is not really an either/or question.

Given that his mother migrated from Puerto Rico in the late nineteenth century, that his father, though born in England, was raised in the Dominican Republic, and that Spanish was his first language, Williams' work is complex in a way that his longstanding label as 'white' American modernist,[358] and more recent identification with linguistic and cultural post-modernity do not begin to suggest. Williams was caught between his own ethnic and national heterogeneity, and social imperatives of the day. In *The Spanish American Roots of William Carlos Williams*, Julio Marzán refers to a critical assessment of Williams which illustrates the difficulties scholars have had in pinning down the poets' relationship to his *latinidad*:

> According to Townley, Williams identified with the peasants he saw in Spain and sometimes spoke in the voice of Carlos, an old Spanish peasant. This assertion makes no sense at all, as Williams consistently looked back at an aristocratic Spanish background [...]. Inexplicably, however, even though Townley continues to identify Carlos as an occasional literary device, he contradicts the force of his own previous observations by subsequently claiming that the significance of Williams' Spanish heritage was 'impossible to understand,' and this declaration is the only justification he gives for simply dropping the subject.[359]

The inconsistencies Marzán draws attention to are instructive. The idea that Williams could not have identified with a 'Spanish peasant' because he 'looked back at an aristocratic Spanish background' attributes Williams with a more stable and unitary identity than was the case. Because his family had established itself in the United States prior to the massive immigration of so many Puerto Ricans, and because they did not share the modest origins of many of these immigrants, he did not identify with the decolonizing Latin American nationalist rhetoric of the early decades of the twentieth century. (In addition to schools in New Jersey, Williams studied in Geneva and Paris, and attended the prestigious

Horace Mann High School before going on to obtain a medical degree from the University of Pennsylvania). Not only were the more stable identities associated with Latin American nationalism most likely unavailable to Williams, he probably had little need for them. The highly textual upper class Spanish legacy bequeathed to Williams by his mother takes on meaning in the context of turn-of-the century Puerto Rico, and distinguishes him from more recent immigrant populations from Latin America, whereas his identification with a popular oral Spanish tradition responds more to the realities of his life in working class New Jersey – a hub of modernity as it were – and, however ironically, to the need to decolonize Anglo-American poetic diction. Because Williams was situated at the intersection of multiple temporalities and cultural and linguistic traditions, the contradictions underscored by Marzán are, in an operative sense, not contradictions at all. In accounting for the various personal and literary lineages Williams had recourse to, the stress should be on multiplicity over consistency, and biographical inventiveness and selection over biographical fact.

In the essay 'Federico García Lorca', Williams may not identify himself as a Spanish peasant, but he does identify with a 'local' and popular Spanish literary tradition. Retrospectively, it may seem surprising that the author of *In the American Grain* looks toward the work of the Spanish writer, Federico García Lorca, as a model for the specifically American vernacular he had in mind. That Williams shared these ideas about Lorca in a speech delivered at the First Inter-American Writers Conference in Puerto Rico in 1941 may seem even more surprising, particularly since Williams believed that a genuinely American writing would be in direct opposition to the English literary tradition represented by T.S. Eliot. As Miguel Mota puts it, Williams seems 'curiously oblivious' to his surroundings, or to how his poetic project might translate in the context of Latin American cultural politics.[360] This failure to identify with (or simply identify) the project of Latin American cultural decolonization reminds us that at this point pan-Hispanism and pan-Americanism are not by definition mutually exclusive – or, in other words, Spain was not yet universally identified as the foil to Latin

American cultural authenticity. Given this non-identification on Williams' part, one might be more inclined to associate his own project of poetic decolonization with the emergence of U.S. hegemony than with the oppositional decolonizing movements which were gaining momentum across Latin America at the time. Williams' choice of a Spanish poet as model, however, points to the precarious place he himself occupies in this emerging hegemony.

In the context of this particular essay, the literary tradition to which Lorca belongs represents not so much an interruption or a decentring of the English literary tradition that Williams found so oppressive, rather a replacement for it. The way that Spain would step in for Britain is evident on another occasion when Williams draws attention to the similarities between the United States and Spain:

> Sixteenth and seventeenth century Spain and Spaniards are nearer to us in the United States today than, perhaps, England ever was. It is a point worth at least taking under consideration. We in the United States are climactically as by latitude and weather much nearer Spain than England, as also in the volatility of our spirits, in racial mixture – much more like Gothic and Moorish Spain.[361]

Similar to Williams' text about Père Sebastian Rasles, this reference to Spain is thematically decentring and formally centring. While Williams may refer to 'racial mixture,' it is in a strangely impersonal way, particularly given the cultural and linguistic hybridity which he himself represents, and which inspired his hosts to invite him to speak in the first place. Spain mirrors an indivisible and uniform social body: 'We in the United States are [...] much nearer to Spain than England.' The 'us' mentioned here ('nearer to us') echoes the type of uniform body Williams' earlier referred to as 'the rest of us', with the important difference that, in the earlier reference, the 'us' is irremediably protestant as opposed to quasi-Spanish. In this instance, Spain is not the heritage of some North Americans, say, certain populations in the Western United States, or certain sectors on the East Coast, but, Williams claims, based on the reality of cultural and geographical kinship (which can almost substitute for historical fact), it represents a more likely heritage for all Americans than England ever did. Williams senses that the case he is pressing upon the reader (or listener) is not entirely credible, however, because at heart it is based on a wish for something that is contrary to historical fact. 'It is a point worth at least taking under consideration [...],' he implores. But Williams dissimulates. While he may write himself out of the picture, this fantasy of an alternative U.S. heritage where Spain just happens to be the logical replacement for England, is in fact profoundly personal (it would probably not be the first choice of an Italian-American, for example), something which belies the ostensible act of centring (mirroring), and alludes to what Spain and the Spanish-speaking world really did mean for many in the United States during the first half of the twentieth century – whether that be Latin American immigration, or the conflictive Spanish-Anglo encounters that took place on what would become U.S. territory. The 'we' that Williams presents as transparent was in fact anything but, and for many, as his proposal of an alternative national lineage suggests, it was an identity that was neither fully accessible nor expendable, hence, the impossible contradictions of the Spanish-speaking Anglo-American modernist, William Carlos Williams.

If a close examination of the strategies and inconsistencies of William Carlos Williams points to linguistic and cultural negotiations that traversed an ostensible mono-culturalism, the dialogue between the Peruvian Marxist José Carlos Mariátegui and North American man of letters, Waldo Frank, offers a point of departure from which to examine the complexities of the inter-American dialogue that took place during the early decades of the twentieth century.[362] While as a whole, North American writers and intellectuals may not have been overly preoccupied with Latin America or their Latin American counterparts in the early decades of the twentieth century, there were those who were, and Frank, who was an historian, a journalist, literary critic and novelist, was the most prominent among them. After a trip to Spain in the early 1920s, he became a devoted hispanophile, something confirmed by his nine-month speaking tour of Latin America in 1929. Though Frank enjoyed enormous popularity in the United

States for quite some time, his star was eclipsed long before the end of his career; during the last two decades of his life, he was all but forgotten, something the Castro government was unaware of when they paid him $25,000 to write about Cuba and its new government, imagining that Frank would be the one to make revolution attractive to a North American audience. While the Spanish translations of his work are at this point out of print, Latin Americans and Spaniards continued to read Frank long after he had disappeared from the North American intellectual arena. Associating with intellectuals and writers such as José Vasconcelos, Victoria Ocampo and José Carlos Mariátegui, Frank had an influence in Latin America that went far beyond that of a cultural dilettante; it was he, for example, who suggested to Ocampo that she found a publication dedicated to the creation of a hemispheric literary community, which would become the highly influential journal, *Sur*.

Until very recently, U.S. scholars have not paid much attention to Waldo Frank. He represents the type of anomaly often left out of intellectual histories, for a variety of reasons. His example contradicts many assumptions about inter-American cultural relations and U.S. intellectual life in the first half of the twentieth century. Moreover, given his philosophical eccentricity, his ideas cannot in themselves compensate for this anomaly or account for the popularity he long enjoyed among Hispanic intellectual communities. Notwithstanding what in retrospect seems this rather inexplicable standing, Frank was well respected in Latin America. Latin Americans regarded him as the rare North American who really understood the Hispanic world, and who viewed Latin American culture as something more than an exotic antidote to Western malaise (which is not to say that this last element was completely absent from Frank's approach to Latin America). Most simply, Latin American intellectuals liked Waldo Frank. The role that language played in this instance cannot be overestimated. The fact that Frank was one of the few North American writers who made the effort to speak and write Spanish with fluency, not only predisposed Latin Americans toward him, it made their friendship possible.

Frank was in certain respects a conventional modernist. He identified North American materialism and U.S. imperialism as two great evils of modernity, and like Williams, equated Puritanism with cultural death. He professed an ideal of 'wholeness'; true 'wholeness', according to Frank, was something that Europe had not known since the Middle Ages – the Renaissance having chipped away at Europe's one-time spiritual and social totality. America, he insisted, was but Europe's 'grave'.[363] While the particular contours of Frank's philosophy of wholeness are uniquely his own, in many respects his ideas are in line with various forms of romantic anti-capitalism, many of which idealized the medieval village as an example of an organic community, an era before the technological rationalism that would befall Europe.

If Frank considered himself first and foremost a novelist, he was better known for his writings about Latin America and his promotion of Latin American culture. Lewis Mumford considered Frank's work on Latin America his most important and lasting intellectual contribution.[364] For Frank, hispanism was more than an antidote to U.S. materialism and modernity – a view that, in itself, would not have been particularly original or unconventional. Frank's 'originality' consisted in his prophetic approach to the Americas.[365] Latin America supplied Frank's philosophy of wholeness with a teleological narrative, with the North bringing order and the South bringing body and soul. This paradigm draws on a binary that is foundational to Western thinking, where North and South America come together like platonic soul mates, with their pairing bringing about the world's redemption. Notwithstanding the platonic nature of this union, as is generally the case with binaries, one side possesses the phallus. Frank tells us that, despite its spiritual bankruptcy, it is Anglo America which possesses the 'tool'; whether Anglo America will be able to effectively wield that tool is another matter, however.[366] Though Frank may have once been regarded by parties as diverse as card-carrying communists and state department officials, as the North American expert on Latin America, the overriding teleological thrust which informs all of his work makes it difficult to appreciate whatever 'expertise' he could rightly lay claim to.

Frank's status within the U.S. intellectual community in the twenties and thirties was not without any justification. Whatever the peculiarities of his philosophy, Frank's prolific output as a scholar and writer was impressive, as was the encyclopaedic character of his knowledge. From classical to contemporary writers, there was no Western intellectual tradition or literary genre he seemed unfamiliar with, and he was a very cogent cultural critic. Though it is true that his representation of the Americas only confirmed the cultural stereotypes of a utilitarian North and a spiritual South, and that neither in the body of his texts nor in the footnotes does he adequately acknowledge the contributions that other scholars made to his own work, his comprehensive approach to Hispanic culture and commitment to learn Spanish displays intellectual integrity and uncommon intellectual ambition.

This uncommon ambition, however, proved to be Frank's weakness as much as his strength. He was a voracious reader and voluminous writer, but the degree to which his interpretations were put at the service of his own status as visionary became ever more astounding over time. Whatever Frank happened to encounter or address invariably confirmed his theories. In his first two books about the Americas, *America Hispana* and *The Re-discovery of America*, Brazil receives scant attention. Frank more than corrects for this oversight in *South American Journey*, a book written after his second speaking tour of Latin America in 1942. This time Frank is not only mindful to include Brazil. Brazil, it turns out, proffers the manna of regeneration that will make the marriage of the Americas possible. If most of what Frank encountered reinforced his notion of a quasi-divine pan-Americanism, what is conspicuously missing is any account of how his theory might become reality. Frank wrote, 'What is needed is an action which immediately brings body and spirit together in the direction of growth', but neither he nor the reader know what such an action would be.[367]

Frank saw himself as Simon Bolívar's heir. The last section of *America Hispana* bears an unmistakable resemblance to Bolívar's analysis of the Americas in his famous text, *Carta de Jamaica*. Frank's version, however, bears none of the historical specificity which made Bolívar's text so remarkable. He distinguishes one region from another largely on the basis of cultural character. Frank regarded Bolívar as more of a poet than a soldier, an evaluation which points to the missing element of praxis in his work. With respect to this element of praxis, however, it is important to acknowledge the discontinuity between Frank's work and life. If Frank's work is characterized by an unqualified idealism, he was on the other hand a committed political actor – something which would later bring him to the attention of the House Un-American Activities Committee.

Given the nature of Frank's pan-American philosophy, the perplexity of U.S. scholars with respect to his long-standing popularity in Latin America is understandable. Some North Americans have speculated that Latin Americans gravitated to Frank because he affirmed an elite conception of culture entertained by certain intellectuals informed by turn of the century aerialist traditions. This conclusion is rather unconvincing (not to mention condescending), however, if we take into account some of Frank's Latin American friends and allies. One of his closest allies was the Peruvian Marxist José Carlos Mariátegui, to whom Frank dedicated *America Hispana*. It is difficult to imagine anyone less likely to be taken in by flattery founded on ideological compromise than Mariátegui.

Mariátegui was an autodidact who, in addition to writing innovative socioeconomic analysis, authored essays on art and literature that ushered in a new era in cultural criticism. As the editor of the hugely influential *Revista Amauta*, and the biweekly workers' magazine, *Labor*, and as the founder of the Peruvian socialist party in 1928, Mariátegui was anything but the traditional Latin American *letrado*. In the extended correspondence the two men carried out before they met in person in 1929, Mariátegui asked Frank his opinion about socialism, to which Frank noted his disappointment with American communists.[368] Mariátegui was unequivocal that without a class analysis and socialist agenda –

neither of which Frank's philosophy of wholeness possessed – anti-capitalism and anti-imperialism served little purpose. Indeed, romantic anti-capitalism, though sometimes a forerunner to Marxist commitment, could just as easily serve a reactionary agenda, something which Frank's appreciation for an Hispanic spiritualism rooted in a vertical Spanish society, as well as his reluctance to unconditionally condemn the fascist forces in the Spanish Civil War, did not contradict.[369] The indiscriminate character of Frank's Latin American alliances – he befriended the conservative woman of letters Victoria Ocampo with the same ease as Mariátegui – underscores the politically ambivalent character of his social theories. Considering what for Mariátegui would have been the ideologically underdeveloped nature of Frank's work, and given the latter's embrace of a pan-Hispanism that contradicted the decolonizing cultural logic at the heart of Mariátegui's political project, where the European and indigenous figure in stark opposition, Mariátegui and Frank's intellectual friendship and collaboration are indeed difficult to understand.

Yet Mariátegui and Frank were friends and mutual admirers. Sections of Frank's book, *The Re-discovery of America*, were published in *Amauta*. Given its idealism and method of analysis, *The Re-discovery of America* could not be more different from Mariátegui's materialist analysis of America, *Siete ensayos de interpretación de la realidad peruana*. On the other hand, Frank's idealism probably did have a great deal to do with his friendship with Mariátegui. Both men professed a spiritual inclination that distinguished them from more conventional Marxists.[370] Frank accurately perceived the integral place of this idealism within Mariátegui's political thought:

> He welcomed [...] the religious impulse freed of its theologic forms. For he knew that the nucleus of religion, the sense of the Whole, must energize the revolution [...]. This organic sense of the Whole he recognized in Marxism dialectic and it was this vital mysticism of the Marxian vision [...].[371]

Contextualized in the respective philosophies and methodologies of Mariátegui and Frank, however, this shared idealism is at the service of radically different if not incompatible approaches to culture and politics. In Frank's description of Mariátegui's philosophy, the latter's rigorous approach to cultural and social analysis disappears. Remarking on the kinship between the two men, Ogorzaly notes that 'Frank [...] characteriz[es] Mariátegui as a co-visionary [...]. Considering the close friendship and correspondence of the two, one can assume that Mariátegui would concur with Frank's interpretation of him.'[372] Actually, quite the contrary is true. The Frank-Mariátegui relationship presents a distinct discontinuity between ideas and methodology, and friendship, since it is difficult to imagine anyone less likely to see themselves as a visionary than José Carlos Mariátegui. Whether as protagonist in or prophet of world history, in works such as *Siete ensayos de interpretación de la realidad peruana*, or *Peruanicemos a Peru*, the author is almost austerely absent.

As much as the incisive political and cultural thinker that he was, however, Mariátegui was also a facilitator – a factor that was every bit as integral to the alliance between the two men as their shared intellectual affinities. Although he once claimed that *Amauta* would not publish works of politically indiscriminate points of view, and that only those works adhering to the 'science' of Marxism would appear in its pages, in practice, almost the opposite was true. There is nothing remotely Marxist about Uriel Garcia's ultimately reactionary *indigenista* essays, or the apolitical poetry of José María Eguren, to mention just two authors whose work found its way into *Amauta*. In *Amauta* Mariátegui brought together tremendously diverse and divergent voices, many of which were every bit as eccentric as Frank's. Taken alone, the ideological meaning of these works might well have been questionable, but in the pages of *Amauta*, works that were extremely heterogeneous, thematically, aesthetically and ideologically, were put at the service of a progressive political agenda. When placed next to pastoral depictions of indigenous communities, quasi-anthropological stories about indigenous life, and Mariátegui's column 'Defensa del Marxismo', Uriel Garcia's semi-disguised conservatism possessed a social meaning quite different from whatever the author may have intended. The intellectual community that took shape around *Amauta*, and *Indigenism* more generally, conforms to Antonio Gramsci's definition of an historically progressive class:

> Certain intellectual formations [...] pertain[ing] to the historically progressive class, exercise such a power of attraction that [...] they end up by subjugating the intellectuals of the other social groups [...] and create a system of solidarity between all the intellectuals. This phenomenon manifests itself 'spontaneously' in the historical periods in which the given social group is really progressive.[373]

Frank's reception in Latin America becomes more understandable if we consider that, whatever the ideological implications of his work when taken alone, his contributions made him part of this truly progressive class. As Luis Alberto Sánchez remarked, 'we recognize Frank as ours, and of our race.'[374]

If Waldo Frank was fascinated with Latin America, the reverse cannot be said of Mariátegui. And were the reverse true – that is, had Mariátegui travelled in fascination to the United States – it would have had entirely different ideological meanings. If, on the one hand, Mariátegui's lack of interest in the United States as anything other than an intellectual subject is evidence of an indifference to the trappings of hegemony, on the other hand, Frank's example of trans-Americanism offers a different perspective on this disinterest. While Mariátegui recognized the increasingly powerful role of the United States within the context of global capitalism, he made little effort to learn English. One gathers that he concurred – in spirit at least – with nineteenth century (descriptive) evaluations of a more pragmatic U.S. culture. Mariátegui visited the United States only once, and then, only because of an unavoidable two-week gap between his arrival to the United States and departure to Europe. Like many Latin American writers – including Vallejo, Huidobro, and (the early) Neruda, to name just three of the most prominent – the intellectual and cultural influence of Spain and France are evident in Mariátegui's choices and intellectual proclivities. While Mariátegui's profoundly generative work is no less remarkable for what the author did not do, the field of trans-American studies inaugurates a hemispheric interpretative map which can contextualize well-known (and lesser-known) works in unexpected ways. It is in this context that Waldo Frank has once again become interesting – and important – not necessarily because of the merit of his ideas (though these are fascinating as cultural meditations), but rather as a trans-American actor. Less an anomaly that fits uneasily with conventional wisdom, his example legitimizes new ways of imagining the Americas, past and present.

In an excellent article on Waldo Frank's trans-American interventions, Sebastiaan Faber asks what Frank's one-time popularity in the Hispanic world can tell us about contemporary Latin Americanist discourse.[375] Following Neil Larsen and Mark Falcoff, Faber points to the parasitical quality of the Latin Americanist discourse emanating from U.S. academic institutions, 'with the Northern intelligentsia mining the Hispanic South for 'spiritual energy,' 'authenticity,' or 'purity' with which to strengthen their own position.'[376] Equally important, as I see it, is how North American discourse can drain a more local Latin American intelligentsia of its authority, something which that intelligentsia perceives in no uncertain terms.[377] In other words, genuine reciprocity remains elusive. U.S. Latin Americanists today do not count on the kind of reception Luis Alberto Sánchez gave Frank in the late twenties. Faber productively redefines these problematic discursive dynamics as an inter-American issue, attenuating the stalemate that a more nationalist framing of the issue creates. Recuperating the all but forgotten Frank, Faber suggests that the latter offers an example of genuine intellectual inquiry. Whatever his foibles, Frank, as he plainly told his Latin American interlocutors, came to Latin America to listen and to learn, and perhaps even more importantly, according to Faber, Frank went to the South open to self-critique.[378]

The extent to which Frank went to Latin America to listen and learn, and in the spirit of self-critique, is something we can never know for certain but is best judged by his writings. In that sense, Latin America did not tweak, modify or challenge the philosophy of wholeness Frank had developed before his encounter with the Hispanic world, but on the contrary supplied that philosophy with a teleological narrative. Comparatively, can there be any more soul-searching acknowledgement about the hermeneutic limitations of knowledge produced in the North American academy than what we have seen over the past two decades? I quote one prominent U.S. Latin Americanist: 'what subaltern studies can or should represent is not so much the subaltern as a concrete social-historical subject, but rather the difficulty of representing the subaltern as such in our disciplinary discourse and practice within the academy.'[379] By today's understanding of democratic exchange, I am not sure that Waldo Frank did much better than contemporary academics. Nor was he more genuinely interested in Latin America than, by and large, are today's U.S.-aligned academics, and nor was his intellectual project without a good dose of self-interest. He did after all build a career around his knowledge of Latin America. Yet there was nothing 'parasitical' about Frank's intervention; quite the contrary.

Waldo Frank reminds us that the word 'parasitic' must be given a clinical rather than a moral value. While self-awareness and individual generosity are not to be discounted, they cannot in themselves grant intellectual authority where systemic imbalance denies it. While Frank's activities are inextricable from a growing U.S. hegemony and U.S. institutions of power (the Vice-President of the United States met with Frank on the night before his departure to Latin America in 1942, hoping that Frank would help bring Latin Americans in line with Allied forces), part of what accounts for the enthusiasm with which he was received by Latin American intellectual communities was his independence from official institutions. This included academia. Frank was a public intellectual with no official university affiliation. The very idiosyncrasy of his ideas made it highly unlikely that they would disenfranchise local Latin American intellectuals. Though Frank played a key role in the development of trans-American cultural alliances, not surprisingly, his platonic inter-Americanism did not give rise to a new Latin Americanist discourse.

Though nothing in Frank's voluminous oeuvre offers the kind of disciplinary foundation for Hemispheric studies as does the work of a figure like Herbert E. Bolton – on the contrary, his is a cautionary tale with respect to theorizing the Americas – he can inspire us to think creatively about inter-American discourse and dialogue, and to better identify what are fruitful or, alternately, what are fruitless avenues. What gave Frank's intervention its reciprocal force was not so much hermeneutic humility or anything close to representational accuracy, nor necessarily an ability to listen? By all accounts, however, he was an engaging conversationalist. Though he probably would not have liked the term, given its association with Puritanism, Frank was a pioneer, and for that reason alone merits admiration. Moreover, it was this pioneering (and iconoclastic) status as much as anything specific that Frank had to say about Latin America that gave his intervention the meaning it had in the context of trans-American exchange. For however much Luis Alberto Sánchez embraced him as one of Latin America's own, Frank expressed his very North American immoderation in every syllable. Indeed, the one thing that you can say for certain about Waldo Frank is that no one more enthusiastically got it wrong.

15. FROM ANACONA WE ARE BORN, THROUGH DÉFILÉE WE REMEMBER: AN ISTWA (HISTORY/STORY) OF MOURNING AND REVOLUTION

Natalie M. Léger (Cornell University)

> From Anacaona we are born. When you take our history – the struggle against the invaders, the war of independence, and everything that came after – there were women there standing strong, right next to the men. But they're rarely told about in history. Only their husbands – unless a woman does the telling. – Josie, *Walking on Fire*

This piece critiques the conventional narration of the Haitian Revolution, specifically; the normative telling's emphasis on the exemplary masculine subject. Like most historical accounts, C. L. R James' *The Black Jacobins* relates the story of the revolution as that of a great man's, namely Toussaint L'Ouverture – an impressive, yet flawed, tragic hero. My reading of Danticat displaces the central positioning of the exceptional male and asks: where are the 'others' in such accounts – the unsung women of the revolution? Closely reading the manner in which Danticat works within the lapses of 'History', within the vast spaces of silence, to unveil the obscured in her story, 'Nineteen Thirty-Seven' I assess how a move to gender the discourse of the Haitian Revolution (and, more broadly, Haitian history) structures the narrative and thus the aesthetics of mourning, I argue, conditions the narrative. I ultimately intend to reveal the manner in which the narrative's aesthetics of mourning is at once an act of historical reclamation and too an expression of faith – specifically, a faith infused conviction in Haiti's future possibility.

During a nightly storytelling session, Josie offers this *istwa*. *Istwa* is a Creole (kreyol) word denoting story and history; the account relayed by Josie is an immensely personal story of historical fact, one that (as we shall soon see) is emblematic of women's existence within Haiti. The account then is thus both a story and a history, more aptly put an *istwa*. It is one she always tells and one the women in attendance, never tire of hearing.[380] Like them (and the majority of women in the nation) Josie is poor, illiterate, and without knowledge of facts that we take for granted, such as our year of birth and a firm assurance of our age. And yet while that is so, she is extensively conversant in Haiti's rich history. She, like her counterparts, can 'reel off a dizzying litany of [historical] personages and events [...] [doing] so with an obvious pride over what their ancestors – Anacaona [a Taino warrior queen], and others more humble – accomplished'.[381] What is the purpose of such extensive knowledge? What is to be gained in being so intimately acquainted with the nation's history? The answer lies in the simple yet poetic phrase, 'From Anacaona we are born'. This phrase forcefully points to a past of female resistance in order to counter the silence surrounding women's achievement and worth within Haitian history. When Josie states 'From Anacaona we are born', she affirmatively lays claim to a history of women's strength as well as accomplishment despite this silence. She points to the pivotal importance of women warriors at crucial junctures in Haiti's past – 'the struggle against the invaders, the war of independence, and everything that came after'. In doing so, she invokes a lineage of warrior women so as to boldly question the sense of nothingness as well as the silence that deliberate exclusion nourishes, essentially: Haitian women are nothing; Haitian women have done nothing.

Anacaona, a Taino monarch of pre-colonial Haiti, is the starting point for a lineage that continues in the present with the 'we [who] are born' and is thus the principal means by which to initiate a critical inquiry into the formidable presence of women in Haitian history. The 'we' of the present are those like Josie, women who in having to make a life in poverty and degradation are warriors. They are warriors who on a daily basis struggle against untimely death and who, in doing so, are primed to begin again Anacaona's fight against 'invaders' of whatever ilk, Haitian and foreign alike. As a chieftain of Jaragua (present day Leogane, Haiti), the poetess Anacaona led an ill-fated resistance campaign against the Spanish, who worked her people to death searching for gold. Although her resistance efforts were unsuccessful, for many a Haitian (from Josie to Danticat, who wrote a young adult novel detailing Anacaona's life) she is a clear instance of the lie of nothingness nurtured by historical omission.[382]

Her presence within history counters the blatant falsehood of female inactivity in revolutionary struggle and hence female insignificance to political events formative to the nation. The phrase, 'From Anacaona we are born', thus allows Josie to assert her own worth and that of other women to the nation. It is the means with which she validates a merit questioned not only in history but daily within a homeland in which women, while shouldering the weight of 'the family, household economy, local economy, and culture' with their industry as market women (*Madan Saras*), professionals, wives and mothers, are afforded minimal legal, economic as well as social equality with men.[383] This paper is concerned with this history as well as social reality in mind, and critically focuses on why Josie feels the need to break the silence with her persistent invocation of Anacaona when recounting Haiti's history of resistance. It is titled keenly aware of the women listening in rapture to Josie's only story, to their desire to see and hear themselves within history. It is so named, fundamentally aware of Danticat's own awareness of this desire when treating the Haitian Revolution. Like Josie, she is moved to name one so as to 'do the telling,' essentially call attention to a history rampant with unnamed female others. In the course of doing so, she reveals that while it is 'from Anacaona [that] we [Haitians] are born', it is, however, through Défilée that 'we' remember.

Marissainte Dédée Bazile[384] is a female revolutionary figure colloquially known, as Défilée-la-folle (Défilée the Madwoman). She is the life force of *Krik? Krak!*, tying the collective of deceased and living warrior women together as the matrilineal origin for the Femme d'Ayiti. She is thus Danticat's Anacaona. Little, of historical fact, is known of Défilée. Her history, as that of most legends, is founded upon conjecture and speculation. We know only that she was born in Cap Français, was a slave, was said to have had a cruel master, and was definitively acknowledged, by all, to be mad.[385] How she became so is unclear. Some point to a sexual assault she suffered (perpetrated by her master), others to the loss of several brothers and sons during one offensive of the revolutionary war, and some to the murder of her parents.[386] All, however, acknowledge that by the time she encounters Jean-Jacques Dessalines and acts as a sutler to his army,[387] following him throughout Haiti selling meat and by some accounts also freely furnishing the regiment and Dessalines with sex, she is already unhinged.[388]

This madness proves the basis for her mythic importance within Haiti, as she is widely read by the country's political and literary elite as the 'embodiment of the [...] nation: crazed and lost, but then redeemed through the body of their [Haitians] savior [Dessalines]'.[389] The nation's 'saviour' became so through a consorted effort by the state to memorialize Dessalines. A formidable black national hero such as Dessalines, the father of Independence and the self-appointed as well as world recognized 'Avenger of the Americas', could not only be used to question mulatto leadership (as was often the case) but he could also be deployed to sustain it, validating mulatto rule by association.[390] Upon his assassination by dismemberment, (he was quite literally hacked to pieces by his fellow revolutionary comrades) state actors and literary scholars reveal that Défilée, in a moment of lucidity, singlehandedly collected his discarded remains so as to afford him a proper burial. This Antigonesque act has immortalized her within Haitian historiography, granting her mythic status as the *mère de Patrie, mère d'Haïti* (mother of the nation, mother of Haiti).[391] Défilée (so it goes) acted when no one else would. When the masses and those in power, drunk from the bloodshed of the war, did nothing when Dessalines was attacked – rejoiced, in fact, upon his murder – she, in madness, rose above the folly of the moment, honouring a man far above the degradation of his death. She redeemed the redeemer.[392] So it goes.

Such a reading is ironic at best and cruel at worst. The 'heroics' of Défilée (read: her burial of Dessalines and thus act of mourning) is at once piteous and valorous. The saviour of the 'saviour', it seems, is paradoxically saved by the saved. When Défilée 'comes to the rescue of Dessalines,' restoring him to human consequence through lamentation, she, herself, is already conceived to be in need of rescue due to her folly. Her 'madness' not her action and thus the wherewithal needed to execute such behaviour shapes her memory for Haiti's political and literary elite. A reading such as this requires then that we at once honour her through her deed and equally pity her for the mental instability that enabled her act, indeed that ensured that 'reason' prevails. This dominant interpretation, romantic and nationalistic in sentiment, does Défilée a great disservice. Not only is it clear that her 'redemption' rests upon a man's salvation, and thus that the very mythification of Défilée subsists only to restore and sustain Dessalines' exception, but it is also quite apparent that in understanding her in such a manner the very power of Défilée goes unnoted. Such a reading requires that we see Défilée, in all other aspects of her existence, however, little we know of it, as irredeemable and hence negligible because of her madness.

In spite of the scant record we have, it is clear that we must not accept such a rendering. Défilée's lunacy does not impede her personal recognition of the revolution's importance. It does not detach her from critical and conscious thought. She chooses to be a sutler. She makes the conscious choice to align herself with the revolutionary struggle and in this way acted, and perhaps always acted, with reason. Joseph Jérémie, a centenarian recalling Défilée in 1916 Haiti, attests to her commitment to the uprising when he relates the origins of her cognomen, 'Défilée', stating: 'As soon as the soldiers stopped somewhere to rest, Dédée also stopped. Abruptly, the madwoman raised the long stick [used for a crutch] held in her hand, and bravely cried out: *défilez, défilez* [march, march]. They obeyed her'.[393] This is a woman whose mind, however, unbalanced, is fixed on one solitary purpose – revolutionary success. 'Crazed' she may be but she is certainly not 'lost'; treating her as such obscures what can be gleaned from her existence: a mythic potency tied to communal perseverance and collectivity. When we critically assess Défilée's sparse biography and madness, what we see then is not simply her devotion to the nation's 'saviour' but, more importantly, her ability to rally and unite a collective toward a communal purpose. We see, in effect, the force that Défilée quite possibly was and thus that she, now recalled through her own efforts, can be.

But can this potency be seen within a contemporary moment shaped by a past in which Défilée is no more then a madwoman, a woman redeemed by the 'saviour' she redeemed? Sadly, that is not the case. Although Défilée, as Jana Evans Braziel notes, is one of the better-known woman figures of the revolution within Haiti, she, like the many other women of the upheaval – Sanite Bélair, Marie-Jeanne Lamartinère, Marie-Claire Heureuse and the others forever lost in time – are mere footnotes within the history of the uprising, addendums to the males through whom they are related.[394] Accordingly when 'named' within contemporary Haitian culture, they are often acknowledged and attested to in silence. When *RAM*, a Haitian *rasin* band, offered homage to Dessalines in their 2008 carnival song tellingly titled 'Defile,' they did so in the tradition of historians and writers at home and abroad – with an eye tuned to the exceptional masculine subject.[395] For, as they praised Dessalines and bemoaned his betrayal, they snubbed the woman through whom this honouring first took place – Défilée. Nowhere is she named within the song as an historical and revolutionary figure like Dessalines. The latter of who in being afforded the affectionate appellation 'papa' is honoured here as founding father and as spiritual elder.[396] Present in the duality of her namesake (*defile*), she is named in absence. With each directive to *defile*, (march) *balanse*, (wave) *pran plezi*, (let loose) *banboche*, (enjoy one's self) and *layité* (see *banboche* and *pran plezi*) and within the interludes of instrumental revelry encouraging all to partake in these commands, her presence is unconsciously alluded to, her importance intimated.[397] She emerges, with such direction, as the collective tie that allows Haitians to carouse in honour of Dessalines. She is what makes remembrance possible. And yet in ensuring that we recall Dessalines, that we keep him near and dear to our hearts, we are urged to forget Défilée. Subsumed within his exception, she becomes no more then a cognitive springboard to Dessalines. What we see then with this look at Défilée within contemporary consciousness is the manner in which she is silenced and her presence within revolutionary history. We see the striking consistency of thought surrounding her some hundred years following her mythification within Haiti, a mythification emergent in tandem to Dessalines in 1845. Thus while she is noted before her fellow female revolutionaries, she is nonetheless also obscured within a national and transnational record devoted to the grandeur of Dessalines, Toussaint L'Ouverture, Henri Christophe, and Alexandre Pétion, among others: men, who, for many an historian, writer and layperson, *are* the revolution.[398]

How do we go about negotiating the enormity of these men and hence the exclusions shrouding women in silence and Défilée to a silence in presence within collective consciousness and, more extensively, within the revolutionary record in Haiti and abroad? We turn to the women themselves. We turn to the women ensuring this negotiation takes place, essentially, the 'nine hundred and ninety-nine women [...] boiling in [Danticat's] blood', shaping her literary artistry so that it is fundamentally concerned with mournful remembrance.[399] Danticat, à la Paule Marshall, dubs these women 'kitchen poets'.[400] As the 'old spirits that reside in [and boil in her] blood', (KK, p. 223) these 'poets' are spirits of the Vodun imaginary, one of three important divine collectives – *lè Marasa* (twins), *lè Mò* (the dead) *lè Mistè* (i.e. *lwa*, demi-gods). Each collective of spiritual entities are genetically passed down, like traits if you will; as such, they are said to dwell in the blood.[401] *Lè Mò* here press Danticat 'to speak through the blunt of [her] pencil' with their incessant 'whispers' and 'murmurs'; with their persistence, they demand to be remembered and hence mourned (KK, p. 222). Compelling her to write so as to attend to their unsung lives, each 'scraping [...] [each] Krik? Krak! Pencil, paper' is made to sound 'like someone crying' and thus made to mourn their unnoted existence (KK, p. 220).

We mourn these women then so as to see them and begin to acknowledge their importance and worth to the nation. In doing so, we come to see the rebellious energy they exude within the 'dark corners' of silence. Danticat writes that these women spend 'their days in dark corners [...] braid[ing] their hair in new shapes and twists in order to control the stiffness, the unruliness, their rebelliousness' (KK, p. 221). Such control is not what they offer Danticat, however; her braids, 'like the diverse women in her family [read: spiritual ancestry]', are 'long, others short. Some thick, others thin. Some are heavy. Others are light (KK, p. 219)'. These spirits thus embolden her with the means by which to rail against silence, with the fire and grit needed to tell their many distinct stories. They teach her to fear silence – 'silence terrifies you more than the pounding of millions of pieces steel chopping away at your flesh' (KK, p. 223) – so as to remain in tune to the 'thousand' hearts pounding with her own; they, however, offset this fear with protection (KK, p. 224). Danticat writes: 'with every step you take, there is an army of women watching over you. We are never any farther than the sweat on your brows or the dust on your toes. Though you walk through the valley of the shadow of death, fear no evil for we are always with you' (KK, pp. 222-23). As an 'army', a blockade in life and death, it is clear that these ancestral spirits can not only be understood as Danticat's protectors but also as women experienced in protecting and hence as women with a rich history of marital service. Such service could be in actual battle or the day-to-day struggles of existing as women in Haiti or as the thrice-burdened black, foreign female in the United States, all of which are treated within *Krik? Krak!* These women then are 'poets' not simply because their 'fables [...] metaphors [...] similes [...] soliloquies [...] diction and *je ne sais quoi* daily slip into [Danticat's] survival soup' but because, like the poetess Anacaona, they are also women warriors. Written in their honour and with the spirit of their rebellion in mind,

Krik? Krak! is a 'testament to the way that these women lived and died and lived again', fighting with each resurrection to be heard, seen and hence remembered (KK, p. 224). It is a literary effort to memorialize so that we may see and continue to see the Josies of past and present, so that we may, in effect, exhume them from silence.

If the dead demand mourning and thus exhumation from silence how are we to go about doing so? The performance convention grounding the collection entitled, 'Krik? Krak!' suggests that we must do so via a relation in which the dead and the living 'never [lose] touch with one and other', (KK, p. 222) enacting always the call and response of 'krik?' and 'krak!' *Krik? Krak!* opens with a poem from Sal Scalora entitled 'White Darkness/Black Dreamings'. The poem offers a descriptive explanation for the terms 'krik' and 'krak', and thus the oral tradition of collective storytelling in which they are associated and which we briefly experienced through Josie. It paints a scene of laughter and mirth ('somewhere by the seacoast I feel a breath of warm sea and hear the laughter of children') in which 'an old granny', pipe in hand, is surrounded by 'village children' as she imparts stories to children, stories constructed so that the latter 'will know what came before them'. The granny and the children engage in a call and response to begin the stories, 'they [storytellers] ask Krik? We [the children] say Krak!' This opening, warm and idyllic (the poem ends touchingly with, 'our stories are kept in our hearts'), immediately grounds us in performance, in a phonic oratory engagement that commands attention and participatory engagement. In this way, it encourages relation, essentially an engagement with multiple histories and realities. It welcomes, in fact, with its warmth, encourages our (i.e. the individual reader-participant) solitary utterance, our thunderous 'krak!' in response to Danticat's written exposition, her equally booming 'krik?' We begin reading the collection, then, with an invitation to enter into relation, one wherein we will be afforded historical instruction ('we tell the stories so that the young ones will know what came before them') and our own knowledge, our histories, our realities, will become a part of an emerging collective.

The short story, like the oral tradition of 'krik' and 'krak', encourages attention to multiple realities and histories. It does this through the array of voices and stories it highlights. The oral convention, unlike the short story, however, lends the many voices within this multiplicity (that of the unnamed narrators in 'Children of the Sea', Ma and Caroline of 'Caroline's Wedding' and Princesse of 'Seeing Things Simply' among others) toward a collective self-fashioning with the reader. We see this upon recognizing the importance of the individual within the collection and the personal nature of each story, namely the manner in which *Krik? Krak!* privileges the individual and his/her story, or more aptly puts his /her *istwa* (a story that is a history, history that is a story). Each *istwa*, aside from the epilogue where a clamour of voices, and hence persons is present, offers individual portraits of life within Haiti and in the Diaspora (NYC). We are afforded portraits of survival that, as aforesaid, humanize Haitians within a transnational context, depictions that purposefully name so as to disassociate Haitians from their many disparaging appellations – 'boat people' or people of 'the poorest country in the Western Hemisphere.' If the focus of each *istwa* is the individual and his/her particular efforts for self-fashioning and survival within the space afforded, be it upon the sea ('Children of the Sea'), within prison ('Nineteen Thirty-Seven'), on factory grounds ('Wall of Rising Fire') or in New York City ('Caroline's Wedding'), then, the phonic performance convention brings these individuals, these voices, in relation. Essentially, it provides the space in which theses *istwas* coalesce within the vociferous giddiness, the tense excitement and thrill manifest in the silence of anticipation that an audience (Scalora's 'children' and we, participants, now embedded within this performance) would feel upon 'hearing' these *istwas*. We are thus located within a raucous silence that consciously makes the unnoted present and that in calling such lives to our attention nurtures a burgeoning collective.

The collection, in being forged within a performance convention, enacts the work of mourning that creates community. In replying to Danticat's 'krik?' with our 'krak!' (our performatory engagement with the text), we partake in an act of remembrance, one that 'enables us to work through our relation to history' to share in 'an act of creating community'.[402] This community in creation is what grounds this text. It forms the basis for Danticat's own literary ancestry, providing the means with which the voices within this collection, the 'living dead', (KK, p. 224) can reply, 'krak!' to her solitary, 'krik?' – 'And over the years when you have needed us, you have always cried 'Krik?' and we have answered 'Krak!' and it has shown us that you have not forgotten us' (KK, p. 224). We (reader-performers) are now invited, in fact encouraged to enter into relation with the text and its *istwas* can include our 'krik' within that of Danticat's. With each encounter with the text, we are encouraged to partake in a vociferous performance that creates a trans-cultural community as it imparts history (*istwas*) and implores us to, at all costs, remember.

Such community, founded upon a relation between reader and writer and the living and dead, provides the basis for my understanding of mourning. Mourning, here, is not used in a Freudian sense, à la Freud's piece 'Mourning and Melancholia,' as a brief spell that can and must be overcome for one's self preservation.[403] It is deployed in a more melancholic manner, as it is presented as an enduring manifestation and experience, one in which the past 'remains steadfastly alive in the present'.[404] Sans the pathology of Freud's rendering, where the sustained attachment to the 'lost object' endangers one's health and very existence,[405] mourning as melancholia allows, as David L. Eng and David Kazanjian in *Loss* note, for a positive 'ongoing and open relationship with the past – bring[ing] its ghosts and specters, its flaring and fleeting images, into the present.'[406] It does so permitting a bygone to illuminate the present so as to 'allow lost pasts to step into the light of a present moment of danger', here a collective's disintegration.[407] In reading mourning through melancholia, I am not simply situating my reading within the extensive scholarship concerning melancholic within the West, but I am firmly grounding my assessment within a Vodun imaginary that is fundamentally melancholic.[408] In Vodun, unlike Judeo-Christian thought, the 'lost object', the dead, never quite goes away even when properly laid to rest. When Défilée provides Dessalines a proper burial following his murder, she does so to ensure that his spirit does not terrorize the locality in which he died.[409] With this burial, his family could potentially call upon his spirit when needed, for advice, protection and/or guidance. The passing of Dessalines is thus a circumstance one need not move beyond as he never truly disappears from existence, from the world which he 'left'. To that end, in Haiti his death (and thus existence in death) is celebrated as a national holiday (17 October) not his birth (2 January) and thus life alone.[410] Moreover, when he renames Saint Domingue as 'Ayiti', reinstating the appellation given to the land by Anacaona's people, he too draws from a Vodun imaginary or at the very least a melancholic imaginary central to the spiritual practice that would fully emerge in his wake. For he ensures that the Tainos are never far from Haitian national and cultural consciousness, granting them a seat with the collective of ancestors, such as himself, who never quite take leave of this earth.[411] When the departed 'kitchen poets' demand mourning they forcefully ask not only to be remembered but to also be recognized as individuals worthy of providing advice and guidance. With their voices in convergence, they insist upon being regarded as ancestors with stories and knowledge that can shed light on the difficulties experienced by their descendents. They insist then to be seen as vital members of a collective. To read mourning through Vodun (and hence as melancholic) is to validate such a desire and thus to see the worth of these 'warrior women' within a 'present moment of [persistent] danger', that is the danger of not only socio-economic deterioration but also of continued silence and thus female insignificance.

In 'Nineteen Thirty-Seven' Danticat writes against this insignificance, using Défilée to offer a way in which to see the revolution's unsung heroines within the present. The *istwa* implicitly treats the uprising through a character named Defile, namesake and great-great-granddaughter of the original Défilée. It also does so through the massacre by which the narrative derives its name – the 1937 Dominican massacre of Haitians, an event known in Haiti as *Kout Kouto-a* (the stabbing).[412] The mastermind behind the mass murder was then Dominican dictator Rafael Leonaidas Trujillo Molina. With the slaughter of 15,000-17,000 Haitians,[413] he claimed to have avenged the innocent children lost during Dessalines' post-revolutionary, 1805 slaughter of the inhabitants at Moca, Santo Domingo.[414] Attempting to conceal the state's hand in the massacre, Trujillo required that his army and corps of civilian volunteers use machetes to facilitate the extermination of Haitians within the Dominican Republic.[415] The massacre could, in this way, appear to be a popular uprising and therefore fundamentally desired by the Dominican people should it draw the attention of the international community.[416] In ordering the use of machetes, Trujillo symbolically re-enacted Dessalines assassination by dismemberment, as he ensured that the latter's progeny (children to the 'Father of Independence') were hacked to pieces; in this way, he provided the literary foundation for Défilée's presence in 'Nineteen Thirty-Seven', since she appears within the *istwa* through mourning, through a rite of lamentation that recreates her burial of Dessalines on a broader scale. As the centrepiece of the narrative's mourning rite, she is no longer symbolically tied to one lost ancestor needing to be properly laid to rest but to the thousands lost during *Kout Kouto-a*.

Défilée's presence is felt within the *istwa* through her descendant's (Josephine) struggle with her mother's (Defile) impending death. Defile tended to a friend's sick baby who died in her care. Upon the child's death, she is denounced as a witch (NTS, pp. 38-39). This results in her subsequent imprisonment and later murder by prison guards (NTS, p. 47). Years prior to this, Defile is among the few who survived *Kout Kouto-a*, leaping across Massacre River from Dominican to Haitian soil. Her mother (Eveline), however, was not as fortunate. She died in the massacre and Defile witnessed her execution. This latter aspect is extremely important as the practice mourning, within the *istwa*, is fundamentally concerned with the psychic bond oft-said to be present between a parent and child, here mothers and daughters. Upon her mother's murder, Defile mourns her loss by returning to the site of the massacre – Massacre River. Year, after year, she makes this pilgrimage, inviting other women whose mothers died in the slaying. By the time of Josephine's fifth birthday, Defile's once solitary act of mourning becomes a collective rite (NTS, p. 40). The women, clad in white, gather every November first (Haiti's day of the dead) to honour their mothers (NTS, p. 41). Together, they preserve what was lost by creating the 'flesh' to take its place.

Near the end of her life, when it is clear that the prison guards intend to execute her, Defile implores Josephine to keep the 'weeping Madonna' that had been in their family for generations. As a gift to the original Defile (Défilée, hereafter), the Madonna embodies the undying presence of the ancestors that have passed (NTS, p. 34). With each tear a past life, an ancestor, was invoked, made 'flesh' through the miracle of the Virgin's weeping. Defile states: 'Keep the Madonna when I am gone [...]. When I am completely gone, maybe you will have someone to take my place. Maybe you will have a person. Maybe you will have some *flesh* to console you. But if you don't, you will always have the Madonna' (emphasis mine NTS, p. 43). When Josephine is first brought to the river as a child, her mother takes her hand and places it into the water and states, 'Here is my child, Josephine. We were saved from the tomb of this river when she was still in my womb. You spared us both, her and me, from this river where I lost my mother' (NTS, p. 40). In doing so, Defile initiates Josephine into a sisterhood in which she is transformed into the 'flesh' that can and does take her grandmother's place. She becomes the mother to the daughter that has lost her mother. Like her mother and the other female survivors, she becomes a 'daughter of the river', and is reborn as daughter and as mother. The text reads: 'when we dipped our hands, I [Josephine] thought that the dead would reach out and haul us in, but only our own faces stared back at us, one indistinguishable from the other' (NTS, p. 40). The dead, in this respect, emerge as the force that renders mother indistinguishable from daughter and daughter indistinguishable from mother. Present in their corporeal absence, the dead reside within our own bodies. We thus bear witness to them by acknowledging the plurality inborn within our bodily composition; essentially, the 'many' departed souls innate to the singular that is

'I', the self of the body. To hear the voiceless within Haiti – those muted by the manner in which the massacre was officially handled by the Haitian government (an incident to be quickly swept under the rug) and also those silenced by the exceptionality of male revolutionary figures – we need only then hear ourselves.[417] The narrative suggests that we need to simply remain aware of the ancestors animating our existence and thus recognize the force that resides in our blood.

This force, as we already know, is that of the spiritually potent dead, one of three principal categories of divine beings within Vodun. Within the larger framework of the collection, this divine collective of the departed are the aforementioned rebellious 'nine hundred and ninety-nine women [...] boiling in [Danticat's] blood'. Knowing this, we should be aware of the deceased's implicit and powerful presence with each reference to blood, their abode, within the story. When Danticat writes that Defile's teeth are 'dark red, as though caked with blood from her initial arrest' (NTS, pp. 36-37), we should see these departed 'kitchen poets' within this description. When she directs our gaze to the scabs and bruises on an unnamed prisoner's scalp, 'a line of blood dripping down her back' (NTS, p. 38) and to the 'blood that never stops flowing at the bottom of the river' (NTS, p. 41), we should see again the dead and thus the rich collective of departed souls the 'daughters of the river' now join. The dead are not, however, the only spiritual beings who reside in blood. When Defile dies, Jacqueline, who also lost her mother during the massacre, comes to Defile's house to impart the news of her death to her daughter; she states: 'your mother is dead [...] her blood calls to me from the ground' (NTS, p. 46). In this way, we should see not only the continued presence of the dead but the manner in which Defile's blood, now married with that of her mother's and her sisters' mothers, nourishes the bond between the 'daughters of the river.' It sustains and cements the community created through Defile's act of mourning as it is now a part of the ancestors through whom Haitians continually remember the past and those lost within it; it is thus posed to become like the Madonna herself – a revered ancestor, a *lwa*.

Lwa and *marasa* are the most revered spiritual ancestors within Vodun, dead who are remembered by all. With their presence, they ensure remembrance, for they not only insist upon being remembered (through spiritual offerings and services) but they are corporeal manifestations of histories and thus embody recollections.[418] Haitians have within their lineage *lwas* that represent the particular characteristics and lived existence of their own ancestors from Africa to the New World. Thus in some parts of Haiti a *lwa* is present that will not be found in another part of the country. That said there are *lwa* that all Haitians have, *lwa* whose deeds within life are so great that they are deified and included within the principal pantheon from Africa and the Americas. Two famed revolutionary figures have been afforded the status of lwa by the Haitian people: Dessalines and Boukman – the former, as aforesaid, led the nation to independence and the latter began the uprising. Haitians, in remembering them, have granted them the psychic power to be and act as *lwa*, to heal the sick and protect Haitians from malfeasance. In 'Ninety Thirty-Seven' Danticat does what Haitians, as a collective, have yet to do – afford Défilée the status of *lwa*. She is made into an Ezili, becoming one of the many manifestations of the *lwa*, who is most commonly (and rather reductively) known as the *lwa* of love. It is no coincidence then that within this narrative she is aligned to the 'weeping Madonna', with the Marian iconography through whom the Ezilis are indentified within Vodun.

Of the three principal emanations of Ezili – Freda, Dantò and Lasyrenn ('The Mermaid') – Défilée is most like Ezili Dantò. Dantò is a *lwa*, like Dessalines and Boukman, of the revolution. She, however, is one whose human history and life story remains (and will always remain) un-chronicled. Haitian as well as Euro-American historiography provides us with few particulars concerning her human existence. The salacious details that cast Dessalines as a rogue, an avid and exceptional dancer and also as a hot-tempered personality, are absent in regards to Dantò. So too are the small biographic details we have concerning Boukman: namely that he, like Henri Christophe, was a West Indian of some learning (hence the name 'Bookman'). Dantò is without this detailed historical record and thus the scholarly interest that ensures such a written record exists. The little that has been preserved through Vodun's oral history is, nonetheless, vastly interesting and tellingly of the profound silence negating female achievement and consequence within Haiti and its historiography.

It is said that Dantò was an African slave who fought valiantly and fiercely during the revolution. She was fearless and despite being wounded (she bears three scars on her face) she stood strong against combatants. Yet even with her strength, with the acclaim she garnered among her comrades, and with her dedication to the struggle she became a victim of the uprising. Her comrades did not trust her. When the moment was ripe, they betrayed her, cutting out her tongue so that she would not reveal their secrets should she be captured.[419] With this sparse vignette we are privy to a woman exemplar; the duplicity she experienced is paradigmatic of the forcibly silenced women within Haiti and its revolutionary history. The women had their tongues quite literally cut out with each historical recounting devoid of their stories, their voices and their pivotal contributions to the nation. To align Défilée with Ezili, and in particular Dantò, through the 'weeping Madonna' is to call attention to this pervasive silence and the betrayal that such an imposed silence is. What is more, in implicitly relating Défilée to Dantò through revolutionary activity is to underscore how Défilée, as a *lwa* and as a Dantò, ensures remembrance.

When a *lwa* is summoned, invoked in name, her presence as a single solitary being is not only solicited but also her very ancestry, the genealogy of existence that brought her into being and that continues to sustain her.[420] The force of the *lwa*, we can say, rests with the collective in memory. It lies with a collective conscious of the ancestors shaping its present being. To invoke a *lwa*, then, is to invoke a history, a history of a people and that of a spiritual being. In invoking Défilée, as one would summon a *lwa*, by naming her and inviting readers to discover her genealogy of existence, we are privy to a particular history. Within the 'condensed [...] shorthand of [her] nomenclature', Défilée, as opposed to Dédée Bazile, we are made aware of a profound silence and the voices therein, essentially the thousands upon thousands who 'marched' in the revolutionary struggle giving their lives, and the women, then and now, who continue to 'march on' despite the hardships they face.[421] Danticat, as the *ch'wal* (the ridden through whom the *lwa* speak, here the newly deified Défilée-Dantò) and hence the 'final issue' of the latter reveals to readers the means in which to 'remember' and thus mourn.[422] She provides a way in which to think back to the women within their lives (the unnamed, the unsung, and the unheralded) those whose daily lives deserve recognition. In doing so through an oblique usage of Défilée (a revolutionary figure of note, however, diminished such stature is by the men of the uprising), our focus is drawn not to Défilée but to those whom we see through Défilée. As the silent but ever-present 'weeping Madonna', she, like the *lwa* with whom she is related, Dantò, a fierce mother who 'tells poor women's stories,' 'mothers' *istwas*.[423] She gives ultimately rise to (and hence births) 're-memberings' – recollections that resurrect the unnoted, past and present. The tears, which would manifest upon Défilée-Dantò's invocation, are thus like the tears shaping the collection's 'krik' and 'krak' and hence prose – tears of recollection. Detailing the significance of *lwas*' tears, Deren states: 'When this occurs [when the *lwa* cry] [...] the loa seem to linger a moment, as one might pause on the threshold of departure, to remember, and to be remembered, and to be perhaps recorded in this luminous light'.[424] In ensuring that Défilée, as she has deified her, weeps and thus pauses 'to remember,' 'to be remembered' and to be recorded in remembering, Danticat, through an aesthetics of mourning, consecrates the move to recall others. She renders sacred the move to attend to a history of silence that however distant and obscure provides the basis for collective perseverance and growth.

Fittingly, 'Nineteen Thirty-Seven' ends upon this note of collective enrichment and determination. Josephine and Jacqueline stand together, awaiting Defile's flight in flame; her corpse is to be burned and her spirit released to join that of her mothers' and sisters'. Josephine, reiterating the closing salutation of her mother's collective rite, states: 'Let her flight be joyful [...] and mine and yours' (NTS, p. 42; p. 49).[425] With this, we are meant to recall Defile's first flight. The narrative states that 'she [leapt] from the Dominican soil into the water, and out again on the Haitian side of the river', glowing 'red when she came out, blood clinging to her skin, which at that moment looked as though it were in flames' (NTS, p. 49). These flames are the very reason why she, and the women like her, are imprisoned, beset as they are with 'wings of flame' (NTS, p. 34). Blazed in Defile's flights are the brutalities endured in her 'dive toward life' (NTS, p. 41) in her struggle to exist in difference. She is denied this while of the Diaspora, as a Haitian in the Dominican Republic, and too within Haiti; there this denial occurs not once but twice, first in leaving Haiti for the economic opportunities of the Dominican Republic and second while a Haitian whose difference (purported religious and socio-economic) warrants her caging and eventual loss of life. Who but the poor and disadvantaged could be contained in the manner depicted here? Who but a conceived Voduist as well? Defile is not a Voduist but she is poor and speaks of flights of flame and thus can be conceived as a Voduist. Her difference, for a state struggling to progress, is too great to bear. And yet, this narrative suggests, that it is her difference and the collectivity it inspires that the nation needs. For what we see of the nation, in this piece, and what we know of it in the narrative that precedes it, 'Children of the Sea', is a nation at war with itself, killing its youth and its women for no other reason than a will to power and a will to progress upon achieving power. The 'daughters of the river', in coming together as they do, rebuild lives shattered by horrific losses through memory; through recollection, they construct a foundation through which to begin anew, a foundation rooted within the well-being of all who have suffered in silence. It is thus significant that Défilée is invoked within this collectivity through the Madonna. For in mourning Dessalines (in 're-member-ing' the remains of he who symbolically stood as the nation), Défilée's act of mourning can be construed as a move to reassemble a divided land, a nation on the verge of being what it would subsequently become: a kingdom in the north and a republic in the south.[426] Implicated within this first act of mournful reconstitution, the 'daughters of the river' do not simply rebuild their lives for their personal futures but for a collective in shatters as well. They, therefore, are rightly termed the 'embers' (mothers) and 'sparks' (daughters) for the present and future (NTS p. 41), as the fire of their flight is not only the blood of those who have passed but also a revolutionary fervour for a new Haiti. To remember, then, is not only to bear witness but it is also to express faith in a re-embodied Haiti. The continual effort to remember, within the narrative, is profoundly concerned with working toward a future of difference for Haiti, for a newly 're-member-ed' and thus reassembled Haiti wherein the collective acts as a collective – as a body politic, seeped in the faith of its own potentiality, in a potentiality rooted in the strength of the past, in the exceptional and the unsung. In attending to the silenced within Haitian history through an aesthetics of mourning, Danticat genders Haitian Revolutionary discourse; drawing our attention to the obscured, she reclaims the unheralded by bearing witness to their existence and by consecrating remembrance. As a sacred act it never ceases precisely because, as she notes, 'once you remember, you always stop looking' (CS, p. 216). The intent here is to continue looking, to continue bearing witness so as to re-conceive the past to re-imagine the present and future.

BIBLIOGRAPHY

Dictionaries and Lexicons

Cirlot, Juan Eduardo, *A Dictionary of Symbols*, trans. by Jack Sage (London: 1971)

Hornblower, Simon and Antony Spawforth, eds., *The Oxford Classical Dictionary*, 3rd edn (New York: Oxford University Press, 2003)

Pearsall, Judy, ed., *Concise Oxford English Dictionary*, 10th edn (Oxford: Oxford University Press, 2002)

Dissertations

Reckley, Alice R., *Looking Ahead through the Past: Nostalgia in the Recent Mexican Novel*. Diss. University of Kansas (Ann Arbor: UMI, 1985)

Films, Lectures, Musical Recordings and Interviews

Como agua para chocolate, dir. by Alfonso Arau (Arau Films International, 1992)

Coupe-Cloue, et le Trio Select. In CD *St.Antoine#2*. 1974, track 1, 6; *Sôciss*, 1976

Danticat, Edwidge, 'A Narrative Look at Haiti', Hazel I. Jackson Memorial Lecture. Millersville University, Millersville, Pennsylvania. 24 March 2010.

Dash, J. Michael, 'Neither France nor Senegal: Bovarysme and Haiti's Hemispheric Identity', keynote address for conference on Haiti and the Americas: Histories, Cultures, Imaginations, Florida Atlantic University, Boca Raton, Florida. 22 October 2010.

Emeline Michel, 'L'odeur de ma Terre', on CD *Rhum & Flamme*, 1993, track 1.

Fuentes, Carlos, *Carlos Fuentes,* interviewed by Lewis MacAdams, videocassette, directed and produced by Lewis MacAdams (Santa Fe, New Mexico: Metropolitan Pictures and EZTV for Lannan Foundation, 1989)

Garaje Olimpo, directed by Marco Bechis (Studio, 1999)

García, Guadalupe Pérez, *Diario argentino/Argentine Journal* [experimental documentary] (Argentina-España: Cine Ojo, Impossible Films and Rizoma Films: 2007)

Martel, Lucrecia, *La Mujer sin Cabeza* (Argentina: Aquafilms, 2008)

———. *La Niña Santa* (Argentina: La Pasionaria, 2006)

———. *La Ciénaga* (Argentina: 4k Films, 2001)

———. *Rey Muerto* (Argentina: Instituto Nacional de Cinematografía y Artes Audiovisuales, 1995)

Martelly, Michel, 'Aloufa', 'Pigeons', on CD *Aloufa*. 1997, track 3, 6. *Mauvaise conduite* or *Improper Conduct*, directed by Néstor Almendros and Orlando Jiménez Leal (Antenne-2, 1984)

PM, directed by Alberto Cabrera Infante and Orlando Jiménez Leal (1961).

Royal bonbon, directed by Charles Najman. Perf. Dominique Battraville, Benji, Anne-Louise Mesadieux, Erol Josue, and Alain Thompson (K. Films Amérique, 2002)

Newspapers and Magazines

Barley, Alexander, 'Before Night Falls – Review', *New Statesman*, (July 9, 2001), p. 56.

Clark, Heather and Jose Manuel Prieto, 'Nocturnal Butterflies of the Russian Empire', *Times Literary Supplement,* 5132 (2001), p. 19

Dandan, Alejandra, 'Distinguía día y noche por los ladridos', *El País*, September 7, 2010, p. 14.

Hutak, Michael, 'Easel Angles', *The Bulletin*, 29 August 2001.

Jaggi, Maya, 'Island Memories', *The Guardian*, 20 November, 2004.

Marshall, Paule, 'From the Poets in the Kitchen', *NY Times*, 1983.

Shewey, Don, 'A Painter's Latest Cinematic Collage', *The New York Times*, Late Edition, 5 November, 2000, 2A, p. 44.

Yuste, Miguel. 'Muere en atentado el jefe de la policía argentina', *El País*, June, 19, 1976

Websites

Alfonso, Alfredo, 'Imagen e imaginario de la crisis: Panorama audiovisual argentino sobre la crisis que tuvo su máxima expresión en diciembre de 2001', *Colección GTs ALAIC* (2003), 116-24 <http://www.alaic.net> [accessed 10 March 2010]

Amado, Ana, 'Velocidades, generaciones y utopías: a propósito de La Ciénaga, de Lucrecia Martel', *ALCEU*, 6 (2006, Enero-Julio), 48-56. <http://publique.rdc.puc-io.br/revistaalceu/media/alceu_n12_Amado.pdf> [accessed 10 March 2010]

Bibliography

Armeindariz, Aitor Ibarrola, 'Danticat's *The Dew Breaker*, a Case Study in Trauma Symptoms and the Recovery Process,' *Journal of English Studies*, 8 (2010) <http://www.jstor.org/stable/3394885 > [accessed 11 October 2010]

Benegas, Diego, 'The Escrache is an Intervention on Collective Ethics.' Hemispheric Institute. Performance and Politics, *Cuadernos*, 2004. <http://hemi.nyu.edu/cuaderno/politicalperformance2004/totalitarianism/WEBSITE/texts/the_escrache_is_an_intervention.htm>[accessed 27 October 2010]

Bernstein, Richard, *The New York Times*, December 25, 2000 <http://www.josemanuelprieto.com/resenas_livadia_nyt.html> [accessed 12 November 2010]

Collins, Jo, 'The Ethics and Aesthetics of Representing Trauma: the Textual Politics of Edwidge Danticat's *The Dew Breaker*,' *Journal of Postcolonial Writing*, 47.1 (2011), 5-17 <http://dx.doi.org/10.1080/17449855.2011.533947> [accessed 5 August 2011]

CONADEP, *Nunca más* (Argentina: Editorial Universitaria de Buenos Aires, 1984) <http://www.nuncamas.org/english/library/nevagain/nevagain_000.htm> [accessed 15 December 2010]

Cruz, Sor Juana Inés de la, 'The Poet's Answer To the Most Illustrious Sor Filotea De La Cruz', trans. by Electa Arenal and Amanda Powell <http://web.archive.org/web/20071205013324/www.auburn.edu/~perryka/files/la_respuesta.htm> [accessed 11 July 2011]

——. 'Respuesta de la poeta a la muy ilustre Sor Filotea de la Cruz', in *Proyecto Ensayo Hispánico* <http://www.ensayistas.org/antologia/XVII/sorjuana/sorjuana1.htm> [accessed 29 June 2011]

Ebert, Roger, 'Like Water for Chocolate', *rogerebert.com* (April 2, 1993). <http://rogerebert.suntimes.com/apps/pbcs.dll/article?AID=/19930402/REVIEWS/304020304> [accessed 29 June 2011]

François, Cécile, *El cine de Lucrecia Martel. Una estética de la opacidad* (Francia: Universidad de Orléans, 2009) <http://www.ucm.es/info/especulo/numero43/lucmarte.html> [accessed 10 March 2010]

García Castro, Antonia, 'Metáforas literales. Diálogo con Lucía Cedrón, cineasta', Cultures & Conflits, 06/11/2008. http://conflits.revues.org/index9822.html > [accessed 30 October 2010]

Gómez, Lía, *Nuevas razones de la imagen. Un estudio sobre Lucrecia Martel y el cine argentino contemporáneo* (La Plata: UNLP Facultad de Periodismo y Comunicación Social, 2009) <http://iigg.sociales.uba.ar/jovenes_investigadores/5jornadasjovenes/EJE4/Mesa%201/Gomez.pdf> [accessed 10 March 2010]

Gómez, Leila, *El cine de Lucrecia Martel: La Medusa en lo recóndito* (Boulder: University of Colorado, 2005) <http://www.lehman.edu/faculty/guinazu/ciberletras/v13/gomez.htm> [accessed 9 March 2010]

ImdbPro<http://pro.imdb.com/boxoffice> [accessed 1 July 2011]

Iribarren, María, 'La política tiene que servirnos como brújula. Entrevista exclusiva con la directora de *Cordero de Dios*, in Revista Zoom. Política y sociedad en foco. 17/04/2008. <http://revista-zoom.com.ar/articulo2103.html> [accessed 30 October 2010]

Johnston, David, 'Ruling Backs Homosexuals on Asylum', *The New York Times*, (June 17, 1994) <http://www.nytimes.com/1994/06/17/us/ruling-backs-homosexuals-on-asylum.html?scp=1&sq=johnston%2C+david&st=nyt?> [accessed 29 June 2011]

Lyberger, Dan, 'Capturing Life on Canvas and with Lense', *Lawrence Journal-World*, (2001) <www.ljworld.com> [accessed 26 May 2003]

Lyons, Bonnie and Edwidge Danticat, 'An Interview with Edwidge Danticat,' *Contemporary Literature*, 44.2 (Summer 2003), < http://www.jstor.org/stable/1209094 > [accessed 28 February 2010]

McDonnell, Dr. Jan, *Evita's Cancer*, June 13, 2000. <http://www.nytimes.com/2000/06/13/science/l-evita-s-cancer-733512.html?ref=eva_duarte_de_peron.> [accessed 25 October 2010]

Miranda, Veerle, (2011), 'Cooking, Caring and Volunteering: Unpaid Work Around the World', *OECD Social, Employment and Migration Working Papers*, No. 116, OECD Publishing. <http://dx.doi.org/10.1787/5kghrjm8s142-en> [accessed 3 July 2011]

Mundo, Daniel, 'Medios, terror e indiferencia', *Página, 12*, 09/23/2009, <http://www.pagina12.com.ar/diario/laventana/26-132249-2009-09-23.html.> [accessed 13 September 2010]

Munro, Martin, 'Avenging History in the Former French Colonies,' *Transition*, 99 (2008) <http://www.jstor.org/stable/20204259 > [accessed 28 February 2010]

National Science Foundation, 'Chore Wars: Men, Women, and Housework,' (April 28, 2008) <http://www.nsf.gov/discoveries/disc_summ.jsp?cntn_id=111458> [accessed 5 July 2011]

Pedraza, Silvia 'Los Marielitos of 1980: Race, Class, Gender, and Sexuality', *Cuba in Transition,* 14 (2004), 89-102 <http://www.ascecuba.org/publications/proceedings/volume14/> [accessed 30 June 2011]

Pérez, Ana Laura, 'Fragementos de un país todavía secreto/Fragments of a Still Secret Country' in *Clarin.com.* 22/11/1998. <http://www.clarin.com/suplementos/cultura/1998/11/22/e-01001d.htm>. [accessed 30 October 2010]

Princeton University African American Studies: <http://www.princeton.edu/africanamericanstudies/news/Newsletter-Fall_2008_Final.pdf> [accessed 20 February 2010]

Ravaschino, Guillermo, 'Garage Olimpo', *Cineismo.com* <http://www.cineismo.com/criticas/garage_olimpo.htm > [accessed 26 October 2010]

Shea, Renee and Edwidge Danticat, 'The Dangerous Job of Edwidge Danticat: An Interview,' *Callaloo*, 19.2 (Spring 1996)
< http://www.jstor.org/stable/3299199 > [accessed 28 February 2010]

Sims, Calvin, 'Eva Peron's Corpse Continues to Haunt Argentina'.
<http://www.alfaguara.com.ar/tomaseloymartinez/prensa/300795.pdf.>[accessed 25 October 2010]

——. 'Eva Peron's Corpse Continues to Haunt Argentina.'
< http://www.nytimes.com/1995/07/30/world/eva-peron-s-corpse-continues-to-haunt-argentina.html > [accessed 02 August 2011].

Sødal, Anna, 'Raza, clase y género en el nuevo cine argentino. Un estudio de las relaciones de dominación en Bolivia y La Ciénaga' (Unpublished Masters Thesis, Universitetet i Bergen, Institutt for Fremmedspråk, 2009)
<https://bora.uib.no/dspace/bitstream/1956/3731/1/65413005.pdf>
[accessed 8 March 2010]

The Official Eva Perón Website. <http://www.evitaperon.org/part2.htm> [accessed 25 October 2010]

Vargas, María, *Mirando hacia adentro: cine dirigido por mujeres* (Alabama: Universidad de Alabama, 2007)
<http://bama.ua.edu/~tatuana/numero3/cinenavaja/Vargascine.pdf>
[accessed 10 March 2010]

Wimmer, Natasha, *The Nation* (Los Angeles)
<www.powells.com/review/2009_06_30.html > [accessed 12 November 2010]

Wucker, Michele, 'The River Massacre: The Real and Imagined Borders of Hispaniola', *Windows on Haiti* <http://haitiforever.com/windowsonhaiti/wucker1.shtml>[accessed 12 November 2010]

Yuste, Miguel. 'Muere en atentado el jefe de la policía argentina', *El País*, June,19,1976<http://www.elpais.com/articulo/internacional/ARGENTINA/Muere/atentado/jefe/policia/federal/argentina/elpepiint/19760619elpepiint_1/Tes?print=1> [accessed 12 November 2010]

Primary Sources

Adorno, Theodor and Max Horkheimer, *Dialectic of Enlightenment* (Stanford: Stanford University Press, 2002)

Alexis, Jacques Stephen, *Compère Général Soleil* (Paris: Gallimard, 1955)

Alix, Juan Antonio, *Décimas:* Colección Estudios (Santo Domingo: Librería Dominicana, 1927)

Allende, Isabel, *Afrodita: Cuentos, Recetas y Otros Afrodsíacos* (New York: Harper Collins, 1997)

——. *Aphrodite: A Memoir of the Senses*, trans. by Margaret Sayers Peden (New York: Harper Collins, 1998)

Anzaldúa, Gloria, *Borderlands/La Frontera: The New Mestiza* (New York and San Francisco: Aunt Lute Books, 1987; repr. 1990)

Bibliography

Arenas, Reinaldo, *Antes que anochezca* (Barcelona: TusQuets Editores, 1992)

——. *Before Night Falls*, trans. by Dolores Koch (New York: Penguin, 1993)

Arendt, Hannah, *On Violence* (New York: Harcourt, Brace & World, 1970)

Bakhtin, Mikhail, *The Dialogic Imagination*, ed. by Michael Holquist (Austin: University of Texas Press, 1981; repr. 1990)

——. *Rabelais and his World*, trans. by Helene Iswolsky (Bloomington: Indiana University Press, 1984)

Benjamin, Walter, *The Origin of German Tragic Drama*, trans. by John Osborne (London: Verso, 1998)

——. ed. by Hannah Arendt, *Illuminations* (New York: Harcourt, 1968)

Césaire, Aimé, *La tragédie du roi Christophe* (Paris: Présence africaine, 1963)

——. *The Tragedy of King Christophe: A Play by Aimé Césaire*, ed. by Ralph Manheim (New York: Grove Press, 1969)

Clitandre, Pierre, *Cathedral of the August Heat* (London: Readers International, 1987)

Danticat, Edwidge, *Krik? Krak!* (New York, NY: Vintage Contemporaries, 1996)

——. *Brother, I am Dying* (New York: Vintage Books, 2007)

——. *Anacaona: Golden Flower, Haiti* (New York: Scholastic Inc, 2005)

―――. *The Dew Breaker* (London: Abacus, 2004)

―――. *The Dew Breaker* (New York: Vintage Books, 2004)

―――. ed., *The Butterfly's Way: Voices from the Haitian Diaspora in the United States* (New York: Soho Press, 2001)

―――. *The Farming of Bones* (London: Abacus, New York: Soho, 1998)

―――. 'Haiti: A Bi-Cultural Experience', *Encuentros*, 12 (1995), 1-9

―――. and others 'Voices from Hispaniola: A Meridians Roundtable with Edwidge Danticat, Loida Maritza Pérez, Myriam J. A. Chancy, and Nelly Rosario', *Meridians: Feminism, Race, Transnationalism*, 5. 1 (2004), 69-91

―――. Patricia Justine Tumanq, and Jenesha de Rivera, eds., *Homelands: Women's Journeys Across Race, Place, and Time* (Jackson, USA: Seal Press, 2007)

Dario, Rubén, *Selected Poems*, trans. by Lysander Kemp, prologue by Octavio Paz (Austin: University of Texas Press, 1988)

Depestre, René, *Alléluia pour une femme-jardin* (Paris: Gallimard, 1981)

Deren, Maya, *Divine Horsemen: The Living Gods of Haiti* (New Paltz, NY: McPherson, 1983)

Derrida, Jacques and Roudinesco, Elisabeth, *For What Tomorrow: A Dialogue*, trans. by Jeff Fort (Stanford: Stanford University Press, 2004)

Enaudeau, Corinne, *La paradoja de la representación* (Buenos Aires: Paidós, 1999)

Esquivel, Laura, *Como agua para chocolate: Novela de entregas mensuales con recetas, amores y remedios caseros* (México: Editorial Planeta, 1990)

———. *Like Water for Chocolate: A Novel in Monthly Installments with Recipes, Romances and Home Remedies,* trans. by Carol Christensen and Thomas Christensen (New York: Anchor Books, 1992)

Foucault, Michel, *Discipline and Punish*, trans. by Alan Sheridan, 2nd edn (New York: Vintage Books, 1979; repr. 1995)

Freud, Sigmund, *Collected Papers* (London: The Hogarth Press, 1953)

Glissant, Édouard, *Le discours antillais* (Paris: Seuil, 1981)

———. *The Poetics of Relation*, trans. by Betsy Wing (Ann Arbor: University of Michigan Press, 1997)

Gramsci, Antonio, *Selections from the Prison Notebooks*, ed. and trans. by Q. Joare and G. Nowell Smith (New York: International Publishers, 1971)

James, Cyril Lionel Robert, *The Black Jacobins: Toussaint L'Ouverture and the San Domingo Revolution* (New York; London: Vintage, 1963; repr. 1989)

Kohan, Martín, *Dos veces junio* (Buenos Aires: Editorial Sudamericana S.A., 2008)

Kristeva, Julia, *Revolution in Poetic Language* (New York: Columbia University Press, 1984)

Laferrière, Dany, *Le goût des jeunes filles* (Montréal: VLB éditeur, 1992)

Lorde, Audre, 'Age, Race, Class, and Sex,' in *Sister Outsider*, ed. by Cheryl Clarke (Berkeley, CA: The Crossing Press, 2007)

Marcelin, Phillipe Thoby-, *The Beast of the Haitian Hills* (New York: Rinehart & Company, Inc., 1946)

Márquez, Gabriel García, *Living to Tell the Tale*, trans. by Edith Grossman (Knopf: New York, 2003)

Paso, Fernando del, *Palinuro of Mexico*, trans. by Elizabeth Plaister (Normal, IL: Dalkey Archive Press, 1996)

———. *Noticias Del Imperio* (Barcelona: Plaza y Janes Editores, S. A., 1994)

———. *News from the Empire*, trans. by Alfonso González and Stella.T. Clark (Champaign, Ill: Dalkey Archive Press, 2009)

Perón, Eva, *In My Own Words*: *Evita*, trans. by Laura Dail (New York: New York Press, 1996)

Prieto González, José Manuel, *Enciclopedia De Una Vida En Rusia* (Grijalbo Mondadori, 2004)

———. *El Tartamudo y La Rusa* (México: Tusquets, 2002)

———. *Livadia* (Barcelona: Literatura Mondadori, 1999)

———. *Rex* (Barcelona: Editorial Anagrama, 2007)

———. *Rex: A Novel*, trans. by Esther Allen (New York: Grove Press, 2009)

Rancière, Jacques, *Dissensus: On Politics and Aesthetics*, trans. and ed. by Steven Corcoran (London & New York: Continuum, 2010)

Taylor, Carol, ed., *Brown Sugar 4: Secret Desires* (New York: Washington Square Press, 2005)

Todorov, Tzvetan, *Los abusos de la memoria*, trans. by Miguel Salazar (Barcelona: Paidós Asterisco, 2000)

Williams, William Carlos, *Selected Essays of William Carlos Williams* (New York: Random House, 1954)

———. *In the American Grain* (New York: New Directions, 1956)

Yunqué, Edgardo Vega. *The Lamentable Journey of Omaha Bigelow into the Impenetrable Loisaida Jungle* (New York: Overlook Press, 2004)

Secondary Sources

Abelove, Henry, Michèle Aina Barale and David M. Halperin, eds., *The Lesbian and Gay Studies Reader* (New York: Routledge, 1993)

Agamben, Giorgio, *Homo Sacer* (Stanford: Stanford University Press, 1998)

——. *Means without End: Notes on Politics* (Minnesota: University Of Minnesota Press, 2000; repr. 2005)

——. *State of Exception* (Chicago: University of Chicago Press, 2005)

Aguilar, Gonzalo, *Other Worlds: New Argentine Film. New Concepts in Latino American Cultures* (New York: Palgrave Macmillan, 2008)

Ahmed, Sara, *Strange Encounters: Embodied Others in Post-Coloniality* (London: Routledge, 2000)

Alba, Alicia Gaspar de and Tomás Ybarra Frausto, eds., *Velvet Barrios: Popular Culture and Chicana/o Sexualities* (New York: Palgrave Macmillan, 2003)

Almeida, Lilian Pestre de, 'Rire haïtien, rire africain: le comique dans *La Tragédie du Roi Christophe* de Césaire', *Présence Francophone: Revue Littéraire*, 10 (1975), 59-71

Álvarez Lobato, Carmen, 'Identidad y Ambivalencia. Una Lectura De *Palinuro De México* Desde El Grotesco', *Nueva Revista De Filología Hispánica*, 56. 1 (2008), 123-39

Anderson, Benedict, *Imagined Communities* (London: Verso, 2006)

Anderson, Danny J., *Cultural Conversation and Constructions of Reality: Mexican Narrative and Literary Theories after 1968*, Siglo XX/20th Century, 8 (1990-91), 11-30

Anderson, Jon Lee, *Che Guevara: A Revolutionary Life* (New York: Grove Press 1997)

Aravamudan, Srinivas, *Tropicopolitans: Colonialism and Agency, 1688-1804. Post-contemporary interventions* (Durham, NC: Duke University Press, 1999)

Archibald, Priscilla, *Imagining Modernity in the Andes* (Lewisburg, PA: Bucknell University Press, 2011)

Arditti, Rita, *Searching For Life: The Grandmothers Of The Plaza De Mayo And The Disappeared Children Of Argentina* (Berkeley, CA: University of California Press, 1999)

Arguelles, Lourdes and Ruby B. Rich, 'Homosexuality, Homophobia, and Revolution: Notes toward an Understanding of the Cuban Lesbian and Gay Male Experience, Part II', *Signs: Journal of Women in Culture and Society*, 11.1 (1985), 120-36

Arnold, A. James, 'D'Haïti à l'Afrique: '*La Tragédie du roi Christoph*e' de Césaire', *Revue de littérature comparée*, 60.2 (1986), 133-48

Arriarán, Samuel, *Barroco y Neobarroco En América Latina: Estudios Sobre La Otra Modernidad* (México, DF: Editorial Itaca, 2007)

Aub-Busher, Gertrude and Beverley Ormerod Noakes, eds., *The Francophone Caribbean Today: Literature, Language, Culture* (Kingston: University of the West Indies Press, 2003)

Avelar, Idelber, *Alegorías de la derrota: La ficción postdictarorial y el trabajo del duelo* (Santiago: Editorial Cuarto Propio, 2000)

Baird, Vanessa, 'Before Night Falls – Review', *New Internationalist*, 336 (2001), 33

Barkan, Elazar and Marie-Denise Shelton, eds., *Borders, Exiles, Diasporas* (Stanford, CA: Stanford University Press, 1998)

Bartra, Roger, ed., *La Jaula De La Melancolía: Identidad y Metamorfosis Del Mexicano* (Mexico: Grijalbo, 1987)

———. *La Democracia Ausente: El Pasado De Una Ilusión* (México, DF: Océano, 2000)

Beckles, Hilary McD., *Natural Rebels: A Social History of Enslaved Black Women in Barbados* (New Brunswick, NJ: Rutgers University Press, 1989)

Bejel, Emilio, 'The (Auto)Biography of a Furious Dissident', *Gay Cuban Nation* (Chicago: University of Chicago Press, 2001)

Bell, Beverly, *Walking on Fire: Haitian Women's Stories of Survival and Resistance* (Ithaca, NY: Cornell University Press, 2001)

Bell-Villada, Gene, *Borges and his Fiction: A Guide to his Mind and Art* (Chapel Hill: University of North Carolina Press, 1981)

Bethell, Leslie, ed., *Cambridge History of Latin America*, 10 vols (Cambridge: Cambridge University Press, 1984-92)

Beverley, John, *Subalternity and Representation: Arguments in Cultural Theory* (Durham, NC: Duke University Press, 1999)

Bilbija, Ksenija, 'Spanish American Women Writers: Simmering Identity Over a Low Fire', *STCL*, 20.1 (1996), 147-61

Birkenmaier, Anke, 'Art of the Pastiche: Jose Manuel Prieto's *Rex* and Cuban Literature of the 1990s', *Revista De Estudios Hispanicos*, 43.1 (2009), 123-48

Bisquert, Jaqueline and Daniel Lvovich, *La cambiante memoria de la dictadura: Discursos politicos, movimientos sociales y legitimidad democrática* (Los Polvorinos, Argentina: Universidad Nacional de General Sarmiento, 2008)

Blodgett, Harriet, 'Mimesis and Metaphor: Food Imagery in International Twentieth-Century Women's Writing', *PLL*, 40.3 (2004), 260-95

Bloom, Harold, *Julio Cortazar: Bloom's Major Short Story Writers* (New York: Chelsea House Publishers, 2005)

Bourdieu, Pierre, *Distinction: A Social Critique of the Judgment of Taste* (Cambridge: Harvard University Press, 1984)

Braziel, Jana Evans, 'Re-membering Défilée: Dédée Bazile as Revolutionary

Lieu de Mémoire', *Small Axe*, 18 (2005), 57-85

Brescia, Pablo, 'La niña santa' (Reseña de película), *Chasqui*, 33 (2004), 202-204

——. 'La Ciénaga (Reseña de película), *Chasqui*, 31 (2002), 152-56

Brooks, Peter, *Reading for the Plot*, 1st edn (New York: Vintage Books, 1984)

Brushwood, John, *La Novela Mexicana (1967-1982)* (México: Grijalbo, 1984)

Bru, José and Dante Medina, eds., *Acercamientos a Fernando Del Paso: Premio FIL 2007* (Guadalajara, Jalisco, México: Universidad de Guadalajara, Centro Universitario de Ciencias Sociales y Humanidades, 2008)

Buck-Morss, Susan, 'Hegel and Haiti', *Critical Inquiry*, 26.4 (2000), 821-65

Burkholder, Mark A. and Lyman L. Johnson, *Colonial Latin America* 6th edn (New York, Oxford: Oxford University Press, 2008)

Burnard, Trevor, 'Slave Naming Patterns: Onomastics and the Taxonomy of Race in Eighteenth-Century Jamaica', *The Journal of Interdisciplinary History*, 31.3 (2001), 325-46

Burt, Daniel S., *The Novel 100: A Ranking of the Greatest Novels of All Time* (New York: Barnes & Noble, 2007)

Burton, Richard D. E., 'Names and naming in Afro-Caribbean cultures', *New West Indian Guide/ Nieuwe West-Indische Gids*, 73.1-2 (1999), 35-58

Caistor, Nick, *Che Guevara: A Life* (Northampton, MA: Interlink, 2010)

Calveiro, Pilar, *Violencia y/o política: Una aproximación a la guerrilla de los años 70* (Buenos Aires: Norma, 2005)

Camp, Roderic, *Los Intelectuales y El Estado En El México Del Siglo XX* (México: Fondo de Cultura Económica, 1988)

Canclini, Nestor Garcia, *Hybrid Cultures: Strategies for Entering and Leaving Modernity* (Minneapolis: University of Minnesota Press, 1995)

Caruth, Cathy, *Unclaimed Experience: Trauma, Narrative, and History* (Baltimore: Johns Hopkins University Press, 1996)

Castellanos, Rosario, *A Rosario Castellanos Reader*, ed. and trans. by Maureen Ahern (Austin: University of Texas Press, 1996)

———. *Álbum de familia* (México: Editorial Joaquín Mortiz, 1971)

Caviglia, Mariana, *Dictadura, vida cotidiana y clases medias: una sociedad fracturada* (Buenos Aires: Prometo, 2006)

———. *Vivir a oscuras: escenas cotidianas durante la dictadura* (Buenos Aires: Aguilar Argentina, 2006)

Cedrón, Lucía, *Cordero de Dios* (Argentina-France: Les Films d'Ici, Goa Films, Lita Stantic Producciones: 2008)

Chancy, Myriam J. A., *Framing Silence: Revolutionary Novels by Haitian Women* (New Brunswick, NJ: Rutgers University Press, 1997)

Charles, Carolle, 'Gender and Politics in Contemporary Haiti: The Duvalierist State, Transnationalism, and the Emergence of a New Feminism', *Feminist Studies*, 21.1 (1995), 1-30

Ching, Erik, Christina Buckley and Angelica Lozano-Alonso, 'Reframing Latin America: A Cultural Theory Reading of the Nineteenth and Twentieth Century', *Hispanic American Historical Review*, 89 (2009), 332-33

Chiu-Olivares, Isela, *La Novela Mexicana Contemporánea (1960-1980)* (México: Pliegos, 1990)

Clark, Stephen, '*Antes que anochezca*: Las paradojas de la autorrepresentación', *Revista del ateneo puertorriqueño*, 5.13-15 (1995), 209-25

Cohen, Jaffee, 'Before Night Falls (Review)', *Gay and Lesbian Review Worldwide*, 8.2 (2001), 38.

Collins, Jo, 'The Ethics and Aesthetics of Representing Trauma: the Textual Politics of Edwidge Danticat's *The Dew Breaker*,' *Journal of Postcolonial Writing*, 47.1 (2011), 5-17

Conteh-Morgan, John, 'A Note on the Image of the Builder in Aimé Césaire's "La Tragédie du roi Christophe"', *The French Review*, 57.2 (1983), 224-30

Corber, Robert J., *Homosexuality in Cold War America: Resistance and the Crisis of Masculinity* (Durham; London: Duke University Press, 1997)

——. *In the Name of National Security: Hitchcock, Homophobia, and the Political Construction of Gender in Postwar America*. New Americanists (Durham, NC: Duke University Press, 1993)

Cosentino, Donald, ed., *The Sacred Arts of Haitian Vodou* (Los Angeles: UCLA Fowler Museum of Cultural History, 1995)

Crenzel, Emilio, *La historia política del Nunca más: la memoria de las desapariciones en la Argentina/ The Political History of Nunca Más: the Memory of the Argentina Disappearances* (Buenos Aires: Siglo XXI, 2008)

Curto, Roxanna, 'The Science of Illusion-making in Aimé Césaire's *La tragédie du roi Christophe* and *Une tempête*', *Research in African Literatures*, 42.1 (2011), 154-71

Dash, J. Michael, 'The Theater of the Haitian Revolution/The Haitian Revolution as Theater', *Small axe*, 18 (2005), 16-23

——. *The Other America*: *Caribbean Literature in a New World Context* (Charlottesville: University Press of Virginia, 1998)

——. 'Farming Bones and Writing Rocks: Rethinking a Caribbean poetics of (dis)location', *Shibboleths: Journal of Comparative Theory*, 1.1 (2006), 64-71

Davies, Lloyd Hughes, *Projections of Peronism in Argentine Autobiography, Biography and Fiction*. (Cardiff, Wales: University of Wales Press, 2007)

Davis, Gregson, *Aimé Césaire* (Cambridge: Cambridge University Press, 1997)

Dawes, James, *That the World May Know: Bearing Witness to Atrocity* (Cambridge: Harvard University Press, 2007)

Dayan, Joan, *Haiti, History and the Gods* (Berkeley, CA: University of California Press, 1995)

Deloughrey, Elizabeth, *Routes and Roots: Navigating Caribbean and Pacific Island Literatures* (Honolulu: University of Hawaii Press, 2007)

Derby, Lauren, 'Haitians, Magic and Money: Raza and Society in the Haitian-Dominican Borderlands, from 1900 to 1937', *Comparative Studies in Society and History*, 36.3 (1994), 488-526

Derby, Lauren, 'In the Shadow of the State: The Politics of Denunciation and Panegyric during the Trujillo Regime in the Dominican Republic, 1940-1958', *Hispanic American Historical Review*, 83.2 (2003), 295-344

Doho, Gilbert, 'Le fou, le rebelle, l'enfant et la révolution haitienne', *Présence Francophone* 64 (2005), 53-72

Domínguez, Christopher M. and José Luis Martínez, *La Literatura Mexicana Del Siglo XX* (Dirección general de publicaciones, Consejo Nacional para la Cultura y las Artes, 1995)

Döring, Tobias, *Caribbean-English Passages: Intertexuality in a Postcolonial Tradition* (London and New York: Routledge, 2002)

Dubois, Laurent, *Avengers of the New World: The Story of the Haitian*

Revolution (Cambridge, MA: Belknap Press of Harvard University Press, 2004)

Dumais, Manon, 'Royal bonbon', *Séquences*, 226 (2003), 57-58

Duncan, J. A., *Voices, and Reality Mexican Fiction since 1970* (Pittsburg: University of Pittsburg Press, 1986)

Durrant, Sam, *Postcolonial Narrative and the Work of Mourning* (Albany, New York: State University of New York, 2004)

D'Emilio, John, and Estelle B. Freedman, *Intimate Matters: A History of Sexuality in America*, 2nd edn (Chicago: University of Chicago Press, 1997)

——. *Sexual Politics, Sexual Communities: The Making of a Homosexual Minority in the United States, 1940-1970*, 2nd edn (Chicago: University of Chicago Press, 1998)

Ellis, Robert Richmond, 'The Gay Lifewriting of Reinaldo Arenas: *Antes que anochezca*,' *A/B: Auto/Biography Studies*, 10.1 (1995), 126-44

Enaudeau, Corinne, *La paradoja de la representación*, 1st edn (Buenos Aires: Paidós, 1999)

Eng, David L. and David Kazanjian, *Loss: Politics of Mourning* (Berkeley, CA: University of California Press, 2003)

Epps, Brad, 'Proper Conduct: Reinaldo Arenas, Fidel Castro, and the Politics of Homosexuality', *Journal of the History of Sexuality*, 6.2 (1995), 231-83

Faber, Sebastiaan, 'Learning from the Latins: Waldo Frank's Progressive Pan-Americanism', *The New Centennial Review*, 1 (2003), 257-95

Farmer, Paul, *The Uses of Haiti* (Monroe, ME.: Common Courage Press, 1994)

Feitlowitz, Marguerite, *A Lexicon of Terror: Argentina and the Legacies of Torture* (New York: Oxford University Press, 1998)

Fernandez, James W., ed., *Beyond Metaphor: The Theory of Tropes in Anthropology* (Stanford, CA: Stanford University Press, 1991)

Fernández-Armesto, Felipe, *The Americas: The History of a Hemisphere* (London: Phoenix, 2003)

Ferré, Rosario and Diana L. Vélez, 'The Writer's Kitchen', *Feminist Studies*, 12.2 (1986), 227-42

Fiddian, Robin W., *The Novels of Fernando Del Paso* (Gainesville: University Press of Florida, 2000)

Fignolé, Jean-Claude, 'Public Opinion (a mother)', *Callaloo*, 15.2 (1992), 435-40

Figueroa, Víctor, 'Between Louverture and Christophe: Aimé Césaire on the Haitian Revolution', *The French Review*, 82.5(2009), 1006-1021

Fischer, Sibylle, *Modernity Disavowed: Haiti and the Cultures of Slavery in the Age of Revolution* (Durham, NC: Duke University Press, 2004)

Fischman, G., 'Hybrid Cultures: Strategies for Entering and Leaving Modernity by Néstor García Canclini', *Comparative Education Review*, (1997), 483.

Fitch, Melissa, *Side Dishes: Latina American Women, Sex, and Cultural Production* (New York, NJ: Rutgers University Press, 2009)

Forcinito, Ana, 'Mirada cinematográfica y género sexual: mímica, erotismo y ambigüedad en Lucrecia Martel', *Chasqui*, 35 (2006), 109-30

Fouchard, Jean, *La Méringue: Danse nationale d'Haïti* (Montreal: Éditions Leméac, 1974)

Franco, Jean, *Marcar Diferencias, Cruzar Fornteras* (Chile: Editorial Cuatro Vientos, 1996)

──. 'The Critique of the Piramid and Mexican Narrative After 1968', *Latin American Fiction Today: A Symposium*, (1979), 49-60

Frank, Waldo, *America Hispana: A Portrait and a Prospect* (New York: Charles Scribner's Sons, 1931)

──. *The Re-discovery of America* (New York: Charles Scribner's Sons, 1929)

Fusco, Coco and Nao Bustamante, 'STUFF', *The Drama Review*, 41.4 (1997), 63-82

Gallagher, Mary, ed., *Ici-Là: Place and Displacement in Caribbean Writing in French* (New York: Rodopi, 2003)

García, Lucía, 'La imaginación del espectador es el major director de cine', *Puentes*, 24 (2008), 71-77

Geggus, David, 'The Naming of Haiti', *New West Indian Guide/Nieuwe West-Indische Gids*, 71.1-2 (1997), 43-68

Góngora, Mario, *Studies in the Colonial History of Spanish America* (Cambridge: Cambridge University Press, 1975)

González, Alfonso, *Voces De La Posmodernidad: Seis Narradores Mexicanos Contemporáneos* (México, DF: Coordinación de Difusión Cultural, Dirección de Literatura/UNAM, 1998)

González, Lisa Sánchez, 'Modernism and Boricua Literature: A Reconsideration of Arturo Schomburg and William Carlos Williams', *American Literary History*, 13 (2001), 242-64

González, Patricia E. and Eliana Ortega, eds., *La sartén por el mango: Encuentro de escritoras latinoamericanas* (Río Piedras, PR: Ediciones Huracán, 1984)

Good, Carl, 'A Chronicle of Poetic Non-Encounter in the Americas,' *The New Centennial Review*, 1, (2003), 225-55

Gutiérrez, Ivonne, *Entre El Silencio y La Estridencia: La Protesta Literaria Del 68* (México: Aldus, 1998)

Haigh, Sam, ed., *An Introduction to Caribbean Francophone Writing: Guadeloupe and Martinique* (New York: Berg, 1999)

Harss, Luis and Barbara Dohmann, *Into the Mainstream: Conversations with Latin American Writers* (New York: Harper & Row, 1967)

Harvey, David, *A Brief History of Neoliberalism* (Oxford University Press, 2005)

Hawkins, Hunt, 'Aimé Césaire's Lesson about Decolonization in *La Tragédie du roi Christophe*', *College Language Association Journal*, 30.2 (1986), 144-53

Haste, Helen, *The Sexual Metaphor* (Cambridge, MA: Harvard University Press, 1994)

Heller, Tamar and Patricia Moran, eds., *Scenes of the Apple: Food and the Female Body in Nineteenth- and Twentieth-Century Women's Writing* (Albany: State University of New York Press, 2003)

Hennessy, Alistair, ed., *Intellectuals in the Twentieth-century Caribbean II* (London: Macmillan Caribbean, 1992)

Hertzberger, David K., *Narrating the Past: Fiction and Historiography in Postwar Spain* (Durham: Duke University Press, 1995)

Inness, Sherrie A., ed., *Pilaf, Pozole, and Pad Thai: American Women and Ethnic Food* (Amherst: University of Massachusetts Press, 2001)

Ippolito, Emilia, *Caribbean Women Writers: Identity and Gender* (Rochester: Camden House, 2000)

Itzigsohnm, José and Matthias vom Hau, 'Unfinished Imagined Communities: the Theoretical Implications of Nationalism in Latin America', *Theory and Society*, 35.2 (2006), 193-212

Jelin, Elizabeth and Diego Sempol, eds., *El pasado en el futuro: Los movimientos juveniles* (Madrid: Siglo XXI Editores, 2006)

——. *State Repression and the Labour of Memory* (Minneapolis: University of Minnesota Press, 2003)

——. and Susan G. Kaufman, eds., *Subjetividad y figuras de la memoria/Subjectivity and figures of memory* (Buenos Aires: Siglo XXI Editora Iberoamericana, 2006)

Jouve, Edmond and Simone Dreyfus, eds., *Les écrivains de la négritude et de la créolité: Actes du 3ème Colloque International Francophone du Canton de Payrac organisé par L'A.D.E.L.F.* (Paris: Sepeg International, 1994)

Keyser, Catherine, *Playing Smart: New York Women Writers and Modern Magazine Culture* (New Brunswick: Rutgers University Press, 2010)

Knudsen, Knud and Kari Wærness, 'National Context and Spouses' Housework in 34 Countries', *European Sociological Review*, 24.1 (2008), 97-113

Kutzinski, Vera M., *Against the American Grain: Myth and History in William Carlos Williams, Jay Wright, and Nicolás Guillén* (Baltimore: The Johns Hopkins University Press, 1987)

Kurt, Andreas, 'La Literatura Mexicana Contemporánea Entre Regionalismo y Cosmopolitismo', *Revista De Literatura Contemporánea,* 21.9 (2003), 17-23

Lakoff, George, and Mark Johnson, *Metaphors We Live By* (Chicago, IL: Chicago University Press, 1980)

Lancaster, Roger N., *Life is Hard: Machismo, Danger, and the Intimacy of Power in Nicaragua* (Berkeley, CA: University of California Press, 1992)

——. 'Sexual Positions: Caveats and Second Thoughts on 'Categories', *The Americas,* 4.1 (1997), 1-16

Langley, Lester D., *The Americas in the Age of Revolution, 1750-1850* (New Haven, CT: Yale University Press, 1998)

Laroche, Maximilien, *L'image comme echo:* essais sur la littérature et la culture haïtiennes (Montréal: Nouvelle Optique, 1978)

——. *La Literature Haitienne: identité, langue, réalité* (Montréal, Canada: Éditions Leméac, 1980)

Lawless, Cecilia, 'Experimental Cooking in *Como agua para chocolate*', *Monographic Review/ Revista Monográfica,* 8 (1992), 261-72

Lecercle, Jean-Jacques, *The Violence of Language* (New York: Routledge, 1990)

Levine, Suzanne Jill, *Manuel Puig and The Spider Woman: His Life and Fictions* (New York: Farrar, Straus and Giroux, 2000)

Lobato, Álvarez, 'Carmen: Identidad y Ambivalencia. Una lectura de Palinuro de México desde el grotesco', *Nueva Revista de Filología Hispánica*, 56. 1 (2008), 123-39

Lockhart, James and Stuart B. Schwarz, *Early Latin America: A History of Colonial Spanish America and Brazil* (Cambridge: Cambridge University Press, 1983, repr. 1999)

Logan, Joy, 'Aphrodite in an Apron or the Erotics of Recipes and Self-Representation in Isabel Allende's *Afrodita*', *Romance Languages Annual*, X (1999), 685-89

Loss, Jacqueline, 'Global Arenas: Narrative and Filmic Translation of Identity', *Nepantla: Views from South*, 4.2 (2003), 317-44

Luther, Eric and Ted Henken, *The Life and Work of Che Guevara* (Indianapolis, IN: Alpha Books, 2001)

McCarthy Brown, Karen, *Mama Lola: A Vodou Priestess in Brooklyn* (Berkeley, CA: University of California Press, 1991)

McFayden, Deidre et alia., *Haiti: Dangerous Crossroads* (Boston, MA: South End Press, 1995)

McLaughlin, Thomas and Frank Lentricchia, eds., *Critical Terms for Literary Study* (Chicago: University of Chicago Press, 1990)

Madiou, Thomas, *Histoire d'Haiti*, 8 vols, ed, by Michèle Oriole (Port-au-Prince: Courtois 1847-48; repr. Éditions Deschamps, 1985-1991)

Mariani, Paul, *William Carlos Williams: A New World Naked* (New York: McGraw Hill, 1981)

Marshall, Paule, 'From the Poets in the Kitchen', *Callaloo*, 24.2 (2001), 627-33

Marzán, Julio, *The Spanish American Roots of William Carlos Williams* (Austin: University of Texas Press, 1994)

Mehuron, Kate, 'Queer Territories in the Americas: Reinaldo Arenas' Prose', *Prose Studies: History, Theory, Criticism*, 17.1 (1994), 39-63

Melis, Antonio, *Leyendo Marieategui 1967-1998* (Lima: Biblioteca Amauta, 1999)

Mintz, Sidney, W., *Tasting Food, Tasting Freedom* (Boston: Beacon Press, 1996)

Moreau, Alain, 'La démesure d'un héros grec, le roi Christophe', *Oeuvres et critiques*, 19.2 (1994), 281-93

Mota, Miguel, 'William Carlos Williams' Contact with the Spanish', *Journal of Modern Literature*, 4 (1993), 447-59

Munro, Martin and Elizabeth Walcot-Hackshaw, eds., *Reinterpreting the Haitian Revolution and its Cultural Aftershocks* (Kingston, Jamaica: University of the West Indies Press, 2006)

Negri, Antonio, *Diálogo sobre la globalización, la multitud y la experiencia argentina* (Buenos Aires: Paidós, 2003)

Nesbitt, Nick, 'History and Nation-Building in Aimé Césaire's *La Tragédie du Roi Christophe*', *Journal of Haitian Studies*, 3-4(1997), 132-48

Niranjana, Tejaswini, *Siting Translation: History, Post-Structuralism, and the Colonial Context* (Berkeley, CA: University of California, 1992)

N'Zengou-Tayo, Marie-José, 'Fanm Sé Poto Mitan: Haitian Women, the Pillar of Society', 59 *Feminist review* (1998), 118-42

Oberg, Larry R., 'How Criminal Was Castro?', *The Gay & Lesbian Review Worldwide*, 8.6 (2001)

Ocasio, Rafael, *Cuba's Political and Sexual Outlaw: Reinaldo Arenas* (Gainesville, FL: University Press of Florida, 2003)

Ogorzaly, Michael A., *Waldo Frank: Prophet of Hispanic Regeneration* (Lewisburg: Bucknell University Press, 1994)

Olds, Linda, E., *Metaphors of Interrelatedness* (New York: State University of New York Press, 1992)

Olivera-Williams, María Rosa, 'La década del 70 en el Cono Sur: Discursos nostálgicos que recuerdan la revolución y escriben la historia', *Romance Quarterly*, 57.1 (2010), 43-62

Oubiña, David, *Estudio Crítico sobre La Ciénaga: Entrevista a Lucrecia Martel* (Buenos Aires: Picnic Editorial, 2007)

Parr, James A., *Don Quixote: An Anatomy of Subversive Discourse* (Newark, Delaware: Juan de la Cuesta, 1988)

Past, Mariana, 'Articulating Haitian Conflicts in a New York City Basement: The Global Stakes of Franketyèn's *Pèlin-tèt*', *The Global South*, 4.2 (2010), 76-98

——.'Toussaint on Trial in *Ti difè boulè sou istoua Ayiti*, or the People's Role in the Haitian Revolution', *Journal of Haitian Studies*, 10.1 (2004), 87-102

Patton, Cindy and Benigno Sánchez-Eppler, eds., *Queer Diasporas* (Durham, NC: Duke University Press, 2000)

Pelayo, Rubén, *Gabriel García Márquez: A Critical Companion* (Westport, CT: Greenwood Press, 2001)

Pena, Jaime, *Historias Extraordinarias: El Nuevo Cine Argentino (1999-2008)* (Barcelona: T&B Editores, 2009)

Perloff, Marjorie, *The Poetics of Indeterminacy: Rimbaud to Cage* (Evanston: Northwestern University Press, 1981)

Petit, Octave, "Défilée-La-Folle," *Revue de la Société d'Histoire et de Géographie d'Haïti*, 3.8 (1932), 1-21

Plummer, Brenda Gayle, *Haiti and the Great Powers, 1902-1915* (Baton Rouge, LA: Louisiana State University Press, 1988)

Powells, H. Jefferson and James Boyd White, eds., *Law and Democracy in the Empire of Force* (Michigan: The University of Michigan Press: 2009)

Puri, Shalini, *The Caribbean Postcolonial: Social Equality, Post-Nationalism, and Cultural Hybridity* (New York: Palgrave Macmillan, 2004)

——. ed., *Marginal Migrations: The Circulation of Culture within the Caribbean* (Oxford: Macmillan, 2003)

Ranciére, Jaques, *Dissensus: On Politics and Aesthetics* (London: Coninuum, 2010)

Rangil, Viviana, ed., *El Cine Argentino de hoy: entre el Arte y la Política* (Buenos Aires: Editorial Biblos, 2007)

Richardson, Brian, *Unnatural Voices: Extreme Narration in Modern and Contemporary Fiction* (Columbus: Ohio State University Press, 2006)

Rooney, David, 'Schnabel's Portrait of a Man', *Variety*, 380.4 (2000)

Rosario, Vanessa Pérez, *Hispanic Caribbean Literature of Migration* (New York: Palgrave Macmillan, 2010)

Ruisánchez Serra, José R., '¿Afuera Del 68? Volpi y Pérez Gay Como Ficciones Inaugurales', *Revista De Literatura Contemporánea*, 21.9 (2003), 41-49

Sáenz, Inés, *Hacia La Novela Total: Fernando Del Paso Madrid* (Madrid: Pliegos, 1994)

Scapp, Ron and Brian Seilz, eds., *Eating Culture* (New York: State University of New York Press, 1988)

Schmidt, Hans, *The United States Occupation of Haiti, 1915-1934* (New

Brunswick, NJ: Rutgers University Press, 1971)

Scott, David, *Conscripts of Modernity: The Tragedy of Colonial Enlightenment* (Durham, NC: Duke University Press, 2004)

Shange, Ntozake, *If I Can Cook/You Know God Can* (Boston: Beacon Press, 1998)

Shapiro, Michael J., and Hayward R. Alker, eds., *Challenging Boundaries: Global Flows, Territorial Identities* (Minneapolis: University of Minnesota Press, 1996)

Shemak, April, 'Re-membering Hispaniola: Edwidge Danticat's *The Farming of Bones*', *Modern Fiction Studies*, 48.1 (2002), 83-112

Sklodowska, Elzbieta, *La Parodia En La Nueva Novela Hispanoamericana* (Amsterdam/Philadelphia: John Benjamins Publishing Company, 1991)

Slotkin, Richard, *Gunfighter Nation: The Myth of the Frontier in Twentieth-Century America* (New York: Atheneum: Maxwell Macmillan, 1992)

Sorrentino, Fernando, *Seven Conversations with Jorge Luis Borges*, trans. by Clark M. Zlotchew (Troy, New York: The Whitston Publishing Company, 1982)

Spanos, Tony, 'The Paradoxical Metaphors of the Kitchen in Laura Esquivel's *Like Water for Chocolate*, *Letras femeninas*, 21.1-2 (1995), 29-36

Standish, Peter, *Understanding Julio Cortázar* (Columbia, SC: University of South Carolina Press, 2001)

Steele, Cynthia, *Politics, Gender, and the Mexican Novel, 1968-1988: Beyond the Pyramid* (Austin: University of Texas Press, 1992)

Stein, William W., and Renato Alarcón, 'José Carlos Mariátegui y Waldo Frank: dos amigos', *Aniversario Mariateguiano*, 1 (1989), 161-84

Stevens, Alta Mae, 'Manje in Haitian Culture: The Symbolic Significance of Manje in Haitian Culture', *Journal of Haitian Studies*, 1.1 (1995)

Trachtenberg, Alan, ed., with an Introduction by Lewis Mumford, *Memoirs of Waldo Frank* (Amherst: University of Massachusetts Press, 1973)

Trouillot, Michel-Rolph, *Haiti: State Against Nation* (New York, NY: Monthly Review Press, 1990)

———. *Silencing the Past: Power and the Production of History* (Boston, MA: Beacon, 1995)

———. *Why the Cocks Fight: Dominicans, Haitians, and the Struggle for Hispaniola* (New York, NY: Hill and Wang, 2000)

Turits, Richard Lee, 'A World Destroyed, A Nation Imposed: The 1937 Haitian Massacre in the Dominican Republic', *Hispanic American Historical Review*, 82. 3 (2002), 590-635

Viart, Dominique, 'En Busca Del Tiempo Perdido, Una Ficción Hermenéutica', *Cuadernos Hispanoamericanos,* 562 (1997), 27-45

Warhol, Robyn R. and Diane Price, eds., *Feminisms: An Anthology of Literary Theory and Criticism* (New Brunswick and New Jersey: Rutgers University, 1991)

Williams, Eric, *From Columbus to Castro* (New York: Vintage Books, 1970)

Williamson, Edwin, *The Penguin History of Latin America* (London: Penguin, 1992; repr. 2009)

Wood, Michael and Jose Manuel Prieto, 'Nocturnal Butterflies of the Russian Empire', *The New York Review of Books*, 49. 4 (2002), 40

Young, J. C. Robert, *White Mythologies* (New York: Routledge, 2004)

Zolov, Eric, *Refried Elvis: The Rise of the Mexican Counterculture* (Berkeley, CA: University of California Press, 1999)

Zubiaurre, Maite, 'Culinary Eros in Contemporary Hispanic Female Fiction: From Kitchen Tales to Table Narratives', *College Literature*, 33.3 (2006), 29-51

NOTES

---

[1] James Lockhart and Stuart B. Schwarz, *Early Latin America: A History of Colonial Spanish America and Brazil* (Cambridge: Cambridge University Press, 1983, repr. 1999). Mark A. Burkholder and Lyman L. Johnson, *Colonial Latin America* 6th edn (New York, Oxford: Oxford University Press, 2008). Felipe Fernández-Armesto, *The Americas: The History of a Hemisphere* (London: Phoenix, 2003). Other notable histories are Mario Góngora, *Studies in the Colonial History of Spanish America* (Cambridge: Cambridge University Press, 1975) and the *Cambridge History of Latin America*, ed. by Leslie Bethell, 10 vols (Cambridge: Cambridge University Press, 1984-92).
[2] For the precise fascinating history of 'Discovery and Conquest' of the region, see Edwin Williamson, *The Penguin History of Latin America* (London: Penguin, 1992; repr. 2009), pp. 3-36.
[3] See http://www.princeton.edu/africanamericanstudies/news/Newsletter-Fall_2008_Final.pdf [Accessed 20.02.2010].
[4] Silvia Pedraza, 'Los Marielitos of 1980: Race, Class, Gender, and Sexuality', *Cuba in Transition*, 14 (2004), 89-102. <http://www.ascecuba.org/publications/proceedings/volume14/>[accessed 30 June 2011], p. 89.
[5] John D'Emilio and Estelle B. Freedman, *Intimate Matters: A History of Sexuality in America*, 2nd edn (Chicago: University of Chicago Press, 1997), p. 346.
[6] For analyses on sexuality and Cold War culture see: John D'Emilio, *Sexual Politics, Sexual Communities: The Making of a Homosexual Minority in the United States, 1940-1970*, 2nd edn (Chicago: University of Chicago Press, 1998), Robert J. Corber, *Homosexuality in Cold War America: Resistance and the Crisis of Masculinity* (Durham; London: Duke University Press, 1997), Robert J. Corber, *In the Name of National Security: Hitchcock, Homophobia, and the Political Construction of Gender in Postwar America*. New Americanists (Durham, NC: Duke University Press, 1993), Richard Slotkin, *Gunfighter Nation: The Myth of the Frontier in Twentieth-Century America* (New York: Atheneum: Maxwell Macmillan, 1992).
[7] David Johnston, 'Ruling Backs Homosexuals on Asylum', *The New York Times*, (June 17, 1994). <http://www.nytimes.com/1994/06/17/us/ruling-backs-homosexuals-on-asylum.html?scp=1&sq=johnston%2C+david&st=nyt?> [accessed 29 June 2011]. For a useful critique of this ruling see: Natasha Tinsley Omise'eke, 'Gender Pirates of the Caribbean: Queering Caribbeanness in the Novels of Zoé Valdés and Christopher John Farley', in *Hispanic Caribbean Literature of Migration*, ed. by Vanessa Pérez Rosario (New York: Palgrave Macmillan, 2010), pp. 153-68 (p. 156).
[8] Lourdes Arguelles and Ruby B. Rich, 'Homosexuality, Homophobia, and Revolution: Notes toward an Understanding of the Cuban Lesbian and Gay Male

Experience, Part II', *Signs: Journal of Women in Culture and Society*, 11.1 (1985), 120-36 (p. 131).

[9] *Mauvaise conduite* or *Improper Conduct*, directed by Néstor Almendros and Orlando Jiménez Leal (Antenne-2, 1984). For a review of *Before Night Falls* that finds middle ground between claims of Cuban cruelty to homosexuals and those of Cuba's progress in guaranteeing civil rights for homosexuals, see: Larry R. Oberg, 'How Criminal Was Castro?', *The Gay & Lesbian Review Worldwide*, 8.6 (2001).

[10] Reinaldo Arenas, *Antes que anochezca* (Barcelona: TusQuets Editores, 1992), p. 132. Translation: [Later, in exile, I found that sexual relations can be tedious and unrewarding. There are categories or divisions in the homosexual world. The queer gets together with the queer and everybody does everything. One sucks first, and then they reverse roles. How can that bring any satisfaction? What we are really looking for is our opposite. The beauty of our relationships then was that we met our opposites [...]. Either conditions here are different, or it is just difficult to duplicate what we had there. Everything here is so regulated that groups and societies have been created in which it is very difficult for a homosexual to find a man, that is, the real object of his desire. I do not know what to call the young Cuban men of those days, whether homosexuals who played the male role or bisexuals. The truth is that they had girlfriends or wives, but when they came to us they enjoyed themselves thoroughly]: Reinaldo Arenas, *Before Night Falls*, trans. by Dolores Koch (New York: Penguin, 1993), pp. 106-107.

[11] Jacqueline Loss, 'Global Arenas: Narrative and Filmic Translation of Identity', *Nepantla: Views from South*, 4.2 (2003), 317-44 (p. 330).

[12] ImdbPro<http://pro.imdb.com/boxoffice> [accessed 1 July 2011].

[13] Max Kozloff, 'Island Paradise, Island Prison – Review', *Art in America*, 89.3 (2011), 69.

[14] Vanessa Baird, 'Before Night Falls – Review', *New Internationalist*, 336 (2001), p. 33. Alexander Barley, 'Before Night Falls – Review', *New Statesman*, (July 9, 2001), p. 56. David Rooney, 'Schnabel's Portrait of a Man', *Variety*, 380.4 (2000), p. 21 and p. 29. Jaffee Cohen, 'Before Night Falls (Review)', *Gay and Lesbian Review Worldwide*, 8.2 (2001), p. 38.

[15] *PM*, dir. by Alberto Cabrera Infante and Orlando Jiménez Leal (1961).

[16] The problems of autobiography – factuality, memory, and desire – cannot be addressed here, but should be considered, especially in light of Arenas' penchant for embellishment and his constant uniting of fantasy and reality. Likewise it is important to note that fidelity is a misleading gauge for the success of a film adaptation. I do not take the memoir as pure 'fact'; nor do I feel the quality of the film depends upon the degree of its fidelity to the memoir.

[17] Jacqueline Loss, arguing that Schnabel perpetuates a myth of authenticity with the film, notes that this choice furthers that agenda: 'That Lázaro Gómez Carriles, whom, in *Before Night Falls*, Arenas calls the 'most authentic person he ever

met,' was also a co writer of the film undoubtedly helps to shape Schnabel's 'fable of intimacy' and lends his production a stamp of authenticity': Loss, p. 330.

[18] Sánchez-Eppler articulates how the memoir 'homosexualizes' revolutionary Cuba: Benigno Sánchez-Eppler, 'The Displacement of Cuban Homosexuality in the Fiction and Autobiography of Reinaldo Arenas', *Challenging Boundaries: Global Flows, Territorial Identities*, ed. by Michael J. Shapiro and Hayward R. Alker (Minneapolis: University of Minnesota Press, 1996).

[19] See Tomás Almaguer whose comparison of U.S. and Latin American definitions of homosexuality summarizes this generalization: 'The structured meaning of homosexuality in the European-American context rests on the sexual object choice one makes – i.e., the biological sex of the person toward whom sexual activity is directed. The Mexican/Latin-American sexual system, on the other hand, confers meaning to homosexual practices according to sexual aim – i.e., the act one wants to perform with another person (of either biological sex)': Tomás Almaguer, 'Chicano Men: A Cartography of Homosexual Identity and Behavior', in *The Lesbian and Gay Studies Reader*, ed. by Henry Abelove, Michèle Aina Barale and David M. Halperin (New York: Routledge, 1993), pp. 255-73 (p. 257). To follow a similar study in Nicaragua, see: Roger N. Lancaster, *Life is Hard: Machismo, Danger, and the Intimacy of Power in Nicaragua* (Berkeley, CA: University of California Press, 1992). Lancaster productively complicates these concepts in his later work: Roger N. Lancaster, 'Sexual Positions: Caveats and Second Thoughts on 'Categories', *The Americas*, 4.1 (1997), 1-16.

[20] Several scholars, including myself, have taken an interest in the ways Arenas' memoir productively situates Arenas to offer a transcultural perspective of both Cuba and the U.S. Of particular interest has been the author's grappling with identity constructions that emerge as he traverses various homophobic spaces in revolutionary Cuba and the U.S. See the following: Kate Mehuron, 'Queer Territories in the Americas: Reinaldo Arenas' Prose', *Prose Studies: History, Theory, Criticism*, 17.1 (1994), 39-63, Ellis, Robert Richmond, 'The Gay Lifewriting of Reinaldo Arenas: *Antes que anochezca*,' *A/B: Auto/Biography Studies*, 10.1 (1995), 126-44, Brad Epps, 'Proper Conduct: Reinaldo Arenas, Fidel Castro, and the Politics of Homosexuality', *Journal of the History of Sexuality*, 6.2 (1995), 231-83, Stephen Clark, '*Antes que anochezca*: Las paradojas de la autorrepresentación', *Revista del ateneo puertorriqueño*, 5.13-15 (1995), 209-25, Benigno Sánchez-Eppler, 'The Displacement of Cuban Homosexuality in the Fiction and Autobiography of Reinaldo Arenas', *Challenging Boundaries: Global Flows, Territorial Identities*, ed. by Michael J. Shapiro and Hayward R. Alker (Minneapolis: University of Minnesota Press, 1996), Ricardo L. Ortíz, 'Pleasure's Exile: Reinaldo Arenas' Last Writing', *Borders, Exiles, Diasporas*, ed. by Elazar Barkan and Marie-Denise Shelton (Stanford, CA: Stanford University Press, 1998), Benigno Sánchez-Eppler, 'Reinaldo Arenas, Re-Writer Revenant, and the Re-Patriation of Cuban Homoerotic Desire', *Queer Diasporas*, ed. by Cindy Patton and Benigno Sánchez-Eppler (Durham, NC: Duke University Press, 2000),

Emilio Bejel, 'The (Auto)Biography of a Furious Dissident', *Gay Cuban Nation* (Chicago: University of Chicago Press, 2001), Rafael Ocasio, *Cuba's Political and Sexual Outlaw: Reinaldo Arenas* (Gainesville, FL: University Press of Florida, 2003).
[21] Arenas, *Antes que anochezca*, p. 132.
[22] Ibid. p. 132.
[23] Ibid. p. 107.
[24] Michael Hutak, 'Easel Angles', *The Bulletin*, 29 August 2001.
[25] Dan Lyberger, 'Capturing Life on Canvas and with Lense', *Lawrence Journal-World*, 8 February, 2001) <www.ljworld.com≥ [accessed 26 May 2003].
[26] Don Shewey, 'A Painter's Latest Cinematic Collage', *The New York Times*, Late Edition, 5 November, 2000, 2A, p. 44.
[27] Pierre Bourdieu, 'The Aristocracy of Culture', in *Distinction: A Social Critique of the Judgment of Taste* (Cambridge: Harvard University Press, 1984), pp. 12-96.
[28] Ana Amado, 'Velocidades, generaciones y utopías: a propósito de La Ciénaga, de Lucrecia Martel', *ALCEU*, 6 (2006), 48-56. <http://publique.rdc.puc-io.br/revistaalceu/media/alceu_n12_Amado.pdf> [accessed 10 Mar 2010].
[29] The Lacanian category used here, 'the Real', will be discussed more thoroughly in the essay ahead. Suffice it to say, for now, that much dissent has ensued as to its definition, if any, for Lacan. Many specialists agree that the Real is that which resists and, for that very reason, instigates symbolic production and linguistic/social/cultural representation.
[30] 'Phantoms' is a well-established category in the psychoanalytic tradition, indicating, among other things, that which, due to subjectivity's constitutive 'lack', kindles fantasy's image-production – or 'phantoms' – of a self-completion movement, by the possibility of integrating an ever-elusive unit, nominally called 'object petit @'.
[31] 'Partial objects' is a complex category, associated in part with Kleinian and the English School of Psychoanalysis. It has usually been opposed to 'total objects'. According to the Kleinian branch of psychoanalysis, the partial object is related to the schizo-paranoid position of the self, and thereby with the way the foetus and newly-born apprehends reality – by fragments.
[32] 'Jouissance' is another deeply engrained term in the psychoanalytic tradition and beyond. In the structuralist phase of Lacanian psychoanalysis, it had at times a rather negative connotation, as opposed to desire. It indicated a totalitarian energetic and affect movement on the subject's part to compensate for its constitutive lack. Desire's movement, on the contrary, is metonymic and thereby residual, not totalitarian. On the other hand, recent cultural theory has much expounded on the rather positive qualities of jouissance in general, elaborating for instance on the 'feminine jouissance'. To make clear my structuralist Lacanian allusion, I have added the modifier 'opaque jouissance'.
[33] The 'desiring machines' is a well-known concept, metaphor, and image used by Deleuze and Guattari to suggest residual signifying economies and agencies that

resist the totalitarian 'capitalist', 'social' or 'technical' machine. Whereas the first is anti-oedipal, anti-triangularist, and anti-familiarist, among others, the second tends towards closure, control, and therefore towards everything the first is against. The desiring machines serve to explain a-signifying or residual-signifying procedures which by their very open-endedness provide 'vantage lines' that further destabilize semiotic or social regimes (*The Anti-Oedipus*).

[34] 'Traversement' or 'to traverse' is a term belonging in part to the psychoanalytic tradition, that connotes a state, experience, or movement where something is not so much overcome as gone through, traversed, and in its very possibility, debilitated, suspended or released.

[35] Interview of Lucrecia Martel, *La Mujer sin Cabeza* (Argentina: Aquafilms, 2008).

[36] The 'acousmatic' refers in film theory in general to sounds of an unidentifiable source.

[37] With the terms 'the vertically inclined and metaphoric axis' I am alluding to the rich semiotic, structuralist, and psychoanalytic traditions that elaborate on two linguistic and signifying axis: the vertical-paradigmatic and metaphoric one, that permits word and semiotic code association or equivalence, and the horizontal, sintagmatic and metonymical one, that permits word and semiotic code combination or concatenation.

[38] Lía Gómez, *Nuevas razones de la imagen: Un estudio sobre Lucrecia Martel y el cine argentino contemporáneo* (La Plata: UNLP Facultad de Periodismo y Comunicación Social, 2009) <http://iigg.sociales.uba.ar/jovenes_investigadores/5jornadasjovenes/EJE4/Mesa%201/Gomez.pdf> [accessed 10 March 2010].

[39] Lucrecia Martel, *La Mujer sin Cabeza* (Argentina: Aquafilms, 2008), *La Niña Santa* (Argentina: La Pasionaria, 2006), *La Ciénaga* (Argentina: 4k Films, 2001), *Rey Muerto* (Argentina: Instituto Nacional de Cinematografía y Artes Audiovisuales, 1995).

[40] Alfredo Alfonso, 'Imagen e imaginario de la crisis: Panorama audiovisual argentino sobre la crisis que tuvo su máxima expresión en diciembre de 2001', *Colección GTs ALAIC* (2003), 116-124 <http://www.alaic.net> [accessed 10 Mar 2010], p. 118.

[41] Ibid. p. 119.

[42] Lía Gómez, *Nuevas razones de la imagen: Un estudio sobre Lucrecia Martel y el cine argentino contemporáneo* (La Plata: UNLP Facultad de Periodismo y Comunicación Social, 2009).

[43] Julia, Kristeva, *Revolution in Poetic Language* (New York: Columbia University Press, 1984), p. 12.

[44] The English School of Psychoanalysis, in dialogue with Melanie Klein's theorization about an unconscious fantasy, the site of partial objects and drives, added a 'ph' to distinguish it from 'fantasy', which could be associated more with conscious image production.

[45] 'Gramene', as a term deriving from a deconstructive and psychoanalytic tradition, refers to that which is 'pure inscription', stemming from its Greek root.
[46] Martel, interview, Making-of *La Niña Santa*, DVD version.
[47] Luce Irigaray, 'This Sex Which Is Not One', in *Feminisms: An Anthology of Literary Theory and Criticism*, ed. by Robyn R. Warhol and Diane Price (New Brunswick and New Jersey: Rutgers University, 1991), p. 350.
[48] See Jaqueline Bisquert and Daniel Lvovich, *La cambiante memoria de la dictadura: Discursos públicos, movimientos sociales y legitimidad democrática* (Los Polvorinos, Argentina: Universidad Nacional de General Sarmiento, 2008) and see Emilio Crenzel, *La historia política del Nunca más: La memoria de las desapariciones en la Argentina* (Buenos Aires: Siglo XXI, 2008).
[49] Tzvetan Todorov, *Los abusos de la memoria*, trans. by Miguel Salazar (Buenos Aires-Barcelona: Paidós, 2000), pp. 30-33.
[50] Nicolas Böhmer, 'An Oresteia for Argentina: Between Fraternity and the Rule of Law' in *Law and Democracy in the Empire of Force*, ed. by H. Jefferson Powells and James Boyd White (Michigan: The University of Michigan Press, 2009), p. 90.
[51] Elizabeth Jelin, *State Repression and the Labour of Memory* (Minneapolis: University of Minnesota Press, 2003).
[52] Ibid. p. 30.
[53] Rita Arditti, *Searching For Life. The Grandmothers Of The Plaza De Mayo And The Disappeared Children Of Argentina* (Berkeley, CA: University of California Press, 1999).
[54] Bisquert and Lvovich, *La cambiante memoria de la dictadura*, p. 17; my translation.
[55] Daniel Mundo, 'Medios, terror e indiferencia' in *Página/12*, 09/23/2009, <http://www.pagina12.com.ar/diario/laventana/26-132249-2009-09-23.html> [Last accessed 09/13/2010].
[56] Marguerite Feitlowitz, *A Lexicon of Terror: Argentina and the Legacies of Torture* (New York: Oxford University Press, 1998).
[57] Pablo D. Bonaldi, 'Hijos de desaparecidos. Entre la construcción de la política y la construcción de la memoria' in *El pasado en el futuro: Los movimientos juveniles*, ed. by Elizabeth Jelin and Diego Sempol (Madrid: Siglo XXI Editores, 2006), pp. 143-55 (p. 161).
[58] Susana G. Kaufman, 'Lo legado y lo propio. Lazos familiares y transmisión de memorias in *Subjetividad y figuras de la memoria*, ed. by Elizabeth Jelin and Susana G. Kaufman (Buenos Aires: Siglo XXI Editora Iberoamericana, 2006), pp. 73-110 (p. 68).
[59] Bisquert and Lvovich, *La cambiante memoria de la dictadura*, pp. 42-3; my translation.
[60] Bonaldi, 'Hijos de desaparecidos. Entre la construcción de la política y la construcción de la memoria', p. 162; my translation.

[61] Their relation to justice has contributed most to their international visibility, more particularly, what they call 'escrache.' Even though they wanted the army trials to happen, they did not trust the good faith of the judges and decided to take it in their own hands by publicly condemning the perpetrators through 'escraches': The practice of exposing the presence of unpunished criminals of the dictatorship by publicly shaming them (See Benegas, 2004).

[62] The prologue refers to the conflict as a war between two demons: the extreme left guerrilla movement and the extreme right military. However, it contradicts this idea by not including the political background of the victims, considered irrelevant for the purpose of investigating the army's crimes. In addition, the prologue observes that the guerrilla movements were outnumbered at the beginning of the dictatorship (according to Arditti, they were 2.000, of whom only 20% were armed, against 200.000 well-equipped soldiers), and advices to initiate the trials against the army. Consequently, both right- and left-wing groups were dissatisfied with the report after its first impact in society.

[63] Translation 'I suspect that my problem is neither physical nor neurological: as all the traumas, it comes from childhood'. Guadalupe Pérez García, *Diario argentino* [experimental documentary] (Argentina-España: Cine Ojo, Impossible Films and Rizoma Films: 2007) All further references are given as (Pérez García, 2007) in parentheses in the text.

[64] DIRECTOR.? Mom... why did you vote for Menem in 1989?
MOTHER. Do you have a little knife to stab me in the stomach?
DIRECTOR. Come on, I also voted for him...
MOTHER. Well... one sometimes believes in stupid things.... What is unforgivable about Menem is his second victory: it is not acceptable to step in the same hole twice. And he started winning all the elections and no one can say he didn't win legally.
DIRECTOR. But the second time we didn't vote for him, why did you vote for him the first time?
MOTHER. But ... who else was one going to vote for?
STEPFATHER. The thing is that Peronism is a political movement; it is a party but is also a movement that included different social classes. Those who remembered Peronism ended up voting for Menem thinking that Menem was Peronist but Menem wasn't Peronist, that's the issue.
DIRECTOR. Then I don't know what it means to be a Peronist because if Menem is in the Peronist party probably he thinks he is Peronist: he must feel like a Peronist.
STEPFATHER. No, but Menem sold the entire country to foreign monopolies. I understand that Peronism for you had lost all meaning because there is no longer such a thing as Peronism: it ended in 1955.
DIRECTOR. But if Peronism became meaningless in 1955, why did Mom and I vote for Menem in 1989: that's my question. See? I don't understand why.
MOTHER. Because people didn't vote for Menem, they voted for the idea of what they thought could be accomplished by Peronism as a movement.

STEPFATHER: People need to make their own experience. Think of how many struggles Argentina has undergone so far. Argentina as a country has suffered a lot because after the downfall of Perón we had four dictatorships and the army took control of the University twice. All those misfortunes are the reason why you had to emigrate to find a job. (Pérez García, 2007).

[65] 'Why are you remembering all of those things? It is a very sad time we all try not to repeat and not to remember'.

[66] 'Because traditionally one always liked Peronism more than radicalism, because of the previous generation, because of my parents'.

[67] 'Who else was one going to vote for?' (Pérez García, 2007).

[68] 'I like to think of a revolutionary Argentina, but that Argentina usually ends badly. Hence, I waited for the first available flight and left.' (Pérez García, 2007).

[69] Ana Laura Pérez, 'Fragementos de un país todavía secreto' in *Clarin.com*. 22/11/1998.<http://www.clarin.com/suplementos/cultura/1998/11/22/e-01001d.htm> [Last accessed: 30/10/2010].

[70] María Iribarren, 'La política tiene que servirnos como brújula. Entrevista exclusiva con la directora de *Cordero de Dios*, in Revista Zoom. Política y sociedad en foco. 17/04/2008. <http://revista-zoom.com.ar/articulo2103.html>. [Last accessed: 10/30/2010].

[71] Lucía García, 'La imaginación del espectador es el major director de cine', *Puentes*, 24 (2008), 71-77 (p. 73); my translation.

[72] Ibid. p. 77.

[73] María Iribarren, (supra).

[74] 'What is the point of so much ideology for you all if you are capable of letting a man die just like that?' Lucía Cedrón, *Cordero de Dios* (Argentina-France: Les Films d'Ici, Goa Films, Lita Stantic Producciones: 2008). All further references are given as (Cedrón, 2008) in parentheses in the text.

[75] 'Because there are some things that don't get resolved by talking' (Cedrón, 2008).

[76] Antonia García Castro, 'Metáforas literales. Diálogo con Lucía Cedrón, cineasta', *Cultures & Conflits*, 06/11/2008, p. 7; my translation.

[77] García Castro, 'Metáforas literales. Diálogo con Lucía Cedrón, cineasta', p. 7; my translation.

[78] María Iribarren, (supra).

[79] Pilar Calveiro, *Violencia y/o política. Una aproximación a la guerrilla de los años 70* (Buenos Aires: Norma, 2005), p. 14; my translation.

[80] Jacques Derrida and Elisabeth Roudinesco, *For What Tomorrow. A Dialogue*, trans. by Jeff Fort (Stanford: Stanford University Press, 2004), p. 3.

[81] Ibid. p. 3.

[82] Ibid. p. 4.

[83] García Castro, p. 5; my translation.

[84] Tzvetan Todorov, *Los abusos de la memoria* (Barcelona: Paidós Asterisco, 2000), p. 31.

[85] See Corinne Enaudeau, *La paradoja de la representación*, 1st edn (Buenos Aires: Paidós, 1999), p. 27.

[86] The military junta was the *de facto* government established as a result of the military coup in the March 24, 1976 and ended in December 10, 1984. Jorge Videla, the first dictator to assume command, was the President at the moment both film and novel centre their fictional representation.

[87] Even though *Garage Olimpo* seems to be a representation of the violence and abuse of power committed by the military dictatorship (the film even ends with some general statistics about the victims of the regime), chances are that the film's plot took place in the specific year of 1978. *El Olimpo* is the clandestine centre of detention in which the movie takes place, and that centre was in operation between August 1978 and January 1979, opening a small window for the plot to take place in 1979.

[88] Martín Kohan, *Dos veces junio*, 5th edn (Buenos Aires: Editorial Sudamericana S.A., 2008), p. 11.

[89] See Idelber Avelar, *Alegorías de la derrota: La ficción postdictatorial y el trabajo del duelo* (Santiago: Editorial Cuarto Propio, 2000), p. 14.

[90] Kohan, p. 15. 'Maybe I acted wrongly, and that is why I felt observed. That was the impression that provoked in me a sense of guilt. When we act wrongly we feel like we are being watched, it does not matter if you are alone.'

[91] Michel Foucault, *Discipline and Punish*, trans. by Alan Sheridan, 2nd edn (New York: Vintage Books, 1995), pp. 35-169.

[92] Jacques Rancière, *Dissensus: On Politics and Aesthetics*, trans. and ed. by Steven Corcoran (London & New York: Continuum, 2010), pp. 30-32. Rancière describes this term as the people within the polis who did not have a right to act and/or to govern. He underlines that, in Classical Greece, to be part of the demos meant to not count.

[93] Kohan, p. 63. '[...] a ring. A golden ring with the letter 'R' carved on the back [...] and on the interior rim a letter so small that I barely had a chance to read it under the poor light of the street. It said 'Raúl and Susana', and a year: '1973' [...]. I don't know why I threw the ring onto the sand of the beach and I covered it with sand using my feet. I covered the ring with sand first and then I smashed the sand flat with my soldier boots, making sure that no one finds the ring again.'

[94] Ibid. p. 137. 'She started to tell me the things that were going on [...]. With a broken voice she started to tell me all the things that they have done to her. At some point I just didn't want to hear anymore and I told her: 'Shut up. Shut your mouth.' But I didn't move. I didn't move because I was afraid of her grabbing my pullover and pushing me back [...]. I didn't move and she kept talking.'

[95] Rancière, p. 40.

[96] Giorgio Agamben, *State of Exception* (Chicago: University of Chicago Press, 2005).

[97] Kohan, p. 35. 'The sergeant said things were to be done with the greatest responsibility, that in the days we were living, any mistake was to be paid dearly;

the enemy was waiting for any distraction on our part to strike, and that in times of war it was essential to face every action with the most complete seriousness.'

[98] This does not mean that the state of exception equals a dictatorship. In fact, Agamben is clear in stressing that one is not a synonym of the other and that the latter can be replaced by the state of exception. However, the state of exception has been the paradigm of contemporary dictatorships, allowing them to exclude all rights guaranteed by law to a group of citizens and establishing an extreme disciplinary state for the rest of the citizens, so they can return to the polis and be protected by the state, as defined by the authoritarian apparatus.

[99] Hannah Arendt, *On Violence* (New York: Harcourt, Brace & World, 1970), p. 9.

[100] In fact, the complete title is *Garage Olimpo: Desaparecidos*.

[101] According to María Rosa Olivera-Williams, the history of Argentina is very similar to Chile and Uruguay because it was inserted within the international politics and economic policies of the United States within the Cold War context. Following the loss of Cuba and its revolution, the United States could not allow other countries to follow their example in the rest of Latin America. See María Rosa Olivera-Williams, 'La década del 70 en el Cono Sur: Discursos nostálgicos que recuerdan la revolución y escriben la historia,' *Romance Quarterly*, 57 (2010), 43-62. The military regimes had to ensure a stabilized market in their countries so private enterprises had a safe ground to do business, setting the agenda for what was later known as neoliberalism. For an understanding of neoliberalism and its historical context, along with the relevance of Chile and South America, see David Harvey, *A Brief History of Neoliberalism* (Oxford University Press, 2005).

[102] There are two versions of this opening scene, the one described above and another without the soundtrack. In that other version the voice-over of a radio announcer substitutes the music.

[103] See Theodor Adorno and Max Horkheimer, *Dialectic of Enlightenment* (Stanford: Stanford University Press, 2002), pp. 120-68. Adorno and Horkheimer focus on American culture, which is what they have in mind with the term Cultural Industry at its best. However, entertainment and spectacle are their main targets, as they allow people to be distracted from their situation in a capitalist society, which they considered as oppressive as any other form of government and economical model.

[104] General Cesareo Cardozo was Chief of the Federal Police after the coup and he was considered to be the third most important man in charge of supervising and torturing militants from the left armed groups ERP and the 'montoneros'. He was killed early into the dictatorship by Gonzales in June 18, 1976. Ana María paid with her life for her attack on January 4, 1977 while trying to escape. The name of Cardozo is never used in the film while the young girl is called 'Ana', a clear reference to the terrorist attack. To read the news, see Miguel Yuste, 'Muere en atentado el jefe de la policía argentina', *El País*, June, 19, 1976.

http://www.elpais.com/articulo/internacional/ARGENTINA/Muere/atentado/jefe/policia/federal/argentina/elpepiint/19760619elpepiint_1/Tes?print=1.

[105] More and more testimonies affirm the use of music as a way to cover up the tortures. As recently as September 6, 2010, Horacio Vivas, a survivor from another Clandestine Centre of Detention called 'El Vesuvio' recounted how the torturers used Spaniard singer Julio Iglesias to cover the screams. Once he got out and went to Spain, he could not hear the singer again. See Alejandra Dandan, *'Distinguía día y noche por los ladridos'*, *El País*, September 7, 2010, p. 14.

[106] 'La aurora' was a hymn sang in schools in honour of the flag. Many people know it as the 'himno a la bandera' (salute to the flag).

[107] Bechis cut to a close-up to the wing in order to show the Argentinean flag.

[108] This is implied because, after the shot to María's silhouette, Bechis cuts to a shot of the river. As Guillermo Ravaschino states, by the time *Garage Olimpo* was released, it was common knowledge in Argentina that the military used those planes to throw drugged bodies to the river, so that no one would find them again. See Guillermo Ravaschino, 'Garage Olimpo', *Cineismo.com* <http://www.cineismo.com/criticas/garage_olimpo.htm > [accessed 26 October 2010].

[109] The idea of a nation as something imagined was first introduced by Benedict Anderson. Ascribing to that idea we can think of the nation as artifice, something imagined and created. See Benedict Anderson, *Imagined Communities*, 3rd edn (London: Verso, 2006).

[110] The name used by the military junta for their politics.

[111] See Antonio Negri, *Diálogo sobre la globalización, la multitud y la experiencia argentina* (Buenos Aires: Paidós, 2003), p. 48.

[112] The film is a co-production with Italy and it was critically acclaimed as an art-film on the international market.

[113] Kohan, p. 120. 'In a war the bodies do not belong to anyone: they are surrendered [...] when you act upon a body during a war, you are acting upon something that does not belong to anybody anymore.'

[114] 'Look who has returned! The little bird who wanted to fly!'

[115] Gabriel García Márquez, *Living to Tell the Tale*, trans. by Edith Grossman (New York: Knopf, 2003), p. 366.

[116] Luis Harss and Barbara Dohmann, *Into the Mainstream: Conversations with Latin American Writers*, trans. by Luis Harss and Barbara Dohmann (New York: Harper & Row, 1967). *Los nuestros* was published in 1966, in Buenos Aires, by Editorial Sudamericana.

[117] Ibid.

[118] Márquez, *Living to Tell the Tale*, p. 366.

[119] Rubén Dario: *Selected Poems*, trans. by Lysander Kemp, prologue by Octavio Paz (Austin: University of Texas Press, 1988), pp. 69-70.

[120] Rubén Pelayo, *Gabriel García Márquez: A Critical Companion* (Westport, CT: Greenwood Press, 2001), p. 16.

[121] James A. Parr, *Don Quixote: An Anatomy of Subversive Discourse* (Newark, Delaware: Juan de la Cuesta, 1988), pp. 21-39.
[122] Carlos Fuentes, *Carlos Fuentes*, interviewed by Lewis MacAdams, videocassette, directed and produced by Lewis MacAdams (Santa Fe, New Mexico: Metropolitan Pictures and EZTV for Lannan Foundation, 1989).
[123] Dr. Jan McDonnell. *Evita's Cancer*, <http://www.nytimes.com/2000/06/13/science/l-evita-s-cancer-733512.html?ref=eva_duarte_de_peron.> [accessed 25 October 2010].
[124] Lloyd Hughes Davies, *Projections of Peronism in Argentine Autobiography, Biography and Fiction* (Cardiff, Wales: University of Wales Press, 2007), p. 23.
[125] The Official Eva Perón Website. <http://www.evitaperon.org/part2.htm> [accessed 25 October 2010].
[126] Eva Perón, *In My Own Words: Evita.* trans. by Laura Dail (New York: New York Press, 1996), p. 9.
[127] Calvin Sims, 'Eva Peron's Corpse Continues to Haunt Argentina.' < http://www.nytimes.com/1995/07/30/world/eva-peron-s-corpse-continues-to-haunt-argentina.html > [accessed 02 August 2011].
[128] Gene Bell-Villada, *Borges and His Fiction: A Guide to his Mind and Art* (Austin, Texas: University of Texas Press, 1999), p. 5.
[129] Eric Luther with Ted Henken, M.A, *The Life and Work of Che Guevara* (Indianapolis, IN: Alpha Books, 2001), p. 4.
[130] Jon Lee Anderson. *Che Guevara: A Revolutionary Life* (New York: Grove Press, 1997), p. 3.
[131] Eric Luther, p. 17.
[132] Ibid. p. 115.
[133] Ibid. p. 56.
[134] Ibid. p. 141. (The emphasis is mine).
[135] Any avid reader or scholar will certainly testify to that. Levine was Puig's close friend. Her biographical account is one of the most complete in English. She translated his first two novels, shared time with him, and had access to a large epistolary where Puig did not hide behind a literary mask. Suzanne Jill Levine, *Manuel Puig and The Spider Woman: His Life and Fictions* (New York: Farrar, Straus and Giroux, 2000), p. xii.
[136] Ibid. p. x.
[137] Suzanne Jill Levine, p. 73. Puig, writes Levine, was not yet twenty. In 1986 Puig was asked to write an homage to Borges on the occasion of his death. The note Puig wrote is worth reading for he draws a realist picture of Borges who was then in his 50s.
[138] According to Borges himself, 'House Taken Over' was published in *Annals of Buenos Aires* Magazine, see: Fernando Sorrentino, *Seven Conversations with Jorge Luis Borges*, trans. by Clark M. Zlotchew (Troy, New York: The Whitston Publishing Company, 1982), p. 61. The story, furthermore, was illustrated by Borges' sister Norah. Harold Bloom, on the other hand, as others often do, quotes

Sur as the magazine where 'House Taken Over' was first published. See Harold Bloom, *Julio Cortazar* (*Bloom's Major Short Story Writers*) (New York: Chelsea House Publishers, 2004), p. 13.

[139] Ibid. p. 2.

[140] Peter Standish, *Understanding Julio Cortázar* (Columbia, SC: University of South Carolina Press, 2001), p. 91.

[141] Was Ugné a wife or a partner? Was Dunlop Canadian or American? Bloom seems to have contradicting information on both accounts. See: Harold Bloom, *Julio Cortázar*, p. 14. Some of the biographical information on Julio Cortázar available leaves us all wondering who is right and who is not.

[142] Tomás Eloy Martínez, Argentine Author Who Merged Fact With Fancy, Dies at 75. http://www.nytimes.com/2010/02/06/arts/06martinez.html.

[143] Rubén Pelayo, p. 103.

[144] Daniel S. Burt, *The Novel 100: A Ranking of the Greatest Novels of All Time* (New York: Barnes & Noble, 2007), p. 2.

[145] Nestor García Canclini asserts Latin America has always been post modern. Problems with post modern discourse emanate from elites circles, since postmodernism tries to break the boundaries of 'high'/'low' culture since in Latin America everything at a point in time was part of popular culture. Postmodernism if properly understood can be a way of contesting the hegemonic idea of culture. Postmodernism allows for a more open space being able to conceptualize Latin American culture; understanding the economy with the inequalities culture (popular/ elite); politisation of culture and the calamity of culture becoming an industry run by private corporations. Despite all, hybridization might once again be a creation of the elite to legitimize oppression, nevertheless it remains people who are the owners of culture, it is for them that it exists and they who must keep it alive.

[146] Fernando del Paso, *Noticias del imperio* (Barcelona: Plaza y Janes Editores, S. A., 1994), pp. 70-71. 'Vienna turned to and then taught the world the delights of pop music – the dizzying waltz, the diabolical violin of Johann Strauss, as well as the mechanical tunes that seemed to come out of nowhere every time a clock struck the half hour (with minutes), or quarter hour (with gavottes) […]. In keeping with the times, the Viennese upper-middle class, who weekly ordered a vat of hot bathwater for their houses, also hung Aeolian harps from trees in their gardens to be played by the Alpine winds.' Fernando Del Paso, *Palinuro of Mexico*, trans. by Elizabeth Plaister (Normal, IL: Dalkey Archive Press, 1996), p. 49.

[147] Palinurus (Palinuro), in Roman mythology, is the helmsman of a ship of the Trojan hero Aeneas, whose descendants would one day found the city of Rome. As the price for the safe passage of Aeneas and his people from Sicily to Italy, Palinurus loses his life, one on behalf of many. Somnus causes Palinurus to fall asleep and fall overboard. (Palinurus' own version at Aeneid 6.349 does not blame the god.) He is then stranded on the coast of Lucania, in southern Italy, where he is killed by a native tribe, the Lucani. When Aeneas and the Sibyl meet

Palinurus in the Underworld, the Sibyl promises that the local people will be moved by signs to provide the helmsman's body with a proper burial, at what is now Cape Palinuro. [*The Oxford Classical Dictionary*, ed. by Simon Hornblower and Antony Spawforth, 3rd edn (New York: Oxford University Press, 2003), p. 1100.

[148] Álvarez Lobato, 'Carmen: Identidad y Ambivalencia. Una lectura de Palinuro de México desde el grotesco', *Nueva Revista de Filología Hispánica*, 56. 1 (2008), 123-39. 'I learned [...] the myth of Palinuro was the symbol of man [...] that is drawn by their dreams, and because of them dies.' Thus individual identity becomes a national identity through idealism, sacrifice and art. This identity is constructed as a grotesque collage of drawings, text, views, fragments, cultures and human disciplines': Fernando Del Paso, *Palinuro of Mexico*, trans. by Elizabeth Plaister, p. 126.

[149] The Plaza de las Tres Culturas in Tlatelolco is a symbolic space because here were located the ruins of the pyramids of Tlatelolco, a satellite city of the Mexican (Aztec) capital Tenochtitlan (what is now Mexico City) which was home to a massive market, as well as a colonial Spanish church and the governmental building for the Mexican Foreign Affairs Secretariat. Hence three cultures plaza: Pre-Columbian era, Colonial era and Modern era.

[150] Samuel Arriarán, *Barroco y Neobarroco En América Latina: Estudios Sobre La Otra Modernidad* (México, DF: Editorial Itaca, 2007), p. 21. Translation: 'It is not a simple addition but a new construction of cultural miscegenation in the context of postmodernity.'

[151] Fernando del Paso, *Palinuro de México* (Madrid: Plaza y Janés, 1977), pp. 183-90. [Palinuro's voice reporting] 'Absolutely nothing so far. We're waiting for replay. The real agitators were poverty, ignorance and hunger. We students are organizing ourselves to put an end to them. These statues, as is to be expected in emergencies, have been witnesses [...]. Certain Hertzian waves in search of a continent washed over the best frock-coat and wig of Primo de Verdad BA, standing permanently at the junction of Paseo de la Reforma and Rio Neva: this was the reply, still hanging in the air, mingling with the floating decrees, while a few pettifogging lawyers, armed with tricolor pen-holders, stir up the dust of old constitutions and other huge necropolis and pick out best-aired laws and arrange them in a posy to offer the judges engaged in suspending constitutional guarantees. That means they're afraid of us: the converted members of the ruling class, the mendicants begging for a little presidential palm grease, ashen writers drowning their thirst for martyrlogy in their inkpots and, with them, bankers expert in churriguersque deals, tumid ministers, congressmen and senators forever standing to attention, like obedient pricks [...]. We will hold another demonstration, we will pour the enthusiasm of five hundred thousand hearts into the Plaza Mayor': Del Paso, *Palinuro of Mexico*, pp. 478-89.

[152] Michael Bakhtin, *Rabelais and his World*, trans. by Helene Iswolsky (Bloomington: Indiana University Press, 1984), pp. 26-27.

[153] The use of a carnival atmosphere in the plot justifies the experimental fiction of a whole range of human experiences, characters, themes, scenes of violence and indifference to the sacrifice of Palinuro. According to Cirlot, during carnival time we celebrate possibilities of human experience, which is an invocation to the essential chaos, a brief escape time. (*Dictionary of Symbols*, pp. 266-67)

[154] Del Paso, *Palinuro of Mexico*, p. 659.

[155] José Manuel Prieto González, *Rex* (Barcelona: Editorial Anagrama, 2007), pp. 183-84. 'The bird opened its mouth, balancing for a second on the edge, and let well up through its breast, with no effort by the neck muscles, a first note, a prolonged sight that flowed out long and *uncontainably* as it tried to open the hands that had remained trapped, slender and fragile, in the bones of its wings [...]. I pushed the door farther to see her better. My hand swinging out over the tessellated floor, I checked the windows, swept the ground with my eyes to try and glimpse the projector or generator of that image, the woman, the bird (I didn't find it) [...] It was Nelly! And I realized this, as well, and right away, from the necklace around her as she sang and slowly turned her head, rays of light meaning from the stones dappling the walls, the windowpanes, the floor, with multicolored points': José Manuel Prieto González, *Rex: A Novel*, trans. by Esther Allen (New York: Grove Press, 2009), p. 249

[156] Heather Clark and Jose Manuel Prieto, 'Nocturnal Butterflies of the Russian Empire', *Times Literary Supplement,* 5132 (2001), p. 19.

[157] Anke Birkenmaier, 'Art of the Pastiche: Jose Manuel Prieto's *Rex* and Cuban Literature of the 1990s', *Revista De Estudios Hispanicos*, 43.1 (2009), 123-48 (pp. 124-26).

[158] Bernstein, *The New York Times* online.

[159] Gloria Anzaldúa, *Borderlands/La Frontera*: *The New Mestiza* (New York: Aunt Lute Books, 1987), p. 25. All further references to this work are given in the text by the abbreviation GA followed by the page number in Arabic script in parentheses in the text.

[160] Audre Lorde, 'Age, Race, Class, and Sex,' in *Sister Outsider*, ed. by Cheryl Clarke (Berkeley, CA: The Crossing Press, 2007), p. 114. All further references to this work are given in the text by the abbreviation AL followed by the page number in Arabic script in parentheses in the text.

[161] Following Yunqué's own convention, I will later refer to his 'character' persona as Vega, in an attempt to clearly demarcate him from the authorial persona (or narrative voice), who I am calling Yunqué.

[162] Edgardo Vega Yunqué, *The Lamentable Journey of Omaha Bigelow into the Impenetrable Loisaida Jungle* (New York: Overlook Press, 2004), p. 9. All future references will be indicated by the capital initial Y followed by the page number in Arabic script.

[163] Hannah Arendt, 'Introduction,' in Walter Benjamin, *Illuminations* (New York: Harcourt, 1968), p. 13.

[164] Ibid. p. 172.

[165] Catherine Keyser, *Playing Smart: New York Women Writers and Modern Magazine Culture* (New Brunswick: Rutgers University Press, 2010), p. 16.
[166] Brian Richardson, *Unnatural Voices: Extreme Narration in Modern and Contemporary Fiction* (Columbus: Ohio State University Press, 2006), p. 21.
[167] Richardson, *Unnatural Voices*, p. 128.
[168] Ibid. pp. 128-29.
[169] Benjamin, *Illuminations*, p. 167.
[170] Michel Foucault, *Discipline and Punish* (New York: Vintage Books, 1979), p. 206.
[171] Edwidge Danticat, *The Dew Breaker* (New York: Vintage Books, 2004), p. 184. All further references will be given in the text marked in parentheses by the abbreviation DB and the page number in Arabic script.
[172] Cathy Caruth, *Unclaimed Experience: Trauma, Narrative, and History* (Baltimore: Johns Hopkins University Press, 1996), p. 11.
[173] Foucault, *Discipline and Punish*, p. 255.
[174] Bonnie Lyons and Edwidge Danticat, 'An Interview with Edwidge Danticat,' *Contemporary Literature*, 44.2 (Summer 2003), < http://www.jstor.org/stable/1209094 > [accessed 28 February 2010], p. 193.
[175] James Dawes, *That the World May Know: Bearing Witness to Atrocity* (Cambridge: Harvard University Press, 2007), p. 166.
[176] Dawes, p. 166.
[177] Cited in Dawes, *That the World May Know*, p. 175.
[178] Ibid. p. 192.
[179] Ibid. p. 193.
[180] Peter Brooks, *Reading for the Plot*, 1st edn (New York: Vintage Books, 1984), p. 61.
[181] Jo Collins, 'The Ethics and Aesthetics of Representing Trauma: the Textual Politics of Edwidge Danticat's *The Dew Breaker*,' *Journal of Postcolonial Writing*, 47.1 (2011), 5-17 <http://dx.doi.org/10.1080/17449855.2011.533947> [accessed 5 August 2011], pp. 9-10.
[182] Ibid. p. 11.
[183] Aitor Ibarrola Armeindariz, 'Danticat's *The Dew Breaker*, a Case Study in Trauma Symptoms and the Recovery Process,' *Journal of English Studies*, 8 (2010) <http://www.jstor.org/stable/3394885 > [accessed 11 October 2010], p. 54.
[184] Ibid. p. 236.
[185] Ibid. p. 247.
[186] Ibid. p. 260.
[187] Collins, 'The Ethics and Aesthetics of Representing Trauma', p. 10.
[188] Martin Munro, 'Avenging History in the Former French Colonies,' *Transition*, 99 (2008) <http://www.jstor.org/stable/20204259 > [accessed 28 February 2010] p. 27.
[189] Munro, p. 31.

[190] Renee Shea and Edwidge Danticat, 'The Dangerous Job of Edwidge Danticat: An Interview,' *Callaloo*, 19.2 (Spring 1996) < http://www.jstor.org/stable/3299199 > [accessed 28 February 2010], p. 385.
[191] Nestor Garcia Canclini, *Hybrid Cultures: Strategies for Entering and Leaving Modernity* (Minneapolis: University of Minnesota Press, 1995), p. 61.
[192] Shalini Puri, *The Caribbean Postcolonial: Social Equality, Post-Nationalism, and Cultural Hybridity* (New York: Palgrave Macmillan, 2004), p. 12.
[193] Mikhail Bakhtin, *The Dialogic Imagination*, trans. by Caryl Emerson and Michael Holquist (Austin: University of Texas Press, 1981), p. 84.
[194] Edwidge Danticat, *The Farming of Bones* (London: Abacus, 1998). All further references to this work will be given in parentheses in the text marked by the abbreviation FB and followed by the page number in Arabic script.
[195] Sara Ahmed, *Strange Encounters: Embodied Others in Post-Coloniality* (London: Routledge, 2000), p. 81.
[196] Francois Duvalier was President of Haiti between 1957 and 1971. He had become a leading figure in a group espousing Black Nationalist ideologies in the late 1930s and 1940s. His administration turned into an extremely repressive dictatorship which caused the mass migration of Haitians to the United States and Canada and to the rest of the Caribbean. On his death in 1971, his nineteen-year-old son Jean-Claude was proclaimed 'president for life'.
[197] Anthea Morrison, 'The Caribbeanness of Haiti: Simone Scharz-Bart's *Ton Beau Capitaine*', in *The Francophone Caribbean Today: Literature, Language, Culture*, ed. by Gertrude Aub-Busher and Beverley Ormerod Noakes (Kingston: University of the West Indies Press, 2003), pp. 114-24 (p. 115).
[198] Edwidge Danticat, 'Haiti: A Bi-Cultural Experience', *Encuentros*, 12 (1995), 1-9 (p. 4), quoted in Morrison, p. 115.
[199] Maya Jaggi, 'Island Memories', *The Guardian*, 20 November, 2004.
[200] Interestingly, the name chosen to baptise the newborn nation, the first Black Republic in history, was the Taino name for the *entire* island, a name that meant 'land of mountains'.
[201] Susan Buck-Morss, 'Hegel and Haiti', *Critical Inquiry*, 26.4 (2000), 821-65, (pp. 836-37). Buck-Morss cites a significant episode that she defines as one of the 'moments of clarity' in history where the 'enlightened' nature of the Haitian revolution came home to the very army that was fighting against it: 'The French soldiers sent by Napoleon to the colony, upon hearing the former slaves singing the 'Marseillaise', wondered aloud if they were not fighting on the wrong side' (p. 865).
[202] Slavery was abolished in the Dominican Republic during the Haitian occupation between 1822-1844.
[203] Buck-Morss, p. 835.
[204] J. Michael Dash, *The Other America: Caribbean Literature in a New World Context* (Charlottesville: University Press of Virginia, 1998), p. 43.
[205] Haiti's financial debt, which extends to the present day, began shortly after the success of the revolution, when France demanded from Haiti the payment of huge

monetary compensation in exchange for the recognition of Haiti as a sovereign republic.

[206] Édouard Glissant, *Le discours antillais* (Paris: Seuil, 1981), p. 267. My translation from the French.

[207] Morrison, p. 117. My emphasis in italics.

[208] Edwidge Danticat, *The Butterfly's Way: Voices from the Haitian Diaspora in the United States* (New York: Soho Press, 2001), p. 57.

[209] Édouard Glissant, *The Poetics of Relation*, trans. by Betsy Wing (Ann Arbor: University of Michigan Press, 1997), p. 111.

[210] Glissant, *Caribbean Discourse*, p. 24.

[211] Lauren Derby, 'Haitians, Magic and Money: Raza and Society in the Haitian-Dominican Borderlands, from 1900 to 1937', *Comparative Studies in Society and History*, 36.3 (1994), 488-526 (p. 500).

[212] Such consistent production of national and racial tropes by the Dominican government may be explained by the complexity of the rivalry between Haiti and the Dominican Republic, stemming from the differences originating from their colonial past (Haiti was once the French Saint-Domingue, while today's Dominican Republic was once the Spanish Santo Domingo). However, the rivalry was further intensified during and after Haiti's occupation of the Dominican Republic (from 1822 to 1844). As Danticat affirmed in our interview: 'The fact that the Dominican Republic celebrates its independence from Haiti and not from Spain makes its definition of itself different from what it would be for Haiti.'

[213] Dash, p. 44.

[214] Marilyn Houlberg, 'Magique Marasa: the Ritual Cosmos of Twins and Other Sacred Children' in *The Sacred Arts of Haitian Vodou*, ed. by Donald Cosentino (Los Angeles: UCLA Fowler Museum of Cultural History, 1995), pp. 267-83 (p. 268), in Shemak, p. 92.

[215] As Lauren Derby explains, '*décimas* were poetry typically recited in parks and *colmados* (corner groceries) and sold in single sheets in the marketplace'. These public poems aired popular or factional complaints about official corruption and ineptitude, and were also anonymous. Lauren Derby, 'In the Shadow of the State: The Politics of Denunciation and Panegyric during the Trujillo Regime in the Dominican Republic, 1940-1958', *Hispanic American Historical Review*, 83.2 (2003), 295-344 (p. 322).

[216] A significant extract of the poem reads: '*El que se crea preocupado/que se largue alla a la Habana/ Que en tierra dominicana/no le da buen resultado. Y el biscochuelo lustrado/ aunque sea con mile de abeja/no de motivo de queja/que todo esto es tonteria/pues esta a la moda hoy dia/el negro tras de la oreja*' ('Whoever is worried should leave for Havana, as on Dominican soil he won't have much success. And the 'refined mulatto', even if covered in honey, should not complain about all this silliness because a little black behind one's ear is in fashion nowadays'). Juan Antonio Alix, *Décimas*. Colección Estudios (Santo Domingo: Librería Dominicana, 1927) (my translation from the Spanish).

[217] The ironic undertone of Alix's poem becomes even more prominent if we consider Derby's reference that 'Alix wrote 'servile praise' for whomever would provide him recompense: governors, generals, [...] even esteemed Dominican gentlemen in New York City': Lauren Derby, 'In the Shadow of the State', p. 307. However, his poem 'El negro tras de las orejas' suggests that behind the seemingly complaisant and celebratory tone, Alix hid a powerfully satirical tone that unmasked the reality of Dominican racism.

[218] In this respect, both Amabelle and Sebastien are the 'children of the waters'; both have left Haiti due to life-changing events caused by the river and the sea, by which they have been orphaned.

[219] Tobias Döring, *Caribbean-English Passages: Intertexuality in a Postcolonial Tradition* (London and New York: Routledge, 2002), p. 7.

[220] April Shemak, 'Re-membering Hispaniola: Edwidge Danticat's *The Farming of Bones*', *Modern Fiction Studies*, 48.1 (2002), 83-112 (p. 105).

[221] 'Voices from Hispaniola: A Meridians Roundtable with Edwidge Danticat, Loida Maritza Pérez, Myriam J. A. Chancy, and Nelly Rosario', *Meridians: Feminism, Race, Transnationalism*, 5. 1 (2004), 69-91 (p. 74).

[222] Ahmed, *Strange Encounters*, p. 93.

[223] In 1806 Henri Christophe was elected President of the new Republic of Haiti in the north, and in 1811 he proclaimed himself the nation's first king; he ruled until his death in 1820.

[224] David Geggus, 'The Naming of Haiti', *New West Indian Guide/Nieuwe West-Indische Gids*, 71.1-2 (1997), 43-68 (p. 43).

[225] Ibid. p. 43.

[226] Geggus continues, 'The reason many Haitians, from Dessalines's secretary Juste Chanlatte to the twentieth-century Indigenists, have viewed the Taíno as a symbol of resistance has much to do with the personal epic of [the indigenous cacique] Enrique and his long campaign in the mountains of Baoruco. More generally, as David Lowenthal (1972:108) remarks, the Caribbean Indians' rapid disappearance has helped foster in the region a romantic stereotype of a population that preferred death to slavery. Enrique's story, however, was particularly apt for Haitians, as he was apparently joined in his mountain retreat by African fugitives from the first generation of plantation slaves' (p. 51).

[227] Ibid. p. 58.

[228] Mariana Past, 'Articulating Haitian Conflicts in a New York City Basement: The Global Stakes of Franketyèn's *Pèlin-tèt*', *The Global South*, 4.2 (2010), 76-98 (pp. 94-97).

[229] Nick Nesbitt proposes in 'Nation-Building in Aimé Césaire's *La tragédie du Roi Christophe*' that Césaire's theatrical works represent a unique practice in Caribbean historiography, and that the writer, 'without lacking in rigor and sophistication, created a form of historical knowledge that dramatically altered fields as diverse as the Parisian post-war intellectual scene, and West-African and Caribbean colonial and post-colonial politics' (p. 133).

[230] Bridget Jones, 'Theatre and Resistance? An Introduction to some French Caribbean Plays', in *An Introduction to Caribbean Francophone Writing: Guadeloupe and Martinique*, ed. by Sam Haigh (New York: Berg, 1999), pp. 83-100 (p. 85).

[231] 'I am reborn from my ashes'.

[232] Najman's critical approach is in concert with Michel-Rolph Trouillot's landmark work of historical fiction, *Ti difè boulè sou istoua Ayiti* (1977), where the writer takes the Haitian people to task for having 'allowed themselves to become accustomed to mistreatment on the part of their leaders, passively accepting and enabling political and socio-economic conditions that have only continued to worsen. His (at times) subtle indictment of Toussaint L'Ouverture prods the Haitian people to re-think who the real heroes of the Revolution really were, and to visualize themselves as a powerful social force' for change: Mariana Past, 'Toussaint on Trial in *Ti difè boulè sou istoua Ayiti*, or the People's Role in the Haitian Revolution', *Journal of Haitian Studies*, 10.1 (2004), 87-102 (p. 99).

[233] David K. Hertzberger, *Narrating the Past: Fiction and Historiography in Postwar Spain* (Durham, NC: Duke University Press, 1995), p. 12.

[234] Aimé Césaire, *La tragédie du roi Christophe* (Paris: Présence africaine, 1963). All further references to this work will be abbreviated to AC followed by the page number given in parentheses in the text.

[235] Víctor Figueroa, 'Between Louverture and Christophe: Aimé Césaire on the Haitian Revolution', *The French Review*, 82.5(2009), 1006-1021(p. 1011).

[236] 'The bastards! They're beating the *mandoucouman*!'

[237] 'It is time for the old king to retire'.

[238] 'With our pompous titles, Duke of Limonade, Duke of Marmelade, Count of Candy Hole, we really look good! [...] The French will roar with laughter'.

[239] 'The mockery of the French doesn't bother me! Why not 'Duke of Marmelade,' why not 'Lemonade?' These are names to sate the appetite. As gastronomic as you would wish! After all, the French too have their 'Duke of Pâté,' their 'Duke of Bouillon' and the like. Is that really any more agreeable to the taste? They are clearly precedents for all this! Did you notice the type of personnel that Europe sent us when we requested international technical aid? Not a single engineer. Not a soldier. Not a professor. Instead: a Master of Ceremonies! Form, my friend, is the essence of civilization!'

[240] Roxanna Curto, 'The Science of Illusion-making in Aimé Césaire's *La tragédie du roi Christophe* and *Une tempête*', *Research in African Literatures*, 42.1(2011), 154-71 (p. 157).

[241] 'Master of ceremonies, upon seeing Christophe: Gentlemen, silence please. I will call out the names: [...] His Majesty the Duke of Limonade / His Majesty the Duke of Pleasure / His Serene Highness the Marquis of Downing / His Highness the Duke of Dondon / His Highness the Duke of Marmelade / The Count of Candy Hole / The Count of Dirty Hole / The Count of the Northern Band [...]. Go ahead, gentlemen!'

[242] Hunt Hawkins, 'Aimé Césaire's Lesson about Decolonization in *La Tragédie du roi Christophe*', *College Language Association Journal*, 30.2 (1986), 144-53 (p. 147).

[243] See Srinivas Aravamudan, *Tropicopolitans: Colonialism andAgency, 1688-1804. Post-contemporary Interventions* (Durham, NC: Duke University Press, 1999).

[244] If one prolongs only slightly one's glance at the map, one notes many other similarly entertaining geographical terms, that are not mentioned in the play: 'Ananas' ('Pineapple'), 'Abricot' ('Apricot'), 'Galette Sèche' ('Dry Wafer'), 'Savane Belle Mère' ('Mother-in-Law Savannah'), 'Caracol' ('Snail'), and 'Grand Gosier' ('Big Throat').

[245] Geggus, 'The Naming of Haiti', p. 54.

[246] Ibid. p. 54. (Referring to Moreau de Saint-Méry 1958, 1:212).

[247] Richard D. E. Burton, 'Names and naming in Afro-Caribbean cultures', *New West Indian Guide/ Nieuwe West-Indische Gids*, 73.1-2 (1999), 35-58 (p. 37).

[248] Ibid. pp. 54-55.

[249] Trevor Burnard, 'Slave Naming Patterns: Onomastics and the Taxonomy of Race in Eighteenth-Century Jamaica', *The Journal of Interdisciplinary History*, 31.3 (2001), 325-46 (pp. 336-40).

[250] 'CHRISTOPHE: These new names, these noble titles, this coronation! Before, we were robbed of our names! Our pride! Our nobility, they, as I say, they robbed us of them! Pierre, Paul, Jacques, Toussaint! These are the humiliating labels that obliterated our real names'.

[251] Richard D. E. Burton, 'Names and naming in Afro-Caribbean cultures', p. 45.

[252] Ibid. p. 48.

[253] Gilbert Doho, 'Le fou, le rebelle, l'enfant et la révolution haitienne', *Présence Francophone* 64 (2005), 53-72.

[254] Ibid. pp. 53-70.

[255] 'Here, the Phoenix is not satisfied with being reborn from his ashes: he is capable of improving himself, of learning, so as to transform his past defeats into future victories': Jean R. Guion, 'L'éternel défi de la négritude face à la normalisation occidentale', in *Les écrivains de la négritude et de la créolité: Actes du 3ème Colloque International Francophone du Canton de Payrac organisé par L'A.D.E.L.F.* ed. by Edmond Jouve and Simone Dreyfus (Paris: Sepeg International, 1994), III, pp. 107-21 (p. 121).

[256] Manon Dumais, 'Royal bonbon'. *Séquences*, 226 (2003), 57-58 (p. 57). 'The destiny of the despotic king is so quickly abandoned that those who are unfamiliar with the history of Haiti will only see [in the film] a naive story with folkloric flavor'.

[257] Víctor Figueroa, 'Between Louverture and Christophe: Aimé Césaire on the Haitian Revolution', p. 1007.

[258] J. Michael Dash, 'Neither France nor Senegal: Bovarysme and Haiti's Hemispheric Identity', keynote address for conference on Haiti and the Americas:

Histories, Cultures, Imaginations, Florida Atlantic University, Boca Raton, Florida. 22 October 2010.
[259] Ntozake Shange, *If I Can Cook/You Know God Can* (Boston: Beacon Press, 1998).
[260] Maximilien Laroche, *La Literature Haitienne: identité, langue, réalité* (Montréal, Canada: Éditions Leméac, 1980), p. 129.
[261] See Maximilien Laroche (supra); Alta Mae Stevens, 'Manje in Haitian Culture: The Symbolic Significance of Manje in Haitian Culture', *Journal of Haitian Studies*, 1.1 (1995); Vèvè A. Clark, 'When Womb Waters Break: The Emergence of Haitian New Theatre (1953-1987)', in *Journal of Haitian Studies*, 1.1 (1995), 89-100, Joan Dayan, *Haiti, History and the Gods* (Berkeley, CA: University of California Press, 1995) and Myriam J. A. Chancy, *Framing Silence: Revolutionary Novels by Haitian Women* (New Brunswick, NJ: Rutgers University Press, 1997).
[262] George Lakoff and Mark Johnson, *Metaphors We Live By* (Chicago, IL: Chicago University Press, 1980), p. 159.
[263] Sidney W. Mintz, *Tasting Food, Tasting Freedom* (Boston: Beacon Press, 1996), p. 11.
[264] Thomas Madiou, *Histoire d'Haiti*, 8 vols, ed. by Michèle Oriole (Port-au-Prince: Courtois 1847-48; repr. Éditions Deschamps, 1985-1991); Cyril Lionel Robert James, *The Black Jacobins: Toussaint L'Ouverture and the San Domingo Revolution* (New York; London: Vintage, 1963; repr. 1989), Eric Williams, *From Columbus to Castro* (New York: Vintage Books, 1970).
[265] James, *The Black Jacobins*, p. 12.
[266] Orchestre Septentrional 1971, track 1.
[267] Lakoff and Johnson, *Metaphors We Live By*, pp. 154-55.
[268] Mintz, *Tasting Food, Tasting Freedom*, p. 9.
[269] Ibid. p. 6.
[270] Edwidge Danticat, *The Farming of Bones* (New York: Soho, 1998), p. 3.
[271] L'odeur de ma Terre, 1993: track1.
[272] *Callaloo* (1992), p. 400.
[273] René Depestre, *Alléluia pour une femme-jardin* (Paris: Gallimard, 1981), p. 128.
[274] Ibid. p. 133.
[275] Alta Mae Stevens, 'Manje in Haitian Culture: The Symbolic Significance of Manje in Haitian Culture', *Journal of Haitian Studies*, 1.1 (1995), p. 75.
[276] Ibid. p. 80.
[277] Thomas McLaughlin, 'Figurative Language', in *Critical Terms for Literary Study*, ed. by Thomas McLaughlin and Frank Lentricchia (Chicago: University of Chicago Press, 1990), p. 86.
[278] Ibid. p. 87.
[279] Ibid. p. 83.
[280] Dayan, *Haiti, History and the Gods*, p. 136.

[281] Ibid. p. 136.
[282] Ibid. p. 79.
[283] Lakoff and Johnson, *Metaphors We Live By*, p. 146.
[284] Mintz, *Tasting Food, Tasting Freedom*, p. 4.
[285] Danticat, *The Farming of Bones*, p. 93.
[286] Phillipe Thoby-Marcelin, *The Beast of the Haitian Hills* (New York: Rinehart & Company, Inc., 1946), p. 41.
[287] Mintz, *Tasting Food, Tasting Freedom*, p. 8.
[288] Jacques Stephen Aléxis, *Compère Général Soleil* (Paris: Gallimard, 1955), p. 11, my translation.
[289] Thoby-Marcelin, *The Beast of the Haitian Hills*, p. 134.
[290] Ibid. p. 134.
[291] Emile Roumer, *The Poets of Haiti: 1782-1934*, trans. by Edna Wothley Underwood (Maine: Mosher Press, 1934), p. 4.
[292] Depestre, *Alléluia pour une femme-jardin*, p. 32, my translation.
[293] Bell Hooks, 'Eating The Other: Desire and Resistance', in *Eating Culture*, ed. by Ron Scapp and Brian Seilz (New York: State University of New York Press, 1988), p. 181.
[294] Helen Haste, *The Sexual Metaphor* (Cambridge, MA: Harvard University Press, 1994) p. 74.
[295] Susan Bordo, 'Hunger as Ideology', in *Eating Culture*, p. 21.
[296] Michel Martelly, 'Aloufa', 'Pigeons', on CD *Aloufa*. 1997, track 6.
[297] Pierre Clitandre, *Cathedral of the August Heat* (London: Readers International, 1987), p. 22.
[298] Ibid. p. 76.
[299] Leslie Casimir, 'Reporting Silence', in *The Butterfly's Way: Voices from the Haitian Diaspora in the United States*, p. 154.
[300] Haste, *The Sexual Metaphor*, p. x.
[301] Ibid. p. 29.
[302] Dany Laferrière, *Le goût des jeunes filles* (Montréal: VLB éditeur, 1992), p. 107, my translation.
[303] Linda E. Olds, *Metaphors of Interrelatedness* (New York: State University of New York Press, 1992), p. 32.
[304] Sor Juna Inés de la Cruz, 'Respuesta de la poeta a la muy ilustre Sor Filotea de la Cruz', in *Proyecto Ensayo Hispánico*: <http://www.ensayistas.org/antologia/XVII/sorjuana/sorjuana1.htm.> 'And what then shall I tell you, my Lady, of the secrets of nature that I have learned while cooking? I observe that an egg becomes solid and cooks in butter or oil, and on the contrary that it dissolves in sugar syrup […]. I shall not weary you with such inanities, which I relate simply to give you a full account of my nature, and I believe this will make you laugh. But in truth, my Lady, what can we women know, save philosophies of the kitchen? It was well put by Lupercio Leonardo [sic] that one can philosophize quite well while preparing supper. I often say, when I make these little observations, 'Had Aristotle cooked, he would have

written a great deal more'": Sor Juana Inés de la Cruz, 'The Poet's Answer To the Most Illustrious Sor Filotea De La Cruz', trans. by Electa Arenal and Amanda Powell.<http://web.archive.org/web/20071205013324/www.auburn.edu/~perryka/files/la_respuesta.htm>.

[305] Rosario Castellanos, 'Lección de cocina', in *Album de familia* (México: Editorial Joaquín Mortiz, 1971), pp. 7-22 (p. 7). 'My place is here. I've been here since the beginning of time': Rosario Castellanos, 'Cooking Lesson', in *A Rosario Castellanos Reader*, ed. and trans. by Maureen Ahern (Austin: University of Texas Press, 1996), pp. 200-15 (p. 207)

[306] Castellanos, 'Lección de cocina', p. 7. 'How could one carry out such an arduous task without the cooperation of society – of all history [...]. What can you suggest to me for today's meal, O experienced housewife, inspiration of mothers here and gone, voice of tradition?' Castellanos, 'Cooking Lesson', p. 207.

[307] Castellanos, 'Lección de cocina', p. 20. 'First there's the piece of meat, on color, one shape, one size. Then it changes, looks even nicer and you feel very happy. Then it starts changing and changing and changing and you just can't tell when you should stop it'. Castellanos, 'Cooking Lesson', p. 214.

[308] Castellanos, 'Lección de cocina', p. 18. 'This piece of meat's mother never told it that it was meat and ought to act like it'. Castellanos, 'Cooking Lesson', p. 213.

[309] Rosario Ferré, 'La cocina de la escritura', in *La sartén por el mango: Encuentro de escritoras latinoamericanas*, ed. by Patricia E. González and Eliana Ortega (Río Piedras, PR: Ediciones Huracán, 1984), pp. 137-54 (p. 154). 'The important thing is to apply that fundamental lesson taught to us by our mothers, who were the first to show us how to summon the spirit of the cooking stove. The secret of writing, like the secret of good cooking, has nothing to do with gender. It has to do with the skill with which we mix the ingredients over the fire': Rosario Ferré and Diana L. Vélez, 'The Writer's Kitchen', *Feminist Studies*, 12.2 (1986), 227-42 (p. 242).

[310] According to Ksenija Bilbija, 'the postmodernist return to the discourses of power leads Esquivel [...] to reclaim the kitchen as a not necessarily gender exclusive space of 'one's own'': Ksenijia Bilbija, 'Spanish American Women Writers: Simmering Identity Over a Low Fire', *STCL*, 20.1 (1996), 147-61 (p. 156).

[311] Cecilia Lawless, 'Experimental Cooking in *Como agua para chocolate*', *Monographic Review/ Revista Monográfica*, 8 (1992), 261-72 (p. 267).

[312] Roger Ebert, 'Like Water for Chocolate', rogerebert.com (April 2, 1993). <http://rogerebert.suntimes.com/apps/pbcs.dll/article?AID=/19930402/REVIEWS/304020304>.

[313] Laura Esquivel, *Como agua para chocolate: Novela de entregas mensuales con recetas, amores, y remedios caseros* (México: Editorial Planeta, 1990), p. 74. 'Under her blouse, her breasts moved freely, since she never wore a brassiere.

Drops of sweat formed on her neck and ran down into the crease between her firm round breasts. Pedro couldn't resist the smells from the kitchen and was heading toward them. But he stopped stock-still in the doorway, transfixed at the sight of Tita in that erotic posture. Tita looked up without stopping her grinding and her eyes met Pedro's. At once their passionate glances fused so perfectly that whoever saw them would have seen but a single look, a single rhythmic and sensual motion, a single trembling breath, a single desire': Laura Esquivel, *Like Water for Chocolate: A Novel in Monthly Installments with Recipes, Romances, and Home Remedies*, trans. by Carol Christensen and Thomas Christensen (New York: Anchor Books, 1992), pp. 64-65.

[314] Maite Zubiaurre, 'Culinary Eros in Contemporary Hispanic Female Fiction: From Kitchen Tales to Table Narratives', *College Literature*, 33.3 (2006), 29-51 (p. 44).

[315] Janice Jaffe, Latin American Women Writers' Novel Recipes and Laura Esquivel's *Like Water for Chocolate*, in *Scenes of the Apple: Food and the Female Body in Nineteenth- and Twentieth Century Women's Writing*, ed. by Tamar Heller and Patricia Moran (Albany: State University of New York Press, 2003), pp. 199-213 (p. 209).

[316] Zubiaurre, p. 31.

[317] This was the late 1970's slogan for *Fnjoli* perfume, where at least the male voice-over in the commercial is so impressed that he exclaims 'Tonight I'm going to cook for the kids!'

[318] Joy Logan points out that the trip is hardly uncharted, given the extremely well-travelled nature of 'the trail bridging food and sex': Joy Logan, 'Aphrodite in an Apron or the Erotics of Recipes and Self-Representation in Isabel Allende's *Afrodita*', *Romance Languages Annual*, X (1999), 685-89 (p. 685).

[319] Isabel Allende, *Afrodita: Cuentos, Recetas y Otros Afrodisíacos* (New York: Harper Collins, 1997), p. 16. 'Toward the end, when I thought we were finished and in the last round of revisions, I realized that among all the aphrodisiacs, from shellfish with herbs and spices to lace chemises, rose-colored lights, and aromatic bath salts, there was one, the most powerful of all, I hadn't included: stories […] the greatest enhancement to eroticism, as effective as the most knowing caresses, is the story': Isabel Allende, *Aphrodite: A Memoir of the Senses*, trans. by Margaret Sayers Peden (New York: Harper Collins, 1998), p. 16.

[320] Zubiaurre, p. 31.

[321] Allende, *Afrodita*, p. 306. 'There's nothing as aphrodisiac as a *mousse au chocolate* on the skin, but try to make sure it's on *you*, because if it's on the other person, you're the one who will have to lick it off and absorb all those calories': Allende, *Aphrodite*, p. 298.

[322] Logan, p. 688.

[323] Miguel Segovia, 'Only Cauldrons Know the Secrets of Their Soups: Queer Romance and *Like Water for Chocolate*', in *Velvet Barrios: Popular Culture and Chicana/o Sexualities*, ed. by Alicia Gaspar de Alba and Tomás Ybarra Frausto (New York: Palgrave Macmillan, 2003), pp. 163-78 (pp. 163-64).

[324] Lisa Heldke, 'Let's Cook Thai: Recipes for Colonialism', in *Pilaf, Pozole, and Pad Thai: American Women and Ethnic Food*, ed. by Sherrie A. Inness (Amherst: University of Massachusetts Press, 2001), pp. 175-98 (p. 176).
[325] Heldke, p. 180.
[326] Segovia, p. 164.
[327] Segovia, p. 166.
[328] Coco Fusco and Nao Bustamante, 'STUFF', in *The Drama Review*, 41.4 (1997), 63-82 (p. 63).
[329] Ibid. p. 63.
[330] Ibid. p. 66.
[331] Ibid. p. 74.
[332] Harriett Blodgett, 'Mimesis and Metaphor: Food Imagery in International Twentieth-Century Women's Writing', *PLL*, 40.3 (2004), 260-95 (p. 262).
[333] Blodgett, p. 265.
[334] Ibid. p. 264.
[335] Tony Spanos, for example, contrasts Sor Juana's and Castellanos' 'belittling and mocking the sacred place of the house' (p. 30) with Esquivel's transformation of the kitchen 'from a place of domination and confinement [...] to one that becomes highly functional and therapeutic': Tony Spanos, 'The Paradoxical Metaphors of the Kitchen in Laura Esquivel's *Like Water for Chocolate*', *Letras femeninas*, 21.1-2 (1995), 29-36 (p. 33). Janice Jaffe, also writing about *Like Water for Chocolate*, says that Castellanos needed to fight against the 1970s patriarchal norms as well as lack of recognition for Latin American women writers, but 'as the contributions of both female and male authors in the world of Latin American fiction today become more equally appreciated, the challenge to speak to the great diversity of female experience opens the doors for new recipes for writing': Jaffe, p. 210.
[336] National Science Foundation, 'Chore Wars: Men, Women, and Housework', (2008).<http://www.nsf.gov/discoveries/disc_summ.jsp?cntn_id=111458>.[accessed July 5, 2011]
[337] Knud Knudsen and Kari Wærness, 'National Context and Spouses' Housework in 34 Countries', *European Sociological Review*, 24.1 (2008), 97-113.
[338] Veerle Miranda, Cooking, Caring and Volunteering: Unpaid Work Around the World', *OECD Social, Employment and Migration Working Papers*, No. 116 (OECD Publishing, 2011). <http://dx.doi.org/10.1787/5kghrjm8s142-en> (p. 26).
[339] Michael A. Ogorzaly, *Waldo Frank: Prophet of Regeneration* (Lewisburg: Bucknell University Press, 1994), p. 121.
[340] Michael Ogorzaly makes this point implicitly in the title of his book on Frank: *Waldo Frank: Prophet of Regeneration*.
[341] William Carlos Williams, 'Federico García Lorca (1919)', in *Selected Essays of William Carlos Williams* (New York: Random House, 1954), pp. 219-30.
[342] Sebastiaan Faber, 'Learning from the Latins: Waldo Frank's Progressive Pan-Americanism', *The New Centennial Review*, 1 (2003), 257-59 (p. 260).

[343] Vera M. Kutzinski, *Against the American Grain: Myth and History in William Carlos Williams, Jay Wright, and Nicolás Guillén* (Baltimore: The Johns Hopkins University Press, 1987), p. 38.
[344] My italics. William Carlos Williams, *In the American Grain* (New York: New Directions, 1956), p. 129.
[345] If Frank and Williams' ethnic alterity is not evident in this blanket description, it was at other times both explicitly and implicitly apparent. Frank will later assign Israel an important role in his vision of world regeneration. To distinguish himself from another William Williams, W. C. Williams deliberately distinguished himself through his middle name, Carlos – a choice which makes his canonization as a white Anglo-American poet all the more ironic.
[346] Kutzinski, *Against the American Grain*, p. 19.
[347] Williams, *In the American Grain*, p. 120.
[348] Ibid. p. 121.
[349] Ibid. p. 177.
[350] Lisa Sánchez González, 'Modernism and Boricua Literature: A Reconsideration of Arturo Schomburg and William Carlos Williams', *American Literary History*, 13 (2001), 242-64 (p. 249).
[351] Marjorie Perloff, *The Poetics of Indeterminacy: Rimbaud to Cage* (Evanston: Northwestern University Press, 1981), p. 111.
[352] Williams, *In the American Grain*, p. 217.
[353] Williams considered Poe the greatest of American authors, precisely because his style was fundamentally 'mathematical'. He believed that the French, attracted as they were to the macabre nature of Poe's work, admired him for the wrong reasons. According to Williams, theirs was a surface appreciation that missed the true value of Poe's work. It was precisely a Frenchman, however, and a pioneer of post-structuralism, who brought the qualities which Williams so admired to the public's attention. I am referring, of course, to Jacques Lacan's landmark essay on 'The Purloined Letter'.
[354] Williams, *In the American Grain*, p. 108.
[355] Ibid. p. 110.
[356] Ibid. p. 129.
[357] Ibid. p. 176.
[358] Sánchez Gonzalez, 'Modernism and Boricua Literature', p. 243.
[359] Julio Marzán, *The Spanish American Roots of William Carlos Williams* (Austin: University of Texas Press, 1994), p. 13.
[360] Miguel Mota, 'William Carlos Williams' Contact with the Spanish', *Journal of Modern Literature*, 4 (1993), 447-59 (p. 449).
[361] Paul Mariani, *William Carlos Williams: A New World Naked* (New York: McGraw Hill, 1981), p. 447.
[362] Faber, 'Learning from the Latins: Waldo Frank's Progressive Pan-Americanism', 257-95.
[363] Waldo Frank, *The Re-discovery of America* (New York: Charles Scribner's Sons, 1929), pp. 19-31 and pp. 56-66.

[364] Lewis Mumford, 'Introduction', *Memoirs of Waldo Frank*, ed. by Alan Trachtenberg (Amherst: University of Massachusetts Press, 1973), p. xxvii.

[365] This originality comes into question if we consider that the theory about the redemptive role of the Americas around which he built his career, may not have originated with him in the first place but rather with the French writer, Romain Rolland. In one of the few in-depth studies of Frank, Michael Ogorzaly claims that the French writer expressed this theory to Frank in a letter dating from 1916; Frank then made this aspect of Rolland's 'thought his own.'[365] Given his open admiration for the French writer, Frank's failure to credit him for the idea is surprising. On the other hand, Frank carried on a life-long correspondence with Rolland and felt a profound kinship with him; in intellectual friendships such as theirs, the origin of ideas is often fluid.

[366] Frank, *The Re-discovery of America*, p. 10.

[367] Waldo Frank, *America Hispana* (New York: Charles Scribner's Sons, 1931), p. 369.

[368] William W. Stein and Renato Alarcón, 'José Carlos Mariátegui y Waldo Frank: dos amigos', *Aniversario Mariateguiano*, 1 (1989), 161-84.

[369] Faber, p. 286.

[370] Ogorzaly, p. 96.

[371] Frank, *America Hispana*, p. 174.

[372] Ogorzaly, p. 96.

[373] Antonio Gramsci, *Selections from the Prison Notebooks*, ed. and trans. by Quintin Joare and Geoffrey Nowell Smith (New York: International Publishers, 1971), p. 60. This quote comes from my book *Imagining Modernity in the Andes* (Bucknell University Press, 2011), p. 34.

[374] Ogorzaly, p. 164.

[375] Faber, p. 262.

[376] Ibid. p. 281.

[377] Ibid. p. 281.

[378] Ibid. p. 280-81.

[379] John Beverley, *Subalternity and Representation: Arguments in Cultural Theory* (Durham, NC: Duke University Press, 1999), p. 1.

[380] Beverly Bell, *Walking on Fire: Haitian Women's Stories of Survival and Resistance* (Ithaca, NY: Cornell University Press, 2001), p. 2.

[381] Ibid. p. 8.

[382] See Danticat's *Anacaona: Golden Flower, Haiti, 1490*.

[383] Bell, *Walking on Fire*, pp. 7-8. Regarding the extensive responsibility of rural Haitian women, Mary-José N'Zengou-Tayo writes, 'As he [Rémy Bastien] interviewed a peasant about his life [in 1951], the latter was angry with his wife and complained about her 'laziness'. Bastien discovered that she was considered lazy because, unlike her female neighbours, she was unable to undertake any commercial activity ('un petit commerce') in addition to her normal household chores and the care of three young children. Thirty-seven years later nothing

much had changed for the peasant woman when, in 1987, a participant at a workshop described the considerable contribution of women to the economy of the northwestern region. She noted that women are entirely responsible for the household economy, organizing the family, raising children, working in the fields and gardens; and that 90 per cent are involved in some form of commercial enterprise, and spend most of the day at the market which they reach on foot or by donkey': Marie-José N'Zengou-Tayo, 'Fanm Sé Poto Mitan: Haitian Women, the Pillar of Society', 59 *Feminist review* (1998), 118-42 (p. 124). While these women shoulder more then their counterparts from the middle and upper class, these latter women are still responsible for 'womanly' activity and are subject to paternalist authority within their own circles; see N'Zengou Tayo (pp. 126-32). Regarding Haitian women, more broadly, Bell provides a plethora of statistical data detailing the inequality shaping their lives. She states: 'According to the United Nations Development Program, Haitian women rank last in a gender development index of countries in the Western Hemisphere, while they rank 150 out of a total of 174 countries surveyed. According to the Inter American Development Bank, of women in twenty-five Latin American countries, Haitian women place at the absolute bottom in female-male life expectancy differential, incidence of teen marriage, contraceptive use, primary school enrollment, secondary school enrollment, and ratio of secondary school teachers. They tie for worst, or rank second worst, in the following: economic equality with men, political and legal equality, social equality, life expectancy, mortality in childbearing years, fertility, rate of widowhood/divorce/separation university enrollment, female adult literacy, discrepancy between male and female literacy, percentage of paid employees, and percentage of professionals. Female life expectancy is 56.4 years; the literacy rate among women is 45.6 percent; and their combined enrollment rate in primary, secondary, and tertiary schools is 24 percent' (pp. 18-19).

[384] Her first name is variously spelled as two names, Marie Sainte.

[385] Jean Fouchard, *La Méringue: Danse nationale d'Haïti* (Montreal: Éditions Leméac, 1974), pp. 77–80; Octave Petit, 'Défilée-La-Folle,' *Revue de la Société d'Histoire et de Géographie d'Haïti*, 3.8 (1932), 1-21 (p. 3). (Conférence prononcée au Cercle Excelsior de Jérémie, le 22 Août 1931. Lue à la Société d'Histoire et de Géographie d'Haïti le 9 Octobre 1932).

[386] See Petit, p. 4, 5, Petit, p. 6 and Joan Dayan, *Haiti, History, and the Gods* (Berkeley, CA: University of California Press, 1995), p. 44, respectively.

[387] Definition of 'sutler': 'A person who followed an army and sold provisions to the soldiers', *Concise Oxford English Dictionary*, 10th edn, ed. by Judy Pearsall (Oxford: Oxford University Press, 2002), p. 1444.

[388] Dayan, p. 44.

[389] Dayan, p. 40 and see Dayan's extensive treatment of Défilée's mythos as constructed by the literary and political elite of Haiti, where she provides detailed summations of prevailing readings of Défilée following the rise of Dessalines' importance in Haiti in the forty years following his assassination (pp. 27-29).

[390] Joan Dayan, *Haiti, History, and the Gods*, pp. 27-28. After securing Haitian independence in 1804, Dessalines is said to have declared: 'I have avenged America.' See Laurent Dubois' aptly titled, *Avengers of the New World* and Lysius Salomon's commemorative utterance thirty-nine years following Dessalines' death, 'Avenger of the black race, liberator of Haiti, founder of independence, Emperor Dessalines! Today is your glory, the sun today burns for you as radiantly as it did in 1804' (quoted in Dayan, *Haiti, History, and the Gods*, p. 27).

[391] Petit, p. 8.

[392] Dayan, *Haiti, History, and the Gods*, p. 45.

[393] Jérémie quoted in Dayan, *Haiti, History, and the Gods*, p. 44; French original Fouchard, p. 56. See Petit, p. 7 as well.

[394] Jana Evans Braziel, 'Re-membering Défilée: Dédée Bazile as Revolutionary Lieu de Mémoire', *Small Axe*, 18 (2005), 57-85 (p. 59) For an indication of the historical significance of these women see Joan Dayan, *Haiti, History and the Gods*: 'Sanite Belair [...] refused to be blindfolded during her execution, [...] Marie-Jeanne Lamartinère [...] led the indigenes in the extraordinary Battle of Crête-á-Pierrot, and [...] Claire Heureuse (her real name was Marie Claire Félicité Guillaume Bonheur), the wife of Dessalines [...] saved many of the French he had ordered massacred' (p. 47).

[395] Rasin is a type of popular music that accompanies carnival festivities. See video, http://www.youtube.com/watch?v=2KMjn-w5i_0.

[396] 'Papa' is among the designations (maitre, *maitresse*) allocated to ancestors who in being honoured by the people have been made into a *lwa*.

[397] *Layité* truly has no English equivalent. It quite literally means to give yourself over to the music so as to let the rhythms course through your body, allowing you to let loose and enjoy yourself. It is a word that calls upon you to both *banboche* and *pran plezi*, all the while imparting the importance of a relaxed body to revelry.

[398] Jana Evans Braziel, whose work on Défilée, Danticat and Haiti has inspired my own, offers a thorough footnote delineating the literature afforded to the revolution and the men through which it is rendered, 'Re-membering Défilée: Dédée Bazile as Revolutionary Lieu de Mémoire,' *Small Axe*, 18 (2005), 57-85. See also the following writers for works on Toussaint, C.L.R James, Nick Nesbitt, Thomas-Prosper Gragnon-Lacoste, George Le Gorgeu, Aimé Cesairé and Victor Schoelcher, among others; on Dessalines, see Massillon Coicou, Hénock Trouillot, Timoléon Brutus, Jean Price-Mars and Luc Dorsinville; on Christophe, see Hubert Cole, Cesairé, Derek Walcott, Vergniaurd Leconte and Eugene O'Neill; and lastly on Pètion, see Horace Pauléus Sannon and Joseph St. Rémy.

[399] Danticat, *Krik? Krak!* (New York, NY: Vintage Books, 1996) p. 224. For ease of reading all further references to this work will follow in parentheses in the text with the abbreviations KK for *Krik? Krak!* Also all references to the short story in *Krik? Krak!*, 'Nineteen Thirty Seven,' will be abbreviated as NTS.

[400] See Paule Marshall, 'From the Poets in the Kitchen', *NY Times*, 1983 and Paule Marshall, 'From the Poets in the Kitchen', *Callaloo*, 24.2 (2001), 627-33.
[401] Maya Deren, *Divine Horsemen: The Living Gods of Haiti* (New Paltz, NY: McPherson, 1983), p. 31.
[402] Sam Durrant, *Postcolonial Narrative and the Work of Mourning* (Albany, New York: State University of New York, 2004), p. 11.
[403] Sigmund Freud, 'Mourning and Melancholia,' in *Collected Papers* (London: The Hogarth Press, 1953), pp. 153-70.
[404] David L. Eng and David Kazanjian, 'Introduction: Mourning Remains,' *Loss: Politics of Mourning* (Berkeley, CA: University of California Press, 2003), p. 4.
[405] Freud, p. 155; p. 166.
[406] Eng and Kazanjian, p. 4.
[407] Ibid. p. 6.
[408] See Eng's and Kazanjian's thorough treatment of Western scholarship concerning melancholia, pp. 7-23.
[409] Dayan, p. 45.
[410] The very first line of the song 'Defile' by *RAM* bemoans this fact, 'Nou fete lamò Dessaline, men nou pa fete lavi Dessalines' ('We celebrate Dessalines' death but we don't celebrate his life').
[411] There is much to be said of Dessalines' symbolic use and deference to Amerindians, essentially to their pivotal presence to his revolutionary action and thought. In addition to re-naming Saint Domingue as *Ayiti*, he is said to have called upon the memory of Amerindians in another instance. Dayan, paraphrasing Thomas Madiou, writes 'Dessalines called the populations subject to his authority 'Incas or children of the sun,' memorializing the 1780 Inca uprising in Peru' (Dayan, p. 22). An examination of the importance of Amerindians to Dessalines could quite possibly further shift the discourse concerning liberal democratic revolution and modernity by pointing to yet another alternative subject position by which to imagine as well as re-imagine existence.
[412] The event is known as 'El Corte' (the cutting) in the Dominican Republic; for critical discussion of the massacre see Richard Lee Turits, 'A World Destroyed, A Nation Imposed: The 1937 Haitian Massacre in the Dominican Republic', *Hispanic American Historical Review*, 82. 3 (2002), 590-635 and Michele Wucker, 'The River Massacre: The Real and Imagined Borders of Hispaniola,' *Windows on Haiti*. http://haitiforever.com/windowsonhaiti/wucker1.shtml.
[413] Turits, p. 590.
[414] Ibid. pp. 633-34.
[415] Ibid. p. 599.
[416] Ibid. p. 615.
[417] The 'official' response to the massacre parallels that of the Haitian government's response to the January 12th earthquake, where the dead were treated, as they are in life, with complete and utter disregard. Regarding *Kout Kouto-a*, Turits writes: 'Haiti did not respond militarily to defend or avenge its compatriots. To the contrary, President [Sténio] Vincent of Haiti acted in every

way possible to avoid a military conflict. It was not only the army that Vincent held back. He prohibited public discussion of the massacre, and refused for a long time even to allow the church to perform masses for the dead. It appears that Vincent was constrained by fear of losing control to his domestic opponents. If troops were sent to the frontier, the palace would be left vulnerable to attack. But under increased domestic pressures due to growing evidence of the extent of the massacre, Vincent did eventually seek an investigation of the atrocities and mediation of the conflict by other countries. Unwilling to submit to an inquiry, Trujillo offered instead a sizeable indemnization to Haiti, while still refusing any admission of official responsibility. One can only speculate as to why Vincent so readily accepted Trujillo's offer of $750,000 (of which only $525,000 was ever paid) in exchange for an end to international arbitration.' (pp. 622-23)

[418] I will not treat the *marasa* here. For a reading that does, see Braziel's 'Remembering Défilée: Dédée Bazile as Revolutionary Lieu de Mémoire', where she reads Défilée as Dessaline's twin.

[419] Karen McCarthy Brown, *Mama Lola: A Vodou Priestess in Brooklyn* (Berkeley, CA: University of California Press, 1991), p. 229.

[420] And here I am thinking of Maya Deren's poetic passage detailing an oungan's (vodun priest) struggle with preserving the sanctity of his spiritual practice or demeaning it by performing for tourists at a government sponsored Vodun ceremony; he summons his *lwa* for guidance. Deren writes: 'To call upon his loa, thus, at this critical moment, was to call upon everything of which he was, himself, the final issue – to call not only upon the generality, the principles of his patrimony, but, beginning with the Marassa, the first men, upon the roll of that ancestral progression which had successively borne that complex forward: the African tribes, the Indian allies, the thousands of individuals whose blood had nourished it and whose diverse personal genius had swelled and elaborated its manifold and various aspect' (p. 81).

[421] Deren, p. 81.

[422] Ibid. p. 81.

[423] McCarthy Brown, p. 255.

[424] Deren, p. 96.

[425] When this phrase first appears in the narrative, it is on the second day of the narrative when Josephine leaves her mother to return to her home in the countryside; her mother's goodbye is a reiteration of this rite closing – 'Let your flight be joyful,' she said, 'and mine too'' (p. 42).

[426] I am indebted to Jana Evans Braziel and her work on Défilée in 'Remembering Défilée' for this insight; see Braziel, pp. 57–85.

INDEX

The index refers to the text, but not to the front matter or the endnotes. Works of literature are listed alphabetically after their author. It is hoped that by placing more emphasis on themes, general concepts and works of literature, in addition to listing important names and geographical places, compilation of this index will enable academic researchers and scholarly readers to more easily access the text.

Adorno, Theodor W., 65, 73
aesthetic (s), 5, 7, 13, 22, 24, 37, Frankfurt School, 65, 65-67, 69, 75-77, 79-81, 107, 109, 114, 203, of mourning, 261-62, 278, 280
African, 10, 184-86, 188, 199, 205, 237, 244, 277, African-American, 247
Afro-Caribbean, 10, 183-84, 191, 193, 198
Aléxis, Jacques Stephen, 203, 215
Alfonsín, Raúl, 47, 50-51, 56
Algerian, women, 169, Algerian War of Independence, 169
Allende, Isabel, 12, 239-40, *Afrodita: Cuentos, Recetas y Otros Afrodisíacos*, 234-7
Amerindian, 10, 184-85, 188, 190
Anacaona, 13, 261-64, 268, 272
Antonioni, Michelangelo, 'Blowup,' 102
Anzaldúa, Gloria Evangelina, 3, 7-8, 119-31, *Borderlands/La Frontera*, 7, 119-22, 124-28, 130
Arenas, Reinaldo, 3-4, 15-31, *Antes que anochezca* (*Before Night Falls*), 3, 15
Arendt, Hannah, 72, 137
Argentina, 3, 6, 34, 38-40, filmmakers, 45-81, 83-93, 95-103
Aristotle, 65, Aristotelian, 111
Asia, 1-2
Augustine, St., 113

Bakhtin, Mikhail Mikhailovich, 109, 113, 162, grotesque realism, 110, heteroglossia, 109
Bardem, Javier, 20-21, 24, 31
Barthes, Roland, 139
Baudelaire, Charles, 8, 134, 137, 146
Bazile, Dédée, 13, 264-65, 277
Bechis, Marco, 3, 5, 73-4, 77, *Garage Olimpo*, 5, 65-6, 72-75, 77-80
Délair, Sanite, 266
Benjamin, Walter, 187, *Illuminations*, 137, 'Some Motifs on Baudelaire,' 134, theory of the flâneur, 8, 134, 137, 142-43, 146
Berlin, 115
Bierce, Ambrose, 109
Bloom, Harold, 6, 84
Bolaño, Roberto, 112
Bolívar, Simon, *Carta de Jamaica*, 254
Bolton, Herbert E., 260
Borges, Jorge Luis, 3, 6, 83, 86, 88-89, 91-93, 98, 101, 104, 108, 112, 115, 'Pierre Menard, autor del Quijote', 108, *The Garden of Forking Paths*, 93
Boukman, Papa, 13, 276
Brazil, 2, 210, 253
Bryant, Anita, 17
Buenos Aires, 49, 59, 73, 89-90, 92-95, 97-101, 103, General Alfredo Oscar Saint-Jean, 49
Bustamante, Nao, 12, 238-39
Butler, Judith, 36

Caetano, Adrián, 37
Caribbean, 3, 10, 161-66, 175, 179, 184-85, 191, 197-99, 203, 205, Caribbean-American, 247
Carpentier, Alejo, 111, 183, 194, *El reino de este mundo*, 197
Carriles, Lázaro Gómez, 22
Carroll, Lewis (Charles Lutwidge Dodgson), 109, 111
Castellanos, Rosario, 12, 232, 233-34, 239-40, 'Lección de cocina, 228-30
Castro, Fidel, 23, 25-26, 28-31, 95-96, 251
Caviglia, Mariana, 57-8
Cedrón, Jorge, 58,
Cedrón, Lucía, 3, 58, 60-63, *Cordero de Dios/Lamb of God* (2008), 5, 47, 52, 58-9, 61-63
Cervantes, Miguel de, (Saavedra), 6, 84, 86-87, 93, 104-05, 111, *Don Quixote* (*Don Quijote de la Mancha*), 6, 84, 86-87, 104-05
Césaire, Aimé, 10, 183-93 195-99, *La tragédie du roi Christophe*, 10, 183, 185-92, 197
Chandler, Raymond, 115
Chekhov, Anton Pavlovich, 115
Chile, 3, 96, 239
China, 2
Christophe, Henri, 13, 187, 191, 194, 197, 267, 276
cinema, 15-81
colonization, Latin America, 1-2, 184, 199, 248-9
Colombia, 2-3, 6, 83-84, 87, 104
Columbus, Christopher, 1, 172, 184, 204
Connolly, Cyril, *The Unquiet Grave*, 109
Conrad, Joseph, 115, *Heart of Darkness*, 154

Cortázar, Julio, 3, 6, 83, 88, 98, 100-03, *62 Modelo para armar*, 102, *Autonautas de la cosmopista*, 102, *Libro de Manuel*, 102, *Los Reyes*, 101, *Presencia*, 101, *Rayuela*, 102, *The End of the Game and Other Stories*, 101, *Blow Up and Other* Stories, 101, *Around the Day in Eighty Worlds*, 101
cosmopolitanism, 7, 13, 83, 107, 241
Creole (Kreyòl), 2, 4, 7, 12, 33, 177, 187-88, 194, 196-97, 202-03, 212, 262
Cruz, Sor Juana Inés de la, 227
Cuba, 3, 7, 15-23, 25-31

Danticat, Edwidge, 3, 9-10, 13-14, 147-82, 185, 261, 263-64, 267-71, 272-75, 278-80, *Breath, Eyes, Memory*, 10, 157, 213, 'Caroline's Wedding', 270, 'Children of the Sea', 270, 279, *Krik? Krak!*, 264, 267-71, 'Nineteen Thirty-Seven', 13, 261, 270, 272-75, 278-80, 'Seeing Things Simply', 270, *The Dew Breaker*, 9-10, 147-59, *The Farming of Bones*, 9, 161-82, 207, 'Wall of Rising Fire', 270
Dantò, Ezili, 276-78
Darío, Rubén, (Félix Rubén García Sarmiento), 85-6
Deleuze, Gilles, 35-36, 42
Depestre, René, *Alléluia pour une femme-jardin*, 209-10, 217
Depp, Johnny, 20, 25
Dessalines, Jean-Jacques, 156, 164, 184, 190, 199, 264-67, 272-73, 276, 279
diaspora, 199, 270, 279, Caribbean, 179, diasporic, 4, 33, 179
Diaz Ordaz, Gustavo, 108, 113

Index

dictatorship, Argentine, 5, 39, 45-63, 66-69, 76, 79, Cuba, 20, Haiti (Duvalier), 163, 220-21, 225, Spain, 91
Dominican Republic, 3, 9, 161-62, 168, 204, 247, 273, 279, Saint-Domingue, 164, 184, 190, 192, 205, 272, act of defiance, 164
Dorismond, Patrick, 149
Dostoevsky, Fyodor, 115
Dreyfuss, Joel, 166
Dunlop, Carol, 102-03
Duvalier, François, 147, 153, 158, 163, 215, 223

Ecuador, 2
East, John, 18
Eguren, José María, 256
Eliot, Thomas Stearns, *The Waste Land*, 158, 243, 248
Esquivel, Laura, 12, 239-40, *Como agua para chocolate*, 231-37

Fanon, Franz, 195, *The Wretched of the Earth*, 169
Faulkner, William, 6, 83-87, 104, *As I Lay Dying*, 85, *The Sound and the Fury*, 83, 85-86
Ferdinand II and V of Aragon, King, 1
Foucault, Michel, 9, 36, 69, 78, 111, 148
France, 58-59, 93, 99, 102, 164, 169, 186, 188, 195, 205-06, 257
Frank, Waldo, 12-13, 242-44, 246, 250-60, *America Hispana*, 253-54, *South American Journey*, 253, *The Re-discovery of America*, 255
Fuentes, Carlos, 84, 102, 112, *Christopher Unborn*, 87, 104
Fusco, Coco, 12, (and Nao Bustamante), 'STUFF', 238-39

Gadea, Hilda, 96-97
Gallegos, Rómulo, 87
García, Lupe Pérez, 3, 5, 53, 55-56, 58, *Diario argentino/Argentine Journal* (2007), 5, 47, 52, 55-57, 63
Garcia, Uriel, 256
Gauguin, Paul, 223-24
gay rights, 17-19, 21, 28
Godard, Jean-Luc, 'Weekend', 102
Góngora, Luis de, 243
Gonzales, Ana María, 73
González, Elían, 20
Guadeloupe, 165
Guattari, Félix, 35-36, 42
Guevara, Che, 25, 93-97, 101, 103

Haiti (Haïti), 2-3, 9-12, 13-14, 147, 150, 153-54, 156, 161-81, 183-91, 194-99, 201-225, 261-80, January 2010 earthquake, 185, Port-au-Prince, 149, 163, slave revolt, 208
Havana, 16, 22, 37, 96, 115, 221
Hegel, Georg Wilhelm Friedrich, 170
Helms, Jesse, 18
Henry, Gesner (a.k.a. Coupe-Cloue), 218
Herskovits, Melville, 212
heteroglossia, 109
Heureuse, Marie-Claire, 266
H.I.J.O.S., 51-52
Hispaniola, 2, 161, 180, 204-05
history, of colonization, 1-2
Homer, *Ulysses*, 109
homosexuality, 3, 4, 15, 17, 19, 23, 25-30
Huidobro, Vicente, 257
Hurt, William, 100
Huxley, Aldous, 115

Immigrants, 3, 16-17, 163, 247-48, 250, immigration, 17, 247, 250

India, 204, 237, 245, Indian, 122-24, 128, 163, 172, 191, culture, 124
Infante, Guillermo Cabrera, 22, *Tres tristes tigres*, 111
Infante, Sabá*P.M.*, 22
intertextual (ity), 7, 34, 107, 109, 111, 114
irony, 9, 112, 133, 140, 166-67, 175, 187-89, 198, 265
Isabella of Castile, Queen, 1

James, C. L. R., *The Black Jacobins*, 261
Japan, 1-2, 93, 204
Jelin, Elizabeth, 48, 51, collective memories, 48
Joyce, James, 83, 86, 87, 104, 109, 111, 113

Kafka, Franz, 71, 86, 104, 115, *Die Verwandlung* (*Metamorphosis*), 86
Kansas, 139, 142
Karvelis, Ugné, 102
Kodama, María, 93
Kohan, Martín, 3, 5, 66, 68, 74, 79, *Dos veces junio*, 5, 65- 69, 73-75, 77-78
Kout Kouto-a, 272-73
Kraków, 115
Kristeva, Julia, 36, 40
Kundera, Milan, 115

Lacan, Jacques, 36, 41-2
Laferrière, Dany, *Le goût des jeunes filles*, 223-24
Lamartinère, Marie-Jeanne, 266
Laroche, Maximilien, 186, 203
Lester, Richard, *A Hard Day's Night*, 138
Lima, Lezama, *Paradiso*, 111
linguistic, 111, 113, 115, 175, 178, 185, 209, 219, 247-50

London, 12, 98, 100, 137, 241
Lorca, Federico García, 243, 248-49
Lorde, Audre, 3, 7-8, 119-31, 'Age, Race, Class, and Sex: Women Redefining Difference', 7, 122-31
Louima, Abner, 149
L'Ouverture, Toussaint, 13, 156, 192, 199, 203, 261, 267

Madrid, 12, 89, 92, 241
magical realism, 107, 114, 136, magical realist, 8, 108, 133-36, 146
Magritte, René François Ghislain, 111
March, Aleida, 97
Mariátegui, José Carlos, 3, 12-13, 242, 250-51, 254-57, *Amauta*, 254-57, *Labor*, 254, *Peruanicemos a Peru*, 256, *Revista Amauta*, 254, *Siete ensayos de interpretación de la realidad peruana*, 255-56
Márquez, Gabriel García, 3, 6, 83-87, 92, 102, 104-05, 115, 133, 136, *Cien años de soledad* (*One Hundred Years of Solitude*), 87, 102, *Leaf Storm*, 85-87
Marshall, Paule, 267
Martel, Lucrecia, 3-4, 33-44, *La Ciénaga* (2001), 36-38, 40, 43, *La mujer sin cabeza* (2008), 37, 39, 44, *La niña santa* (2004), 37, 38, 43, *Rey Muerto* (1995), 37, 41
Martelly, Michel (a.k.a. Sweet Micky), 183, 218
Martinique, 165, 193
Marxist, 3, 48, 97, 242, 250, 254-56
Menem, Carlos Saúl, 51, 53-54, 56
metaphor, 41, 57, 59, 68-9, 107, 115, gastronomical, 11-12, 201-25, 238, 239, 268Mexican, 3, 122-23,

126, 227, 228, 230, 233, 237, 243, Mexican-American, 86
Mexico, 2-3, 7, 93, 87, 100, 113, 231, 240, Mexico City, 84, 96, 99, 109, Emperors of, 108
Miami, 16
Milk, Harvey, 16-17
Millán, Elsa Helena Astete, 93
modernist, 7, 13, 85, 87, 104, 111, 241, 242, 246, 247, 250, 252
Molina, Rafael Leonaidas Trujillo, 273
Morrison, Toni, 133
Mozart, Wolfgang Amadeus, *Die Entführung aus dem Serail*, 116

Nabokov, Vladimir Vladimirovich, 115
Najman, Charles, 185, 199, 'Royal bonbon' (2002), 10, 183-87, 194-95, 196, 198
Neruda, Pablo, 257
New Jersey, 247-48
New York, 8, 16, 28-29, 98-100, 102, 133-36, 139, 141, 147, 270, *New York Times*, 19, Manhattan, 137
Nuevo Cine Argentino, 37

Ocampo, Victoria, 251, 255
Ordaz, Gustavo Díaz, 108, 113
Ovid (Publius Ovidius Naso), 115

Paris, 13, 58, 98, 100-01, 103, 137, 210, 241, 247
parody, 10, 112-13, 116, 184, 197-98
Paso, Fernando Del, 3, 6-7, 107-17, *Noticias del imperio* (1987), 108, *Palinuro de México*, 7, 107-10, 113-14, 116
Penn, Sean, 20
Perón, Eva, 87, 89, 91-93,

Perón, Juan Domingo, 53, 87-88, 89-90, 94, 99, 103
Peronism, 6, 54, 56, 83, 88, 103
Peru, 2-3, 96-97, 242, Peruvian Embassy, 16, Peruvian Socialist Party, 254
Pétion, Alexandre Sabès, 13, 187, 267
Piglia, Ricardo, 112
Poe, Edgar Allan, 101,115,137, 245
Prieto, José Manuel, *El tartamudo y la rusa*, 6, *Encyclopedia of a Life in* Russia, 107, 116, *Nocturnal Butterflies of the Russian Empire* (*Livadia*), 107-08, 115-16, *Rex*, 7, 107, 113, 116
Proust, Marcel, 115-16
Protestant, 243-46, 249
psychoanalysis, 36, 40, psychoanalytic, 34
Puig, Manuel, 3, 6, 83, 88, 97-100, *Boquitas pintadas*, 99, *El beso de la mujer araña*, 98, 100, *El lugar sin límites*, 99, *La traición de Rita Hayworth*, 98, *The Buenos Aires Affair*, 99
Puerto Rico, 3, 243, 247-48, Puerto Rican, 3, 8, 13, 133, 136, 244, 247
Pushkin, Alexander Sergeyevich, 115

Queer Theory, 4, 34, 36
Quevedo, Francisco Gómez de, 111

Rabelais, François, 113, *La vie de Gargantua* et de *Pantagruel*, 104
Rama, Ángel, 86, 111
Rasles, Père Sebastian, 245-46, 249
Reagan, Ronald, 16-17
Rejtman, Martín, 37
revolution, 1-3, 9, Argentinian, 94-6, Cuban, 20-23, 25-26, 97, 101,

103, French, 164, Guatemalan, 97, Haitian, 9, 10, 13, 164-65, 170, 184-87, 190-191, 194, 196, 198-99, 205, Mexican, 109, 231, 261-67, 272-80
Rivera, José Eustasio, 87
Roosevelt, Theodore, 86
Roth, Philip, 144, 146
Roumer, Emile, 217
Ruiz, Saturnino Montero, 58
Rulfo, Juan, 84
Sábato, Ernesto, 47, 52
Saint-Méry, Moreau de, 190, 203
Sánchez, Luis Alberto, 257-58, 260
Saussure, Ferdinand de, 133
Schnabel, Julian, 3, 15, 19-23, 28-30, *Before Night Falls* (2000), 3, 15, 21, 28, 30
Scilingo, Adolfo, 51
Shakespeare, William, *Hamlet*, 156
Shikibu, Murasaki, *The Tale of Genji*, 115
South America, 2-3, 6, 83, 241, 252
Sophocles, *Antigone*, 85
Spain, 89, 91-93, 99, 205-06, 243, 247-50, 257
Spanish Civil War, 94, 255
Stagnaro, Bruno, 37
Sterne, Laurence, 87, 104, *Tristram Shandy*, 111
Swift, Jonathan, *Gulliver's Travels*, 104

Tahiti, 223-24
Taino, 167-68, 184, 190, 205, 262, 272
Todorov, Tzvetan, 47, 62-63
Trapero, Pablo, 37

Trujillo, Rafaél Léonida, 162, 167-68, 170-74, 176-80, 273
Turkey, Istanbul, 108
Twain, Mark, 111

Unamuno, Miguel de, 111
United States, 3-4, 6, 10, 83-85, 102, 149, 163-64, 206, 224, 237, 239, 243-44, 247, 249-50, 257, 259, 268

Vallejo, César, 257
Vargas Llosa, Mario, 102, 133
Vasconcelos, José, 243, 251
Venezuela, 2
Verne, Jules, 100
Videla, Jorge Rafael, 47
Vodun, 218, 267, 271-72, 275-77

War, American Civil, 85, Chaco War, 94, Cold War, 4, 15, 17, Falklands, 53, Haitian War of Independence, 261-62, 265, Spanish Civil, 2, 94, 255
Wender, Wim (with Ry Cooder), *The Buena Vista Social Club*, 20
Werleigh, Christian, 203
Wilde, Oscar, 115
Williams, William Carlos, 3, 12-13, 241, 247-50, 252, *In the American Grain*, 245, 248
Woolf, Virginia, 12, 86, 228

Yunqué, Edgardo Vega, 3, 8, 133-46, *The Lamentable Journey of Omaha Bigelow into the Impenetrable Loisaida Jungle*, 8, 133-46